# ANNUAL REVIEW of
# GERONTOLOGY AND GERIATRICS

## Volume 5, 1985

# ANNUAL REVIEW OF
# GERONTOLOGY AND GERIATRICS

## Volume 5, 1985

**Carl Eisdorfer, Ph.D., M.D.**
*EDITOR-IN-CHIEF*

**M. Powell Lawton, Ph.D.**
**George L. Maddox, Ph.D.**
*SPECIAL VOLUME EDITORS*

SPRINGER PUBLISHING COMPANY
New York

Springer Publishing Company, Inc.
536 Broadway
New York, New York 10012

85  86  87  88  89  /  5  4  3  2  1

ISBN 0-8261-3084-4
ISSN 0198-8794

Printed in the United States of America

# Contents

# Introduction

The choice of topics for this volume of the *Annual Review of Gerontology and Geriatrics,* which deals exclusively with the social and psychological aspects of aging, was guided by the wish to emphasize issues that have been relatively neglected in some ways. There was also a wish that the topics should have a degree of commonality without sacrificing a broad range of currently important issues. The editors' selections of specific areas meriting critical review focus on social lifestyle, intrapersonal (as contrasted with interactional) processes of aging, and interventions designed to benefit the quality of life in the later years. This volume should advance our present understanding of the older person in a social context.

The chapters are grouped in sections to illustrate and highlight personal determinants of lifestyle, variations in social lifestyle, and interventions. The section on personal determinants of lifestyle is focused on what may be the single most cogent current issue in the psychology of aging: personal control and efficacy. Personal control is far from being a neglected topic. New reports on this construct appear every month. What has been neglected is the broad, critical review which the authors of the first two chapters of this volume provide. Both the methods and the conclusions reported in studies of personal control have been so diverse as to verge on the incomprehensible. The review by Rodin, Timko, and Harris provides the relief from the chaos of conflicting conclusions for which we have all been looking. The clear organization of their critical review allows us to see where there has and where there has not been consensus among the findings of different investigators. Further, their overview portrays how some dissonances may have been produced by methodological differences. Most importantly, their strong theoretical position provides a series of points from which new research hypotheses may be formulated and tested.

It was by design that both an American and a European were asked to review the same general topic. Arnetz, a Swedish investigator trained as both a physician and a behavioral scientist, focuses his review of the literature on aging, efficacy, and the effects of psychosocial interventions primarily on European publications. His frequent references to U.S. publications, however, illustrate that scientific information in gerontology and geriatrics travels across national boundaries. Interest in personal control and efficacy is now international and so is the perception that we now know enough about the determinants and modifiability of perceived personal control and efficacy to design and test beneficial interventions. Arnetz stresses particularly the importance of investigating simultaneously the biological and psychosocial effects of interventions with older adults. He reviews research in Sweden, including his own, that suggests positive physiological as well as psychosocial responses to social interventions.

The conclusions from research on personal control and efficacy are made more comprehensible by these critiques. It seems safe at this point to suggest to future researchers that the quest for age differences in personal control is likely to be less fruitful than the quest for age-related factors that influence control and for moderators of the relationship between control and more distal social and psychological outcomes. In underlining the diversity among older people in actual, perceived, expected, and desired control, both chapters point out the inevitable need for a transactional view of person and context and for a view that includes the interaction of biological and psychosocial variables. Thus, even though control is seen by many as a personality need or trait, this cannot be understood without reference to the environmental barriers and constraints on the exercise of personal choice or the social effects of exercising choice. And the more visible psychosocial responses to environmental stimuli also have biological concomitants. The net import of these two chapters is to affirm the need to see the older person as a creating, proactive force, a perception that is a very appropriate antidote to the frequent portrayal of old age as a time of passivity and reactivity.

Section Two deals with four domains of everyday life which together illustrate important aspects of how older people characteristically live: their lifestyles as reflected in their sexuality, leisure, interpersonal relationships, and living arrangements. Lifestyles are recognized to be determined both by the personal and social characteristics and needs of people, and by the restraints and resources of the environmental context. Far from being steady states, lifestyles are dynamic. They can and do change. The observed changes reflect age-related factors such as health, the experience of different age cohorts, social values, and sociopolitical institutions. Each of the chapters in Section Two deals to some extent with the issue of the contributions of age, in relation to other influences, on lifestyle, and the diversity within the older group in determining the social behaviors marking each lifestyle domain.

Starr's chapter on sexuality reviews the long tradition of popular and scientific writing that has invoked age alone as the explanation for late-life changes in sex behavior. The blindness of this body of literature to the effect of other influences on sexual behavior such as the availability of a sex partner, introjected negative social stereotypes by older people themselves, and a relatively narrow socially defined concept of "sex" is forcefully portrayed by Starr. In suggesting the expansion of our definition of fulfilling sexuality, Starr underlines the diversity of the older person as well. Orgasmic sex may or may not represent either a particular individual's wish or capability. "Pleasuring," in Starr's terms, is a more comprehensive concept that subsumes diversity among both individuals and behavioral avenues to sexual fulfillment.

By contrast to sexuality, leisure behavior is one of the traditional concerns of gerontologists. Interestingly enough, however, leisure as a focus for research seemed to go out of fashion for a period, and Lawton's review is the first general review of this topic to appear in more than a decade. At the present time there seems to be a renewal of interest in leisure, and a new stream of research findings may be forthcoming in the next few years.

Lawton's goal is primarily to link the study of leisure in old age to some of the basic fields of psychological knowledge in which activity choices are embedded: motivation, personal control, and stimulus regulation. His discussion of personal control complements the more general presentation of Rodin, Timko, and Harris. The function of leisure activity and other uses of time will never be completely understood until we know how they fit into the other domains of the person as he or she functions in the physiological, psychological, and social arenas. Lawton also finds in his literature review that age is a relatively poor predictor of activity level or leisure behavior. Contextual factors like socioeconomic status and the personal factor of health are much more potent. His use of "the diversity principle" concentrates particularly on differentiating among the many meanings that an activity can have for an individual. It is these meanings that moderate the relationship between time allocations to different activities and outcomes like satisfaction and psychological well-being.

The chapters by Rubinstein on living alone and Horowitz on family caregiving both deal explicitly with the social relationships of older people. They differ in that Rubinstein focuses on the older person and on one social status, that of living alone, while Horowitz focuses on caregiving behavior, which is a transaction between the older person and others.

As Rubinstein's literature review shows, research has not neglected the lifestyle of older people living alone. But he demonstrates that investigations rarely have been designed to yield clear conclusions about the effects of living alone per se. That is, especially in later life, the statuses of gender, marital situation, and living arrangement are confounded with one another. To varying degrees, studies of "older people" are likely, for example, to consist of a plurality of older women living alone. Rubinstein points to the ways we might expect age, gender, and marital status to affect lifestyle but simultaneously warns us that it will require a great deal more research to understand the experiences and consequences of living alone. He takes pains to review how living arrangement is determined by a variety of factors and how living arrangement in turn affects other outcomes in a very complex interactive manner. The bottom line of knowledge on the lifestyle of those living alone permits no easy generalization. Its quality is also diverse; for older persons "outcomes associated with living alone appear to represent a mixed blessing for older persons." One concludes that the quality of life when lived alone can be explained neither by age nor by the fact of living alone, but by a diversity of moderating factors, chief among which is the quality of social relationships.

Rubinstein notes the differences between social network and a more limited variety of social relationships, social support. Horowitz's chapter is specifically about social support, but she makes clear how social support, in turn, takes different forms and has multiple attributes. One cannot say that family caregiving is neglected in the gerontological literature. If anything, the literature is littered with material on this topic. What makes this topic suitable for the *Annual Review* is that the plethora of recent written material taxes any reader's capacity to make critical order of it. The *Review* meets this need by organizing for us the recent research findings on the facts about caregiving as they fall into a larger historical perspective.

The diversity of the caregiving experience is then documented at length, including the important aspects of burden, affective experience, and psychological outcomes. Change and diversity also are seen in temporal perspective. The policy implications of the reviewed knowledge are discussed in a way that makes apparent how well her clear structural view of caregiving serves our ability to apply the knowledge on behalf of society. Her summary of research needs again flows from the gaps repeatedly noted in her review.

Horowitz's chapter provides a bridge to Section Three, dealing with interventions. One function of caregiving is intervention, a desired favorable effect on an impaired or marginally dependent older person. The last section acknowledges that even though the majority of older people are relatively independent, the focus of some substantial proportion of our total social effort is the frankly impaired segment of the older population. Focusing on this segment now will prepare us better for the growth in the dependent portion of the older population that is expected until at least 2030.

The chapters by Gallagher on supports for caregivers serving mentally ill older persons and by Smyer and Frysinger on mental health services in institutions differ in many ways from those in the preceding sections. First, they are meant to anticipate and create a recognition of the need for more research and service in two relatively new areas. Unlike the other areas discussed in this volume, there is a very limited body of literature from which the important parameters of the intervention process or their outcomes have been identified. The authors of both chapters are relatively on their own in using a very small amount of literature to stimulate their thinking and that of the reader. They had no choice, in making some early order of the area, other than to use concepts from other areas, to identify many issues in a priori fashion, and to concentrate on research that needs to be done, programs that should be created, and methodologies that should be applied. At the same time, both chapters demonstrate that the advancement of knowledge regarding intervention schemes benefits greatly from the use of theory and more basic social scientific knowledge.

Gallagher finds theoretical approaches derived from the child caregiving literature useful: a stage model, anticipatory grief, and adaptive coping styles. The major portion of her chapter offers for the first time a collation of information from a number of recent or ongoing attempts to give support to caregivers of impaired older people. Common threads and differing therapeutic or supportive techniques are discussed. The compendium is detailed enough to offer assistance to professionals who wish to operate such programs, but it is critical in calling attention to the many sources of error in drawing conclusions about the efficacy of any of the approaches. Such methodological critiques lead to the statement of a set of research needs, which is the next step toward a firmer knowledge base.

The target group selected for intervention by Smyer and Frysinger is more appropriately referred to as a community, that is, the system that includes the older resident, the family, and the staff in institutions for the aged. Their focus is on the mental health, broadly defined, of all three groups; the authors emphasize the mental health relevance of a variety of psychosocial interventions. They have provided an invaluable compendium of published research on mental health programs for residents, relatives, and staff. Like Gallagher, they include methodological comments about each study, resulting in an excellent base from which future research can expect to benefit.

Together these two chapters are the first of a series of reviews of ameliorative approaches to a variety of problems of older people that are planned for future volumes of the *Annual Review*. Early interventive efforts are inevitably evaluated in a qualitative manner, if at all. This stage is followed by quantitative assessments that tend to be elemental and often methodologically flawed, yet provide enough suggestive evidence in favor of or against the efficacy of a program to warrant further, more sophisticated evaluation. It is during the early stages of careful evaluative effort that reviews such as those in this volume may be most helpful in collating the best of what has preceded it and pointing toward new investigations that will use improved concepts and methods.

M. Powell Lawton, Ph.D.
George L. Maddox, Ph.D.

# Contributors

**Bengt B. Arnetz, M.D., Ph.D.**
Laboratory for Clinical Stress
   Research
Karolinska Institute
National Institute for
   Psychosocial Factors and
   Health
Stockholm, Sweden

**Margaret Frysinger, B.S.**
Department of Individual and
   Family Studies
College of Human Development
Pennsylvania State University
University Park, Pennsylvania

**Dolores E. Gallagher, Ph.D.**
Geriatric Research, Education
   and Clinical Center (GRECC)
Veterans Administration
   Medical Center
Palo Alto, California
Stanford University School of
   Medicine
Stanford, California

**Susan Harris, B.A.**
Department of Psychology
Yale University
New Haven, Connecticut

**Amy Horowitz, D.S.W.**
The Lighthouse: New York
   Association for the Blind
New York, New York

**M. Powell Lawton, Ph.D.**
Philadelphia Geriatric Center
Philadelphia, Pennsylvania

**George L. Maddox, Ph.D.**
University Council on Aging
   and Human Development
Duke University
Durham, North Carolina

**Judith Rodin, Ph.D.**
Department of Psychology
Yale University
New Haven, Connecticut

**Robert L. Rubinstein, Ph.D.**
Philadelphia Geriatric Center
Philadelphia, Pennsylvania

**Michael A. Smyer, Ph.D.**
Department of Individual and
   Family Studies
College of Human Development
Pennsylvania State University
University Park, Pennsylvania

**Bernard D. Starr, Ph.D.**
School of Education
City University of New York
Brooklyn College
Brooklyn, New York

**Christine Timko, Ph.D.**
Department of Psychology
Yale University
New Haven, Connecticut

**FORTHCOMING**

**THE ANNUAL REVIEW OF
GERONTOLOGY AND GERIATRICS, Volume 6**

**Tentative Contents**

# Some Individual Determinants of Lifestyle: American and European Views

## CHAPTER 1

# The Construct of Control:
# Biological and Psychosocial Correlates

Judith Rodin, Ph.D.,
Christine Timko, Ph.D., and
Susan Harris, B.A.
Department of Psychology
Yale University
New Haven, Connecticut

## INTRODUCTION

The need for mastery and control of one's environment has long been viewed as basic to human motivation (cf. Adler, 1929; deCharms, 1968; Erickson, 1950; Piaget, 1952; White, 1959). More recently it has been suggested that the presence or absence of control has profound effects on people's emotional, cognitive, and physical well-being (e.g., Glass & Singer, 1972; Seligman, 1975; Wortman & Brehm, 1975). One of the purposes of the present review is to examine the relationship between opportunities for both actual and perceived control and aging. Do opportunities for the exercise of control and perceptions of competence change with old age, and if so, how do they change? After we review studies of the control–aging relationship, and discuss the methodological and theoretical issues they raise, we turn to the second major question of the chapter: What are the positive and negative effects, especially as they relate to health, of variations in older persons' expectancies of and opportunities for control? An examination of the links between aging and control on one hand, and control and well-being on the other, leads us to address a third and final question:

The first author's work is supported by NIH grant AG02455.

Is the impact of enhanced or diminished control influenced by age and age-related events, and if so, why?

## Definitions of Control

The construct of control has been formally defined within several research traditions, and its definition has been influenced by the particular domain of inquiry. For example, in a sociological analysis of the reciprocal effects between job conditions and human functioning, Kohn (1976; Kohn & Schooler, 1978, 1982) defined occupational self-direction as the use of initiative, thought, and independent judgment in work. The environmental determinants of occupational self-direction included degree of substantive complexity and extent of routinization of the work as well as closeness of supervision. In learned helplessness research, which is based on psychological learning theory, control is defined as a function of the degree of contingency between a response and an outcome (Seligman, 1975; Seligman, Maier, & Solomon, 1971). Here studies have been conducted primarily in the performance domain. In another learning theory approach, Rotter (1966) differentiated between generalized expectancies for internal and external control of reinforcements. According to Rotter's theory, when people perceive events as contingent upon their own behavior or their own personal characteristics, they have an internal locus of control orientation. When, however, events are perceived as resulting from chance, or the control of powerful others, or as unpredictable, such perceptions represent a belief in external control. Because much of the research on control and aging has utilized Rotter's (1966) I-E Scale or variations of it, the construct of locus of control will be discussed at length later in this chapter.

Also derived from the social learning theory tradition, Bandura's (1977) notions of self-efficacy and outcome expectations are closely tied to conceptions of perceived personal control. Perceived self-efficacy refers to people's judgments of their own capabilities to execute different levels of performance in different domains. Self-efficacy expectations have been shown to influence subjects' levels of motivation, cognitions, emotions, and behaviors in coping with aversive events. Bandura makes an important distinction between judgments of self-efficacy and judgments of the likely consequences of one's behavior, termed outcome expectations. He pointed out that Rotter's (1966) conceptual scheme is primarily concerned with people's causal beliefs about action–outcome contingencies, rather than with personal efficacy, and that learned helplessness (Maier & Seligman, 1976) focuses exclusively on response–outcome expectations. The distinction between judgments of self-competence and environmental responsiveness will also be discussed in a later section of this review, since it has proved useful in understanding the control–aging literature.

Baron and Rodin (1978) operationally defined objective or actual control as the ability to regulate or influence intended outcomes through selective responding. They defined perceived control as the expectation of having the power to participate in making decisions in order to obtain desirable consequences. One aspect of perceived control involves a sense of freedom of choice, or being aware of opportunities so that preferred goals and means may be selected. A second aspect, perceived control over outcomes, refers to an individual's belief in a causal link between his or her own actions and the consequences that follow. The crucial component in perceived control is the assumption people make that they are responsible for their outcomes through their own efforts. Baron and Rodin's explicit differentiation between actual and perceived control is necessary from both theoretical and empirical standpoints, because people's perceptions of control have often been found to be inaccurate assessments of their objective levels of control (cf. Abramson & Alloy, 1980; Langer, 1975; Weisz, 1983). Since judgments of control are not always veridical, it is important to maintain the distinction between objective and subjective control in discussing control and aging.


## THE CONTROL–AGING RELATIONSHIP

### Hypotheses

Much has been written on how and why personal control is influenced by growing old, and the majority of theorists have hypothesized that the elderly experience a decline in both objective and subjective control. Specifically, environmental and biological events are thought to decrease the two types of control, which are postulated to act as determinants of one another. Rodin (in press-a, in press-b), for example, suggested that aging frequently produces lowered perceived control because many environmental events that accompany old age result in limits on the range of outcomes that actually are attainable. These environmental factors include the losses of roles, norms, and appropriate reference groups, which are often created by major life events such as retirement and bereavement (cf. Kuypers & Bengtson, 1973). Weisz (1983) emphasized the association between old age and loss of actual contingency for a number of important outcomes; for instance, retirement entails a loss of contingency in the world of work, and one's health status depends less on voluntary behaviors and more on biological forces. Indeed, the biological changes that occur in late adulthood, particularly acquired deficits in one's physical abilities, may induce generalized feelings of lack of control, as well as actual helplessness (Rodin, 1980, in press-a, in press-b; Schulz, 1980).

Yet another challenge to the sense of control of older people is presented by negative stereotypes that exist about the aging process (cf. Butler, 1970). Aging labels such as "old" and "institutionalized" connote an inferior status in themselves (Avorn & Langer, 1982). Kuypers and Bengtson (1973) argued specifically that the elderly are quite susceptible to social labeling, and that the consequences of generally negative aging labels in Western societies involve the loss of coping abilities and the internalization of a sense of incompetence. Similarly, Rodin and Langer (1980) suggested that negative labeling and stigmatization contribute to behavior on the part of older individuals that confirms the prevalent stereotypes of old age and so lead to lowered self-esteem and diminished feelings of control. In a developmental analysis of self-efficacy, Bandura (1981) described the elderly as a group particularly likely to underestimate their true competence in a number of important life areas. Again, Bandura attributed some of this underestimation to widespread social stereotypes about characteristics of the aged. He also stated that mistaken perceptions of declining competence in intellectual and physical abilities can be stimulated by using younger groups rather than one's peers as a basis for social comparison.

Not only do negative stereotypes of aging influence judgments of self-efficacy, but an older person's observations of other, less competent elderly, through the media or personal contact, also may lead to modeling of helpless behaviors (cf. Bandura, 1977). In a study of the acquisition of learned helplessness, DeVellis, DeVellis, and McCauley (1978) demonstrated experimentally that expecting a low degree of contingency in a given situation can result from vicarious exposure to noncontingency. Although this experiment was conducted with college students, its results have implications for older people. For example, vicarious exposure to dependency and passivity is especially likely to occur in a nursing home setting, where independent activities are rarely reinforced by staff (cf. Baltes & Reisenzein, in press). Within and outside of institutions, people in contact with older individuals may be apt to assist with tasks that were formerly implemented independently. Such assistance, although well-intentioned, may undermine the individual's sense of control as well as his or her task performance (Avorn & Langer, 1982; Langer & Imber, 1979).

Based on these numerous hypotheses concerning a possible association between growing old and loss of control, several studies have examined the relationship between age per se and people's feelings of control. These studies, however, taken together, do not provide clear evidence that perceived control either increases or decreases as a function of age. We will review these studies briefly and then consider why such a weak relationship has been obtained.

## Studies of the Relationship between Age and Feelings of Control

Many studies in this area have used Rotter's (1966) I-E scale or modifications of it. Rotter's scale treats locus of control orientation as a unidimensional construct, with beliefs in internal and external control representing opposite poles of a continuum. Using this scale, investigators have found greater internality, greater externality, and no differences when comparing older and younger subjects. For example, Rotella and Bunker (1978) and Wolk and Kurtz (1975) found that the scores of samples of noninstitutionalized elderly were more internal than normative scores for younger samples. In a cross-sectional study, Gatz and Siegler (1981) found that middle-aged and elderly subjects were higher in internality than college students. However, subsequently Siegler and Gatz (1985) evaluated data from a six-year longitudinal study of a cohort of 46- to 69-year-olds, and found a decrease in internality over time. Similarly, Cicirelli (1980) showed increasing externality with progressing age, and Lao (1975) showed that people over 60 and teenagers were more external than middle-aged subjects.

In addition to findings of greater internality and greater externality among older adults, findings of no difference as a function of age have also been reported. Using elderly non-institutionalized samples, many studies found no association between age and internal–external perceptions of control (Brown & Granick, 1983; Hunter, Linn, Harris, & Pratt, 1980; Krantz & Stone, 1978; Kuypers, 1972). In studies of institutionalized elderly, Duke, Shaheen, and Nowicki (1974) and Fawcett, Stonner, and Zepelin (1980) also found no difference in locus of control scores from norms for college students. Wolk's (1976) elderly subjects who lived in a retirement village were similar to college students on average level of internal control, but residents of an institution were significantly lower in internality than both of the other groups. Nehrke, Hulicka, and Morganti (1980) compared three groups of hospitalized inpatients—men in their 50s, 60s, and 70 or older—and no differences among the groups were revealed in locus of control orientation.

The lack of consistency in the results of studies using unidimensional measures of locus of control makes it impossible to state conclusively whether or how control perceptions change in old age. Let us consider some reasons why the data appear so confusing.

*Dimensionality.*   One reason for the contradictory results of investigations of the control–aging relationship involves questions about the Rotter scale itself. Although it has been widely used within and outside of the field of gerontology, it has also been widely criticized. One of the major criticisms concerns Rotter's (1966) original assumption that locus of control orientation represents a one-dimensional construct (Lefcourt, 1966, 1981; Phares, 1973, 1976). Factor analytic studies of the I-E scale (e.g., Gurin, Gurin, Lao, & Beattie, 1969; Mirels, 1970) support the notion that control should be conceptualized multidimensionally. In one factor analytic study by Gurin, Gurin, and Morrison (1978), three factors were revealed: the first for personal efficacy, the second for control ideology, and the third for political control.

In response to criticisms of the unidimensional view of locus of control, multidimensional measures have been suggested (e.g., Lefcourt, 1981). One multidimensional measure was designed by Levenson (1974), based on the Rotter scale. Levenson hypothesized that, contrary to Rotter's homogeneous conceptualization of externals, those people who believe the world is not ordered behave and think differently from those who believe the world is ordered, but controlled by powerful others. In addition, Levenson speculated that a person who believes in chance control of reinforcements is cognitively and behaviorally different from a person who is simply low in internality. To test her hypotheses, Levenson designed a scale to measure three orthogonal dimensions of personal control. The Internal dimension represents beliefs in personal mastery and the effectiveness of one's own actions. The Chance factor assesses the belief that events happen randomly and are due to external forces such as fate or luck. The Powerful Others dimension also measures beliefs in external forces, but in this case the source of control is powerful people and is therefore nonrandom.

The issue of whether control is most usefully conceptualized as a uni- or multidimensional construct is crucial to gerontologists, because age might be differentially related to different control dimensions (cf. Lachman, in press-a; Rodin, in press-b). For example, Lachman (in press-a) hypothesized that because aging sensitizes people to the role of chance and luck in their lives, and because the aged come to see younger people as more powerful than themselves, the elderly should appear more externally oriented on Levenson's Chance and Powerful Others scales. At the same time, because older individuals have accumulated a vast number of mastery experiences in at least a few domains, their belief in Internal control may increase, especially if realistic adjustments are made in particular expectations or goals. Lachman's own work has not confirmed these hypotheses, however.

In one investigation using Levenson's locus of control scale, Lachman (1983) conducted a longitudinal study in which a sample of noninstitutionalized elderly subjects completed a battery of personality and intelligence tests on two occasions two years apart. Results showed that Internal control scores declined from the first testing to the second, while Chance and Powerful Others scores remained stable. However, in subsequent cross-sectional studies, Lachman (1984) found no effects of age on any of the Levenson subscales.

A cross-sectional study by Saltz and Magruder-Habib (1982) of subjects from 21 to 88 years old found that the elderly appeared more external than young adults on the Chance factor, but no differences appeared on the Internal or Powerful Others control dimensions. In another cross-sectional investigation, Ryckman and Malikioski (1975) administered Levenson's scale to respondents ranging in age from 17 to 79 years. The oldest subjects were not different from any other age-group in internality, and were actually less external than middle-aged subjects on scales measuring beliefs in chance and control by powerful others.

Thus, despite Levenson's refinement of the measurement of locus of control, studies using her multidimensional measure have been no more conclusive regarding age–control relationships than studies that used unidimensional measures. Using another approach, some investigators have considered distinctions between outcome and self-efficacy expectations in an effort to elucidate a possible relationship between aging and control.

Weisz (1983), in considering whether control perceptions are veridical over the life course, specified that for people to make accurate judgments of their capacity for control, they must be able to gauge two factors. First, they must be able to judge the degree to which an outcome is contingent upon their behavior, and second, they must be able to judge their degree of competence in producing the behaviors upon which a desired outcome depends. Additionally, individuals must be able to combine these two factors correctly into a composite control judgment. Weisz stated that studies to date had provided little direct evidence as to the accuracy of contingency reasoning among the elderly, or on the veridicality of self-assessments of competence by older people.

Building on earlier factor analytic studies of Rotter's I-E scale, Gurin (1980) distinguished perceptions of personal competence from perceived environmental responsiveness. At the same time, Brim (1980) made a similar distinction between a person's sense of self-confidence and his or her action–outcome expectancies. Together, they (Gurin & Brim, 1984) evaluated data gathered in the Institute for Social Research's national cross-sectional surveys that have been conducted nearly every two years since 1952. While these surveys assessed only the perceived responsiveness of political institutions and authorities rather than measuring perceptions of environmental responsiveness in general, personal efficacy measures assessed self-perceptions of both general competence and competence in the political arena specifically.

Analyses of historical trends in both control dimensions revealed that overall there was little variation in estimates of personal control since the surveys began. However, perceptions of political responsiveness reached a high in the late 1950s through the mid-1960s, and then declined continuously until 1980. These results suggest that evaluations of the external, political world are more influenced by public events than are evaluations of self-efficacy. Unfortunately, analyses of age effects in the data did not yield definite conclusions about perceptions of political responsiveness—or generalized personal self-efficacy—as lifespan issues. Regarding self-efficacy, Gurin and Brim did suggest that as people age, new roles may provide direct substitutes for former roles; therefore, one's overall level of self-efficacy may remain stable, although the domains in which one feels competent are likely to change. The age effect on the measure of political self-efficacy was significant and curvilinear, with the highest sense of competence expressed by middle-aged respondents.

Lachman (in press-b) analyzed data collected for the Michigan Panel Study of Income Dynamics. Subjects were 36 to 63 years old at the first of three measurement occasions. In her study, Lachman divided the sample into seven age-cohort groups and used a sequential strategy in order to examine both ontogenic and historical change patterns in a measure of personal efficacy. Lachman's oldest cohort showed the highest average level of perceived self-efficacy. Results also showed that although all of the age-cohort groups were relatively stable in self-efficacy perceptions over time, the oldest cohort showed the lowest degree of correlational stability. This suggests that there may be increasing interindividual variability in perceived self-efficacy in the later years.

Although the field appears to be reaching a consensus that the crucial dimensions of perceived control include both perceptions of personal competence and behavior–outcome contingencies, even studies using these multidimensional measures have yet to yield agreement concerning the relationship between aging and control. A further explanation for the conflicting findings may involve the global nature of the measures discussed thus far. This explanation is best presented by going back to Rotter's initial position on locus of control expectancies.

*Generality.*    While some studies criticized Rotter's (1966) unidimensional construct of control, others criticized his initial assertion that locus of control orientation represents a generalized personality trait. Rotter described expectancy as a global characteristic that is stable over time and across situations. However, as reviewed by Lefcourt (1981), evidence accumulated showing that individuals' control beliefs often changed in response to a variety of life events such as draft lotteries, employment experiences, and clinical or educational interventions. Furthermore, studies convincingly demonstrated that a person who displays internally oriented behaviors in some situations will as likely as not display externally oriented behaviors in other settings (Endler & Edwards, 1978; Reid, 1977).

Responding to the body of research indicating that control orientations are at least partially situationally determined, Rotter later (1975) acknowledged this influence. Although he stated that generalized assessments concerning locus of control are appropriate and meaningful for many research purposes, Rotter also noted that some research goals may require the development and use of domain-specific measures. Such research goals would include achievement of a high level of predictability within a particular domain. In accordance with this reasoning, a number of investigators have constructed domain-specific control measures, and some of these measures have been administered to elderly samples.

Lachman (in press-a) and Rodin (in press-b) have both argued that domain-specific measures of perceived control may be more appropriate for use with the aged than generalized measures. They hypothesized that locus of control expectancies may show differential age changes across different domains, so that general measures may mask important age changes. Underlying this hypothesis is also the assumption that situations do not have uniform meanings across the life span. For example, health and intellectual functioning are two areas in which expectancies of personal efficacy may change with old age.

Bradley and Webb (1976) conducted a cross-sectional study of four age groups—adolescents, and young, middle-aged, and elderly adults—assessing locus of control beliefs with respect to the domains of physical, intellectual, and social achievement. Results showed that subjects over 60 scored the most externality on physical functioning, whereas both the elderly and teenage groups were more external on perceived social ability. No differences appeared on locus of control for achievement in the intellectual domain.

In Lachman's (1984) two cross-sectional studies, the domains of intellectual functioning and health were evaluated. In both studies, older people were more likely than college students to believe that a decline in intellectual abilities was inevitable in later life (Chance scale). In one of the two studies, they were also more likely to believe that they needed help to successfully complete cognitive tasks (Powerful Others scale) and less likely to believe that they were responsible for maintaining their levels of intellectual functioning (Internal scale) than younger subjects.

As part of Lachman's second study, all subjects completed the Multidimensional Health Locus of Control (MHLC) scale (Wallston & Wallston, 1981), which includes Internal, Chance, and Powerful Other factors specific to the health domain. Compared to the college students, older people believed that powerful other people have greater control over their health. Beliefs in one's own control over health outcomes and in chance as a health determinant were equivalent between the two groups. Another study that examined age differences on the MHLC scales showed results similar to Lachman's, in that elderly subjects more strongly endorsed the Powerful Others scale than a group of middle-aged adults (Saltz & Magruder-Habib, 1982). Taken together, these studies suggest that domain-specific assessments of perceived control may be more sensitive to age effects than global measures.

It may be particularly important to use domain-specific measures of locus of control when the purpose of the research is prediction. Lachman (1984) conducted hierarchical regression analyses to test the relative advantage of domain-specific and generalized scales for the prediction of intellectual performance by elderly subjects. The analyses showed that when the generalized measures were entered in the regression equation in the first stage, the domain-specific scores accounted for additional variance at the second stage. However, when the domain-specific measures were entered first, the generalized scales did not explain addditional variance at the second step. Lachman concluded that when the goal is to maximize the amount of variance accounted for within a domain, generalized and domain-specific measures of locus of control should be used in conjunction with one another.

Rodin has been conducting a longitudinal study of several hundred community-residing elderly for five years, in which multidimensional, domain-specific assessments of control are obtained every two months for each subject. Through extensive pilot-testing, Rodin defined nine domains of importance to people 60 and over: relationships with spouse, with immediate family members, and with friends, plus personal safety, personal economic conditions, health, housing, transportation, and daily activities and/or work. For each domain, importance of the domain, outcome expectancies, and feelings of personal efficacy are assessed at regular intervals. It is intended that this type of study will help to explain more fully both stability and change in perceived control, as well as their antecedents and consequences.

*Cohort Effects.* A final issue in interpreting the studies examining the relationship between aging per se and feelings of control is overreliance on cross-sectional data. As has been noted many times in the study of aging, conventional cross-sectional investigations of age-related changes confound age-related and cohort effects. Only certain types of longitudinal data, with multiple cohorts, can simultaneously address the issues of intra-individual variability, cohort differences, and intra-cohort differences, all of which are necessary for determining the extent of actual developmental change in perceived control (cf. Gurin & Brim, 1984; Lachman, 1983, in press-a; Rodin, in press-b). The studies reviewed here on the aging–control relationship have been conducted over a period of 10 or 15 years, beginning about 1970. This body of data may well reflect historical effects on perceived control, for Rotter (1975) found that even college students have become increasingly external, as measured by the I-E Scale, over a 15-year period.

In addition to cohort effects on control expectations, there is likely to be intra-cohort variability. Such demographic factors as gender, socioeconomic status, education, and race have all been found in some studies to be related to various measures of perceived control, within and across different age groups, including the elderly. It is unclear from the data presently available whether patterns of change in control perceptions vary as a function of these factors. With longitudinal data, intra-cohort variability may be evaluated by examining the relative ordering of individual subjects on control measures from one time to another, using indices of correlational stability.

**Variations in the
Impact of Control**

So far we have focused on the measurement and methodological problems of studies that have examined the aging–control relationship, in
attempting to explain the conflicting results of such studies. However, a
theoretical interpretation of the inconsistent findings is also possible,
and this hypothesis is amenable to empirical investigation. We suggest
that the studies just reviewed appear contradictory and unclear because
age per se may not bear a direct relationship to control expectancies.
Rather we propose that age may exert its effects by influencing the
relationship between variations in personal control and psychological
and physical well-being. Thus one would look for correlations between
age and the effects of control-relevant manipulations on psychological
and physical well-being, rather than for direct correlations between control and age per se. While lack of personal control is potentially damag-
ing for people of all ages, the elderly may be psychologically and physically more vulnerable to the negative effects of uncontrollability
because of environmental and physiological changes that commonly occur in old age.

    In the sections that follow, we review evidence suggesting that
personal control is associated with beneficial effects among older individuals, and that the loss of control is related to poor outcomes. Specifically, we first review studies that investigated the correlates of perceived control in four areas: psychological adjustment, intellectual
abilities, activity, and physical health. We then describe interventions
with the aged that have manipulated control to determine its effects in
these four areas of functioning. Unfortunately, there are as yet no
studies that have directly compared the strength of these associations
for subjects of different ages, but we hope to point to the types of
studies that should be done.

## CORRELATES OF CONTROL

There is extensive literature on the correlates of differences in perceived control among older people. Much of that research has investigated the association between control and psychological adjustment,
but the areas of physical health, cognitive functioning, and activity
level have also been explored. As is the case for studies just reviewed
concerning the relationship between control and age per se, many
studies of the correlates of control have utilized variations of Rotter's

I-E scale, while fewer were based on the investigators' own measures of control expectancies. Although studies varied widely as to how psychological adjustment, health, intellectual functioning, and activity were operationalized, certain indicators were more commonly used. Psychological adjustment was typically equated with greater life satisfaction, positive self-concept, positive affect, and feeling young for one's age. Health was frequently indicated by global self-reports of health status, but more specific measures were also used, such as pain and illness experiences and utilization of medical services. Similarly, activity measures often referred to general activity level, but sometimes were broken down into social, work, and organizational activity indices. Tests indexing intellectual functioning most often consisted of WAIS subtests and were usually quite narrow in focus.

The age and characteristics of the samples chosen for study also varied widely in this body of research. Reports of studies usually specified the residential settings of subjects, but did not always describe other sample characteristics that may have been related to locus of control expectancies. Elderly samples residing in various settings were often compared in these studies, on the assumption that different settings afford residents different levels of objective control.

## Psychological Adjustment

*Life Satisfaction*    Investigations of the relationship between perceived control and psychological adjustment frequently used life satisfaction as the primary indicator of adjustment, in conjunction with other indicators. In an early study of noninstitutionalized elderly, Palmore and Luikart (1972) found that locus of control was the third strongest predictor of life satisfaction (after self-rated health and organizational activity), with internality making a significant positive contribution to satisfaction. Wolk and Kurtz (1975) reported that internal, noninstitutionalized elderly were both more satisfied with their lives and better adjusted than their external counterparts, and Mancini (1980–1981) similarly found that internally oriented residents of public housing were higher on life satisfaction scores. In a study of residents of nursing homes, private homes, and public housing, Nehrke, Bellucci, and Gabriel (1977–78) reported that internality was positively correlated with life satisfaction within each setting. However, Hulicka, Morganti, and Cataldo (1975) found that perceived choice was not related to life satisfaction among institutionalized and community-residing women, but was related to positive self-concept.

Reid and his colleagues developed their own measure of locus of control orientation. Their instrument measured both desire and expectancy for control with the measures combined into one overall desired control score. The scores were related to numerous variables including life satisfaction, mood state, and self-concept. Studies of both institutionalized and noninstitutionalized older subjects (Reid, Haas, & Hawkings, 1977; Reid & Ziegler, 1980; Ziegler & Reid, 1979) showed positive correlations between perceived internal control and life satisfaction. Feelings of control were also highly related to positive self-concept and feelings of tranquility. Data on the relationship between mood and depression were more variable from study to study.

In more recent work, Reid and Ziegler (1980; Ziegler & Reid, 1983) have studied the same subjects prospectively, taking measures at two or three points in time. While internality scores continued to be correlated with life satisfaction, hierarchical regressions to predict later satisfaction from earlier measures of control did not yield significant findings. Such data suggest that life satisfaction and feelings of control measured at the same time may be correlated because both reflect good feelings about one's current life situation. If we accept this assumption, which views feelings of control as a measure of state rather than trait, we would not necessarily expect feelings of control at time one to predict life satisfaction at time two, but would expect time two measures of these variables to be correlated. Such correlations were obtained in the Reid and Ziegler (1980), Ziegler and Reid (1983), and Storandt, Wittels, and Botwinick (1975) studies.

The only study to find that external rather than internal locus of control was correlated with life satisfaction was reported by Felton and Kahana (1974). Whether this exceptional finding was due to their unusual measure of control, which was based on residents' solutions to hypothetical problems, or to the fact that the environment of the nursing home setting they tested was so constrained that only external patients could feel satisfied, can only be speculated upon. There is, however, support for the hypothesis that the degree of constraint in a setting interacts with individual predispositions for control to affect life satisfaction.

Wolk (1976) studied elderly residents of a retirement village—a setting with low situational constraint—and elderly residents of an institution—a setting high in situational constraint. Within the low-constraint sample, internality was positively correlated with life satisfaction, self-concept, and developmental task adjustment. No significant correlates of perceived control were found among residents of the high-constraint home. In a similar study, Wolk and Telleen (1976) again compared nursing home residents to retirement village occupants. In the low-constraint setting, perceived personal autonomy was positively correlated with having greater life satisfaction, a positive self-concept, and more adequate developmental task accomplishment, while in the high-constraint setting perceived autonomy was positively related to life satisfaction only.

Conceptually related to studies comparing settings according to degree of constraint are those that looked at other setting variables that might relate to restrictiveness of one sort or another. For example, Fawcett et al. (1980) studied elderly women in two homes for the aged where the women in one home had been institutionalized for a much greater number of years on the average than subjects in the second home. Internality was found to be positively related to life satisfaction in the home where there was a shorter average length of institutionalization, but was unrelated to satisfaction in the second setting. In a multiple regression analysis predicting life satisfaction scores, perceived institutional constraint accounted for more variance than locus of control scores.

*Morale.* Slight variants of the studies relating control to life satisfaction are those that used morale as the measure of psychological adjustment. In general, the same type of relationship accrues, with various measures of perceived control and choice correlating positively with higher morale (Brown & Granick, 1983; Chang, 1978; Pohl & Fuller, 1980). Other studies have found similar relationships between feelings of control and self-esteem (Hunter, Linn, & Harris, 1981–82) or feeling young for one's age (Linn & Hunter, 1979), both of which may also be taken to reflect morale.

*Coping.* Kuypers (1972) reported that internal locus of control scores among noninstitutionalized elderly were positively related to better coping abilities, in that internals showed greater adaptability and less defensiveness than externals. Holahan, Holahan, and Belk (1984) hypothesized that factors fostering elderly persons' perceptions of self-efficacy may be an essential aspect of coping with both life change events and daily hassles. For men, self-efficacy with respect to life events was negatively correlated with depression and the experience of psychosomatic symptoms, whereas self-efficacy regarding daily hassles was negatively correlated with symptomatology only. Among women, life events self-efficacy was negatively correlated with loneliness, while hassles self-efficacy was negatively correlated with agitation, loneliness, positive attitudes toward one's own aging, and depression.

*Social Support.* Studies by Cicirelli (1980) and Bohm (1983) both examined the relationship between control expectancies and variables related to social support. Cicirelli found that internal control was positively associated with elderly subjects' greater feelings of cohesiveness with their siblings and children. In forming the hypotheses for her study, Bohm drew on Cicirelli's results and the results of other studies showing that higher perceived control is associated with greater social support, as well as research showing that greater social support benefits psychological and physical functioning. Bohm hypothesized that since control and social support have such a strong positive relationship, the association between social support and level of functioning might be due to variations in perceived control. Her findings confirmed this hypothesis. After entering the control variables in hierarchical regression analyses, various measures of social support did not, in general, make a significant additional contribution to predicting psychological and physical well-being. Elderly subjects who were higher in perceived control showed better psychological and physical functioning.

**Health**

Most of the studies investigating health correlates of locus of control expectancies among older adults have utilized global self-report measures of health status. Studies by Mancini (1980–81) and Brothen and Detzner (1983) both found that internals reported that they were in better overall health than externals. Studies by Hunter and her colleagues found inconsistent relationships between locus of control and health measures including self-report of health, disability, and degree of daily pain (Hunter et al., 1980; Hunter et al., 1981–82; Linn & Hunter, 1979). No relationship between perceived control and overall health was found by Wolk (1976) for subjects living in either high- or low-constraint settings.

The studies conducted by Reid and his colleagues also yielded inconsistent results regarding the control–health relationship with findings of both positive and no correlations between internality and self-reports of good health (Reid & Ziegler, 1980; Ziegler & Reid, 1979). Ziegler and Reid's (1983) study of elderly persons who relocated to a new residence suggested that locus of control was uncorrelated with health status at six months after relocation, but that internality was positively associated with better health at the 18-month follow-up.

Brown and Granick (1983) and Hunter et al. (1980) tested specific health-related behaviors and outcomes for their relationship to personal control. Both studies suggested that control perceptions were unrelated to the number of previous hospitalizations elderly subjects reported. While Brown and Granick found that externals reported a greater number of doctor visits, in the Hunter et al. study, locus of control was not related to the number of times subjects had seen a doctor in the past six months. Among the subjects of Hunter et al., externals were more likely to be taking medications and had more problems with their hearing and eyesight, while Brown and Granick's external subjects had fewer hearing problems but were more likely to have high blood pressure. Both studies found that subjects' reports concerning a large variety of other health problems and illnesses (e.g., trouble with walking, headaches) were not associated with control perceptions.

Bohm (1983) also tested specific health indicators for their relationships to control, but added two facets to her study that were not included in other investigations of this issue. First, she specified three different types of perceived control on the basis of factor analyses: global control, ability to mobilize support when needed, and ease with which elderly people feel that they get their needs met. Second, Bohm statistically controlled for the severity of subjects' actual illness status in tests of the efficacy–health relationship. Her data showed that global control was inversely related to use of medications and frequency of doctor visits. Both global and support mobilization control were negatively correlated with number of self-treatments, but were positively related to compliance with medication regimens. Finally, perceived ease in getting one's needs met was negatively correlated with number of emergency room visits.

## Intellectual Abilities

Only a few studies have examined the intellectual correlates of locus of control perceptions in the elderly population. In an early study, Kuypers (1972) characterized internals as having greater intellectual and cognitive abilities, as well as greater cognitive sensitivity and awareness, in comparison to externals. Brown and Granick (1983) found that internals performed better than externals on four subtests of the WAIS, but that eight other standard IQ measures were unrelated to locus of control. Poorer memory for recent events was reported by externals in the Hunter et al. (1980) study.

Lachman, Baltes, Nesselroade, and Willis (1982) gave elderly subjects a test battery that included Levenson's multidimensional I-E scale, intelligence-specific scales, and 17 psychometric ability tests representing the factors of general reasoning, crystallized intelligence, perceptual speed, and memory span. There was a high positive correlation between measures of internal locus of control and various measures of intellectual performance.

In a longitudinal study, Lachman (1983) gave a sample of older subjects a battery of intelligence and personality tests on two occasions two years apart. Causal modeling techniques were used to test alternative directional hypotheses regarding changes in personal control and intellectual functioning. Support was found for the position that higher initial levels of global feelings of control and fluid intelligence predicted positive changes in perceived efficacy on the intellectual sphere.

## Activity

Only four studies have included measures of elderly subjects' activity level in investigating the correlates of locus of control. Wolk and Kurtz (1975) found that internals were more active than externals, as reflected in scores of daily behavioral involvement in the environment over the preceding month. Among elderly subjects who had very recently relocated to a new apartment complex, internality was positively associated with a higher frequency of participation in activities offered by the complex (Ziegler & Reid, 1983). Using more specific indicators of activity, Hunter et al. (1980) found that externals attended organizational meetings less often than internals, did less volunteer work, and also had more problems with grocery shopping and handling finances. The two groups were equivalent on amount of TV watching, frequency of seeing friends, and having problems doing household chores. In Wolk's (1976) study comparing elderly residents of high- and low-constraint settings, internality was positively correlated with activity level for the low-constraint sample, but locus of control was unrelated to activity among highly constrained residents.

## Summary

On the whole, the research just reviewed indicates that greater perceived control is strongly associated with better psychological adjustment and cognitive functioning among older people. Although some studies found that control expectancies were unrelated to certain indicators of subjects' adjustment and intellectual ability, only one study found any evidence that externality is linked with more adequate adaptation. The number of studies examining activity in relation to locus of control is very small, but they do suggest that internality appears to be positively correlated with greater activity in general.

The evidence that internality is associated with better physical health appears relatively weak on the basis of the studies just reviewed. However, measures of health were also less consistent among studies, ranging from global self-reports to experiences with specific health problems and use of the medical care system. Additionally, most studies examining health correlates of control failed to account for severity of illness, which would clearly influence health-related behaviors. In contrast to correlational studies, intervention studies with older, and usually infirm, subjects have suggested strongly that increased control benefits subjects' health outcomes. We now consider these intervention studies.

## INTERVENTIONS USING CONTROL

None of the studies examining the correlates of perceived control was able to address the question of whether or not there is a causal relationship between feelings of control and functional ability, and if so, what the causal direction between the variables might be. Is perceived control an antecedent or a consequence of functional ability? It is possible that there is a reciprocal relationship, or that the correlation is due to the fact that both have a third, causal variable in common. Several investigators have manipulated objective control in interventions with older people to begin to determine how level of actual control influences psychological and physical health. We describe these manipulations in a bit more detail than we have other studies because their effects on specific outcomes often appear tied to the operationalization of control used.

### Relocation Studies

In a review and analysis of the literature on relocation of the aged, Schulz and Brenner (1977) presented a conceptual model that emphasized the importance of control and predictability as mediators of relocation outcomes. The model posited that one's response to the stress of relocation is determined largely by the perceived controllability and predictability of the move, as well as by differences between the pre- and post-relocation environments in terms of the degree of control afforded. Schulz and Brenner found support for their model in numerous relocation studies that commonly used mortality rate as the dependent variable.

Krantz and Schulz (1980) tested one aspect of the model proposed by Schulz and Brenner. They hypothesized that increasing the predictability of the institutional environment for people just entering a long-term care facility would inhibit the psychological and physical deficits typically associated with relocation. Older people recently admitted to a nursing home were randomly assigned to one of three experimental conditions. In the relevant information condition, new residents received information designed to enhance the predictability of the institution; for example, they were given directions for finding various facilities. Subjects in the irrelevant information condition received the same amount of information, but this information did not help to make the environment predictable. Control condition subjects were given the usual short orientation message by staff members of the institution.

After the intervention, subjects in the relevant information group were more likely than control group subjects to say that their emotional health had improved since arriving at the institution, and that their physical health had improved in the previous two weeks. In comparison to the control group, the relevant information group was judged by nurses to be healthier and to have a greater zest for life. Additionally, the relevant information group participated in more activities requiring physical effort. On most measures, the irrelevant information group fell between the other groups but did not differ significantly from either one. Measures taken two months after the intervention found no decline in health or psychological status among subjects provided with predictability-enhancing information.

Bers, Bohm, and Rodin (described in Rodin, in press-a) also conducted a relocation study that suggested an important influence on health outcomes of perceived control over the decision to relocate. The sample for the study consisted of hospitalized patients over the age of 65 who were to be discharged to nursing homes within the subsequent week. Half participated in a family interaction task designed to increase feelings of control over the entry decision. The other subjects received no control-relevant treatment. Measures obtained at the time of hospitalization were used to predict which subjects were still in a nursing home one year later, and which subjects had returned home from an institution by that time. The variable that best discriminated between groups was whether or not subjects believed they had control over deciding to move to the nursing home; having control was a better predictor of ultimate return to home than variables related to coping style, self-concept, and illness severity during hospitalization. A multiple regression analysis was performed to predict subjects' health status at one year after discharge from the hospital. This analysis also included a group of subjects that had gone directly home from the hospital. The best predictors of poor health status were illness severity at the time of discharge and entering a nursing home following discharge. However, the third best predictor was perceived control over the decision to relocate, with greater control making a positive contribution to better health.

Taken together, the two relocation studies described here provide further support for the conclusions reached by Schulz and Brenner (1977). Specifically, it appears that the greater the perceived choice an individual has in being relocated, and the more predictable the new environment is, the less negative the effects of the relocation. In addition, decreases in environmental controllability are associated with negative outcomes, while increases in controllability are associated with positive outcomes. Strong support for the second conclusion is provided by a different series of field studies conducted by Rodin and her colleagues and by Schulz and his colleagues with patients already in nursing homes for various periods of time.

## Nursing Home Studies

Langer, Rodin, Beck, Weinman, and Spitzer (1979) randomly assigned elderly nursing home residents to one of three conditions that varied objective control, to determine whether declines in memory and health could be slowed or reversed by enhanced control. Residents in the contingent condition were visited regularly by an experimenter, who asked them to seek out and obtain specific information about the nursing home and then to remember it until the next visit, so that they could receive poker chips redeemable for a gift. In the noncontingent condition, the content and form of the visits were exactly the same, except that no contingency was established between obtaining and remembering the information and earning the chips. In the no-treatment condition subjects were visited once at the beginning and once at the end of the study.

The results revealed that only the contingent group—the group that was afforded the most control—showed significant improvements on memory tasks and overall health as a result of the intervention. The memory tasks consisted of tests for immediate memory, and recent and remote events. Health status was assessed from subjects' medical records, use of major tranquilizers and other medications taken, and vital signs. After the intervention, the contingent group was also more likely to complain when they felt that something was wrong. Complaints were taken as a positive sign in that complaining makes sense only when people believe they can have an effect on their environment.

In another study Langer and Rodin (1976) assessed the effects of a different type of manipulation of control on health and activity. Subjects in one group were called together by the hospital administrator, who delivered a communication that emphasized the residents' responsibility for themselves, enumerated activities that were possible for them to do, and explicated when decisionmaking was possible. A second group was given a talk by the administrator that made explicit what was essentially the implicit message in the nursing home, that it was the staff's responsibility to care for them as patients. Residents for whom responsibility had been emphasized became more active and alert, felt less unhappy, and became increasingly involved in a variety of activities (e.g., movies, contests, socializing with staff, seeing friends), in comparison to the group whose feelings of personal control were not explicitly enhanced. These results have been replicated in two other studies (Banziger & Roush, 1983; Mercer & Kane, 1979). Rodin and Langer (1977) found that most of these group differences remained at 18 months following the intervention. Additionally, during this 18-month period the "responsible" patients showed a significantly greater improvement in health; in fact, only 15 percent of the "responsible" group died within this time, compared to 30 percent of the "nonresponsible" group.

Using a third type of intervention to increase feelings of control, Schulz (1976) organized visits by college undergraduates to nursing home patients. When the patients were given control over the length and timing of the visits, or were told in advance when the visits would take place, or both, they showed improvements in psychological adjustment (e.g., self-reports of happiness, hopelessness; staff's ratings of subjects' zest for life), health (e.g., staff's ratings of subjects' health, quantity of medications taken), and activity (e.g., self-reports of perceived activity level and time devoted to active pursuits, future commitments). However, when the visits were both uncontrollable and unpredictable, patients did not show comparable benefits.

**Failures to Find**
**Positive Outcomes**

In a follow-up study of the long-term effects of Schulz's (1976) intervention, Schulz and Hanusa (1978) collected data from the same subjects at 24, 30, and 42 months after the intervention's end. Results showed that health and zest for life, as judged by staff, declined among subjects who were originally given control or predictability over the student visits. Schulz and Hanusa's findings stand in sharp contrast to the follow-up results obtained by Rodin and Langer (1977), who found that the positive impact of their intervention persisted over time.

Schulz and Hanusa (1978) offered two possible explanations for the declines exhibited by subjects in Schulz's (1976) study. The first explanation was that subjects' expectations for controlling or predicting events in their lives may have been raised by the interventions used and then abruptly violated by the termination of the visits. This explanation suggests that the loss of control may be more aversive than the initial lack of control (Rodin, 1983; in press-a). There are animal studies that have experimentally compared loss to lack of control, indicating that the former is more profound both physiologically and psychologically (e.g., Hanson, Larson, & Snowden, 1976). In a later paper, Schulz and Hanusa (1980) expanded further on the implications of their first explanation for the results of their study. They suggested that, for the majority of older individuals, degree of well-being is more likely the result of relative changes in control opportunities occurring over a short period of time than absolute levels of control. More precisely, it may be only when individuals undergo a sudden change in level of control, as they might due to an experimental intervention, that positive or negative outcomes result. Certainly changes in one's level of control are more salient than one's absolute level, and for this reason loss of control may have a more dramatic effect.

Schulz and Hanusa (1978) also suggested that different attributional patterns may have been generated between subjects in Langer and Rodin's (1976) and Schulz's (1976) studies. Langer and Rodin's manipulation may have altered subjects' beliefs about their ability to control outcomes in the institution. More precisely, the communication given to the experimental group, which emphasized their responsibility for themselves and their outcomes, may have encouraged subjects to believe that their ability to control events would persist over time and across situations. The termination of the experiment need not have affected these beliefs. In contrast, Schulz's intervention may have caused subjects to feel that the opportunity to exercise control was dependent upon the presence of an external agent and so it would not remain in other situations or when the agent was removed. This explanation focuses on the fact that control may only have positive effects when the locus of control is attributed to internal, stable, and global sources (cf. Abramson, Seligman, & Teasdale, 1978; Weiner, 1974).

A third explanation for the different results of Langer and Rodin

(1976) and Schulz (1976) was offered by Ransen (1981), who argued that Langer and Rodin's intervention actually changed the institutional setting while Schulz's did not. Rodin and Langer (1977) suggested that, because different floors in the nursing home were assigned to different experimental conditions, the probability was enhanced that patterns of interaction among residents and staff members would be affected. In addition, as Ransen noted, Langer and Rodin's agent of change was a full-time member of the institution, and the target behaviors involved many aspects of the setting. By contrast, the agents of change in Schulz's study were outsiders—the student visitors—and the visits were the only target behaviors. Thus it is likely that changes in control occur in institutional settings when the progressive mutual accommodation made between people and their physical and social environments is altered.

Schulz and Hanusa's (1978) follow-up study raised two major conceptual issues relevant to how control exerts its effects. The first concerned the potentially important role of subjects' attributions for success and failure in exerting control as mediators of the effects of control on health and psychological state. The second involved the question of what types of control manipulations have psychological and health benefits for institutionalized elderly, and what types have no or detrimental effects. Each of these issues has been addressed empirically but indirectly thus far.

Krantz and Stone (1978) measured the performance of college-aged women and women over 65 on a set of problems before and after they were given feedback regarding their success or failure. For half the subjects, success was attributed to their own actions and for half the subjects failure was attributed to their own actions. Thus all subjects were made to feel that they had control over outcomes that accrued to them; the only difference was whether the outcomes signified success or failure. Subjects who felt their own actions had led to failure performed significantly more poorly on the second problem task than they had on the first problem set; for subjects whose success appeared contingent on their own actions, performance improved. Interestingly, there was no difference in the effects of this manipulation on older versus younger women, or internals versus externals. This study does not inform us, however, about the role of attributions for success or failure on perceived control. Given the importance recently ascribed to attributional phenomena in control-related processes (e.g., Abramson et al., 1978; Rehm, 1977; Seligman, 1978), such studies would seem to be quite important.

Schulz and Hanusa (1979) attempted an orthogonal manipulation of competence and control as they continued their investigation of the effects of control-relevant interventions. Here competence corresponds to perceived self-efficacy and control to the nature of the response–outcome contingencies available. Perceived control and perceived competence were manipulated over a five-week period in order to test the hypothesis that elderly who were both made to feel competent and were given control over an outcome would exhibit better functioning than subjects exposed to either manipulation alone. Subjects receiving the high-competence manipulation were given positive feedback as they worked on cognitive and social skills tasks; subjects assigned to the low-competence condition received the same amount of feedback as they worked on the tasks, but the feedback was ambiguous. In the high-control condition, subjects' receipt of payment for participating in the experiment was made to appear contingent on their performance; in the low-control condition, subjects received payment before beginning the tasks.

Post-intervention self-reports by subjects showed that participants in all treatment conditions were healthier, more active, and higher in perceived control over daily activities than subjects in the no-treatment condition. However, subjects who were exposed to either the high-competence or high-control manipulation demonstrated more positive change in health status and greater zest for life, as rated by staff, than subjects who were exposed to both. The authors explained the unexpected results for the group with high competence and high control by suggesting that the combined manipulation may have raised subjects' perceived control to a level at which the environment was no longer able to provide them with opportunities for exercising their competence (cf. Lawton, Windley, & Byerts, 1982), resulting in relatively greater declines in functional ability.

To test their explanation, Schulz and Hanusa (1979) carried out a conceptual replication of their experiment with college freshmen. They chose college students for their sample because they assumed that opportunities to exercise competence are virtually limitless in a college environment, so that the positive effects of control- and competence-enhancing interventions should be additive. The results of the college study supported the hypothesis that the combined effects of increased competence and control had a greater positive impact than either intervention alone. These studies suggest that for enhanced competence to have positive effects, there must be environmental opportunities to exhibit one's competence. Rodin and Langer (1977) made a similar point in evaluating why their intervention may have had such strong effects. To obtain an appropriate match, environmental alterations may be needed in order to increase opportunities for competent behaviors, or to decrease the difficulty level of required behaviors to prevent expectations for self-efficacy from exceeding actual abilities.

Recently, Rodin (1983) carried out an intervention consisting of explicit skills training to increase self-regulatory behaviors. Rodin randomly assigned residents of a home for older persons to one of several conditions and examined psychological and physiological outcomes. The experimental group received six sessions of self-regulation coping skills training by a psychologist. In these sessions, subjects were made aware of their own forms of negative self-statements, and were taught and practiced positive self-statements (cf. Meichenbaum, 1974, 1977). Finally, they were given opportunities to apply these new coping techniques in attempting to resolve a number of hypothetical "helplessness-provoking" problems that could be encountered in their daily lives (e.g., an expected visitor suddenly cancels). A second group spent as much time with the psychologist but did not receive explicit skills instruction to enhance control. There was also a no-treatment group. One month after the intervention, subjects in the self-instructional group reported feeling that they had significantly more control and perceived the value of control to be greater than subjects in the other conditions. In addition, the percentage of time that self-instructional subjects spent in more energetic activities increased, and they reported less stress and experienced less difficulty with problems that commonly arose in the nursing home.

In the same study, Rodin (1983) examined changes in urinary free cortisol. Subjects in all the groups except the no-treatment controls showed substantial reductions in urinary free cortisol levels (presumably as a function of reduced stress) from pre- to post-intervention measures. However, only the self-regulation skills group was found to have maintained lower cortisol levels at an 18-month follow-up. Declines in cortisol levels were significantly related to subjects' increased participation in active and planned activities, increased energy, perceived freedom to effect change in the environment, and perceived say in determining outcomes.

While at one-month post-intervention none of the groups was judged by a physician to be significantly changed in health, 18 months later the self-instructional group was judged as showing some improvement relative to the other conditions. At the 18-month follow-up, the self-instructional group had decreased in overall number of analgesics, major and minor tranquilizers, and sleeping pills taken while the other groups increased. Also significant were decreases in reports of dizziness, headaches, weakness, urinary infections, and gastrointestinal problems in the self-instruction group subjects.

## Summary

The control-related interventions described above support three broad conclusions. First, increasing provision of control over the environment and greater perceived self-efficacy have a positive impact on the physical and psychological status of the institutionalized aged. Second, this effect is obtainable with different operationalizations of control. Third, predictable positive events also have a positive impact on health and psychological variables. Thus various types of interventions aimed at increasing control often appear to mitigate environmental challenges to the older person's adaptive resources; however, their long-term efficacy depends on the nature of the intervention and how it is terminated.

## MECHANISMS MEDIATING THE EFFECTS OF CONTROL

Although intervention studies suggest that increased control often benefits the psychological and physical functioning of older people, they do not necessarily specify the mechanisms by which control brings about positive outcomes. Some studies have attempted to test possible mediating mechanisms. In general, this work suggests that control contributes to better physical and psychological functioning through the mechanisms of behavioral and cognitive change, and physiological adaptations.

### Mediators Proposed by Various Theoretical Approaches to Control

According to Rotter (1966), expectancies for internal and external locus of control differentially affect learning. If an individual perceives reinforcement to be contingent on his or her own behavior (i.e., has an internal locus of control), then the occurrence of either a positive or negative reinforcer will strengthen or weaken the potential for that behavior to recur in the same or a similar situation. If, however, the individual believes that reinforcement is externally controlled, then the preceding behavior is less likely to be strengthened or weakened. On the basis of several studies, Rotter concluded that individuals high in internality are therefore more likely than externals to be alert to aspects of their environment that provide useful information for future behavior, to take steps to improve their environmental conditions, and to place value on skill and achievement situations.

Bandura (1977) suggested that self-efficacy expectations influence both the initiation and persistance of coping behaviors in the face of aversive experiences. Thus his theory focused more on the stress-reducing benefits of control-related behavior than on the learning that might result from that behavior. According to Bandura, expectations of personal mastery are a major determinant of people's choice of behavioral settings and activities, in that individuals avoid situations that are believed to exceed their coping abilities. Subjects higher in perceived self-efficacy exert more effort and sustain their effort for longer periods of time in dealing with stressful situations.

The theory of learned helplessness informs the discussion of the mechanisms by which control may have beneficial effects, although it is based on an investigation of the detrimental effects of uncontrollability. Animals and humans exposed to uncontrollable experiences (i.e., noncontingency between their responses and outcomes) show cognitive, motivational, and emotional deficits (Hiroto & Seligman, 1975; Klein, Fencil-Morse, & Seligman, 1976; Overmier & Seligman, 1967; Seligman & Maier, 1967). A reformulation of the original theory proposes that in humans the generality of learned helplessness over time and across situations, and its relationship to various outcomes, are determined by causal interpretations of the uncontrollable events (Abramson et al., 1978). If events are attributed to internal rather than external sources, helplessness is hypothesized to involve loss of self-esteem; if events are attributed to stable rather than unstable causes, helplessness is expected to persist over time; and if events are attributed to global as opposed to specific sources, helplessness should generalize across a variety of domains.

Other investigators have offered less formal theories of control, but their work provides additional insights into how control might have its effects. These are reviewed below, differentiating between mediators of psychological and of biological outcomes.

**Possible Mechanisms
Mediating the Relationship
between Control
and Psychological Well-being**

*Perceived Distress.*  It has been suggested that perceived control reduces the distress generated by an aversive event even when the individual with control does not actually execute the controlling response (Miller, 1980). According to Miller (1979), having control over an aversive event provides the individual with a guaranteed upper limit on how bad the situation can become, and this guarantee improves outcome expectations, thereby reducing distress to lower levels. In some situations, variations in perceived control may influence whether an event is appraised as stressful at all (Lazarus & DeLongis, 1983). Holding environmental events constant, controllable events may be significantly less likely to be perceived as stressful than uncontrollable events. For example, Turk, Kerns, and Rudy (1984) have shown that appraisal of the degree to which pain interferes with one's life—and the degree of control one holds over this interference—mediate the association between chronic pain and depression.

People who perceive events as controllable by their own responses and who are reinforced for making those responses are further afforded a more predictable environment, and predictability in itself has a strongly positive effect on psychological well-being (e.g., Berlyne, 1960; Seligman, 1968; Weiss, 1971). Berlyne (1960) demonstrated that uncertainty causes conflict and heightens arousal and surprise, so that when individuals are faced with uncertainty they seek out information to increase the predictability of the environment. Predictability allows people to relax when aversive events are not expected, whereas the absence of safety signals results in anticipatory arousal (Seligman, 1968). Thus predictability reduces the psychological distress associated with uncontrollability by making safety more salient.

*Attributions.*   The attributions people make for uncontrollable events are another mediator between control and psychological state, in that attributions are linked to levels of self-esteem and depression. We previously pointed out that the reformulated model of learned helplessness proposed that internal attributions for uncontrollable experiences reflect negatively on one's self-esteem (Abramson et al., 1978). Janoff-Bulman (1979) distinguished two kinds of internal attributions—behavioral and characterological self-blame—and found evidence that only characterological attributions were esteem related. Characterological self-blame involves attributions to a relatively nonmodifiable source—one's personality or character traits—and is associated with a belief in personal deservingness for past negative outcomes. Behavioral self-blame involves attributions to a modifiable source—the behaviors one engaged in or failed to engage in—and is associated with a belief in the future avoidability of the negative outcome.

Like Janoff-Bulman, Rodin (1978) focused on the potentially harmful effects of attributing negative outcomes to nonmodifiable sources. Specifically, she presented an analysis of older people's tendency to overattribute negative physical symptoms to aging per se, and underattribute health problems to situational factors, such as the occurrence of stress-inducing events. When physical declines are attributed to the aging process, they may be seen as inevitable and thus nonmodifiable, so that remedial steps that could be beneficial may not be undertaken. Using a nursing home patient sample, Rodin and Langer (1980) found that encouraging plausible environmental attributions for physical problems (e.g., slippery floors cause difficulty walking) resulted in more activity, better health, and reduced experience of stress.

Not only do attributional processes mediate the consequences of loss of control, but according to some theoreticians (e.g., Kelley, 1967, 1971), motivation to attain control may determine which attributions are made. The purpose of explanatory inference—the function that it serves—is effective control. The tendency for individuals to overestimate their degree of personal control in events that are objectively random (e.g., Langer, 1975; Wortman, 1976) is consistent with the assumption that they are motivated to believe that they are able to control their environment.

## Possible Mechanisms Mediating the Relationship between Control and Physical Well-being

*Behavioral and Cognitive Mechanisms.* Perceptions of control may influence whether actions are taken to prevent and remedy health problems. These include gathering health-related information, engaging in self-care behaviors, being active in interactions with medical providers, and showing better compliance with medical regimens. While the intervention studies reviewed above indicate that subjects afforded relatively high control tended to improve their health status relative to those with lower levels of control, we are suggesting that even holding illness severity constant, people high in perceived control may be more likely to take action to enhance their health status. Some health-related measures do not adequately separate the effects of illness severity from the effects of taking an active role in one's health enhancement; for example, an increased number of doctor visits may indicate that the individual has suffered an illness, or that he or she has decided to participate more actively in his or her own health care. Research investigating the control–health relationship must address this measurement issue more clearly.

Research on the construct of health locus of control (cf. Wallston

& Wallston, 1982) supports the hypothesis that individuals with higher levels of perceived control take greater responsibility for meeting their health needs. For example, one study of information-seeking found that people classified as internals who highly valued health indicated a greater willingness to read information on hypertension than externals who also valued health highly (Wallston, Maides, & Wallston, 1976). In a similar study by Toner and Manuck (1979), willingness to read hypertension information did not differ between young adult internals and externals, but older adult internals were more willing to read the information than externals of their age. Sproles' (1977) study of information-seeking by renal dialysis patients suggested that internals knew more about their condition, desired to know even more, and were more willing to attend patient education classes. Among participants in an exercise program, internals were less likely to drop out than externals (Dishman, Ickes, & Morgan, 1980), and among people trying to quit smoking, internals were more successful in reducing cigarette consumption and maintaining the reduction (Kaplan & Cowles, 1978; Shipley, 1980; Wildman et al., 1979). Studies of compliance and health beliefs showed that hypertensive internals reported better dietary compliance (Wallston & McLeod, 1979), and medication compliance (Lewis, Morisky, & Flynn, 1978) than externals. Similarly, dialysis patients with an internal locus of control adhered more closely to their prescribed diet and were more likely to restrict weight gain (Levin & Schulz, 1980). These studies indicate that there may well be direct effects of feelings of control on behavior in health-related areas, which in turn improve health or modify disease.

Research based on Bandura's theory of self-efficacy provides further support for behavioral change as a mediator of the relationship between feelings of control and health outcomes. The suggestion that self-judgments of efficacy determine people's choice of behaviors implies that attempts to reduce drug, alcohol, or cigarette consumption, for example, could be affected by such judgments. Since self-efficacy also affects the amount of effort devoted to a task, and the length of persistence, adherence to medical regimens might be more consistent and longer-lasting among people high in self-efficacy expectations. These types of hypotheses have been confirmed in research on the construct of self-efficacy. Studies on smoking cessation have shown that perceived self-efficacy is a reliable predictor of whether relapses occur and the circumstances surrounding relapses (e.g., Condiotte & Lichtenstein, 1981). Studies using overweight subjects have similarly shown that self-efficacy perceptions regarding eating and weight management predict success at weight reduction attempts (e.g., Chambliss

& Murray, 1979). Beliefs in one's ability to manage pain have been found to increase both laboratory and clinical pain tolerance (e.g., Manning & Wright, 1983; Neufeld & Thomas, 1977), and recovery from myocardial infarction is facilitated by enhancing patients' and their spouses' judgments of their cardiac and physical capabilities (e.g., Ewart, Taylor, Reese, & Debusk, 1984; Taylor et al., 1984). These results strongly uphold the notion that perceived competence to engage in preventive and curative health behaviors increases the likelihood of undertaking and continuing health-enhancing actions.

A cognitive mechanism by which control may be linked to health involves the labeling of symptoms. Extensive work has been done on how people come to experience and label bodily sensations as symptoms relevant to health or illness (e.g., Leventhal & Everhart, 1979; Mechanic, 1972; Pennebaker, 1982; Schachter & Singer, 1962), and control appears to be one variable that influences the labeling process. When level of perceived control over environmental events is manipulated experimentally, subjects who are given low or no control report more physical symptoms than those who feel more in control (Matthews, Scheier, Brunson, & Carducci, 1980; Pennebaker, Burnam, Schaeffer, & Harper, 1977; Weidner & Matthews, 1978).

There are at least three possible explanations for the results concerning symptom perception and labeling. First, experiences of uncontrollability may influence people's cognitive strategies such that subjects try harder and pay more attention (Matthews et al., 1980), with the "psychic cost" of the increased attention experienced physiologically (Pennebaker, 1982). Second, loss of control experiences may cause individuals to adopt symptom-relevant schemas and then selectively search their bodies in greater detail for symptoms (Pennebaker, 1982). This second hypothesis is based on the assumption that people adopt schemas that direct their search and processing of information. Subjects who are aroused and upset, as they would be in an uncontrollable situation, often attribute their distress to being ill (Mechanic, 1972). The third explanation for the relationship between loss of control and increased symptomatology is that failure to control the environment affects physiological activity in both the neuroendocrine and immune systems. Thus, the individual may actually experience more symptoms as a function of physiological activation. In the next section, we review evidence on the physiological effects of variations in control that impact on health status.

*Physiological Mechanisms.*    The hypothesis that increased control may directly affect a large variety of physiological states has been supported by the results of numerous laboratory studies. For example,

Glass, Reim, and Singer (1971) found that subjects given perceived control over the termination of aversive noise exhibited significantly less autonomic reactivity (vasoconstriction) than subjects who were not able to predict the noise. An experiment by Geer and Maisel (1972) showed that subjects given control over aversive stimuli displayed lower galvanic skin response reactivity than did subjects who did not have control. Weiss (1970, 1971, 1972) investigated the physiological consequences of helplessness in rats. He demonstrated in a series of studies that the amount of gastric ulceration and weight loss in rats was significantly reduced when an aversive event such as electric shock was made either predictable or controllable.

Other studies indicate that the experience of uncontrollability results in activation of the sympathetic adrenal medullary system and the pituitary adrenal cortical axis. As we review below, both catecholamines, secreted by the sympathetic system, and corticosteroids, secreted by the pituitary system, have been shown to increase in response to uncontrollability. Fluctuations in these hormones influence bodily systems of relevance to the development of coronary disease and suppression of the immune system.

The association between catecholamine levels and control has been demonstrated in animal and in human studies. Weiss (1970, 1971, 1972) has shown that the amount of neurotransmitter norepinephrine was highly responsive to manipulations of control. Uncontrollable stress has been shown strongly by Frankenhaeuser and her colleagues to elevate peripheral levels of catecholamines in people (Frankenhaeuser, 1975; Frankenhaeuser, Lundberg, & Forsman, 1978; Lundberg & Frankenhaeuser, 1978).

Peripheral catecholamine secretions are associated with increased blood pressure and heart rate, elevation of blood lipids, induction of myocardial lesions, and provocation of ventricular arrythmias (Krantz, Glass, Contrada, & Miller, 1981). Thus the catecholamine increase that occurs in response to uncontrollability may be one mechanism accounting for the reported relationship between coronary disease and control-related variables. Response to uncontrollability is one of the most significant contributors to stress and the Type A coronary-prone behavior pattern (i.e., competitive achievement striving, sense of time urgency, and hostility), which in turn are the most promising psychosocial risk factors for cardiovascular disease (Engel, 1978; Friedman, Byers, Diamant, & Rosenman, 1975; Glass et al., 1980a, 1980b; Greene, Moss, & Goldstein, 1974).

In addition to demonstrating that catecholamines are responsive to loss of control, animal studies show a clear relationship between control and level of plasma cortisol. For example, Levine and his colleagues (Davis, Porter, Livingstone, Herrman, MacFadden, & Levine, 1977) found that corticosteroid levels remained elevated over experimental sessions for subjects that could not escape an aversive stimulus; those that could exert control by escaping showed a significant decrease in corticosteroid levels by the last trial. Hanson et al. (1976) found similar results. Changes from predictable to unpredictable events are also a sufficient condition to cause increases in adrenal corticosteroid levels (Levine & Coover, 1976).

In a typical study showing the effects of loss of control on corticosteroids in humans, subjects who were able to choose among noise intensities and their yoked partners were exposed to the same noise levels (Lundberg & Frankenhaeuser, 1978). The group that was unable to choose its own intensity secreted significantly more cortisol.

Like catecholamines, pituitary adrenal secretions have been implicated in the development of cardiovascular disease. Corticosteroids regulate the metabolism of cholesterol and other lipids involved in the atherosclerotic process and play a role in regulating electrolyte balance and blood pressure. Since corticosteroids are elevated in response to lack of control and are a factor in heart disease, they may mediate the control–disease relationship.

Frankenhaeuser, Lundberg, and Forsman (1978) have argued that the controllability of a task is a major determinant of the degree of effort expended and/or distress experienced, and hence of the balance between sympathetic adrenal and pituitary adrenal arousal as measured by catecholamine and cortisol excretion. In laboratory experiments using demanding tasks, Frankenhaeuser and her co-workers showed that effort is related to catecholamine secretion, whereas distress is related to cortisol secretion. Personal control appears to be the important modulating factor in these tasks because it tends to reduce the negative and enhance the positive aspects of arousal, thereby changing the balance between sympathetic adrenal and pituitary adrenal activity.

While the psychoendocrine effects of control variations have been replicated and extended by numerous laboratories, the relationship between control and responses of the immune system is less well understood and accepted. Two animal studies showed a direct effect of uncontrollable stress on the immune system. Monjan and Collector (1977) found that uncontrollable noise produced T and B cell suppression in mice. Laudenslager et al. (1983) exposed rats to a series of either escapable shocks or identical inescapable shocks and measured cellular immune response. Lymphocyte proliferation and response to the mitogens PHA and Con-A were suppressed in the inescapable-shock group but not in the escapable-shock group, suggesting that the controllability of the stressors can modulate immune functioning.

There are several possibilities for the mechanism whereby inescapable shock can lead to changes in the functioning of the immune system. As discussed above, uncontrollable stressors produce higher levels of circulating corticosteroids than controllable stressors (Davis et al., 1977; Weiss, Stone, & Harrell, 1970). Adrenal corticosteroids can suppress a variety of immune system functions, including lymphocyte proliferation in response to mitogens (Monjan & Collector, 1977). Another possible mechanism whereby inescapable shock may lead to changes in immune functioning involves endogenous opioids. Shavit et al. (1983) found that conditions which produced opioid analgesia were immunosuppressive, while conditions that produced nonopioid analgesia were not. Lymphocytes and neutrophils do possess opiate receptors (Hazum, Chang, & Cuatrecascas, 1979).

Animal data also argue strongly for a link between loss of control and tumor growth and proliferation. Sklar and Anisman (1979) found that tumors grew more quickly in mice given inescapable shock than in mice given escapable shock or no shock. However, since the dose of tumor cells was large enough to ensure tumor development in every animal, the effect of inescapable shock on the process of tumor rejection could not be assessed. Moreover, the physiological mechanisms that promote the growth of an established tumor are different from those that influence the rejection or initial development of a tumor and subsequent metastasis (Herberman et al., 1977; Oehler & Herberman, 1978; Pross & Barnes, 1977). To assess the effects of uncontrollability on tumor rejection, Visintainer, Volpicelli, and Seligman (1982) used a dose of tumor cells designed to induce tumors in 50 percent of unshocked rats. With this dose, rats receiving inescapable shock were only half as likely to reject the tumor and twice as likely to die as rats receiving escapable shock or no shock.

We have emphasized the relationship between control and the immune system because it may play a dramatic role in the health of aged people in particular. Environmental and psychosocial stressors that have been shown to affect immunity may be more common among the elderly; bereavement is one example (Palmblad, 1981). The immune system itself also clearly changes with aging (Siskind, 1981). In general, the loss of immunologic competence in the aged reflects both intrinsic deficiencies in the competence of specific cell populations and extrinsic deficiencies in the environment of the cells. For example, it has been suggested that suppressor T cells—thymus-dependent cells with immunosuppressive properties—increase in number and/or activity with age and that this increase plays a major role in the age-related decline of immune potential. Whereas the response to exogenous antigens decreases with age, the reverse occurs with respect to endogenous antigens, leading to an increase in the incidence and severity of the so-called autoimmune diseases (Timiras, 1972).

Numerous studies have shown that the rates of secretion and metabolism of adrenocortical hormones decline with age, possibly in relation to decreases in weight and alteration in tissue components of the cortex (Grad, Kral, Payne, & Berenson, 1967; Romanoff et al., 1963; Serio et al., 1969). It has also been reported that cortisol may disappear from the circulation of older subjects at a slower rate than in younger persons (West et al., 1961). Some data have suggested that elevated levels of cortisol can reduce immune functioning since corticosteroids display immunosuppressive properties (Munck, Guyre, & Holbrook, 1984). There have also been reports of an adverse relationship between corticosterone level and the capacity of the spleen to synthesize antibodies (Gabrielson & Good, 1967; Gisler, 1974). In healthy people homeostatic regulatory mechanisms usually counteract the suppressive properties of corticosteroids. But in chronically ill or aged individuals, homeostatic regulatory mechanisms may be less effective (Timiras, 1972).

The age changes that occur in immune and neuroendocrine functioning suggest that the loss of control may have an especially debilitating effect on the health of elderly persons through its effects on the pituitary adrenal system (Rodin, 1980, 1983, in press-a). One segment of Rodin's longitudinal study (unpublished data) was designed to test this hypothesis. A subsample of subjects, free of endocrine disease (e.g., diabetes) and the most obvious immunologic disease (e.g., cancer, rheumatoid arthritis), was tested at the baseline period for immunocompetency (see Rodin, in press-a, for details). A first type of analysis was to relate the baseline immunologic parameters to the psychosocial data also collected at baseline. Results revealed that the strongest correlates of immunosuppression were the recency of major stressful life events and effect of these events on the subjects' sense of control. The major impact of feeling lack of control over stressors was to suppress the number of helper cells and to lower the ability of the T cells to mobilize an effective response to an antigen challenge.

Rodin is also examining subjects who have so far experienced a significant stressor during the course of the study to date. Pre- to post-stressor change scores in biological measures showed that a reduction in the number of helper cells occurred in response to stress and that the reduction was related to both health and nutritional status, as well as to the psychological variables of expectancy and control. Reduction in ability to mobilize a response to antigen was strongly affected by these psychological parameters.

From these preliminary data, it may be tentatively concluded that perceived losses in predictability and control related to a highly stressful event are related to reductions in the number of helper T cells and to the body's reduced efficiency in counteracting a foreign histocompatibility antigen. It is important to recognize that it may not be the occurrence of a stressor per se that determines effects on the immune system, but rather the predictability of the stressor and its effects on perceived control, in combination and/or interaction with health and nutritional status.

Further data are required in the future to determine whether the relationship between control and health is stronger as a function of age per se, whether older people rebound from these challenges more slowly, and whether the course of disease is affected by immunosuppression differentially as a function of age. Although we expect detrimental effects on health, it is possible that stress may affect intervening mechanisms such as the immune system in some individuals, but not manifest itself in an alteration in overall health.

## LIMITS OF CONTROL

Throughout this chapter we have emphasized the benefits to be derived from increased personal control for older people in particular. Before concluding, however, we must emphasize that we do not mean to suggest that it is universally beneficial to feel increased control. People differ in their desire for personal control, and there are some conditions in which perceived control is more likely to induce stress than to have a beneficial impact (cf. Averill, 1973). Consistent with our proposal that variations in control have the most impact on the aged, we further propose that their individual preferences for control may show greater variability than do younger groups. Moreover, we speculate that in situations in which having control is stress-inducing, the negative effects may be more disruptive for older than younger people. It is important, therefore, that future research determine the interactions among age, individual preferences for control, situational factors, and variations in opportunities for control that produce positive psychological and physical outcomes.

There is evidence that individuals' preferences for control vary widely. In laboratory studies, there is always a minority of subjects who opt for uncontrollable rather than controllable aversive events when they are given a choice (e.g., Averill & Rosenn, 1972). Field experiments in health care settings have shown that some individuals benefit more than others from being highly informed about and/or involved in their own medical treatment. In studies that made patients more active participants in treatment (e.g., Cromwell, Butterfield, Brayfield, & Curry, 1977), heightened the patients' sense of choice (e.g., Mills & Krantz, 1979), or provided for self-monitoring or self-care (Berg & LoGerfo, 1979), there were substantial individual differences in reactions to treatment interventions. We suspect that variability in optimal or preferred levels of control increases with age, in line with increasing variability in perceptions of control (cf. Lachman, in press-b).

Research has indicated that medical patients whose treatments offer options congruent with their control beliefs show the best psychological and physical adjustment (Cromwell et al., 1977; Lewis et al., 1978; Wallston, Wallston, Kaplan, & Maides, 1976). If it is true that people's preferences for control increase in variability with aging, then the difficulty of attaining a match between an elderly individual's control expectancies and the levels of actual control afforded by an environment is increased. It is also important to note that among both institutionalized and noninstitutionalized elderly, options for exerting control offered by the environment are likely to be reduced, as may the array of responses a particular individual is able to make. Both of these factors may widen the gap between preferred level of control and actual level of control for some individuals.

Engaging in futile attempts to control events that are actually uncontrollable is likely to have psychological and physiological costs (Janoff-Bulman & Brickman, 1980; Schulz & Hanusa, 1980; Wortman & Brehm, 1975). Excessive feelings of responsibility may be aversive (Averill, 1973; Rodin, Rennert, & Solomon, 1980; Thompson, 1981), and personal control often places heavy demands on people in the form of a high investment of time, effort, resources, and the risk of the consequences of failure. Lack of sufficient information to support effective control over an outcome has also been proposed to decrease the desirability of control (Rodin et al., 1980). The psychological cost of control may be greater for older people because they may have more extreme reactions to stress than other age groups, and because stress may accelerate the aging process (Eisdorfer & Wilkie, 1977).

The possible physiological costs of control also merit attention. Specifically, there is evidence that in some individuals, excessive efforts to assert control can have negative effects on many of the same physiological systems that show benefits with increased control. The work of Glass (1977), for example, considers Type A individuals who are so hard driving that they exert continued effort to exercise control even in the face of maladaptive outcomes or uncontrollable situations. Glass postulates that this repeated and frustrated desire for control may be related to increased catecholamine output, which in turn contributes to atherosclerosis. The effects of control-relevant, self-regulation on biological processes are not simple and straightforward. Research has yet to explore fully the conditions under which exercising control is beneficial and when it is not.

## CONCLUSIONS

We began the chapter by hypothesizing that cultural, environmental, and personal factors associated with growing old could contribute to diminished opportunities for control in later life. While these events tend to increase as one grows old, they do not necessarily lead to strong correlations between perceived control and chronological age per se, since older people may vary in the extent to which they desire control and in the nature of the environmental and personal factors to which they are exposed.

We have hypothesized that aging-related events can influence perceptions of both personal competence and response–outcome contingencies. Before discussing this hypothesis further, it will be helpful for us to present a model of perceived control and the mechanisms by which its variations have beneficial or detrimental effects on well-being. The model is displayed in Figure 1.1.

In the model, perceptions of self-efficacy and environmental responsiveness influence one another in a reciprocal relationship, and these perceptions are combined to form an overall judgment of level of perceived control (cf. Weisz, 1983). Presumably both variables could be affected by sociocultural and individual difference variables that might be changing as one grows old. At present, little is known about how people combine judgments of self-competence and contingency, and this is clearly an area in which research is needed. It is possible that the weight each control component receives changes developmentally, or that the combinatorial process itself undergoes life-span changes.

Figure 1.1 also lists some mechanisms that we proposed might account for the positive impact of control. We hypothesized that attributional processes and variations in predictability link control to psy-

42

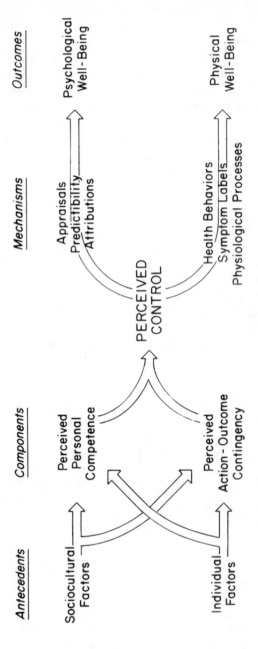

**Figure 1.1** Hypothetical model of the antecedents, components, mechanisms, and outcomes of perceived control.

chological parameters, while health-related cognitions and behaviors, symptom labels, and physiological processes mediate the control–health relationship. Because aging and age-related events may have a direct effect on each of these mechanisms, the elderly may be the most vulnerable to the negative effects of loss of control experiences in terms of psychological and physical functioning. For example, we proposed that those individuals lower in perceived control may engage in fewer health-related behaviors, and we suspect that this relationship may become stronger in old age. Weaker beliefs in personal control might be especially likely to decrease health-promoting activity among older people because physical declines are frequently viewed as an unalterable part of the aging process.

The perception of oneself as undergoing the inevitable declines of aging might also lead older people to have a greater tendency to label their bodily sensations as symptoms of disability or illness. The aged may be more likely to focus on bodily sensations, not only because they may intentionally search for physical signs of aging, but also because they may have less environmental stimulation, particularly if they are institutionalized. In addition, most elderly people actually experience a greater number of symptoms due to biological changes regardless of attentional focus. While we concentrated on neuroendocrine and immune system changes, numerous other physiological changes also occur with aging, including DNA damage and changes in protein synthesis, cells, and tissues (Schimke, 1981).

Future research is needed to explore the hypothesis that the negative effects of loss of control are most profound for the aged and to clarify the mechanisms by which increased control benefits the psychological and physical health of older and younger age groups. Studies are also needed to specify how various aspects of control relate to different health-relevant outcomes. Based on our present understanding, however, we may conclude that perceived competence and environmental contingency figure importantly in the health and well-being of older people. The theoretical and clinical significance of these observations is considerable.

## REFERENCES

Abramson, L.Y., & Alloy, L.B. Judgment of contingency: Errors and their implications. In A. Baum & J.E. Singer (Eds.), *Advances in environmental psychology*, Vol. 2. Hillsdale, NJ: Erlbaum, 1980, pp. 112–130.

Abramson, L.Y., Seligman, M.E.P., & Teasdale, J.D. Learned helplessness in humans: Critique and reformulation. *Journal of Abnormal Psychology,* 1978, *87,* 49–74.

Adler, A. *The science of living.* Greenberg, New York, 1929.

Averill, J.R. Personal control over aversive stimuli and its relationship to stress. *Psychological Bulletin,* 1973, *80,* 286–303.

Averill, J.R., & Rosenn, M. Vigilant and non-vigilant coping strategies and pathophysiological stress reactions during the anticipation of electric shock. *Journal of Personality and Social Psychology,* 1972, *23,* 128–141.

Avorn, J., & Langer, E.J. Induced disability in nursing home patients: A controlled trial. *Journal of the American Geriatrics Society,* 1982, *30,* 397–400.

Baltes, M.M., & Reisenzein, R. The social world in long-term care institutions: Psychosocial control toward dependency? In M.M. Baltes & P.B. Baltes (Eds.), *The psychology of control and aging.* Hillsdale, NJ: Erlbaum, in press.

Bandura, A. Self-efficacy: Toward a unifying theory of behavioral change. *Psychological Review,* 1977, *84,* 191–215.

Bandura, A. Self-referent thought: A developmental analysis of self-efficacy. In J.H. Flavell & L. Ross (Eds.), *Social cognitive development: Frontiers and possible futures.* New York: Cambridge University Press, 1981, pp. 200–239.

Banziger, G. & Roush, S. Nursing homes for the birds: A control-relevant intervention with bird feeders. *The Gerontologist,* 1983, *23,* 527–531.

Baron, R., & Rodin, J. Perceived control and crowding stress. In A. Baum, J.E. Singer, & S. Valins (Eds.), *Advances in environmental psychology.* Hillsdale, NJ: Erlbaum, 1978, pp. 145–190.

Berg, A.O., & Logerfo, J.P. Potential effect of self-care algorithms on the number of physician visits. *New England Journal of Medicine,* 1979, *300,* 535–537.

Berlyne, D.E. *Conflict, arousal and curiosity.* New York: McGraw-Hill, 1960.

Bohm, L.C. Social support and well-being in older adults: The impact of perceived control. Unpublished doctoral dissertation, Yale University, 1983.

Bradley, R.H., & Webb, R. Age-related differences in three behavior domains. *Human Development,* 1976, *19,* 49–55.

Brim, O.G. How a person controls the sense of efficacy through the life span. Paper presented at the Social Science Research Council Conference on the Self and Perceived Control Through the Life Span, New York, 1980.

Brothen, T., & Detzner, D. Perceived health and locus of control in the aged. *Perceptual and Motor Skills,* 1983, *56,* 946.

Brown, B.R., & Granick, S. Cognitive and psychosocial differences between I and E locus of control aged persons. *Experimental Aging Research,* 1983, *9,* 107–110.

Butler, R. Myths and realities of clinical geriatrics. *Image and Commentary,* 1970, *12,* 26–29.

Chambliss, C.A., & Murray, E.J. Efficacy attribution, locus of control, and weight loss. *Cognitive Therapy and Research*, 1979, *3*, 349–353.

Chang, B.L. Generalized expectancy, situational perception, and morale among institutionalized aged. *Nursing Research*, 1978, *27*, 316–324.

Cicirelli, V.G. Relationship of family background variables to locus of control in the elderly. *Journal of Gerontology*, 1980, *35*, 108–114.

Condiotte, M.M., & Lichtenstein, E. Self-efficacy and relapse in smoking cessation programs. *Journal of Consulting and Clinical Psychology*, 1981, *49*, 648–658.

Cromwell, R.L., Butterfield, D.C., Brayfield, F.M., & Curry, J.J. *Acute myocardial infarction: Reaction and recovery.* St. Louis: Mosby, 1977.

Davis, H., Porter, J.W., Livingstone, J., Herrman, J., MacFadden, L., & Levine, S. Pituitary-adrenal activity and lever press shock escape behavior. *Physiological Psychology*, 1977, *5*, 280.

deCharms, R. *Personal causation.* Academic Press, New York, 1968.

DeVellis, R.F., DeVellis, B.M., & McCauley, C. Vicarious acquisition of learned helplessness. *Journal of Personality and Social Psychology*, 1978, *36*, 894–899.

Dishman, R.K., Ickes, W., & Morgan, W.P. Self-motivation and adherence to habitual physical activity. *Journal of Applied Social Psychology*, 1980, *10*, 115–132.

Duke, M.P., Shaheen, J., & Nowicki, S. The determination of control in a geriatric population and a subsequent test of the social learning model for interpersonal distances. *The Journal of Psychology*, 1974, *86*, 277–285.

Eisdorfer, C., & Wilkie, F. Stress, disease, aging and behavior. In J.E. Birren & K.W. Schaie (Eds.), *Handbook of the psychology of aging.* New York: Van Nostrand Reinhold, 1977, pp. 251–275.

Endler, N.S., & Edwards, J. Person by treatment interactions in personality research. In L.A. Pervin & M. Lewis (Eds.), *Perspectives in interactional psychology.* New York: Plenum, 1978, pp. 141–170.

Engel, G.L. Psychological stress vasodepressor (vasobasal) syncope, and sudden death. *Annals of Internal Medicine*, 1978, *89*, 403–412.

Erickson, E.H. *Childhood and society.* New York: Norton, 1950.

Ewart, C.K., Taylor, C.B., Reese, L.B., & Debusk, R.F. Effects of early postmyocardial infarction exercise testing on self-perception and subsequent physical activity. *The American Journal of Cardiology*, 1984, *51*, 1076–1080.

Fawcett, G., Stonner, D., & Zepelin, H. Locus of control, perceived constraint, and morale among institutionalized aged. *International Journal of Aging and Human Development*, 1980, *11*, 13–23.

Felton, B., & Kahana, E. Adjustment and situationally-bound locus of control among institutionalized aged. *Journal of Gerontology*, 1974, *29*, 295–301.

Frankenhaeuser, M. Experimental approaches to the study of catecholamines and emotion. In L. Levi (Ed.), *Emotions: Their parameters and measurement.* New York: Raven Press, 1975.

Frankenhaeuser, M., Lundberg, U., & Forsman, L. Dissociation between sympathetic adrenal and pituitary-adrenal responses to an achievement situation characterized by high controllability: Comparison between Type A and Type B males and females. Tech Rep. No. 540, University of Stockholm, 1978.

Friedman, M., Byers, S.O., Diamant, J., & Rosenman, R.H. Plasma catecholamine response of coronary-prone subjects (Type A) to a specific challenge. *Metabolism,* 1975, *24,* 205–210.

Gabrielson, A.E., & Good, R.A. Chemical suppression of adapted immunity. *Advances in Immunology,* 1967, *6,* 90–229.

Gatz, M., & Siegler, I.C. Locus of control: A retrospective. Paper presented at the meeting of the American Psychological Association, Los Angeles, August, 1981.

Geer, J., & Maisel, E. Evaluating the effects of the prediction-control confound. *Journal of Personality and Social Psychology,* 1972, *23,* 314–319.

Gisler, R.H. Stress and the hormonal regulation of the immune response in mice. *Psychotherapy & Psychosomatics,* 1974, *23,* 197–208.

Glass, D.C. *Behavior patterns, stress and coronary disease.* Hillsdale, NJ: Erlbaum, 1977.

Glass, D.C., Krakoff, L.R., Contrada, R., Hilton, W.C., Kehoe, K., Mannucci, E.G., Collins, C., Snow, B., & Elting, E. Effects of harrassment and competition upon cardiovascular and plasma catecholamine response in Type A and Type B individuals. *Psychophysiology,* 1980a, *17,* 453–463.

Glass, D.C., Krakoff, L.R., Finkelman, J., Snow, B., Contrada, R., Kehoe, K., Mannucci, E.G., Isecke, W., Collins, C., Hilton, W.F., & Elting, E. Effect of task overload upon cardiovascular and plasma catecholamine responses in Type A and Type B individuals. *Basic and Applied Social Psychology,* 1980b, *1,* 199–218.

Glass, D.C., Reim, B., & Singer, J. Behavioral consequences of adaptation to controllable and uncontrollable noise. *Journal of Experimental Social Psychology,* 1971, *7,* 244–257.

Glass, D.C., & Singer, J.E. *Urban Stress.* Academic Press, New York, 1972.

Grad, B., Kral, V.A., Payne, R.C., & Berenson, J. Plasma and urinary corticoids in young and old persons. *Journal of Gerontology,* 1967, *22,* 66.

Greene, W.H., Moss, A.J., & Goldstein, S. Delay, denial, and death in coronary heart disease. In R.S. Eliot (Ed.), *Stress and the heart.* Mount Kisko, NY: Futura, 1974.

Gurin, P. The situation and other neglected issues in personal causation. Reported in Thematic Minutes V of the Social Science Research Council Conference on the Self and Perceived Personal Control through the Life Span, New York, 1980.

Gurin, P., & Brim, O.G. Change in self in adulthood: The example of sense of control. In P.B. Baltes & O.G. Brim (Eds.), *Life-span development and behavior,* Vol. 6. New York: Academic Press, 1984, pp. 281–334.

Gurin, P., Gurin, G., Lao, R.C., & Beattie, M. Internal-external control in the motivational dynamics of Negro youth. *Journal of Social Issues,* 1969, *25,* 29–53.

Gurin, P., Gurin, G., & Morrison, B.M. Personal and ideological aspects of internal and external control. *Social Psychology,* 1978, *41,* 275–296.

Hanson, J.D., Larson, M.E., & Snowden, C.T. The effects of control over high intensity noise of plasma cortisol levels in rhesus monkeys. *Behavioral Biology,* 1976, *16,* 333.

Hazum, E., Chang, K.J., & Cuatrecascas, P. Specific non opiate receptors for beta-endorphin. *Science,* 1979, *205,* 1033–1035.

Herberman, R.B., Nunn, M.E., Holden, H.T., Staal, S., & Djeu, J.Y. Augmentation of natural cytotoxic reactivity of mouse lymphoid cells against syngeneic and allogeneic target cells. *International Journal of Cancer,* 1977, *19,* 555–564.

Hiroto, D.S., & Seligman, M.E.P. Generality of learned helplessness in man. *Journal of Personality and Social Psychology,* 1975, *31,* 311–327.

Holahan, C.K., Holahan, C.J., & Belk, S. Adjustment in aging: The roles of life stress, hassles, and self-efficacy. *Health Psychology,* 1984, *3,* 315–328.

Hulicka, I.M., Morganti, J.B., & Cataldo, J.F. Perceived latitude of choice of institutionalized and noninstitutionalized elderly women. *Experimental Aging Research,* 1975, *1,* 27–40.

Hunter, K.I., Linn, M.W., & Harris, R. Characteristics of high and low self-esteem in the elderly. *International Journal of Aging and Human Development,* 1981–82, *14,* 117–126.

Hunter, K.I., Linn, M.W., Harris, R., & Pratt, T. Discriminators of internal and external locus of control orientation in the elderly. *Research on Aging,* 1980, *2,* 49–60.

Janoff-Bulman, R. Characterological versus behavioral self-blame: Inquiries into depression and rape. *Journal of Personality and Social Psychology,* 1979, *37,* 1798–1809.

Janoff-Bulman, R., & Brickman, P. Expectations and what people learn from failure. In N.T. Feather (Ed.), *Expectancy, incentive and action.* Hillsdale, NJ: Erlbaum, 1980.

Kaplan, G.D., & Cowles, A. Health locus of control and health value in prediction of smoking reduction. *Health Education Monographs,* 1978, *6,* 129–137.

Kelley, H.H. Attribution theory in social psychology. In D. Levine (Eds.), *Nebraska Symposium on Motivation,* Vol. 15. Lincoln: University of Nebraska Press, 1967.

Kelley, H.H. *Attribution in social interaction.* Morristown, NJ: General Learning Press, 1971.

Klein, D.C., Fencil-Morse, E., & Seligman, M.E.P. Learned helplessness, depression, and the attribution of failure. *Journal of Personality and Social Psychology,* 1976, *33,* 508–516.

Kohn, M.L. Occupational structure and alienation. *American Journal of Sociology,* 1976, *82,* 111–130.

Kohn, M.L., & Schooler, C. The reciprocal effects of the substantive complexity of work and intellectual flexibility: A longitudinal assessment. *American Journal of Sociology*, 1978, *84*, 24–52.

Kohn, M.L., & Schooler, C. Job conditions and personality: A longitudinal assessment of reciprocal effects. *American Journal of Sociology*, 1982, *87*, 1257–1286.

Krantz, D.S., Glass, D.C., Contrada, R., & Miller, N.E. Behavior and health. In *The five-year outlook on science and technology*, Vol. 2. Washington, DC: Government Printing Office, National Science Foundation, 1981.

Krantz, D.S., & Schulz, R. Personal control and health: Some applications to crises of middle and old age. In A. Baum & J.E. Singer (Eds.), *Advances in environmental psychology*, Vol. 2. New York: Academic Press, 1980, pp. 23–57.

Krantz, D.S., & Stone, V. Locus of control and the effects of success and failure in young and community-residing aged women. *Journal of Personality*, 1978, *46*, 536–551.

Kuypers, J.A. Internal-external locus of control, ego functioning, and personality characteristics in old age. *The Gerontologist*, 1972, *12*, 168–173.

Kuypers, J.A., & Bengtson, V.L. Social breakdown and competence. *Human Development*, 1973, *16*, 181–201.

Lachman, M.E. Perceptions of intellectual aging: Antecedent or consequence of intellectual functioning? *Developmental Psychology*, 1983, *19*, 482–498.

Lachman, M.E. Locus of control in aging research: A case for multidimensional and domain-specific assessment. Unpublished manuscript, Brandeis University, 1984.

Lachman, M.E. Personal control in later life: Stability, change, and cognitive correlates. In M.M. Baltes & P.B. Baltes (Eds.), *Aging and the psychology of control*. Hillsdale, NJ: Erlbaum, in press-a.

Lachman, M.E. Personal efficacy in middle and old age: Differential and normative patterns of change. In G.H. Elder (Ed.), *Life-course dynamics: Trajectories and transitions, 1968–1980*. Ithaca, NY: Cornell University Press, in press-b.

Lachman, M.E., Baltes, P.B., Nesselroade, J.R., & Willis, S.L. Examination of personality-ability relationships in the elderly: The role of contextual (interface) assessment mode. *Journal of Research in Personality*, 1982, *16*, 485–501.

Langer, E.J. The illusion of control. *Journal of Personality and Social Psychology*, 1975, *32*, 311–328.

Langer, E.J., & Imber, L. When practice makes perfect: The debilitating effects of overlearning. *Journal of Personality and Social Psychology*, 1979, *37*, 2014.

Langer, E.J., & Rodin, J. The effects of choice and enhanced personal responsibility for the aged: A field experiment in an institutional setting. *Journal of Personality and Social Psychology*, 1976, *34*, 191–198.

Langer, E., Rodin, J., Beck, P., Weinman, C., & Spitzer, L. Environmental determinants of memory improvement in late adulthood. *Journal of Personality and Social Psychology,* 1979, *27,* 2000–2013.

Lao, R.C. Developmental trend of the locus of control. *Personality and Social Psychology Bulletin,* 1975, *1,* 348–350.

Laudenslager, M.L., Ryan, S.M., Drugan, R.C., Hyson, R.L., & Maier, S.F. Coping and immunosuppression: Inescapable but not escapable shock suppresses lymphocyte proliferation. *Science,* 1983, *221,* 568–570.

Lawton, M.P., Windley, P.G., & Byerts, T.O. *Environment and aging: Theoretical approaches.* New York: Springer Publishing Company, 1982.

Lazarus, R.S., & DeLongis, A. Psychological stress and coping in aging. *American Psychologist,* 1983, *38,* 245–254.

Lefcourt, H.M. Internal versus external control of reinforcement. *Psychological Bulletin,* 1966, *65,* 206–220.

Lefcourt, H.M. *Research with the locus of control construct, Vol. 1: Assessment methods.* New York: Academic Press, 1981.

Levenson, H. Activism and powerful others: Distinctions within the concept of internal-external control. *Journal of Personality Assessment,* 1974, *38,* 377–383.

Leventhal, H., & Everhart, D. Emotion, pain, and physical illness. In C.F. Izard (Ed.), *Emotions and psychopathology.* New York: Plenum, 1979.

Levin, A., & Schulz, M.A. Multidimensional health locus of control and compliance in low and high participation hemodialysis. Unpublished manuscript, University of Wisconsin, Madison, 1980.

Levine, S., & Coover, G.D. Environmental control of suppression of the pituitary-adrenal system. *Physiology and Behavior,* 1976, *17,* 35–37.

Lewis, F.M., Morisky, D.E., & Flynn, B.S. A test of the construct validity of health locus of control: Effects of a self-reported compliance for hypertensive patients. *Health Education Monographs,* 1978, *6,* 138–148.

Linn, M.W., & Hunter, K. Perception of age in the elderly. *Journal of Gerontology,* 1979, *34,* 46–52.

Lundberg, U., & Frankenhaeuser, M. Psychophysiological reactions to noise as modified by personal control over stimulus intensity. *Biological Psychology,* 1978, *6,* 51.

Maier, S.F., & Seligman, M.E.P. Learned helplessness: Theory and evidence. *Journal of Experimental Psychology,* 1976, *105,* 3–46.

Mancini, J.A. Effects of health and income on control orientation and life satisfaction among aged public housing residents. *International Journal of Aging and Human Development,* 1980–81, *12,* 215–220.

Manning, M.M., & Wright, T.L. Self-efficacy expectancies, outcome expectancies, and the persistance of pain control in childbirth. *Journal of Personality and Social Psychology,* 1983, *45,* 421–431.

Matthews, K., Scheier, M.F., Brunson, B.I., & Carducci, B. Attention, unpredictability and reports of physical symptoms. *Journal of Personality and Social Psychology,* 1980, *38,* 525–537.

Mechanic, D. Social psychologic factors affecting the presentation of bodily complaints. *New England Journal of Medicine,* 1972, *286,* 1132–1139.

Meichenbaum, D. Self-instructional strategy training: A cognitive prosthesis for the aged. *Human Development,* 1974, *17,* 273.

Meichenbaum, D. *Cognitive-behavior modification: An integrative approach.* New York: Plenum, 1977.

Mercer, S., & Kane, R.A. Helplessness and hopelessness among the institutionalized aged: An experiment. *Health and Social Work,* 1979, *4,* 90–116.

Miller, S.M. Controllability and human stress: Method, evidence, and theory. *Behavior Research and Therapy,* 1979, *17,* 287–304.

Miller, S.M. Why having control reduces stress: If I can stop the roller coaster, I don't want to get off. In J. Garber & M.E.P. Seligman (Eds.), *Human helplessness: Theory and application.* New York: Academic Press, 1980, pp. 71–95.

Mills, R.T., & Krantz, D.S. Information, choice and reactions to stress: A field experiment in a blood bank with laboratory analogue. *Journal of Personality and Social Psychology,* 1979, *37,* 608–620.

Mirels, H.L. Dimensions of internal versus external control. *Journal of Consulting and Clinical Psychology,* 1970, *34,* 226–228.

Monjan, A., & Collector, M. Stress induced modulation of the immune response. *Science,* 1977, *196,* 307–308.

Munck, A., Guyre, P.M., & Holbrook, N.J. Physiological functions of glucocorticoids in stress and their relation to pharmacological actions. *Endocrine Reviews,* 1984, *5,* 25–43.

Nehrke, M.F., Bellucci, G., & Gabriel, S.J. Death anxiety, locus of control and life satisfaction in the elderly: Toward a definition of ego-integrity. *Omega,* 1977–78, *8,* 359–368.

Nehrke, M.F., Hulicka, I.M., & Morganti, J.B. Age differences in life satisfaction, locus of control, and self-concept. *International Journal of Aging and Human Development,* 1980, *11,* 25–33.

Neufeld, R.W.J., & Thomas, P. Effects of perceived self-efficacy of a prophylactic controlling mechanism on self-control under painful stimulation. *Canadian Journal of Behavioral Science,* 1977, *9,* 224–232.

Oehler, J.R., & Herberman, R.B. Natural cell-mediated cytotoxicity in rats. III. Effects of immunopharmacologic treatments on natural reactivity and on reactivity augmented by polyinosinic-polycytidylic acid. *International Journal of Cancer,* 1978, *21,* 221–229.

Overmier, J.B., & Seligman, M.E.P. Effects of inescapable shock upon subsequent escape and avoidance learning. *Journal of Comparative and Physiological Psychology,* 1967, *63,* 23–33.

Palmblad, J. Stress and immunologic competence: Studies in man. In R. Ader (Ed.), *Psychoneuroimmunology.* New York: Academic Press, 1981, pp. 229–257.

Palmore, E., & Luikart, C. Health and social factors related to life satisfaction. *Journal of Health and Social Behavior,* 1972, *13,* 68–80.

Pennebaker, J.W. *The psychology of physical symptoms.* New York: Springer-Verlag, 1982.

Pennebaker, J.W., Burnam, M.A., Schaeffer, M.A., & Harper, D. Lack of control as a determinant of perceived physical symptoms. *Journal of Personality and Social Psychology,* 1977, *35,* 167–174.

Phares, E.J. *Locus of control: A personality determinant of behavior.* Morristown, NJ: General Learning Press, 1973.

Phares, E.J. *Locus of control in personality.* Morristown, NJ: General Learning Press, 1976.

Piaget, J. *The origins of intelligence in children.* New York: International Universities Press, 1952.

Pohl, J.M., & Fuller, S.S. Perceived choice, social interaction, and dimensions of morale of residents in a home for the aged. *Research in Nursing and Health,* 1980, *3,* 147–157.

Pross, H.F., & Barnes, M.G. Spontaneous human lymphocyte-mediated cytotoxicity against tumour target cells. I. The effect of malignant disease. *International Journal of Cancer,* 1977, *18,* 593–604.

Ransen, D.L. Long-term effects of two interventions with the aged: An ecological analysis. *Journal of Applied Developmental Psychology,* 1981, *2,* 13–27.

Rehm, L.P. A self-control model of depression. *Behavior Therapy,* 1977, *8,* 787–804.

Reid, D.W. Locus of control as an important concept for an interactionist approach to behavior. In D. Magnusson & N.S. Endler (Eds.), *Personality at the crossroads: Current issues in international psychology.* Hillsdale, NJ: Erlbaum, 1977, pp. 185–192.

Reid, D.W., Haas, G., & Hawkings, D. Locus of desired control and positive self-concept of the elderly. *Journal of Gerontology,* 1977, *32,* 441–450.

Reid, D.W., & Ziegler, M. Validity and stability of a new desired control measure pertaining to psychological adjustment of the elderly. *Journal of Gerontology,* 1980, *35,* 395–402.

Rodin, J. Somatopsychics and attribution. *Personality and Social Psychology Bulletin,* 1978, *4,* 531–540.

Rodin, J. Managing the stress of aging: The role of control and coping. In S. Levine & H. Ursin (Eds.), *NATO conference on coping and health.* New York: Academic Press, 1980.

Rodin, J. Behavioral medicine: Beneficial effects of self-control training in aging. *International Review of Applied Psychology,* 1983, *32,* 153–181.

Rodin, J. Health, control, and aging. In M.M. Baltes and P.B. Baltes (Eds.), *Aging and the psychology of control.* Hillsdale, NJ: Erlbaum, in press-a.

Rodin, J. Personal control through the life course. In R. Abeles (Ed.), *Implications of the life span perspective for social psychology.* Hillsdale, NJ: Erlbaum, in press-b.

Rodin, J., & Langer, E.J. Long term effects of a control-relevant intervention with the institutionalized aged. *Journal of Personality and Social Psychology,* 1977, *35,* 897–902.

Rodin, J., & Langer, E. Aging labels: The decline of control and the fall of self-esteem. *Journal of Social Issues*, 1980, *36*, 12–29.

Rodin, J., Rennert, K., & Solomon, S.K. Intrinsic motivation for control: Fact or fiction. In A. Baum & J.E. Singer (Eds.), *Advances in environmental psychology*, Vol. 2. Hillsdale, NJ: Erlbaum, 1980, 131–148.

Romanoff, L.P., Morris, C.W., Welch, P., Grace, M.P., & Pincus, G. Metabolism of progesterone-4-c in young and elderly men. *Journal of Clinical and Endocrine Metabolism*, 1963, *23*, 286.

Rotella, R.J., & Bunker, L.K. Locus of control and achievement motivation in the active aged (65 years and over). *Perceptual and Motor Skills*, 1978, *46*, 1043–1046.

Rotter, J.B. Generalized expectancies for internal versus external control of reinforcement. *Psychological Monographs: General and Applied*, 1966, *80*, (Whole No. 609), 1–28.

Rotter, J.B. Some problems and misconceptions related to the construct of internal versus external control of reinforcement. *Journal of Consulting and Clinical Psychology*, 1975, *43*, 56–67.

Ryckman, R.M., & Malikioski, M.X. Relationship between locus of control and chronological age. *Psychological Reports*, 1975, *36*, 655–658.

Saltz, C., & Magruder-Habib, K. Age as an indicator of depression and locus of control among non-psychiatric inpatients. Paper presented at the meeting of the Gerontological Society of America, Boston, November, 1982.

Schachter, S., & Singer, J. Cognitive, social and physiological determinants of emotional state. *Psychological Review*, 1962, *69*, 379–399.

Schimke, R.T. *Biological mechanisms in aging*. NIH Publication No. 81-2194, 1981.

Schulz, R. Effects of control and predictability on the physical and psychological well-being of the institutionalized aged. *Journal of Personality and Social Psychology*, 1976, *33*, 563–573.

Schulz, R. Aging and control. In J. Garber & M.E.P. Seligman (Eds.), *Human helplessness: Theory and applications*. New York: Academic Press, 1980, pp. 261–277.

Schulz, R., & Brenner, G. Relocation of the aged: A review and theoretical analysis. *Journal of Gerontology*, 1977, *32*, 323–333.

Schulz, R., & Hanusa, B.H. Long-term effects of control and predictability-enhancing interventions: Findings and ethical issues. *Journal of Personality and Social Psychology*, 1978, *36*, 1194–1201.

Schulz, R., & Hanusa, B.H. Environmental influences on the effectiveness of control- and competence-enhancing intervention. In L.C. Perlmutter & R. A. Monty (Eds.), *Choice and perceived control*. Hillsdale, NJ: Erlbaum, 1979, pp. 315–337.

Schulz, R., & Hanusa, B.H. Experimental social gerontology: A social psychological perspective. *Journal of Social Issues*, 1980, *36*, 30–46.

Seligman, M.E.P. Chronic fear produced by unpredictable electric shock. *Journal of Comparative and Physiological Psychology*, 1968, *66*, 402–411.

Seligman, M.E.P. *Helplessness.* San Francisco: W.H. Freeman, 1975.

Seligman, M.E.P. Comment and integration. *Journal of Abnormal Psychology,* 1978, *87,* 165–179.

Seligman, M.E.P., & Maier, S.F. Failure to escape traumatic shock. *Journal of Experimental Psychology,* 1967, *74,* 1–9.

Seligman, M.E.P., Maier, S.F., & Solomon, R.L. Unpredictable and uncontrollable aversive events. In F.R. Brush (Ed.), *Aversive conditioning and learning.* New York: Academic Press, 1971, pp. 347–400.

Serio, M., Piolanti, P., Capelli, G., Magistris, L., Ricci, F., Anzalone, M., & Giusti, G. The miscible pool and turnover rate of cortisol in the aged, and variations in relation to time of day. *Experimental Gerontology,* 1969, *4,* 95.

Shavit, Y., Lewis, J.W., Terman, G.W., Gale, R.P., & Liebeskind, J.C. Endogenous opioids may mediate the effects of stress on tumor growth and immune function. *Proceedings of the Western Pharmacology Society,* 1983, *8,* 53–56.

Shipley, R.H. Effect of followup letters on maintenance of smoking abstinence. Paper presented at the meeting of the Midwestern Psychological Association, St. Louis, 1980.

Siegler, I.C., & Gatz, M. Age patterns in locus of control. In E. Palmore, J. Nowlin, E. Busse, I. Siegler, & G. Maddox (Eds.), *Normal aging III.* Durham, NC: Duke University Press, 1985.

Siskind, G. Immunological aspects of aging: An overview. In R.T. Schimke (Ed.), *Biological mechanisms in aging.* NIH Publication No. 81-2194, 1981, 455–466.

Sklar, L.S., & Anisman, H. Stress and coping factors influence tumor growth. *Science,* 1979, *205,* 513–515.

Sproles, K.J. Health locus of control and knowledge of hemodialysis and health maintenance of patients with chronic renal failure. Unpublished manuscript, Virginia Commonwealth University, 1977.

Storandt, M., Wittels, I., & Botwinick, J. Predictors of a dimension of well-being in the relocated healthy aged. *Journal of Gerontology,* 1975, *30,* 97–102.

Taylor, C.B., Bandura, A., Ewart, C.K., Miller, N.H., & Debusk, R.F. Raising spouse's and patient's perception of his cardiac capabilities following a myocardial infarction. Unpublished manuscript, Stanford University, 1984.

Thompson, S. Will it hurt less if I can control it? A complex answer to a simple question. *Psychological Bulletin,* 1981, *90,* 89–101.

Timiras, P.S. *Developmental physiology and aging.* New York: Macmillan, 1972.

Toner, J.B., & Manuck, S.B. Health locus of control and health-related information seeking at a hypertension screening. *Social Science and Medicine,* 1979, *13A,* 823.

Turk, D.C., Kerns, R.D., & Rudy, T.E. Chronic illness and depression. In

P.H. Blaney (Chair), *Investigations of Variables Buffering Life Stress: Current Trends.* Symposium conducted at meeting of the American Psychological Association, 1984.

Visintainer, M.A., Volpicelli, J.R., & Seligman, M.E.P. Tumor rejection in rats after inescapable or escapable shock. *Science,* 1982, *216,* 437–439.

Wallston, B.S., Wallston, K.A., Kaplan, G.D., & Maides, S.A. Development and validation of the health locus of control (HLC) scale. *Journal of Consulting and Clinical Psychology,* 1976, *44,* 580–585.

Wallston, K.A., Maides, S., & Wallston, B.S. Health-related information seeking as a function of health-related locus of control and health value. *Journal of Research in Personality,* 1976, *10,* 215–222.

Wallston, K.A., & McLeod, E. Predictive factors in the adherence to an anti-hypertensive regimen among adult male outpatients. Unpublished manuscript, Vanderbilt University, 1979.

Wallston, K.A., & Wallston, B.S. Health locus of control scales. In H. Lefcourt (Ed.), *Research with the locus of control construct,* Vol. 1. New York: Academic Press, 1981.

Wallston, K.A., & Wallston, B.S. Who is responsible for your health? The construct of health locus of control. In G.S. Sanders & J. Suls (Eds.), *Social psychology of health and illness.* Hillsdale, NJ: Erlbaum, 1982.

Weidner, G., & Matthews, K. Reported physical symptoms elicited by unpredictable events and the Type A coronary-prone behavior pattern. *Journal of Personality and Social Psychology,* 1978, *36,* 1213–1220.

Weiner, B. Achievement motivation as conceptualized by an attribution theorist. In B. Weiner (Ed.), *Achievement motivation and attribution theory.* Morristown, NJ: General Learning Press, 1974, 3–48.

Weiss, J.M. Somatic effects of predictable and unpredictable shock. *Psychosomatic Medicine,* 1970, *32,* 397–409.

Weiss, J.M. Effects of coping behavior with and without a feedback signal in stress pathology in rats. *Journal of Comparative and Physiological Psychology,* 1971, *77,* 22–30.

Weiss, J.M. Psychological factors in stress and disease. *Scientific American,* 1972, *226,* 104–113.

Weiss, J.M., Stone, E.A., & Harrell, N. Coping behavior and brain norepinephrine level in rats. *Journal of Comparative and Physiological Psychology,* 1970, *72,* 153–160.

Weisz, J.R. Can I control it? The pursuit of veridical answers across the life span. *Life-span Development and Behavior,* 1983, *5,* 233–300.

West, C.D., Brown, H., Simons, E.L., Carter, D.B., Kumagi, L.F., & Englert, E. Adrenocortisol function and cortisol metabolism in old age. *Journal of Clinical and Endocrine Metabolism,* 1961, *21,* 1197.

White, R.W. Motivation reconsidered: The concept of competence. *Psychological Review,* 1959, *66,* 297–333.

Wildman, H.E., Rosenbaum, M.S., Framer, E.M., Keane, T.M., & Johnson, W.G. Smoking cessation: Predicting success with the health locus of control scale. Paper presented at the meeting of the Association for the Advancement of Behavior Therapy, San Francisco, 1979.

Wolk, S. Situational constraint as a moderator of the locus of control-adjustment relationship. *Journal of Consulting and Clinical Psychology*, 1976, *44*, 420–427.

Wolk, S., & Kurtz, J. Positive adjustment and involvement during aging and expectancy for internal control. *Journal of Consulting and Clinical Psychology*, 1975, *43*, 173–178.

Wolk, S., & Telleen, S. Psychological and social correlates of life satisfaction as a function of residential constraints. *Journal of Gerontology*, 1976, *31*, 89–98.

Wortman, C.B. Causal attributions and personal control. In J. Harvey, W. Ickes, & R.F. Kidd (Eds.), *New directions in attribution research*. Hillsdale, NJ: Erlbaum, 1976, 28–52.

Wortman, C.B., & Brehm, J.W. Responses to uncontrollable outcomes: An integration of reactance theory and the learned helplessness model. In L. Berkowitz (Ed.), *Advances in experimental social psychology*, Vol 8. New York: Academic Press, 1975.

Ziegler, M., & Reid, D.W. Correlates of locus of desired control in two samples of elderly persons: Community residents and hospitalized patients. *Journal of Consulting and Clinical Psychology*, 1979, *47*, 977–979.

Ziegler, M., & Reid, D.W. Correlates of changes in desired control scores and in life satisfaction scores among elderly persons. *International Journal of Aging and Human Development*, 1983, *16*, 135–146.

## CHAPTER 2

# Interaction of Biomedical and Psychosocial Factors in Research on Aging: A European Perspective

Bengt B. Arnetz, M.D., Ph.D.
Laboratory for Clinical Stress Research
Karolinska Institute and National Institute for
Psychosocial Factors and Health
Stockholm, Sweden

## INTRODUCTION

In Europe as in the United States scientific interest in population aging and in factors which affect health and functioning has increased significantly in recent decades. This chapter will document the reasons for this increased interest and will illustrate an emphasis in Europe, particularly in Sweden, on studies of the interaction of biomedical and psychosocial factors in aging and on intervention studies. While attention will be given to research in Europe, some of the research cited has been done in the United States. This fact makes an important point regarding the complementarity of research on issues which are recognized to have international significance.

The chapter begins with a brief review of the demographic aspects of population aging in Europe not only to document that populations are aging rapidly; it is also relevant to identify subpopulations among the elderly who have elevated risks for morbidity and mortality in part because they are in high-risk situations likely to involve lack of personal control, perception of incompetence, and social understimulation or isolation. Age-related risks for stress and for being in stressful situations have generated an interest in research on possible mechanisms by which physical and psychosocial stress may be involved in physical and mental changes which lead ultimately to disease and to death.

Psychophysiological research on younger adults has produced important information on how endocrine, metabolic, and cardiovascular systems are affected by psychosocial factors. Of particular importance is research on how psychosocial *under*stimulation may result in *over*stimulation of human neurophysiological systems and altered immune functions. Such research is given attention in this chapter.

Finally, as understanding of the mechanisms involved with stress and reaction to stress has improved, attention has focused increasingly on the possibility that experimental intervention studies can help in understanding not only how biomedical and psychosocial factors interact in later life but also how any deleterious effects of this interaction might be ameliorated or avoided. The chapter will end with illustrations of experimental interventions with which the author has been involved or is familiar.


## DEMOGRAPHIC BACKGROUND DATA

Even though the European population has increased in general, the proportion of elderly people 65 years of age and older has increased considerably faster. Table 2.1 depicts percentage increase in total population and in the age group 65 and over in nine European countries in recent decades.

The greatest proportionate increase among the elderly has in fact occurred among those 80 years and older. In the next 15 years, for example, this age group is projected to increase by 33 percent in Sweden in contrast to an increase of from 3.4 to 4.5 percent for the total population. The United States, which has a younger population than most countries in Europe, during the period of 1960–1970 experienced an increase in the elderly from 9.2 to 9.8 percent of the population (U.S. Bureau of the Census, 1982). Thus, countries in Europe might be looked upon as a forecast for American researchers, policymakers, and administrators with regard to future issues in managing a growing proportion of elderly in American society. At present, 16.8 percent of the Swedish population is 65 years of age or older, compared with 11.4 percent for the United States (U.S. Bureau of the Census, 1982). The United States is not projected to reach the proportion of elderly observed currently in Sweden for another 50 years (Butler & Lewis, 1982). However, even though Sweden and the

**Table 2.1**

Percentage Intercensal Increase in Total Population and in Population Aged 65 and Over, in Nine European Countries.

| Country | Census Years | Percentage Increase in Population | | | |
|---|---|---|---|---|---|
| | | Total | | Aged 65 and Over | |
| | | Males | Females | Males | Females |
| Bulgaria | 1970–80 | 4.0 | 4.7 | 29.7 | 28.6 |
| Czechoslovakia | 1968–78 | 5.2 | 5.5 | 22.2 | 23.3 |
| Finland | 1973–83 | 3.6 | 3.4 | 19.9 | 28.1 |
| France | 1972–82 | 4.7 | 4.3 | 4.6 | 4.1 |
| Hungary | 1970–80 | 3.9 | 3.6 | 17.1 | 23.6 |
| Iceland | 1973–83 | 9.2 | 10.4 | 22.2 | 18.2 |
| Netherlands | 1970–80 | 7.5 | 8.7 | 14.4 | 27.7 |
| Norway | 1973–83 | 3.3 | 4.2 | 15.7 | 20.1 |
| Sweden | 1973–83 | 1.6 | 3.3 | 16.4 | 22.0 |

*Source: Statistical abstract of Sweden* (*Statistisk årsbok*), Statistics Sweden, Stockholm. 1971, 1973, 1976, 1985.

United States differ with regard to the proportion of older people, both countries show the fastest growing age segments in the 75–85 and 85+ age groups. This is of great social, economic, psychological, and medical/health care importance, since these age groups, compared with younger age groups, have a dramatically increased need for formal and informal care.

The risk of poor health increases with advancing age. Figure 2.1, for example, depicts the age-related increase in the number of treatment days from the very young to very old age groups in Sweden. The probability of treatment days increases dramatically after age 70 from about 5 days annually per person for both males and females at age 60–69 to more than 20 days for males and 30 days for females annually at age 70 and older. Since 1970–1971, a multidisciplinary team of research workers in Gothenburg, Sweden, has followed representative groups of 70-year-olds in three cohorts—those born in 1901/02, in 1906/07, and in 1911/12. Due to the fact that marked cohort differences both in vitality and state of health have been observed, a broad-gauged intervention program has been added to the longitudinal study of those born in 1911/12. The Gothenburg study is unique from two points of view. It concerns samples that have been shown to be representative of the total population of 70-year-olds in Gothenburg. Furthermore, the study scope is unusually wide, covering, for example, basic biological factors and the incidence and prevalence of definable disorders in the

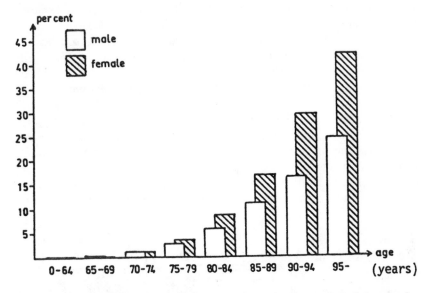

**Figure 2.1.**    Long-term care. Distribution of patients in percent of the population in the respective age group. (Reprinted from *Statistical Yearbook of Countries*, 1982.)

elderly as well as psychological and sociological factors, odontological studies, studies of housing, and social networks. [More than 200 publications are available from this study; for general descriptions, see Rinder, Roupe, Steen, & Svanborg (1975), Svanborg (1977), Steen, Isaksson, & Svanborg (1977), Berg (1980), Svanborg, Bergström, & Mellström (1982), Svanborg, Landahl, & Mellström (1982).] The study has, among many other things, shown that both underdiagnosis and overdiagnosis of health problems are common in the elderly. Observed health care consumption is, therefore, not the same as stating that the person seeking or receiving care is actually physically sick and in need of treatment. Another important observation from longitudinal research is that a considerable proportion of the elderly at ages 70, 75, and 79 is still healthy, that is, without symptoms of any definable disorders. Some of the reports from the Gothenburg group, however, illustrate the need for additional clinical information about the health of the elderly (Landahl, Jagenburg, & Svanborg, 1981). Furthermore, single people and persons who report feeling lonely (for a review see Berg, Mellström, Persson, & Svanborg, 1981) were found to have a decreased sense of subjective well-being. They also consumed more health care than those who do not have these characteristics. Loneliness and inactivity caused mental and somatic symptoms which appear typically to be overdiagnosed and overtreated. The increased health consumption in these groups did not necessarily result in an improved objective health state. This finding is one basis for increased societal concern about the health and health care of aging populations.

With advancing age an increasing proportion of elderly will be found in institutions (Figure 2.2). Thus, among those Swedes 80 years of age and older, approximately 37 percent are living in some kind of institution. The probability of living at home decreases monotonically with age after age 65. At age 65–69, almost all older Swedes live at home. By age 95 and older only about 10 percent live at home. With regard to gender differences, the majority of older people in institu-

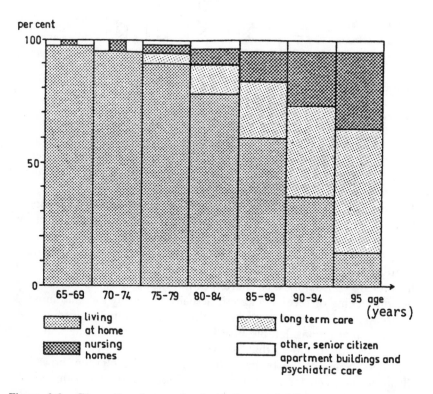

**Figure 2.2.**  Proportion (percent) of elderly people living at home and in various institutions (related to age). (Reprinted from *Official Statistics of Sweden*, 1981.)

tional settings are women. The proportion of the population living in long-term care settings (Figure 2.3) is consistently higher for females at age 75 and beyond. With aging in general, and institutionalization specifically, an increased risk of suffering from learned helplessness (Seligman, 1975), perceived lack of control (Langer & Rodin, 1976), and illusions of incompetence (Langer, 1979) has been noted.

## Risk Groups and Risk Situations
## with Regard to Morbidity
## and Mortality Risks, with Special
## Reference to Elderly People

In general, European and U.S. investigators have similar views of elderly risk groups and situations. An international literature documents the special importance of sociodemographic characteristics (marital status in particular), disease, role loss, psychosocial factors (such as perceived loss of personal controls), and response to stress.

   *Marital Status, Gender, and Race—Macro Data.*  Gender is known to be an important predictor of morbidity and mortality among elderly people. Thus, at present the average life expectancy for the Swedish male at birth is 73.6 years and for women 79.6 years. The equivalents

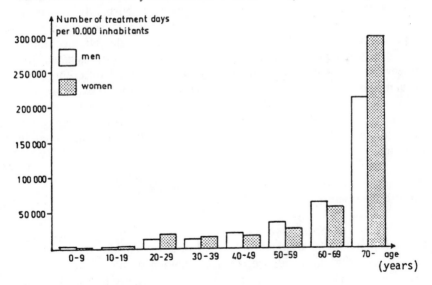

**Figure 2.3.**  Total health care treatment per 10,000 inhabitants by age and sex, 1979. (Reprinted from *Statistical Yearbook of Countries*, 1982.)

in the United States are (for whites) 70.6 and 78.2, respectively (U.S. Bureau of the Census, 1982). The sex ratio (females/males) in life expectancy was in the early 1900s 1.02 for the United States and 1.04 for Sweden. Today, these ratios are 1.10 and 1.08, respectively. For U.S. "blacks and other" (U.S. Bureau of the Census, 1982), the ratio in early 1900 was 0.99 and at present is 1.13. Most recent Swedish data indicate that this relative improvement in life expectancy for women compared with men may have come to a halt. During the last 5 years the average Swedish female improved her life expectancy by 11 months, compared with 13 months for the average male. However, U.S. "blacks and others" have moved from no gender differences to a ratio in favor of women that is even more pronounced than that for American whites. In addition to these gender differences in life expectancies, women tend, in general, to marry older men. This increases the risks that women may live up to 10 years in widowhood.

*The Risk of Singlehood.*   Marital status is an important predictor with regard to life expectancy for 50-year-olds (Table 2.2). Recently this problem has been investigated in the total Swedish population (Mellström et al., 1982). In this study it was shown that, with regard to further life expectancy at the age of 50, widowers survive on an average more than three years less than men still living together with their wives. Among females fewer remaining years of life were observed among widows than among those living with the husband. Similar indices of a shorter life expectancy for widows and widowers have been reported in other European countries as well as the United States. Social-psychological correlates of longevity by marital status have been reviewed thoroughly by Lehr (1982). The observed differences between married elders and widowers, with regard to life expectancy at 50 years of age is, as noted, approximately 3 years. This is the same as the impact all deaths from cancer have on life expectancy at age 50. The equivalent decrease for widows in life expectancy is approximately 1 year.

## Health Characteristics

*Stress and Specific Disorders.*   Several investigators have suggested that loss of a significant other and subsequent grief may be associated with the incidence of cancer among survivors. Leshan and Worthington (1958) reported in a retrospective study that unspecified neoplasms were more common in people who had suffered significant

**Table 2.2**
Swedish Life Expectancy in Years at 50 Years of Age,
Related to Marital Status and Gender.

| Marital Status | Male | Female |
|---|---|---|
| Never married | 24.2 | 29.7 |
| Married | 27.0 | 31.7 |
| Divorced | 21.8 | 29.9 |
| Widows/widowers | 23.9 | 30.4 |

Source: D. Mellström, Å. Nilsson, A. Odén, Å. Rundgren, & A. Svanborg. Mortality among widowed in Sweden. *Scandinavian Journal of Social Medicine*, 1982. With permission from Swedish Society of Medicine, Stockholm.

loss such as death of a spouse and that persons experiencing changes in or loss of job had a significantly higher prevalence of neoplasms than did controls. Kraus and Lilienfeld (1959) reported a doubled frequency of neoplasms for both sexes among bereaved persons compared with controls. Klerman and Izen (1977) have reviewed the literature with regard to specific neoplasms and the possible effects of bereavement. In general, the review supports the notion that bereavement may act as a psychosocial stressor, which in the long run affects the body's immunologic competence and thus the resistance to neoplastic cell transformations.

Cardiovascular disease is one of the major causes of ill-health and death among the elderly. Death rates from heart disease increase drastically with age. While it is known from a number of epidemiologic studies that age, sex, triglycerides, cholesterol, blood pressure, weight, and smoking habits are among the classical risk factors for developing heart disease (Böttiger & Carlson, 1980; Kannel & Gordon, 1980), most epidemiologic heart disease studies have been carried out on age groups below 65 years of age. Further research on risk factors for heart disease in later life is clearly needed, since all traditional risk factors taken together can predict currently only some 50 percent of the heart disease victims (Fuller et al., 1983). Particular attention to psychosocial factors in later life is warranted. For example, "broken heart" is a term commonly used in describing people suffering from bereavement. Parkes, Benjamin, and Fitzgerald (1969) prospectively followed some 4,000 widowers aged 55 years and older for a 9-year period. The mortality rate from heart disease was 40 percent higher during the first 6 months of bereavement than expected for the population in general. It is of interest that death due to coronary thrombosis was 67 percent higher than expected, and it should be noted that stress is reported to be able to increase blood clotting. The finding of increased death rates among widowers as well as widows is supported in a Swedish study by Mellström et al. (1982). He studied all widowed elderly during an 11-year period in Sweden (some 360,000 people). For widowers in the age group 70–74 years, the death rate was 48 percent over the expected during the first 3 months after bereavement. The equivalent figure for widows was 22 percent.

Traditionally it was believed that blood pressure (especially systolic) rises with age (Grane, 1978). However, data from the Framingham study (Kannel & Gordon, 1980) and the gerontological and the geriatric population study in Gothenburg (Landahl, Bengtsson, Sigurdsson, & Svanborg, 1983) have shown that, while there is in older populations an age-related increase in blood pressure, at least up to age 70–75, after age 75 blood pressure may actually decline somewhat. Jenkins, Somerville, and Hames (1983) confirm the need for caution in generalizations about age-related changes in blood pressure. Their study prospectively followed blood pressure development for men 23–64 years of age for 7–13 years. As expected for relatively younger adults, 45 percent of the men had no increase in systolic blood pressure and 60 percent no systemic increase in diastolic pressure. However, blood pressure increases were found in older and heavier men. Furthermore, men with higher anxiety and hostility exhibited higher mean pressures. The blood pressure slope increased the most for those men reporting a *lower* amount of stress.

*Hypertension and Increased Dependency.*   Since increased blood pressure implies a greater morbidity and mortality risk, older people, particularly very old people, should be carefully monitored and treated if need be. This is underlined by the findings from the Framingham study in the United States of men and women 45–74 years old. "Even borderline elevations of pressure in the elderly double the risk" of cardiovascular disease (Kannel & Gordon, 1980, p. 68). Despite findings in recent studies that elderly people may also benefit from antihypertensive treatment, however, they are less likely to receive adequate treatment (Kannel & Gordon, 1980). If untreated, elderly with hypertension run a significant increased risk of suffering from cerebrovascular and cardiovascular disease. Disease in turn may lead to unnecessary dependency on other people, both professionals and family, because disease increases the risk of perceived lack of personal control, learned helplessness, and institutionalization. The psychosocial concomitants of chronic diseases exacerbate poor health, a conclusion shared by both European and U.S. investigators.

## Psychosocial Factors

*Perceived Lack of Control and Competence.* Studies linking theories of perceived lack of control, social incompetence, decreased choice, learned helplessness, external locus of control, and a spiral of senility reflected in increased age-related susceptibility to poor health and early death have been prominent in the international literature on aging. Kuypers and Bengtson (1973) have created a social breakdown syndrome model of aging which focuses on social competence. In their model "an individual's sense of self, his (her) ability to mediate between self and society, and his (her) orientation to personal mastery are functions of the kinds of social labeling experienced in life" (p. 181). The authors suggest that "the elderly in Western society are susceptible to, and dependent on, social labeling because of unique social reorganizations in late life, e.g., role loss, vague or inappropriate normative information, and lack of reference groups" (p. 81). According to the Kuypers–Bengtson model, elderly people gradually become more dependent on external labeling, which is generally more negative for elderly (see also Thomas, 1981). The results of such negative labeling may be *feelings* of incompetence. The staff in long-stay institutions, for example, may tend to take over more and more Activities of Daily Living (ADL) functions and other responsibilities. The elderly may gradually lose their social function and perceived social competence. The end result may very well be an incompetent person, entirely dependent on others. Loss of role functions and role expectations increases the risk that many elderly people will feel helpless in institutions (Seligman, 1975). A syndrome of perceived helplessness may encourage institutionalized elderly to be passive and amenable and to become patients considered by the staff to be "nice patients" since they do not make any demands and just obey the staff (Arnetz & Theorell, 1983a). Such negative role expectations encountered by many elderly in institutions may also have negative effects on mental capacities. In the model of the "spiral of senility," lowered self-esteem leads hypothetically to failing physical health and signs of mental impairment. At this stage the elderly may become "confused," "uncooperative," or "docile." The next expected stage is apathy and acceptance of the situation. This stage gradually worsens and the individual becomes continuously more withdrawn and uninterested in the present. At this stage the staff considers the elderly person to be "hopelessly senile." The end result of this vicious spiral, which is a self-fulfilling prophecy, is complete dependency, helplessness, and, eventually, death (Barns, Sack, & Shore, 1973).

Another aspect of aging and adaptation to institutional life is suggested by the concept of *locus of control*. Rotter's (1966) characterization of internally controlled individuals as more striving, more self-confident, and less anxious and apathetic than externals has been investigated in some studies of older people. Thus, Palmore and Luikart (1972) reported *internal locus of control* to be a good predictor of life satisfaction among people over the age of 60. *Perceived locus of control* has been studied considerably less among *institutionalized* elderly. However, Felton and Kahana (1974) have developed a situationally bound locus of control scale for institutionalized elderly people. In groups of residents in three homes for the aged, locus of control was conceptualized in terms of nine hypothetical problems—monotony, privacy, conformity, emotional expression, activity, environmental ambiguity, affective intensity, motor control, and autonomy. Relationships between locus of control and satisfaction/morale were calculated. In contrast to studies in younger people, adjustment "appears in our study to be related to finding the locus of control in others" (Felton & Kahana, 1974), suggesting better adjustment among institutionalized elderly with *external* locus of control. This is in line with previously noted concomitants of institutionalization, that is, social breakdown, loss of competence, the spiral of senility and learned helplessness. Elderly people who can adjust to a rigid institutional environment by relinquishing personal control may be more situationally adapted than those who wish to continue an independent or at least an interdependent life after they have moved into an institution. Yet this situational adaptation may have negative consequences for health in the long run.

In another study of institutionalized elderly by Reid, Haas, and Hawkings (1977), somewhat different results were reported. In this study, items related to desire and expectancy were used for assessing locus of control. They demonstrated a positive correlation between the preference for and expectation of internal locus of control and psychological adjustment to institutional living. They also found a correlation between nurse's ratings of subjects in terms of happiness and internality. The positive relationship between desired locus of control and favorable self-concept was stronger for males than females.

An important factor in understanding contradictory results in the relationship between locus of control and adaptation may be length of stay in the institution. Reid et al. (1977) reported a negative correlation between length of stay and internality. Situations characterized by a bad fit between an individual's wishes and needs and the demands of the environment may lead to psychological strain which, in turn, may result in neurophysiological and immune changes in the human system.

Since, as we will discuss below, the elderly organism has a diminished capacity for adapting to stress, the risk of deleterious physical and psychosocial responses to stress increases with age.

*Psychosocial Factors, Poor Health, and Death.* It is a complex matter to prove that psychosocial factors cause poor health and even death. Proof requires that all the conventional risk factors have to be controlled for (e.g., heredity, lifestyle, occupational history, smoking habits, blood levels of cholesterol, triglycerides and lipoproteins, and blood pressure). Furthermore, there is still no uniform definition of what is "normal" aging and "pathologic" aging. Finally, drug treatment and patient compliance must be controlled for, and perceived stress and coping strategies adopted by the individual must be assessed. It is quite obvious that studies meeting such stringent conditions are indeed complex, demand multidisciplinary approaches, and are scarce.

In the international literature there are a number of retrospective as well as prospective studies of elderly persons reporting relationships among psychosocial stressors and poor health, even death. Sterling and Eyer (1981) concluded in an extensive review article that "modern society does not generally recognize the importance to health of disruptions of intimate social relationships. Yet, such disruptions are associated with large elevations of morbidity and mortality" (p. 4). They illustrate this conclusion by reporting that standardized death rate is higher for almost all causes [e.g., tuberculosis, cancer, diabetes (males), cerebral hemorrhage (especially males), and pneumonia] for single and divorced people than for married ones. Lefcourt (1973) states that "the illusion that one can exercise personal choice has a definite and a positive role in sustaining life" (p. 424). Since older people are a high-risk group with regard to the risks of losing a significant other, that is, "disruptions of intimate social relationships" and of threats to personal control (Sterling & Eyer, 1981), it is probable that they may also have higher morbidity and mortality risks even after control for traditional risk factors. Langer and Rodin (1976) reviewed studies linking lack of choice and control to increased susceptibility to ill-health and death and conclude that lack of choice and personal control does in fact appear to increase physiological arousal and the risks of both ill-health and, eventually, early death.

The importance of *choice* and *control* for longevity is further stressed by the finding that old people who relocated voluntarily to institutions and believed the institutions offered a better treatment environment had higher morale scores, and they had significantly higher survival rates two years later than elderly whose institutionalization was involuntary and who felt less control over the decision to move to an institution (Noelker & Harel, 1978). Other studies note the potential effects of voluntary and involuntary relocation (Bourestom & Tars, 1974; Lawton & Yaffe, 1970; Wittels & Botwinick, 1974; Zweig and Csank, 1976). Booth et al. (1983) recently reported patterns of mortality in 175 homes for the elderly in England. During a 12-month follow-up period, mortality varied between 7 percent among well-established independent residents under age 80 to 53 percent among severely dependent residents aged 90 or over. Naturally, many complex factors cause such varied death rates, and the effects of the relocation process on mortality, described as a trauma by some investigators, clearly needs further attention (Coffman, 1983).

Finally, one should be aware that hospitalization may have deleterious side-effects. Gillick, Serrell, and Gillick (1982) reported that hospitalized elderly people "are at high risk of developing symptoms of depressed psychophysiologic functioning and of sustaining medical intervention as a result of these symptoms, with attendant medical complications" (p. 1033.) It is hypothesized, as well as partly supported by data from the literature, that unsuitable psychosocial environments may act as psychophysiological stressors causing physiological changes leading to increased demands on an already more stress-sensitive older person.

Psychosocial *overstimulation* is widely recognized as a potent stressor that may have various psychological and physiologic effects. Considerably less attention has been focused on the psychobiologic effects of *social understimulation*. Laboratory experiments have shown a wide range of psychoendocrine changes that may result from understimulation (Arnetz et al., 1983). There are, however, various limitations to the interpretation of such data. Participants are, for example, aware of the artificiality of the experiment. Some have normal social interactions outside the laboratory. Others live in situations characterized by lack of personal control, social understimulation, and monotony. It is difficult to assess how these different experiences affect their responses in the laboratory.

Only a very limited number of controlled studies outside laboratories exist relating psychosocial factors to physiological changes in the elderly. Müller, Grad, and Engelsman (1975) studied 206 geriatric patients in terms of a number of biological variables such as electroencephalograms (EEG), plasma corticosteroid levels before and after the EEG test, body weight, amplitude of the galvanic skin response (GSR), and blood pressure to combined light and sound stimuli. After 5 years 87 percent of this geriatric population was reassessed. No differences were noticed between survivors and those who died, with regard to gender, educational level, hearing deficits, and visual impairments. Survivors were 5 years younger, and their body weight was 14 kilograms higher than those who had died during the 5 years. Those who had died during the 5-year period had slower (theta) EEG activity than those who did not. Plasma corticosteroids were higher in the nonsurvivors (assessment followed the EEG test). Corticosteroids are hormones known to be "stress-sensitive" (Henry & Stephens, 1977; Mason, 1968). Thus, it is plausible that the elderly people with the highest plasma cortisol values at the first assessment exhibited the highest psychophysiological arousal, increasing the risks for early death.

Elevated plasma cortisol values have also been associated with depressive moods, lack of control, subordination, and distress (Arnetz et al., 1983; Henry & Stephens, 1977; Lundberg & Frankenhaeuser, 1980). Arnetz et al. (1983) reported that the highest plasma cortisol values concurred with feelings of monotony and boredom among institutionalized elderly. The importance of a sense of control in alleviating stress or coping with stress in institutionalized elderly has been shown by Rodin (1980). She reported decreased excretion of free cortisol in urine following an experimental intervention to improve sense of control among institutionalized elderly. Arnetz et al. (1983) have also reported a relative decrease in anabolic hormones (dehydroepiandrosterone, estradiol, and testosterone) and increased hemoglobin $A_{1c}$ levels in elderly people reporting understimulation. Thus, biological studies indicate that at least subgroups of institutionalized elderly people show signs of increased autonomic arousal and physiologic stress.

*Stress Response and Age.*    Stress responsiveness in elderly people has been considerably less investigated than in younger age groups. Palmer, Ziegler, and Lake (1978) reported that during rest younger subjects had lower mean arterial pressure than older subjects and lower circulating levels of noradrenaline (norepinephrine). After standing and performing an isometric exercise stress, old subjects increased their circulating levels of noradrenaline more than the younger age group. However, no uniform finding was reported for changes in pulse rates between the two age groups. A recent study by Arnetz (1985) reported a decreased plasma prolactin stress response in elderly people undergoing surgery for inguinal hernias under general anesthesia. Wiggins, Ratner, and Wise (1983) reported a similar diminished prolactin responsiveness to orbital sinus puncture under ether anesthesia in older female rats. Overall, integrated central nervous system response to certain stressors appears to diminish with age. Elderly have reduced β-adrenergic receptor sensitivity to agonists (e.g., isoproterenol) possibly due to changes in properties of the β-receptor-adenylate cyclase complex (Feldman et al., 1984). These changes in β-receptor affinity for agonists are associated with higher levels of circulating catecholamines in elderly people. In order to reach the same desired systemic effect (e.g., metabolic adaptations or pressure responses during stress), the elderly may have to compensate for decreased peripheral receptor sensitivity by enhanced hormonal secretions.

Eisdorfer suggests "that deficits in performance among the aged may be associated with heightened autonomic nervous system receptor activity in specific organs" (Eisdorfer & Wilkie, 1979, p. 50), after observing improved performance in an experimental task by older men who were administered a β-adrenergic blocking agent (propranolol); this agent reduced autonomic nervous system and organ activity as reflected in such indices as heart rate and free fatty acid levels. Further studies of the hormonal as well as the metabolic responses during strain in elderly people is clearly indicated. By measuring other functions such as galvanic skin response, heart rate, blood pressure, circulating levels of catecholamines, corticosteroids, prolactin, and growth hormones, we will get a better picture of overall autonomic arousal in the elderly.

In general, then, elderly people appear to have a diminished stressor responsiveness in various endocrine organs and glands as well as a decreased peripheral response to set levels of circulating mediators like hormones. Taken together, if survival is enhanced or diminished by the organism's reaction to strain by appropriate physiologic arousal, then elderly people exhibit in certain circumstances a hampered stress response and experience a greater risk when subjected to stress.

We now know enough about stress and stress responses in later life, however, to consider multidisciplinary studies intended to counteract, slow, postpone, or reverse age-related psychological, social, and physiologic/medical changes in later life. In the next section several relevant intervention studies will be reviewed.

### Gerontologic and Geriatric Multidisciplinary Intervention Studies

*Existing Knowledge and Need for New Knowledge.*    The literature cited so far supports the assumption that social understimulation and isolation among elderly have negative psychological effects. Feelings of depression, psychosomatic symptoms, and negative self-concept appear to be potential consequences of social understimulation. Some elderly living in the community have been reported to withdraw from social interactions as they age. This gradual withdrawal tends to be more and more difficult to block and reverse as years go by. Social withdrawal and feelings of loneliness appear to be even more of a problem among institutionalized elderly people. Social isolation and understimulation are accompanied not only by psychosocial problems but also by somatic problems which increase the risk of morbidity and mortality.

A social support network is one possible determinant of both somatic and mental well-being. Although various programs have been implemented to counteract isolation and passivity among institutionalized elderly, there is a paucity of experimental studies designed to assess the effects of mobilizing the elderly's own resources and interests and the involvement of the nursing staff, so that institutionalized elderly are helped to master the content and timing of personal activities so as to gain a positive sense of control over their own lives. The attitudes of staff toward elderly people and their insufficient knowledge about aging and elderly people may be major obstacles in creating a more stimulating and active atmosphere for institutionalized elderly people. While some planned interventions designed to increase activity of institutionalized elderly do have staff development and education as part of the intervention program, most of them do not. Another deficiency in previous interventions designed to activate elderly people is the potential but unrecognized influence that psychosocial factors may have on the biochemical reactions of possible pathogenic and/or salutogenic significance in various living situations. Even though epidemiologic data indicate increased mortality and morbidity risks among socially understimulated and isolated elderly, literally no studies have been designed to evaluate physiologic effects of such isolation in real life. Thus, it is of value to assess systematically and simultaneously in intervention studies not only emotional, behavioral, and social reactions but also physiologic changes. We will illustrate below the potential and limitations of studies, primarily those performed in Europe, which describe interventions with elderly persons.

There are a number of different ways to care for the disabled elderly. At present there is a strong preference for caring for the elderly at home as long as possible. Another preference is that small, local nursing homes and senior citizens apartment buildings where the elderly can still keep in touch with their pre-institutional social environment be used when possible. It is, however, rather unusual to encounter in the literature adequate comparisons of the effects of different living arrangements. Several studies illustrate the potential and limitations of intervention studies with older persons.

*Dementia: The Importance of Psychosocial Factors in Care.* The prevalence of dementia increases with age and may reach the 50 percent level at the age of 95 years (Gottfries, 1982). Thus, caring for the demented elderly is a major concern for modern society. It is also a potential burden not only for society but also for the family. Näslund and von Essen (1983) recently reported a project carried out in a major hospital in Stockholm. The aims were to provide day care for demented elderly and assess whether this care prevented or postponed admission to long-term care institutions. Patients were selected from a catchment area of 14,000 people aged 70 and older. A regular ward was made more home-like by furnishing it with functional but ordinary furniture. Some space was furnished as living rooms and some was designed as a resting-relaxation room. Other rooms were used for various planned activities. Twenty-four patients were referred to the day-care group (experimental) and 19 constituted the control group. Both groups underwent a careful physical and mental check-up as well as assessment of ADL status. Nurse's aides functioned as contact persons to the group of demented patients. The contact person and an instructor were responsible for treatment. All contacts with the social welfare organization, family, and other caregivers were the responsibility of the contact person. If a demented person could not come to the day-care center for some reason, the contact person went to the home to find out what help could be provided in the home. Being a contact person meant getting a very complete picture of the patient's life. It also meant great responsibility, traditionally not part of the role of nurse's aides. The contact person and the instructor developed an open and supportive relationship intended to preserve and train the functions the elderly person had left in an environment as stimulatory as possible. In order to stress the home-like environment, no staff wore hospital clothes. Furthermore, all patients were called guests. Much attention was given to ADL training such as personal hygiene, cooking, and the use of public transportation. The experimental and control groups were comparable with regard to age (majority 80–85 years) and sex (majority females). In the experimental group 20 of 24 lived alone compared with 11 of 19 in the control group. Thus, the social network was somewhat less developed in the experimental group.

After six months the two groups were compared. None of the subjects in the experimental group had been admitted to hospitals during the six-month period of day care. In the control groups the equivalent figure was 26 percent (5 of 19, $p < 0.01$, chi-square test). Sixty-two percent of the subjects (15 of 24) in the experimental group improved or showed no decrease in ADL functions during the six-month period. The equivalent figure in the control group was 5 percent (1 of 19). Thirty-eight percent (9 of 24) patients in the experimental group showed a decrease in ADL functions compared with 74 percent (14 of 19) in the control group. There was also a trend toward an improved rating on a scale measuring dementia in the experimental group, compared with the control group over the six-month period. Three of 12 subscales on the Psychotic Inpatient Profile scale (PIP) were used to measure depressive tendencies, anxiety, and worry (Näslund & von Essen, 1983). Seventy-four percent of patients in the experimental group improved or showed no changes on the PIP scale. In the control group, all patients either showed no change or got worse. Thus, these results show that despite the fact that more subjects in the experimental group lived by themselves, a multidisciplinary day-care service postponed the need to admit demented patients to long-term care institutions. ADL functions improved in the experimental group, and depressive moods, anxiety, and worry decreased among those elderly who were part of the day-care service. Regular day-care service helped demented people to return to a more normal day–night rhythm.

In another study by Karlsson et al. (1984) at St. Jörgen's Hospital, Gothenburg, and Gerontology Center, Lund, Sweden, the effects of mental activation of demented patients were evaluated with attention given to biological factors. They tested the hypothesis that environmental stimulation can alter the monoamine metabolism in patients with moderate degrees of dementia. Such an experiment is of interest since Green, Greenough, and Schlumpf (1983) reported that the adult rat brain showed increased dendritic length after environmental stimulation. Patients from two long-stay wards were selected. In one ward no major changes were enacted. In the other, the staff was taught about the possible effects of emotional and intellectual stimulation and ways of activating the patients. Groups of four or five patients were activated by members of the staff during two sessions of 60 minutes each twice a week over a period of two months. Patients were assessed before and after the activation program with regard to motoric, intellectual, and emotional qualities. Monoamine metabolites were analyzed in cerebrospinal fluid. HVA (homovanillic acid), a metabolite formed in the breakdown of dopamine, increased in the activated group.

The psychiatric ratings did not change in the experimental group but worsened in the control group. The increase in HVA correlated positively with improvement of managing personal hygiene ($p < 0.02$) and wakefulness ($p < 0.03$). The study shows that a more humane and stimulating environment may lead not only to psychosocial improvements but also to improved dopamine metabolism in the brain. Thus, data presented by Karlsson et al. (1984) suggest that insufficient environmental stimulation is one factor behind the intellectual deterioration so often seen in later life.

Götestam (in press) has studied effects of reality orientation in older patients (mean age as high as 81 years) with severe dementia. He found that it was possible to improve reality orientation in patients with advanced stages of dementia by means of training (e.g., orientation to time, person, and room), but the effects were of short-term duration. The importance of persistence in environmental changes in long-term care institutions is stressed by Götestam's work. Melin and Götestam (1981) reported in another study the beneficial behavioral effects on psychogeriatric patients of simple interventions like rearranging furniture in a way that would be more conducive to conversation and offering more freedom in choosing the composition of meals and having longer eating periods. Even these minor environmental changes led to improved social interactions as well as improved eating behavior in the experimental group submitted to these changes. Few changes in the control group where no changes were enacted were noted. Similarly, Quattrochi-Tubin and Jason (1980) have shown that a simple stimulus such as offering refreshments can increase the participation and interactions among institutionalized elderly people.

Individualized activity programs for elderly people have also been designed. Salter and Salter (1975) have reported beneficial effects of programs which consisted of actions aimed at improving reality orientation, activities of daily living, and recreational activities. One of the goals of simple social activation programs is to reestablish behavior which was once, but is no longer, present among institutionalized elderly. The attitude of the staff toward elderly people plays an important role for the outcome of a social activation program. Very little change will occur unless the staff has a positive view of elderly people and their possibilities and translates that view actively in their interaction with patients. Salter and Salter (1975) make this point in illustrating measures for staff development as an integral part of activation programs. In another study, Sperbeck and Whitbourne (1981) worked to counteract staff-dependency formulation in institutionalized elderly. Independence among the elderly was encouraged by training staff in the principles of behavioral analysis focusing on cognitive and attitudinal restructuring on the part of both staff and patients. Elderly persons themselves must be encouraged to perform as many ADL activities as possible. Interaction of staff with elderly should be encouraged. Formation of staff–elderly councils on wards is a way to encourage beneficial interaction.

Available data from the reviewed literature, in brief, indicate that mental stimulation as well as environmental modifications to enhance activity can, at least temporarily, reverse or slow age-related deleterious mental and neuroendocrine changes. Simple measures may be taken to prevent the development of decreased personal control associated with institutionalization. The importance of environmental factors in the development of dependency in older people is shown in a study by Finlay, Bayles, Rosen, and Milling (1983). They assessed optimal height of seating for elderly ambulant residents in three social service homes. When seat height was 16–17 inches and arm height some 10 inches above the seat level, 77 percent of those who usually were chair-fast could rise. Thus, even though traditional chairs in institutional settings which are of suboptimal height may be comfortable, they encourage dependence on staff.

*Age-related Muscle Involution: The Effects of Passivity.* Age-related decrease in muscular strength and volume contributes to decreased mobility among elderly. It is still not quite clear how much of the muscle involution is primary (i.e., age-dependent) and how much is secondary (i.e., lack of exercise, passivity, and changes in diet regimens). Aniansson, Grimby, and Rundgren (1980) reported the effects on muscle function of a 12-week training program (3 × 45-minute sessions/week) in elderly aged 67–76 years. Training led to decreased heart rate during submaximal work (100 W). Maximal oxygen uptake increased 22 percent, and static and dynamic muscle strength also increased. Type II fibers increased significantly with training. This study shows that regular training has beneficial effects on elderly people and that age-related changes in muscle morphology and function can be partially counteracted through simple exercise.

Reiter (1982) reports that a physical exercise program for elderly women (aged 65–90 years) living in senior centers or residences was associated with improved mood status, reduced state of anxiety, and improvement in feelings of well-being. There were also indications of better sleep patterns.

*Modifying Psychophysiological Effects of Loneliness.* At the Laboratory for Clinical Stress Research, Karolinska Institute, Stockholm, two multidisciplinary gerontologic intervention studies have been carried out during the last four-year period. One project, "The Aging and Loneliness Project," illustrates an intervention with elderly exhibiting maladaptive strategies in coping with loneliness. Elderly women living in their own homes who had applied for a flat in a senior citizens apartment building but who had a low priority for admission were selected. Mean age was 77 years. Some 63 percent were widows, 24 percent unmarried, and 13 percent divorced. Feelings of loneliness had been reported by 108 of the selected 207 subjects. Subjects reporting feelings of loneliness were allocated to an experimental (n = 68) and control group (n = 40). Both groups were interviewed before and after an intervention project designed as follows had been implemented:

Interviewers (home-help assistants) formed groups of three to five elderly subjects living close together. The groups met four times. At each meeting a particular subject was to be discussed (e.g., the residential area; roles of retirees; social and medical services; and summing up the first three meetings and opportunities for leisure activities). Both experimental and control subjects were given a number of different psychological and social evaluations, and blood pressure was taken before and after the intervention. Andersson (1985) found that the experimental group exhibited lower feelings of loneliness, more social contacts, less feelings of meaninglessness, higher self-esteem, greater ability to trust, and lower systolic and diastolic blood pressure. When the more stringent analysis of covariance was applied to adjust for any initial group differences, the statistically significant changes were found in the intervention group. Social contacts, systolic blood pressure, and number of leisure activities improved. Mean blood pressure before the intervention in experimental group was 159/86 (systolic/diastolic) and following the intervention 150/80; the equivalent figures in the control group were 161/87 and 161/85 (Andersson, 1983). Systolic blood pressure decreased between the two assessment times 10 mm Hg or more in 48.5 percent of the participants in the experimental group and for 38.9 percent in the control group. Diastolic pressure, on the other hand, decreased 10 mm Hg or more for 39.4 percent in the experimental group compared with 22.2 percent in the controls. Availability of a confidant and a sense of personal control decreased loneliness. However, social isolation and loneliness were not found to be related to blood pressure. These findings indicate that the intervention affected blood pressure through mechanisms other than those responsible for improvement in psychosocial variables. It is likely that socially isolated and understimulated elderly as well as those reporting loneliness experienced psychosocial stress, causing physiologic arousal with subsequent increase in blood pressure. The lability in such pressure increases is probably dependent on how long the psychosocial stressor has been in effect. By intervening and offering social activation in groups, feelings of psychosocial strain may have been attenuated, partly explaining the lowered blood pressure. Endocrine changes, other than catecholamines, may be involved in mediating the observed improvement in blood pressure. However, direct measurements of other functions were not carried out.

## A Systematic Study
## of Intervention

In another Swedish study, also carried out at the Laboratory for Clinical Stress Research, Karolinska Institute, the psychophysiologic effects of social understimulation among institutionalized elderly were systematically studied in a six-month controlled intervention study (Arnetz, Eyre, & Theorell, 1982a; Arnetz, Theorell, Levi, Kallner & Eneroth, 1983; Arnetz & Theorell, 1983b).

The aims of the study were to:

1. Devise a social activation program in collaboration with the elderly and the staff with the goal of increasing not only social activation but also personal control over one's own situation.
2. Study possible age-related differences in the effects of social activation on a broad spectrum of physiologic variables in an elderly population.
3. Describe psychological, sociological, physiologic, and health correlates of social understimulation and evaluate the psychosocial and physiologic effects of increased social activation.
4. Design a framework within which staff development in the caring process was possible.
5. Evaluate changes in staff's attitudes toward the elderly people during the course of such a program.
6. Provide administrators of institutions and policymakers with practical information that might be used to improve the psychosocial environment in institutions for the elderly.

The design, implementation, and outcomes of this intervention study illustrate the problems and the potentials of research on the intersection of biomedical and psychosocial factors in aging processes and on ways in which these processes might be modified beneficially.

*Principal Hypotheses.* The principal hypotheses tested in the study were:

1.  *Social understimulation* is frequently observed among residents of institutions for the elderly.
2.  Social understimulation is an *abnormal situation* to which the elderly person cannot and does not readily adapt.
3.  The lack of complete adaptation to the situation causes the human organism to react with *increased* psychophysiologic *arousal*.
4.  The increase in psychophysiologic arousal is reflected in *increased* circulating levels of *catabolic* hormones and *decreased* concentration of circulating *anabolic* hormones.
5.  The change toward higher catabolic metabolism is reflected in *increased* concentrations of overall blood glucose (measured as hemoglobin $A_{1c}$), triglycerides, and urea, and a *decreased* concentration of the ratio HDL-cholesterol/total cholesterol.
6.  The elderly's interests and resources affect response to and the effects of social activation programs.
7.  Cooperation of staff and the elderly in activation programs affects response to and the effects of the program.
8.  Staff development affects the implementation of social activation programs.
9.  Increased social activation, participation, and perceived personal control among institutionalized elderly are accompanied by decreased physiologic arousal and improved physical, psychological, and psychosomatic well-being.
10. Social activation interventions increase the beneficial interaction of staff and elderly patients.

*What Was Measured, and Why.*   First, an impressive amount of psychophysiologic research clearly points to the responsiveness of the neuroendocrine system to psychosocial stressors. Earlier research primarily studied the effects on the hypophysioadrenocortical and the hypothalamicoadrenomedullary response factors. Subsequent studies have also pointed out the sensitivity of the *anabolic* hormones (e.g., estrogen, testosterone, and dehydroepiandrosterone), the secretions of pituitary neuropeptides (e.g., growth hormone), and prolactin to various stressors. It is also well known that changes in hormonal secretions elicited by psychosocial stressors are accompanied by metabolic responses. Thus, it was considered meaningful to study biochemical variables previously shown to be sensitive to social *overstimulation* under conditions of social *understimulation*.

Second, as reviewed earlier, epidemiologic data indicate an increased morbidity and mortality risk among socially understimulated as well as lonely people. It was therefore of interest to study possible pathogenic mechanisms that could explain this increased morbidity and mortality risk.

Some of the physiologic variables chosen (e.g., triglycerides, cholesterol, systolic and diastolic blood pressure, hemoglobin, and erythrocyte sedimentation rate) have been reported to be single-risk factors for myocardial infarction, "a great killer" in the older age group studied (Böttiger & Carlson, 1980). Possible age-related differences in biochemical variables in response to social stimulation was therefore of interest. It was also of interest to examine whether a rather moderate activation program for the elderly people would be accompanied by an improved hormonal and metabolic balance.

*Methodological Considerations in Designing the Intervention Program.* An intervention study to examine biopsychosociological effects of an increased social activity level might be designed in at least two different ways: (1) an investigator might select two different groups of institutionalized elderly people—(a) one with a very low level of social activity and (b) one with a rather high level—and compare the two groups. This design produces a number of uncontrollable factors. (2) The other possibility is to select two matched groups and introduce to one a social activation program, while the other, offered no changes, is followed as a control group.

This latter choice was made for the present study. Even though experiments in real-life settings cannot control all relevant factors, they are more appropriate than laboratory studies for answering the hypotheses in the study described.

*Population and Setting.* Two floors at a senior citizen apartment building (Enskededalen's Service House) were selected for the study. The building is located three kilometers (1.8 miles) from the city center of Stockholm. It was erected in 1979 and consists of 279 apartments. Space on two floors was identical and the same number of staff were available; on each floor there were 11 nurse's aides and the equivalent of 1¾ supervisory staff. One floor was designated the experimental group (Floor E) and the other the control (Floor C). The nurse's aides in both groups had an average of less than one year of health care education. Each floor had approximately 65 tenants, 30 of whom were selected at random to participate in the study. The sex and age distribution of the participants as well as some medical and pharmacologic characteristics are depicted in Table 2.3. The two groups were similar with regard to the characteristics studied and representative of their age group with regard to medical ailments and drug consumption. Health and medical care utilization were assessed by (1)

**Table 2.3**
Age Distribution, Medical Status, and Drug Consumption of the Participants.

|  | Floor $E^a$ (n = 30) | Floor $C^a$(n = 30) |
|---|---|---|
| Number of women | 20 | 20 |
| Number of men | 10 | 10 |
| Mean age (years) | 77.6 | 78.8 |
| Number of subjects $\geq$ 90 years | 0 | 1 |
| Number of subjects 80–89 years | 12 | 14 |
| Number of subjects 70-79 years | 14 | 10 |
| Number of subjects 60-69 years | 3 | 5 |
| Number of subjects 50-59 years | 1 | 0 |
| Number of married couples | 4 | 4 |
| Number of subjects in need of a wheelchair | 7 | 4 |
| Number of subjects with severely impaired vision | 7 | 8 |
| Number of subjects with severe hearing loss | 5 | 8 |
| Number of diabetes mellitus patients | 3 | 6 |
| Number of subjects on diuretics (excluding thiazides) | 6 | 8 |
| Number of subjects on thiazides | 6 | 7 |
| Number of subjects on β-blockers | 1 | 1 |
| Number of subjects on analgesics | 5 | 6 |
| Number of subjects on hypnotics and sedatives | 6 | 7 |

There were no statistical differences between the two groups (chi-square tests).
$^a$E = experimental; C = control.
*Source:* B.B. Arnetz & T. Theorell. Psychological, sociological and health behaviour aspects of a long term activation programme for institutionalized elderly people. *Social Science and Medicine*, 1983, *17*, 8, 449-456. With permission from Pergamon Press, Oxford.

direct interviews with all participants; (2) routine clinical check-ups; and (3) review of medical records. Actual consumption of drugs cannot be determined reliably by any of these methods. Patient compliance is known to be low, especially among multi-drug consumers. Blood screening and/or analysis of urine and feces for drug content, the only reliable ways to determine actual drug use, was not carried out in the present study.

Originally, 63 people were asked to participate and three refused. The reason for non-participation in all three cases was that each individual traveled regularly to local hospitals for medical treatment and did not wish to be involved in additional medical investigations.

*Evaluating the Activation Program.*    Tenants and the staff of the experimental group formed together a "social activation" program. The aim of the program was to increase the tenants' social activity and independence and to counteract social isolation and passivity. The design and implementation of the program is described in detail in Arnetz et al. (1982a).

Changes associated with the activation program were evaluated by a broad spectrum of psychological, sociological, and physiologic/medical parameters. The evaluation was carried out immediately before the start of the activation program and both three and six months after the social activation in the experimental group began. The control group was subjected to the same evaluations at the same points in time. Furthermore, evaluations of interactions within the staff groups were carried out by means of tape recorded personnel meetings.

Data used in psychological and sociological evaluations, described in detail in Arnetz et al. (1982a) and Arnetz and Theorell (1983b), were collected during an approximately one-hour long structured interview with all participants and by staff evaluations of participants' behavior. Activity levels were measured by daily ratings by staff and by direct interviews with the older subjects.

Physiologic/medical evaluations, described in detail in Arnetz et al. (1983), included hemoglobin $A_{1c}$ (Hb$A_{1c}$) and hemoglobin and plasma glucose (see Arnetz et al., 1982b). Height was measured in a standing position without shoes, using a fixed measurement device. Weight was determined on fasting individuals without shoes and with only light clothing. Blood pressure and heart rate were measured immediately before the blood sampling, with the participants resting in their beds. Phase 1 of the Korotkoff sound was chosen for systolic, and phase 5 for diastolic pressure. A standard physical examination of the heart, lungs, and peripheral vessels was performed. A history of smoking, alcohol consumption, and medications was obtained in the structured interview. Furthermore, medical records of the participants were used to complement the oral history.

*Results.* Social activity increased three-fold in the experimental group with few changes in the control group over the six-month period (Arnetz et al., 1982a). An Activation Index monitored by the staff showed that the number of activities per week per person involving at least two persons was 2.3 ($\pm$ 0.5) before the program started and 7.9 ($\pm$ 1.0) after six months ($p < 0.001$). Participants in the experimental group, which was not significantly different from controls at the outset, started to attend activities outside the actual program and in general spent more time out of doors; these changes were observed after both three and six months (Table 2.4).

**Table 2.4**

Participation in Activities Arranged by the Organization of Retired People.

| | | Activation Period | |
| --- | --- | --- | --- |
| | Pre-activation | 3 Months | 6 Months |
| "Did you participate?" | yes (%) | yes (%) | yes (%) |
| Experimental | 12 | 67 | 72 |
| Control | 23 | 37 | 38 |
| p between groups | NS | 0.05 | 0.008 |

*Source:* B.B. Arnetz & T. Theorell. Psychological, sociological and health behaviour aspects of a long term activation programme for institutionalized elderly people. *Social Science and Medicine,* 1983, *17,* 8, 449-456. With permission from Pergamon Press, Oxford.

Seasonal variations were found in feelings of depression, with the lowest values in May and the highest in February and August; visits to country/summer houses, as well as visits by children/neighbors, were more common during the summer months. Most elderly reported that they were quite satisfied with the frequencies of visits from family and friends but that they wanted to see their grandchildren more, especially during the winter period.

Feelings of restlessness decreased significantly in the experimental group during the study, possibly reflecting an improved mood level. Twenty percent of the participants reported that they often felt lonely. No differences were noticed between the two groups with regard to reported psychosomatic and psychological symptoms or in hours of sleep per night (Table 2.5).

The reported consumption of digoxin/digitoxin increased during the six-month period in the experimental group. Two possible explanations exist: (1) there may have been an actual deterioration in cardiac functions. However, no clinical findings were observed supporting such a hypothesis. (2) The other plausible explanation is that increased *mental* and *physical* activation increased the demands on cardiac output. The elderly perceived this and therefore increased their compliance to already prescribed digoxin/digitoxin medicine.

Staff and elderly began to interact more with one another. Furthermore, the elderly in the experimental group started to become less helpless and made more demands and exhibited less amenability to external control according to ratings made by the staff (Arnetz & Theorell, 1983a; Arnetz et al., 1982a).

Changes were noticed not only in psychosocial variables but also in endocrine, metabolic, and weight and height variables (Arnetz

**Table 2.5**
Scoring on Psychosomatic and Psychological Indices Before and Following 3 and 6 months of Activation.

| Question, in Structured Interview | Group | Absolute Score During the 6-month Period | | | Two-Way Analysis of Variance | | | | | |
|---|---|---|---|---|---|---|---|---|---|---|
| | | | | | Time × Group Effect | | Group Effect | | Time Effect | |
| | | $T_1$ | $T_2$ | $T_3$ | F | p | F | p | F | p |
| 10) Psychosomatic index (headaches, palpitation, dizziness and/or respiratory problems) <br><br> No complaints = 0 <br> High frequency of complaints = 1 | Experim. <br> Control | 0.43 <br> 0.37 | 0.23 <br> 0.40 | 0.30 <br> 0.30 | 1.81 | 0.17 | 0.11 | 0.74 | 1.44 | 0.24 |
| 11) Psychological index (irritation, restlessness, depressive mood, worriness, and/or tiredness without any obvious reason) <br><br> No complaints = 0 <br> High frequency of complaints = 1 | E <br> C | 0.47 <br> 0.50 | 0.27 <br> 0.20 | 0.27 <br> 0.23 | 0.32 | 0.73 | 0.06 | 0.81 | 9.55 | 0.0001 |
| 11b) How many *hours* of sleep do you usually get per night, including naps? | E <br> C | 6.93 <br> 6.72 | 7.31 <br> 7.07 | 7.07 <br> 7.07 | 0.13 | 0.88 | 0.15 | 0.70 | 1.06 | 0.35 |

*Source*: B.B. Arnetz & T. Theorell. Psychological, sociological, and health behaviour aspects of a long term activation programme for institutionalized elderly people. *Social Science and Medicine*, 1983, *17*, 8, 449-456. With permission from Pergamon Press, Oxford.

et al., 1983c). Height decreased in the control group compared to the experimental subjects during the six-month period (Fig. 2.4). Plasma levels of testosterone, dehydroepiandrosterone (DHA), and estradiol (Fig. 2.5) increased significantly in the experimental group over the study period compared to the control group. Hemoglobin $A_{1c}$ (HbA$_{1c}$), an indicator of overall blood glucose, on the other hand, decreased in the experimental group during the intervention (Fig. 2.6). The decrease in HbA$_{1c}$, indicating improved blood glucose levels, correlated significantly with social activity levels (Arnetz, 1984). There was a marked increase in plasma cortisol in the control group at the time of the second measurement. Furthermore, a significantly lower level of plasma cortisol was observed in the experimental group at this time (Fig. 2.7).

These findings concurred with the participants' own ratings indicating reduced monotony and boredom. The greatest intergroup differences were found for these variables at the second measurement, when three times as many people in the control group compared with the experimental group reported that they often felt their days were monotonous and boring. This finding supports the view that plasma corti-

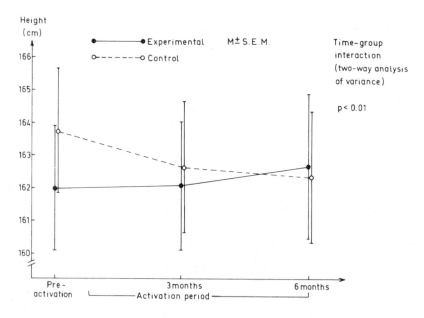

**Figure 2.4.**   Body height before and following three and six months of activation.

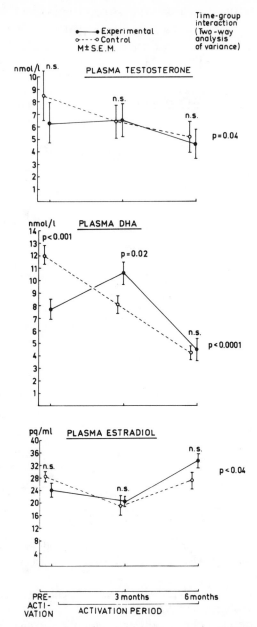

**Figure 2.5** Plasma testosterone, dehydroepiandrosterone (DHA), and estradiol before and following three and six months of activation. (Reprinted by permission of Elsevier Science Publishing Co., Inc. from *An experimental study of social isolation of elderly people: Psychoendocrine and metabolic effects* by B.B. Arnetz, T. Theorell, L. Levi, A. Kallner, & P. Eneroth. PSYCHOSOMATIC MEDICINE, Vol. 45, pp. 395–406. Copyright 1983 by The American Psychosomatic Society, Inc.

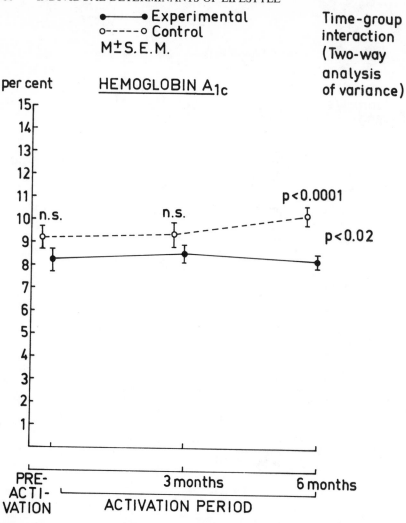

**Figure 2.6.** Hemoglobin $A_{1c}$ (HbA$_{1c}$) before and following three and six months of activation. (Reprinted with permission from Arnetz, 1984.)

sol is associated with depressive moods (Sachar et al., 1980; Schlesser, Winokur, & Sherman, 1980).

The different balance between catabolic and anabolic hormones in the group could partly explain why body weight tended continuously to decrease in the control group (from $65.0 \pm 2.4$ kg to $64.2 \pm 2.4$ kg) but not in the experimental group (from $66.0 \pm 2.8$ kg to $67.1 \pm 3.2$ kg) during the study (Arnetz et al., 1983).

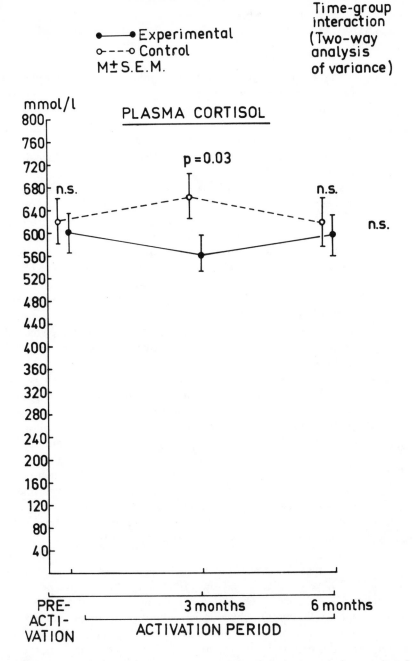

**Figure 2.7.** Plasma cortisol before and following three and six months of activation.

*Overall Conclusions.*  In summary, this intervention study suggests that:

1.  Social understimulation in institutionalized elderly is reflected in psychophysiologic reactions.
2.  The human organism does not seem to adapt to prolonged social understimulation but continues to show a *physiologic arousal response* to the situation.
3.  A state of apparent dulled mental alertness in institutionalized elderly people may be associated with an increased physiologic arousal. The long-term result may be an increased wear and tear on the organism, thus increasing the demands on an ailing body (Leeper, 1982). During such physiologic arousal, the body balance between anabolic and catabolic hormones may be reset with a relative increase in catabolic stress hormones, such as cortisol, catecholamines (dopamine, noradrenaline, and adrenaline), and growth hormone with a simultaneous inhibition of the secretion of anabolic hormones (e.g., estradiol, testosterone, and dehydroepiandrosterone). Ursin (1978) hypothesizes that the absence of challenge and stress may cause disease, just as overload may produce pathology.
4.  From both the present study and previous research it is evident that an increased level of social activity and participation is associated with an improved sense of psychosocial well-being as well as with changes in behavior. Even though most psychological factors were quite stable in the present study, some important changes were noticed, such as a decreased feeling of restlessness, decreased amenability, and increased social interaction in the experimental group. The experimental group also started to interact significantly more with the staff than the control group. The former group also tended to become more talkative and were judged to be happier.

These findings are consistent with those reported by Langer and Rodin (1976), who investigated the effects on behavior and personal well-being of enhanced personal control among institutionalized elderly (range 65–90 years). Their design involved a control and experimental group with pre- and post-experimental evaluations. Elderly residents in the experimental group were given a communication emphasizing their responsibility for themselves, whereas the communication given to a second (control) group stressed the staff's responsibility for them. Residents in the experimental group reported increased happiness and being more active than those in the control group. Furthermore, interviewers' ratings also showed an increased rating score for alertness in the experimental group. In the study of Arnetz and Theorell (1983b) as in the Langer and Rodin (1976) study, increased social interaction among the tenants and between tenants and staff was found. The tenants who could control, for instance, when they wanted to see a movie (or participate in another activity), also attended the movie (or participated in another activity) to a higher degree than the control group who were told when and what to do.

One difference between the Swedish and New Haven studies is the time factor. Langer and Rodin (1976) carried out their study during a three-week period. The Swedish study used a six-month period. However, even during the shorter time span in the Langer and Rodin study, they found that a greater proportion of the elderly in the control were rated as having become more debilitated over a period as short as three weeks. In the experimental group, on the other hand, a majority showed improvements. This is consistent with the Swedish findings on height and weight among experimental and control subjects. Social activation had a beneficial effect and its absence had deleterious effects. These findings taken together suggest that some of the presumptively age-related consequences of aging may be retarded, reversed, or perhaps even in some cases prevented by offering elderly people an improved psychosocial environment, an environment that invites participation and offers the elderly a chance to control their immediate environment.

## ACKNOWLEDGMENTS

Part of the work presented here was supported by the Karolinska Institute's research funds, the Delegation for Social Research with the Ministry of Health and Social Affairs, the Municipality of Stockholm, Lars Hierta's Memorial Foundation, Clas Groschinsky's Memorial Foundation, and the Swedish Academy of Sciences. Thanks are due to Mrs. Birgitta Hartstein for typing the manuscript, to Mrs. Isabella Levi for literature searches, and to Prof. Alvar Svanborg for offering valuable comments and suggestions on earlier drafts of this manuscript.

## REFERENCES

Andersson, L. Intervention against loneliness—effects on blood pressure. (Intervention mot ensamhet—effekter på blodtryck.) 6th Nordic Congress in Gerontology, Copenhagen, 1983, Abstract No. 122.

Andersson, L. Intervention against loneliness in a group of elderly women—an impact evaluation. *Social Science and Medicine*, 1985, *20*, 355–364.

Aniansson, A., Grimby, G., & Rundgren, A. Muscle function and muscle morphology in elderly—effect of training. (Muskelfunktion och muskelmorfologi hos äldre—effekt av träning.) *Swedish Medical Journal (Läkartidningen)*, 1980, *77*, 3749–3751.

Arnetz, B.B. The potential role of psychosocial stress on levels of hemoglobin $A_{1c}$ (HbA$_{1c}$) and fasting plasma glucose in elderly people. *Journal of Gerontology*, 1984, *39*, 424–429.

Arnetz, B.B. Endocrine reactions during standardized surgical stress. The effects of age and methods of anaesthesia. *Age and Ageing*, 1985, *14*, 96–101.

Arnetz, B.B., Eyre, M., & Theorell, T. Social activation of the elderly. A social experiment. *Social Science and Medicine*, 1982a, *16*, 1685–1690.

Arnetz, B.B., Kallner, A., & Theorell, T. The influence of aging on hemoglobin $A_{1c}$ (HbA$_{1c}$). *Journal of Gerontology*, 1982b, *37*, 648–650.

Arnetz, B.B., & Theorell, T. Dateline Sweden, research on activation for the elderly. *Journal of Gerontological Nursing*, 1983a, *9*, 615–619.

Arnetz, B.B., & Theorell, T. Psychological, sociological, and health behaviour aspects of a long term activation programme for institutionalized elderly people. *Social Science and Medicine*, 1983b, *17*, 449–456.

Arnetz, B.B., Theorell, T., Levi, L., Kallner, A., & Eneroth, P. An experimental study of social isolation of elderly people: Psychoendocrine and metabolic effects. *Psychosomatic Medicine*, 1983, *45*, 395–406.

Barns, E.K., Sack, A., & Shore, A. Guidelines to treatment approaches. Modalities and methods for use with the aged. *The Gerontologist*, 1973, *13*, 513–527.

Berg, S. Psychological functioning in 70- and 75-year-old people. A study in an industrialized city. *Acta Psychiatrica Scandinavica*, 1980, Suppl. 288, 1–47.

Berg, S., Mellström, D., Persson, G., & Svanborg, A. Loneliness in the Swedish aged. *Journal of Gerontology*, 1981, *36*, 342–349.

Booth, T., Phillips, D., Barritt, A., Berry, S., Martin, D.N., & Melotte, C. Patterns of mortality in homes for the elderly. *Age and Ageing*, 1983, *12*, 240–244.

Böttiger, L.E., & Carlson, L.A. Mortality and entry characteristics ("risk factors") in the Stockholm prospective study. In H. Boström & N. Ljungstedt (Eds.), *Medical aspects of mortality statistics*. Stockholm: Almquist & Wiksell, 1980, pp. 89–116.

Bourestom, N., & Tars, S. Alterations in life patterns following nursing home relocation. *The Gerontologist*, 1974, *14*, 506–510.

Butler, R.W., & Lewis, M.I. *Aging and mental health. Positive psychosocial and biomedical approaches*, 3rd ed. St. Louis: C.V. Mosby, 1982.

Coffman, T.L. Toward an understanding of geriatric relocation. *The Gerontologist*, 1983, *23*, 453–459.

Eisdorfer, C., & Wilkie, F.L. Stress and behavior in the aged. *Gynaekologische Rundschau*, 1979, *19* (Suppl. 2), 45–56.

Feldman, R.D., Limbird, L.E., Nadeau, J., Robertson, D., & Wood, J.J. Alterations in leukocyte β-receptor affinity with aging. A potential explanation for altered β-adrenergic sensitivity in the elderly. *The New England Journal of Medicine*, 1984, *310*, 815–819.

Felton, B., & Kahana, E. Adjustment and situationally bound locus of control among institutionalized aged. *Journal of Gerontology*, 1974, *29*, 295–301.

Finlay, O.E., Bayles, T.B., Rosen, C., & Milling, J. Effects of chair design, age and cognitive status on mobility. *Age and Ageing*, 1983, *12*, 324–335.

Fuller, J.H., Shipley, M.J., Rose, G., Jarrett, R.J., & Keen, H. Mortality from coronary heart disease and stroke in relation to degree of glycaemia: the Whitehall study. *British Medical Journal*, 1983, *287*, 867–870.

Gillick, M.R., Serrell, N.A., & Gillick, L.S. Adverse consequences of hospitalization in the elderly. *Social Science & Medicine*, 1982, *16*, 1033–1038.

Gottfries, C.G. Senile dementia of Alzheimer's type: clinical, genetic and pathogenetic aspects. Presented at the International Conference of Lifespan Research. Berlin, September, 1982, pp. 16–21.

Grane, M.G. Hypertension in the aged. In R.B. Greenblatt (Ed.), *Geriatric endocrinology, Aging*, Vol. 5. New York: Raven Press, 1978, pp. 115–131.

Green, E.J., Greenough, W.T., & Schlumpf, B.E. Effects of complex or isolated environments on corticol dendrites of middle-aged rats. *Brain Research*, 1983, *264*, 233–240.

Götestam, K.G. Training in reality orientation of patients with senile dementia. In L. Levi (Ed.), *Society, stress, and disease: Vol. 5 Aging and old age*. London: Oxford University Press. In press.

Henry, I.P., & Stephens, P.M. *Stress, health and the social environment. A socio-biologic approach to medicine*. New York: Springer-Verlag, 1977.

Jenkins, C.D., Somervell, P.O., & Hames, C.G. Does blood pressure usually rise with age?—or with stress? *Journal of Human Stress*, 1983, *9*, 4–12.

Kannel, W.B., & Gordon, T. Cardiovascular risk factors in the aged: the Framingham study. In S.G. Haynes & M. Feinleb (Eds.), *2nd Conference on the Epidemiology of Aging*. Washington, D.C.: U.S. Department of Health and Human Services, NIH Publ. No. 80-969, 1980, pp. 65–89.

Karlsson, I., Bråne, G., Melin, E., Nüth, A-L., & Rybo, E. Mental activation—brain plasticity. Abstract, *Collegicum Internationale*, Neuropsychopharmacollegicum, 14th C.I.M.P. Congress, Florence, June 19–23, 1984.

Klerman, G.L., & Izen, J.E. The effects of bereavement and grief on physical health and general well-being. *Advances in Psychosomatic Medicine*, 1977, *9*, 63–104.

Kraus, A.S., & Lilienfeld, A.M. Some epidemiological aspects of the high mortality rate in the young widowed group. *Journal of Chronic Diseases*, 1959, *10*, 207–217.

Kuypers, J.A., & Bengtson, V.L. Social breakdown and competence. A model of normal aging. *Human Development*, 1973, *16*, 181–201.

Landahl, S., Bengtsson, C., Sigurdsson, J., Svanborg, A., & Svärdsudd, K. Changes in blood pressure with advancing age—data from three longitudinal population studies. (Förändring i blodtryck med stigande ålder—data från tre longitudinella populationsstudier.) Sixth Nordic Congress in Gerontology, Abstract, 51, 1983.

Landahl, S., Jagenburg, R., & Svanborg, A. Blood components in a 70-year-old population. *Clinica Chimica Acta*, 1981, *112*, 301–304.

Langer, E.J. The illusion of incompetence. In L.C. Perlmuter & R.A. Monty (Eds.), *Choice and perceived control*. Hillsdale, NJ: Erlbaum, 1979.

Langer, E.J., & Rodin, J. The effects of choice and enhanced personal responsibility for the aged: A field experiment in an institutional setting. *Journal of Personality and Social Psychology*, 1976, *34*, 191–198.

Lawton, M., & Yaffe, S. Mortality, morbidity, and voluntary changes of residency on the well-being of older people. *Journal of the American Geriatrics Society*, 1970, *18*, 823–831.

Leeper, E.M. It's clear that stress can lead to illness, but it's not clear how. *News Report. National Academy of Sciences*, 1982, *32*, 2–6.

Lefcourt, H. The function of the illusion of control and freedom. *American Psychologist*, 1973, *28*, 417–425.

Lehr, U.M. Social-psychological correlates of longevity. In C. Eisdorfer (Ed.-in-chief). *Annual Review of Gerontology and Geriatrics*, Vol. 3. New York: Springer, 1982, pp. 102–147.

Leshan, L., & Worthington, R.E. Loss of cathexes as a common psychosomatic characteristic of cancer patients. An attempt at statistical validation of a clinical hypothesis. *Psychological Reports*, 1958, *2*, 183–193.

Lundberg, U., & Frankenhaeuser, M. Pituitary-adrenal and sympathetic-adrenal correlates of distress and effort. *Journal of Psychosomatic Research*, 1980, *24*, 125–130.

Mason, J.W. Organization of psychoendocrine mechanisms. *Psychosomatic Medicine*, 1968, *30*, 565–808.

Melin, L., & Götestam, K.G. The effects of rearranging ward routines on communication and eating behaviour of psychogeriatric patients. *Journal of Applied Behavior Analysis*, 1981, *14*, 47–51.

Mellström, D. Do environmental factors influence aging? (Påverkar omgivningsfaktorer åldrandet?) In: Aging—problem and strategy (Åldrandet—problem och strategi). *Acta Societatis Medicorum Svecanae*, 1982, *91*, 58–65.

Mellström, D., Nilsson, Å., Odén, A., Rundgren, Å, & Svanborg, A. Mortality among widowed in Sweden. *Scandinavian Journal of Social Medicine*, 1982, *10*, 33–41.

Müller, H.F., Grad, B., & Engelsmann, F. Biological and psychological predictors of survival in a psychogeriatric population. *Journal of Gerontology*, 1975, *30*, 47–52.

Näslund, E., & von Essen, E. To stay in your home—a human right: Day care for demented. (Att bo kvar hemma—en rättighet. Dagvård för åldersdementa.) *Report from National Board of Health and Welfare* (Socialstyrelsen) 1983, *1*, 1–96.

Noelker, L., & Harel, Z. Predictors of well-being and survival among institutionalized aged. *The Gerontologist*, 1978, *18*, 562–567.

Official Statistics of Sweden, Stockholm. *Poor health and consumption of health care.* (*Ohälsa och vårdutnyttjande.*) Report no. 2, 1981, Government Printing Office, Stockholm.

Palmer, G.J., Ziegler, M.G., & Lake, C.R. Response of norepinephrine and blood pressure to stress increases with age. *Journal of Gerontology*, 1978, *33*, 482–487.

Palmore, E., & Luikart, C. Health and social factors related to life satisfaction. *Journal of Health and Social Behavior*, 1972, *13*, 68–80.

Parkes, C.M., Benjamin, B., & Fitzgerald, R.G. Broken heart: A statistical study of increased mortality among widowers. *British Medical Journal*, 1969, *1*, 740.

Quattrochi-Tubin, S., & Jason, L.A. Enhancing social interactions and activity among the elderly through stimulus control. *Journal of Applied Behavior Analysis*, 1980, *13*, 159–163.

Reid, D.W., Haas, G., & Hawkings, D. Locus of desired control and positive self-concept of the elderly. *Journal of Gerontology*, 1977, *32*, 441–450.

Reiter, M.A. *Effects of a physical exercise program on selected mood states in a group of women over 65.* Doctoral dissertation, Columbia University, Teachers College. Dissertation International, 1982, 42(S-A).

Rinder, L., Roupe, S., Steen, B., & Svanborg, A. Seventy-year-old people in Gothenburg. A population study in an industrialized Swedish city. *Acta Medica Scandinavica*, 1975, *198*, 397–407.

Rodin, J. Managing the stress of aging: The role of control and coping. In S. Levine & H. Ursin (Eds.), *Coping and health.* New York: Plenum, 1980, pp. 171–202.

Rotter, J.B. Generalized experiences for internal versus external control of reinforcement. *Psychological Abstract*, 1966, *80*, Whole No. 609.

Sachar, E.J., Asnis, G., Nathan, R.S., Halbreich, U., Tabrizi, M.A., & Halpern, F.S. Dextroamphetamine and cortisol in depression. Morning plasma cortisol levels suppressed. *Archives of General Psychiatry*, 1980, *37*, 755–757.

Salter, C.L., & Salter, C.A. Effects of an individualized activity program on elderly patients. *The Gerontologist*, 1975, *15*, 404–406.

Schlesser, M.A., Winokur, G., & Sherman, E.M. Hypothalamic-pituitary-adrenal axis activity in depressive illness. Its relationship to classification. *Archives of General Psychiatry*, 1980, *37*, 737–743.

Seligman, M.E.P. *Helplessness: On depression, development, and health.* San Francisco: W. H. Freeman, 1975.

Sperbeck, D.J., & Whitbourne, S.K. Dependency in the institutional setting: A behavioral training program for geriatric staff. *The Gerontologist,* 1981, *21,* 268–275.

Statistical abstract of Sweden (*Statistisk årsbok*), Statistics Sweden, Stockholm, 1971, 1973, 1976, 1985.

*Statistical yearbook of counties (Statistisk årsbok för landsting),* Landstingsförbundet (The Organization of County Boards), Stockholm, 1982.

Steen, B., Isaksson, B., & Svanborg, A. Intake of energy and nutrients and meal habits in 70-year-old males and females in Gothenburg, Sweden. A population study. *Acta Medica Scandinavica,* 1977, Suppl. 611, 39–86.

Sterling, P., & Eyer, J. Biological basis of stress-related mortality. *Social Science and Medicine,* 1981, *15E,* 3–42.

Svanborg, A., Bergström, G., & Mellström, D. Epidemiological studies on social and medical conditions of the elderly. World Health Organization, *EURO Reports and Studies,* 1982, *62,* 1–38.

Svanborg, A., Landahl, S., & Mellström, D. Basic issues of health care. In H. Thomae & G.L. Maddox (Eds.), *New perspectives in old age. A message to decision makers.* New York: Springer, 1982, pp. 31–52.

Thomas, W.C. The expectation gap and the stereotype of the stereotype: Images of old people. *The Gerontologist,* 1981, *21,* 402–407.

Ursin, H. Activation, coping, and psychosomatics. In H. Ursin, E. Baade, & S. Levine (Eds.), *Psychobiology of stress. A study of coping man.* New York: Academic Press, 1978, pp. 201–228.

U.S. Bureau of the Census. Statistical abstract of the United States 1982–1983, 103rd ed., Washington, DC, 1982.

Wiggins, C., Ratner, A., & Wise, P.M. Differences in the stress response of prolactin in young and aged female rats. *Life Sciences,* 1983, *32,* 1911–1917.

Wittels, I., & Botwinick, J. Survival in relocation. *Journal of Gerontology,* 1974, *29,* 440–443.

World Health Organization (WHO). *The prevention of mental disorders in the elderly. Report on a symposium. Working group on prevention of mental disorders in the elderly.* Munich, April 1–5, 1974.

Zweig, J.P., & Csank, J.Z. Mortality fluctuations among chronically ill medical geriatric patients as an indicator of stress before and after relocation. *Journal of the American Geriatrics Society,* 1976, *24,* 264–277.

# The Social Lifestyles of Older People

## CHAPTER 3

# Sexuality and Aging

BERNARD D. STARR, PH.D.
SCHOOL OF EDUCATION
CITY UNIVERSITY OF NEW YORK
BROOKLYN COLLEGE
BROOKLYN, NEW YORK

This chapter will strive to provide a balance in the sexuality and aging literature by highlighting the more positive aspects of sexuality in the later years. (For a more general review see Botwinick, 1984.) We will explore the key historical factors that led to a narrow quantitative conceptualization of sexuality. Then we will discuss the value of a phenomenological approach to sexuality in revealing important aspects of sexuality that are masked by quantitative measures. The importance of looking at sexuality in the context of developmental and motivational theory will be elaborated. Then recent findings on sex and aging from the phenomenological perspective will be presented and their methodological problems explored. Factors limiting the sexuality of older people will be reexamined in the context of a new definition of sexuality that emphasizes pleasuring. Finally we will conjecture about sexual and social relationships among the elderly in the future, in the light of cohort differences and changing mores and social factors.

## A HISTORICAL VIEW

If ageism typifies the history of attitudes toward the elderly, then nowhere is this prejudice more apparent than in the area of sexuality. Not only have we traditionally been prudish about sex in the United States, but we have until recently harbored a special aversion to the idea of older people engaging in sexual activity (Botwinick, 1984; But-

97

ler & Lewis, 1976; Comfort, 1976; Ludeman, 1981; Rubin, 1965; Starr & Weiner, 1981). Indeed, in one study young college students barely believed in the existence of sex after 40 (Pocs, Godow, Tolone, & Walsh, 1977). When asked to project about the sexual activities of their parents, the students came up with performance frequencies far lower than Kinsey found for their parents' age group many decades earlier. What might these young people think about sexual activities among their grandparents or older people in general? It is not hard to imagine when we consider the unfavorable characteristics and derogatory epithets we assign to older people who display sexual interest. Media images of older people make it amply clear that sex is the province of the young (Abramson & Mechanic, 1983; Bishop & Krause, 1984; Smith, 1979). Even humorous birthday cards portray the stereotype: "Birthday Greetings: You're at an age when you should give up half your sex life . . . Which half will it be, talking about it or thinking about it?" (Demos & Jache, 1981, p. 212).

The heritage of this legacy is that studies of sex and aging prior to the last few years found low levels of sexual activity, sharply declining levels, or little if any sexual activity or interest among most of the elderly studied (Kinsey, Pomeroy, & Martin, 1948, 1953; Masters & Johnson, 1966; Pfeiffer & Davis, 1972; Pfeiffer, Verwoerdt, & Wang, 1968; Verwoerdt, Pfeiffer, & Wang, 1969). In contrast, a number of recent studies have detailed extensive sexual activity and interest for those over 60 (Brecher, 1984; Starr & Weiner, 1981). Do these distinctly different findings reflect a shift in methodology, or does the discrepancy point to a significant change in the sexual behavior of older people?

In examining this discrepancy we must look at a number of factors—first, the data base from which the findings were obtained. The three most widely cited of the earlier studies—the first Duke University Longitudinal Study (Verwoerdt, Pfeiffer, & Wang, 1969) and the work of Kinsey et al. (1948, 1953) and Masters and Johnson (1966)— based their findings on a relatively small number of subjects over age 60. Over the three stages of the Duke University Longitudinal Study the number of subjects declined from 254 to 126. Kinsey, Pomeroy, and Martin (1948, 1953) included 126 males and 56 females over age 60—and only 10 of the females were over age 70. But Kinsey did not have complete histories on his over-60 group and included them in only a few analyses. Masters and Johnson (1966) based their conclusions about sex and aging on 20 men and 11 women over age 60. By aging females and males Masters and Johnson meant women over 40 and men over 50. When we consider the attrition rates in these studies and the subjects for whom data were incomplete, it appears that up until recently much of our knowledge about sex and aging has been based on perhaps fewer than 300 subjects. Add to this the conceptual and methodological problems of these studies (Botwinick, 1984; George & Weiler, 1981; Starr & Weiner, 1981) and we are compelled to conclude that our empirical knowledge about sex and aging has been skimpy. Even the 800 subjects of the Starr and Weiner survey (1981) obtained on site in senior centers in four regions of the United States, and the recent Consumer Union survey (Brecher, 1984) of 2,622 subjects over age 60 obtained from polling the readers of a consumer magazine, still constitute only a beginning.

Another factor in the discrepancy between earlier findings of low levels of sexual activity and interest among the elderly and recent findings to the contrary is that earlier studies were guided by the prevailing self-fulfilling prophecy—little sex was expected and consequently little was found. Researchers were even discouraged from pursuing the topic in the belief that older people would be resistant or unresponsive to sexual queries (Kinsey et al., 1948, 1953) or that their adult children would stop them from participating in such research (Pfeiffer, 1969). The fact is that most older people live independently—75% of those over 65 are homeowners (Rabushka & Jacobs, 1980) and 80 to 90 percent over age 60 live with spouse, alone, or with an unrelated person (Glick, 1979; *Statistical Abstracts of the U.S.,* 1984); their adult children have little control over what they do. Starr and Weiner (1981) have documented their difficulties in getting past the "gatekeepers," those professionals at senior centers and senior residences who thought sex was inappropriate or of little interest for their elderly clients. But when given the opportunity to speak in their own voices, older people said otherwise.

Another problem is that cross-sectional data were interpreted as if they were longitudinal, overlooking important cohort differences (Kinsey et al., 1948, 1953). There were other methodological question marks. In one major study (Pfeiffer & Davis, 1972; Verwoerdt et al., 1969), sexuality was included as a small part of a more general medical evaluation within a longitudinal study of aging. The data of sexuality were obtained as part of the medical history. This medical context for exploring sexuality is not necessarily conducive to finding high levels of sexuality, especially when many of the subjects reported chronic illness and other physical complaints. Further complicating matters is that the structured interviews in this study were conducted by men who were identified with the mental health professions, a fact that may have made people, especially the older women of the 1950s, uncomfortable.

We have presented this critical picture of early sexuality and aging research to give a clear delineation of the "state of the art." But on a more generous note we must recognize that sexuality research in the 1950s was not easy to do and the subject of sex and aging was even more problematic to investigate directly. Probably whatever approach would have been used would have had severe limitations because of the status of sexuality and beliefs about the elderly. Those researchers who ventured into the arena were courageous and made significant inroads in helping us get to where we are today.

However, from the scientific point of view, previous research on sex and aging is of interest for reflections on ageism exhibited by the general public and research professionals. It also tells us a great deal about the methodological problems and hazards of sexuality and gerontology research. More important, in the light of recent findings the earlier studies remind us of the fluid nature of aging and the sensitivity of older people to the social forces of their times.

## ERRONEOUS ASSUMPTIONS ABOUT
## SEX AND AGING

Kinsey et al. (1948, 1953) gave us the most comprehensive data on sexuality in history and at the same time made the study of sex respectable in the eyes of the general public. Much to his own surprise and the delight of his publisher, *Sexual Behavior in the Human Male* (1948) was an instant best seller. If not for Kinsey's pioneering work and his popular acceptance, it is doubtful that it would be possible to explore sex among the elderly today. Yet surprisingly, it was Kinsey who inadvertently set the stage for the assumption that there was little worth in investigating the sex lives of the elderly—an assumption that pervaded sex and aging research for many decades. For example, one of the most powerful statements that Kinsey made about the status of sex and aging is the number of pages he devoted to the subject: four pages on older women and three pages on older men, out of 1,646 pages in his two volumes.

However, sex after 60 was not of particular interest to Kinsey. There were many other populations that were more compelling, given the dearth of scientific data about sexual behavior at the time. The 186 older subjects were a small token, compared with his total sample of 12,000, and Kinsey himself acknowledged that older people were inadequately represented. Furthermore, he did not give his complete interview to his older subjects, nor did he include them in most of his statistical analyses because the data were incomplete. The primary statistic for his older subjects is on frequency of intercourse, which is reported to decline sharply in the later years: from 2–3 times a week at age 20 to .5–.6 times a week at age 60; and masturbation for his 70-year-old men is virtually nonexistent.

Kinsey's findings are no doubt accurate but need further explanation. The fact that his 60-year-olds were born around 1880 is extremely significant. People of this generation were probably much less accustomed to talking about sexuality than would be true of 60-year-olds today. Also, the assumption that Kinsey's cross-sectional data were indicative of what the sexual behavior of his younger subjects would be like decades later would clearly be misleading, as recent research has indicated (Brecher, 1984; George & Weiler, 1981; Martin, 1981; Starr & Weiner, 1981). For example, it appears that for those elderly who remain sexually active and have a regular partner, the rate of decline in sexual performance may not be as great as heretofore believed (Brecher, 1984; George & Weiler, 1981; Starr & Weiner, 1981). A number of studies have now established that current rates of sexual activity for the elderly are consistent with rates earlier in adulthood (George & Weiler, 1981; Martin, 1981). Starr and Weiner (1981) have indicated that for many of the elderly over age 60, frequency may not decline at all compared with when they were in their 40s and 50s. Yet it was Kinsey's conclusion of sharp decline based on cross-sectional data that steered researchers away from elderly populations or directed them to narrowly conceived questions of frequency of intercourse and rates of decline.

## Contradictory Evidence

Even in those studies that emphasized decline in sexual activity among the elderly, contradictory evidence was underemphasized, probably because it did not fit in with existing conceptions of the elderly. For example, some elderly in every study continued to be sexually active in every decade investigated (Comfort, 1976). In one study 10–20 percent of the over-78 group were still active, and some showed increased activity compared with earlier decades (Pfeiffer, Verwoerdt, & Wang, 1968). Kinsey, who said that by age 75 half of the men were impotent, cites the case of one 70-year-old in his sample "whose ejaculations were averaging seven per week" (Kinsey et al., 1948, p. 235). To emphasize the point, another study showed that 34 percent of post prostatectomy patients over age 70 were still sexually active with varying degrees of frequency (Finkle, Moyers, & Tobenkin,

1969). Aside from having partners, why were they active? What made them different from those who abandoned sexuality? It would seem more useful to study in depth the ones who continue to be active than those who do not. How can we account for the wide range of individual differences? (One older woman, for example, told Starr and Weiner that her husband was so responsive to sexual stimuli that the mere mention of the word *impotence* could give him an erection.) While biological differences could account for many of the variations, so could psychological and social variables play an important role (Starr & Weiner, 1981).

In contradiction to the decline hypothesis, Kinsey et al. (1953) and later Masters and Johnson (1966) firmly established that the female sexual response in terms of orgasmic potential and pleasure does not decline in the later years. The female sexual response reaches a peak in the mid-30s and pretty much remains there throughout the life cycle. These investigators suspected what psychiatrist Mary Jane Sherfy (1973) later stated even more explicitly about female sexuality throughout adulthood: "The human female is sexually insatiable in the presence of the highest degree of sexual satisfaction" (p. 112). Also, Kinsey's data show a rising frequency of orgasm throughout adulthood for married women. The statistical direction of his data would suggest that women would probably continue to be highly orgasmic into old age. Unfortunately, his data on this issue stop at age 60. The Starr–Weiner data indicate that women over 60 are more orgasmic than when they were younger. Contrary to the popular belief that menopause is the "pause that doesn't refresh," most investigators report that sexual response remains the same or improves after menopause (Hite, 1976; Starr & Weiner, 1981; Tavris & Sadd, 1977). If there is essentially no decline in physiologic capability and gratification for older women and if their sexuality continues to be as powerful as Sherfy indicates, where do their sexual feelings and needs go if they are not active? This is certainly something we would ask about younger women who were not sexually active, and especially if they were unhappy or depressed. Furthermore, what are the physiologic and psychological consequences of older women with vibrant sexual potential and need relinquishing their sexuality for whatever reasons?

It is curious that while many researchers and writers are basically positive and supportive about the possibilities for sex in the later years, there is a subtle defensiveness and negativism present. We learn that the ejaculatory urgency is weak, the erection less turgid if not limp, penile entry not always possible, the seminal flow more like a trickle, the vaginal walls thin and fragile, vaginal lubrication diminished or absent, the refractory period for erection longer (sometimes days or weeks), intercourse at times painful, and other aspects of sexual intercourse altered in the direction of marked decline. In spite of all this we are assured that sexual intercourse for most of the elderly is still possible, even into the 80s. In reading these descriptions one gets the sense that sex after 60 is strained or forced, and of questionable pleasure. Although not stated explicitly, sex in the later years is made to seem pale compared with sex among younger people. One even wonders why older people bother to do it at all.

## THE PHENOMENOLOGY OF
## THE SEXUAL EXPERIENCE

In fact, had the question of "why" they engaged in sex been posed, the responses might have pointed to a more fertile and fruitful direction for sex and aging research—namely, how sex is experienced and what it means in the lives of older people. A phenomenological approach to sex asserts that understanding of sexuality is attainable only in terms of the unique meaning of sexual feelings to the person. This approach may be contrasted with the objective approach, with its emphasis on sexual performance. Whether the incidence of sexual problems increases or not, the physiologic facts of decline do not speak to or reveal the experienced pleasure and satisfaction of sexual activity expressed by sexually active older people. For example, 75 percent of the respondents in the Starr–Weiner survey (1981) said that sex feels as good or better compared with when they were younger (36 percent said better). The enthusiasm and exuberance of many of these phenomenological descriptions of sexuality in later life were often compelling in emphasizing that something important had been missed by the physiologic descriptions and statistical frequencies of earlier research. Brecher (1984) presented similar subjective data that corroborated these findings.

There is a vast difference between a phenomenological approach and a purely quantitative behavioral one. For example, one person says, "I'm interested in travel" but actually travels once in three years. Another person is interested in travel but travels at least six times a year. Who is more interested in travel? In terms of frequency count, it is no contest. But the measure of interest, importance, value, and the overall role that events play in adding joy and meaning to a person's life is reflected more in the phenomenology of experiences than in frequency counts. Frequency could not convey what this 69-year-old woman reported to Starr and Weiner (1981): "Sex is much more enjoyable and satisfying now. It used to be more frequent, and while pleasurable it now has become less frequent, but each time lasts longer and has much greater sensory impact during climax for both of us" (p. 16).

The performance emphasis that has characterized the history of sexuality research was altered by Hite (1976) in her investigation of how women felt about sex and sexual experiences. Her observation that no one had seriously looked into the feeling domain with respect to female sexuality was also true for the study of sexuality in men, and certainly for the elderly.

## Continuity and Discontinuity in Development

The assumption of a neuter or sexless older person implies that important human motives, needs, and interests are somehow lost beyond a certain age. Not only does this negative view favor a biological-reductionist view of human development and a devaluation of psychological phenomena and processes, but it also contradicts what we otherwise accept as invariant processes applicable to all stages of development. If needs are lost or surrendered, where do they go and what comes to replace them? What becomes the motivational force of life if previous basic ones disappear?

This disregard for basic motivational issues points up the danger of looking at a function or area of behavior, such as sexuality, outside of human development in general. It suggests an obligation to anchor analyses of aging in general psychological theory. Invariant processes, whether they be cognitive, emotional, or motivational, must be assumed to be present in the later years. When they appear to be absent we must offer explanations, not accept their absence as natural. When a clinical psychologist examines a patient and finds through observation and test results the total absence of aggression, she does not conclude that the patient lacks an aggressive drive. Rather, knowing that aggression is a universal invariant of human functioning, she looks for the ways in which aggression is concealed or hiding behind defenses. We must apply the same thinking to the assertion that there is an absence of basic drives such as sexuality in older people.

**The Centrality of Sexuality**

Sexuality is a psychological as well as a physiologic need. All major theories of personality development (psychoanalytic-psychodynamic, social learning, cognitive) emphasize the role of sexuality in an individual's identification as a male or a female. Reinforcing the psychological dimension of sexuality is the media attention to the subject, which almost mandates that we be sexual. Alex Comfort (1976) has pointed out that the very sense of personhood is tied to sexual functioning and feeling sexual. Supporting the positive health benefits of active sexuality is the statement by Butler and Lewis (1976) that sexual activity is associated with reduced insomnia and relief from the pain of arthritis by raising the cortisone levels in the blood. Others have cited the role of withdrawal or absence of sexuality in depression (Beck, 1968; Sviland, 1978). Leviton (1973) has even postulated that sexuality can be a deterrent to suicide in the aging. The pervasive role that sexuality plays in feelings about and identification of self would suggest the need to examine sexuality beyond actual performance frequencies. Given that there are physiologic changes in sexual functioning with age, what are their effects on need, drive, feelings about self, compensations, and other psychological concomitants? Where there is the apparent absence of sexuality, we want to know how the sexual drive is being dealt with intrapsychically. If a low activity level is due to circumstances—for example, the lack of a partner—then there is a host of feeling areas to probe. Renshaw (1982) recommends that "with the same casual comfort that we have always asked intimate questions of women about vaginal discharge, urinary flow, and constipation, so now let us also ask older women: How do you handle normal sexual feelings?" (p. 139). When Starr and Weiner (1981) investigated sexual feelings and alternatives, they found, typical of all unfulfilled needs, a variety of adjustment techniques: denial, compensation, sublimation, resignation, and feelings of persistent frustration, among others. But more research is needed to explore the broad spectrum of possible consequences of different activity and frustration levels with respect to sexuality in the later years.

**RECENT RESEARCH FINDINGS**

Starr and Weiner (1981) probed a broad spectrum of sexuality among the elderly using a 50-item open-ended questionnaire that required respondents to write answers. Their questions can be grouped according to those that reflect behavior, interest, needs, attitudes, preferences and satisfaction, and frustration. Their findings along with the corroborating data of Brecher (1984) suggest that it is perhaps time to go beyond the questions, "Do they or don't they?" and if they do, "How often?" The unmistakable conclusion is that indeed older people do it. What is more important and needs to be explored further is that they like sex, want sex, feel they need sex for their physical and psychological well-being, and are frustrated when they do not have sex. Furthermore, their sexual experiences are not "cute" old people's experiences. They want and prize orgasm as part of a sexual experience. When they do not have orgasm many are frustrated and seek other sources of release such as masturbation—this is especially true of women. Older people also practice a variety of sexual techniques including oral sex. Many are curious and experiment with techniques they heard about or learned from the media. Also, most older people have satisfying sexual experiences that feel as good as or better than sex when they were younger. Finally, despite the lack of any enlightened sex education when they were children, many have absorbed and responded to the sexual revolution to liberate and broaden their sexuality. Some of the statistical highlights supporting these conclusions are as follows (Starr & Weiner, 1981):

*Like sex:* 95 percent said they liked sex.
*Want sex:* 99 percent indicated they would like to have sex if it were available; varying degrees of preferred frequencies were stated.
*Orgasm:* 70 percent said that orgasm is an important part of a good sexual experience. 99 percent of the women indicate that they are orgasmic sometimes, most of the time, or always.
*Masturbation:* While 82 percent accept masturbation in principle, 46 percent acknowledge masturbating. Masturbation is highest for single (81 percent), divorced (66 percent), and widowed (47 percent) women.
*Touching and cuddling:* 93 percent consider these important.
*Oral sex:* Although there was no specific question on oral sex, 15 percent make reference to it as a common and most enjoyable part of sex. Brecher (1984), who asked about oral sex directly, found that 43 percent of older women and 56 percent of older men engaged in oral sex.
*Sexy pictures, books, or movies:* 62 percent say they get aroused by these.
*Sexual experimentation:* 39 percent would like to try new sexual experi-

ences that they have heard about, read about, or thought about; most of these indicated they would like to try a greater variety of techniques.

*Nudity:* 80 percent felt positive about nudity during lovemaking.

*Younger lovers:* 84 percent of the women and 90 percent of the men endorsed the idea of older people having younger lovers.

*Sex and living together without marriage:* 91 percent approve of this in principle for older people.

*Regrets:* When asked what they would like to change in their sex life, past and present, 50 percent indicated the desire for greater freedom and openness and more varied experiences and partners.

*Homosexuality:* 64 percent accept the current open attitude toward homosexuality. Similarly, in the Consumer Union Survey (Brecher, 1984) 70 percent agreed that homosexual relations between older people "are nobody else's business."

*Health:* 76 percent felt that sex had a positive effect on their health.

*Satisfaction:* 75 percent say sex feels the same or better compared with when they were younger—36 percent say better, 39 percent the same. More women (41 percent) than men (27 percent) say better.

*Sex education:* 88 percent received a negative sex education or none at all when they were children.

On reflection we should not be surprised by these findings despite their wide diversion from earlier conceptions and conclusions. Kinsey, who is the most widely quoted, started his interviewing in 1938. Therefore, the Starr and Weiner data reflect cohort differences influenced by the sexual revolution as well as other social changes that have had an impact on older people. Of crucial importance is that older people today, in light of the many social changes that have taken place, are more receptive to sex surveys, and the open atmosphere about sex encourages people to talk more freely. Also, older people today are healthier, live longer, have more leisure time, and above all have had their consciousness raised. Increasingly, the elderly see themselves as whole, complete people with the full range of needs and potential for gratification as much as adults of any age. Fueling the fires of these social changes are social activism, advocacy, key spokespeople in powerful positions, and the appearance of up-beat magazines catering exclusively to the retired and elderly.

## Quantitative and Qualitative
## Responding

The use of indirect and open-ended questions as well as structured questions enabled Starr and Weiner to uncover nuances and subtleties. For example, question #21, "How often do you have sexual relations?" can reveal interest for those who have partners and are active. But question #6, "How often would you like to have sexual relations if you could as often as you wanted to?" offers an opportunity to express interest to those who are not active as well as those who are more interested in sex than their actual level of activity would suggest (health problems, no partner, uncooperative partner, strained relationship, etc.). Similarly, responses to question #20.5, "What do you do when you are not satisfied (in a sexual experience)?" provides revealing data that complements the dry statistics provided by responses to question #37, "How often do you achieve orgasm in your sexual experiences?"

Sometimes a powerful need comes through in the elaborations that project a different image of the reality and possibilities for sexual experience in the later years that have been masked by studies highlighting exclusively current frequencies in the context of a decline model. Those reports could not convey the intensity of feeling expressed by this 71-year-old woman: "When I don't have an orgasm (in a heterosexual experience) if I'm horny, I masturbate it through to climax." Another 66-year-old woman said: "I get jittery (i.e., I don't have an orgasm) and can't sleep" (Starr & Weiner, 1981, pp. 137–140). What these and many other phenomenological reports suggest is that sex after 60 is not only enjoyable but is often experienced as a powerful need. What makes this the case for some and not for others needs to be better understood.

## Sampling and Other
## Methodological Problems

Whether we are looking at phenomenological or quantitative data, there are invariably methodological problems connected to any kind of sex research. One of the most frequent methodological criticisms of sex research is the sampling (George & Weiler, 1981). It is unlikely that sex research will ever find a true random sample in which each member of the sample has an equal chance of being selected by the researcher. More likely, the subjects will continue to select the researchers. Ultimately, one is stuck with those who are willing to respond. This always leaves a question about the motives and biases of those volunteer subjects. In one study comparing a small sample of volunteer and nonvolunteer subjects (Farkas, Sine, & Evans, 1978), it was found that there were no personality differences between the two groups, but volunteer subjects were less guilty, less fearful, and more experienced sexually and had more sexual problems.

The methodological blemish of volunteer subjects plagued Kinsey as well as all later sex researchers. Some surveys that polled large magazine readerships claim to have achieved national population samples corresponding to the census statistics for each group included, but these studies appear to have selectively included respondents to approximate a national population (Hite, 1976, 1978; Tavris & Sadd, 1977). Nevertheless, the respondents are still volunteers from biased and skewed sources—the readers of those magazines.

Does the recognition and acknowledgment that sex surveys are not based on random samples make them invalid? Within the realm of nonrandom samples, there are vast differences in degree of bias. For example, surveying the readers of *Playboy, Cosmopolitan,* or *Consumer Reports* magazines is different from surveying broader or more representative community groups. While both samples may not be random, the latter has a greater probability of approximating the true population measures. Since the goal of sampling and statistical analysis is to make the best approximations of population measures, a research survey of sexuality meeting this condition would be regarded as valid from the sampling point of view, given the limitations inherent in human and sexuality research.

For the "Starr–Weiner Report of Sex and Sexuality in the Mature Years" the 800 respondents (518 females and 282 males between the ages of 60 and 91) were from senior centers in four regions in the United States. The centers were selected to cover a wide range of social, economic, and ethnic backgrounds. Some of the centers were in difficult areas for sex researchers to gain entry but were pursued because they were thought to be important—for example, rural Georgia and inner-city senior centers in Chicago and New York. Some of the areas not thought likely to produce high incidences of activity or interest in sex (based on the existing literature) were included to offset those affluent areas that might be thought more likely to produce high incidences of activity and interest. In short, there were no intended biases, and efforts were made to cancel or counterbalance possible ones. It would have been far easier and quicker to do the study in a sunbelt retirement community where there are more than 50,000 elderly and closed-circuit television systems convenient for easy advertisement access. But Starr and Weiner concluded that senior centers would better reflect the general population of elderly who live in the communities where they have been living for most of their lives. The estimates say that only about 5 percent of the elderly live in retirement communities (Morgan, 1982).

There are two possible major sources of bias in the Starr-Weiner method and sampling. Before distributing questionnaires, which were to be filled out anonymously at home and mailed to a post office box, Starr and Weiner conducted discussions at the senior center on problems of aging and the need to know more about the sexuality of the elderly. While these discussions were not directly on sexuality, they were open ended and varied considerably. These discussions could have affected subsequent responses to the questionnaires, although the direction of this possible bias is unclear. The other source of possible bias is the 14 percent response rate. While this is higher than rates obtained in some similar surveys with younger populations which are presumed to be more responsive to sex surveys (Hite in her female sexuality survey in 1976 obtained a 3 percent response rate), it still leaves open the question of the 86 percent who did not respond. But now that the door has been opened to an area of research previously thought to be inaccessible, later investigators should be able to obtain better response rates and test the validity of the Starr–Weiner findings.

One other methodological question may pertain more broadly to gerontological research than sexuality per se. Not all elderly attend senior centers. Those who do attend are likely to be more active and socially oriented. What about shut-ins, depressives, the frail, and others who do not attend senior centers? Does surveying the elderly at senior centers then pose an additional bias? Perhaps, but when we look at sexuality or other personality and behavior characteristics of the elderly that are influenced by self-fulfilling prophecies and other constraining beliefs and attitudes, it is the potential and possibilities that are of greater interest than the present manifestations. For example, what are the elderly capable of sexually and what are the optimal level and forms of sexual functioning and expression for different people? Even the healthy and sexually active elderly of the present generation can provide only clues and hints about the answers to these questions. But they can indicate a clear direction for our thinking and research. The turned-off and shutdown older person who may be the greatest victim of the self-fulfilling prophesies may tell us the least about potential and possibilities. Therefore, if we recognize the fluid and evolutionary nature of aging and maintain a futuristic view, the so-called biased sample of active and involved elderly may be the most appropriate for certain types of research.

## Male Erection Problems
## and Withdrawal from Sexuality

The declining male erectile response with aging is, no doubt, the most limiting factor in the sexual relationships of the elderly. This fact in part explains why the male in the later years sets the lower limit on sexual activity (Christenson & Gagnon, 1965; Kinsey, Pomeroy, & Martin, 1948, 1953). Many men even withdraw from sex because of erection problems or the fear of failure. Masters and Johnson (1966) have noted that "there is no way to overemphasize the importance of the factor of fear of failure plays in the aging male's withdrawal from sexual performance" (pp. 269–270). They further elaborated that many men withdraw totally from the sexual arena "rather than face the ego shattering experience of repeated episodes of sexual inadequacy" (p. 270). Butler and Lewis have noted that most men start worrying about sexual aging some time in their 30s. Kaplan (1979) introduced a new sexual disorder, "inhibited sexual desire," to explain the loss of interest in sex displayed by many individuals, especially older men. While Kaplan introduces a number of psychodynamic factors to explain the disorder, Starr in an ongoing unpublished study of the male fear of sexual failure suggests that low sexual desire in many older men may stem from this fear. Many older men who otherwise say they are not interested in sex or say that it is not that important to them project a different picture when asked: "If you could have an erection whenever you wanted one, how would that affect your sexual behavior and your feelings about yourself?" One such 72-year-old man, for example, said, "I would feel ten feet tall—I would have sex frequently—lots of affairs." McCarthy (1984) recently reported clinical data to support the importance of the fear of sexual failure in inhibition of sexual desire.

Starr also asked men and women of all ages, "At what point during lovemaking do you expect (or the man to have) an erection?" Preliminary findings showed varied responses. They range from the expectation (from both men and women) of an instant erection being present prior to foreplay and to the expectation that considerable foreplay including direct genital stimulation would be necessary. Since expectations play an important role in perceived pleasure and success and failure of an experience, what sexual partners expect in terms of erection may be crucial for setting the tone of the sexual encounter. This is especially true because the erectile response is so sensitive to anxiety (Green, 1981b; Norton & Jehu, 1984). We do not know very much about how discrepancies in expectations affect performance and withdrawal from sexuality. For some older men the erection not occurring as quickly or firmly as desired may be as much of a blow to their egos as failure itself. In the private discussions with older people for the Starr–Weiner study, men often spoke longingly about how "they were always ready" in adolescence and early adulthood. Women sometimes felt that they had "lost" their excitement value because their husbands had erection problems or were slow to respond.

According to McCarthy (1984), "Most males believe the myth: to be a real man you should be able to have sex with any woman, any time, in any situation" (p. 98). What the physiologic changes in response patterns do to relationships and sexual functioning needs to be better understood. Also, for many couples in their early years of marriage, sex was a quick act of intercourse with little foreplay. Remember that Kinsey reporting in the 1940s and 1950s on the population that is now elderly stated that the average length of the sex act was two minutes—"sex, American style" as it was humorously referred to in Europe. Such a style could only have been supported by a youthful erectile response. While the length of time devoted to lovemaking seems to have changed, and is much more varied (Starr & Weiner, 1981), one wonders how many retain the earlier quick response and release as the ideal or usual expectation for gauging sexual potency or success, and if so how that affects sexual experiences. Also, the changing male erectile response with aging that requires more sustained direct stimulation may be taxing or impossible in strained relationships or those that are distant and lack intimacy. At younger ages the spontaneous erection could bypass interpersonal factors.

**Total Impotence**

It is difficult to estimate how many men are totally impotent because of definitional problems and the difficulty of separating psychogenic and organic impotence. Also, we do not know how many men consider themselves impotent because of occasional failures or the fear of failure that leads them to withdraw from sexuality and define themselves as impotent. In the Starr–Weiner survey 56 percent of the men said they had experienced difficulty in getting an erection at one time or another; this was confirmed by 57 percent of the women, who indicated that they had experienced their partner having erectile difficulty at some time. Brecher (1984) reported that 50 percent of his male respondents said it took longer to get an erection and 32 percent confirmed that they more frequently lost the erection during intercourse. But we do not know how these experiences are integrated or translated into the individual's sexual experiences and behavior.

It is, therefore, not surprising that controversy and confusion abound on the subject. Bennett and Rivard (1982) state that most impotence is organic and that when impotence appears after age 50 in a male whose sexual functioning was previously normal it "is almost always organic." On the other hand, Masters and Johnson (1970) found only 10 percent of their cases to be organic and Kaplan (1974) attributes 85 percent of impotence to psychogenic causes. According to Wagner (1981a), "the postulated ratio of psychogenic to organic dysfunctions in impotence varies from 20-1 to 1-7" (p. 89). One explanation for such a wide divergence of views is that the erection is a complex neurologic, vascular, hormonal, and psychological event that is not completely understood (Finkle, 1983; Wagner, 1981c). There are identifiable disorders in each of the aforementioned areas but differential diagnosis is often difficult (Wagner, 1981a; Wagner & Green, 1981). Adding to the confusion is that all methods of treatment including psychotherapy, hormonal replacement, surgical implants, and surgical correction of the arterial supply report success on selected cases (Felstein, 1983; Green, 1981a, 1981c; Wagner, 1981b). Further complicating matters is the caution that psychological factors can play a role in physiologically based impotence such as with diabetes. The anxiety and fear associated with reduced erectile response due to these diseases exacerbate the situation and tip the balance toward impotence. Also, "the disease may be used in the psychodynamic relationship of the partners" (Wagner, Hilsted, & Jensen, 1981, p. 58). Consequently, psychotherapy has helped in these cases, which are primarily organically based.

Surgical prosthesis appears to be very promising (Bennett, 1982; Felstein, 1983; Wagner, 1981b). The success rate for surgical implants is reported to be high, especially when good selection procedures are used. However, physicians are reluctant to use these procedures except in cases where organic dysfunction can be clearly established. Men with primarily psychological problems around sexuality and erection are considered poor candidates because difficulties are likely to persist or resurface soon afterwards. According to Wagner (1981b), the anxiety around erectile failure is so great that even when there are no pathologic findings, patients will seek the quick fix of a mechanical device rather than sex therapy. He adds that these patients will put great pressure on physicians and surgeons for "any kind of operation that may give some type of penile rigidity" (p. 155).

Despite the source or degree of erectile problems, many forms of sexual stimulation and gratification are possible for men as well as couples. Clearly many of those seeking the quick fix of surgery are focusing on performance and the defense of a mythical masculinity rather than pleasure. Even the total inability to have an erection is no explanation or justification for complete withdrawal from sexuality. With this in mind a reexamination of sexuality has emerged.

## PLEASURING:
## THE NEW SEXUALITY

Sex to most people means sexual intercourse, with its concomitant goal of orgasm. Indeed, when sex surveys ask, "How often do you have sex?" they mean sexual intercourse. Kinsey studied six different methods of achieving the goal of orgasm with intercourse being the chief means. But over the last two decades since the emergence and popularization of sex therapy, the traditional definition of sex has been questioned. Many sex therapists and researchers prefer to emphasize pleasuring rather than any particular act as the defining characteristic of sexual relations. In this context, intercourse and orgasm as necessary goals of a sexual experience are regarded as limiting rather than promoting sexual gratification. The pressurized sex act in which a person feels he or she must reach a particular goal can generate so much anxiety that acts are pursued and even achieved but not experienced. As McCarthy (1977) points out, our terminology about sexual performance even emphasizes the "getting to" rather than the "experiencing of." So we talk about foreplay and afterplay again emphasizing the act and relegating pleasure to a preparatory or winding down role in the service of the "big event." The traditional goal-oriented definition of sex can be particularly inhibiting and troublesome for older couples since most men will experience slowing of the erectile response, occasional or frequent failure, or the fear of failure.

Consider also the social and sexual impact of the traditional definition of sexuality on the lives of impotent men, those with erection problems, and those who fear sexual failure. The negative impact of this definition embraced by older people has sweeping effects, as exemplified by the 68-year-old widower who said, "If I could get an erection there are ten women in my condominium who I could have an affair with" (Starr & Weiner, 1981, p. 214). This type of attitude suggests that many older men who have erection problems or concerns withdraw not only from all heterosexual activities but all social and intimate contacts with women as well. The equation for men with this view that sex = erection plus intercourse, along with its corollary of no erection = no sex, is perceived as logical and absolute. Since the number of single older women is far greater than single men—four times as many after age 65 (Corby & Zarit 1983)—the withdrawal from socialization factor based on erection problems further reduces the pool of available men and further limits the sexual outlets for older women. But at the same time many women both married and single accept the equation of sex as erection and intercourse so that a 68-year-old married woman still vibrant in terms of sexual interest, need, and desire may report no sexual activity for the past 15 years— "since her husband became impotent" (Starr & Weiner, 1981). Brecher (1984) gives similar anecdotal accounts of women relinquishing their sexuality to male impotence or the fear of sexual failure. These examples illustrate the tyranny that the male erection holds over the potential for intimacy, physical stimulation, and sexual pleasuring.

Furthermore, feminist researchers such as Hite (1976) began to see the emphasis on sexual intercourse as a male definition based on the fragility of the erectile response and the macho need to prove they can perform. Hite's phenomenological exploration of female sexuality found that women enjoyed the intimacy, tactile, and arousal aspects of sexual relations more than intercourse per se. She also astutely noted that whereas many men prefer oral sex to intercourse, they still feel compelled to have intercourse as part of the sexual experience to prove their masculinity. These observations have been supported by other researchers. For example, Denney, Field, and Quadagno (1984) have also found in a sample of young men and women that women enjoy foreplay and afterplay more than intercourse, while men prefer intercourse. Out of these various perspectives and observations the concept of pleasuring has emerged.

Pleasuring refers to any sexual experience that feels good. With pleasuring there is no one act that measures or validates the success of the experience. There are just different events, intercourse and orgasm being just two, neither of which is necessary or essential for a pleasurable experience. Within the context of the pleasuring definition of sexuality, adults of all ages are on an equal par. Frequency and degree of sexual pleasure are limited only by interest, desire, and imagination. While the frequency of different acts may vary (e.g., some may have more frequent intercourse than others), the potential for pleasuring is open to couples with whatever frequency is desired, regardless of erectile response or age. From this point of view, some of those who seek and achieve intercourse could conceivably experience less pleasure and, therefore, less sexuality than those open to and skillful at a variety of forms of sexual pleasuring.

Starr and Weiner (1981) describe exercises suitable for older people garnered from the sex therapy literature that explores pleasure apart from sexual intercourse (Gochros & Fisher, 1980; Kaplan, 1974; Kass & Strauss, 1975; LoPiccolo, 1978; Sviland, 1978). These techniques developed originally for treating male impotence have now been recommended for all couples interested in developing their pleasuring potential. They initially recommend (some *require*) no sexual intercourse or orgasm while couples explore various forms of mutual and self-stimulation. The couple can then find out—and many for the first time—what really stimulates, arouses, and makes them feel good without feeling pressured about getting to the end. Surprisingly (or perhaps not so), "impotent" men concentrating on the pleasuring of these exercises sometimes find that they are able to achieve erection. Typical of their earlier experiences, as soon as they achieved anything approaching an erection they would anxiously attempt entry with the usual complete loss of the mini-erection and the consequent disappointment and negative air cast over the whole experience—hardly pleasurable for the man or the woman. When value judgments and goals are removed, there are sex experiences and pleasuring that can be as satisfying or better than intercourse and/or orgasm. This does not mean that the latter two should not be sought or valued. The aim is to see pleasuring as the goal and to eliminate what Albert Ellis calls MUSTurbatory activities.

If pleasuring were truly accepted as the index of sexuality, then older people and even those men who regard themselves as impotent or inadequate would have great potential for positive sexual experience. It is ironic when looked at from the pleasuring perspective that couples deprive themselves of all physical contact because of "impotence" or feared sexual inadequacy. Laury (1981) reports that older men can have orgasmic ejaculation and pleasure without having an erection. He also cites a survey that reported that 25 percent of the male respondents had masturbated without erection. This is especially noteworthy since older people say that sexual activity makes them feel better and that relinquishing it makes them feel less whole (Starr & Weiner, 1981).

Apparently many older couples who are active sexually, despite problems, have discovered the pleasuring principle on their own. Here is a 67-year-old widow speaking about sex with her lover: "If he doesn't get an erection we have oral sex; he likes it even if he doesn't climax. I feel the same way." Or the 76-year-old married man who commented: "What's the hurry? We can try again tomorrow or the next day. We like sex" (Starr & Weiner, 1981, p. 214).

## Women and the New Sexuality

Women have a special interest in supporting the new sexuality since they are at a severe disadvantage sexually in the later years. Their sexual response potential is at a high level comparable with their early adult years, but there are fewer and fewer available men to share intimacy and sexuality. Added to this there are those men who withdraw from socialization with women because of actual or feared sexual inadequacy. These problems are likely to increase with succeeding generations of elderly women who will be more sexually demanding and assertive, having been nurtured on the sexual revolution and the feminist movement.

One of the reasons given for even younger men today withdrawing from sex or displaying "loss of sexual desire" is that their fear of sexual failure is on the line in today's more equalized sexual encounters. Unlike previous generations, the young women of today are as likely as young men to seek sex, even on the first date. Previously, men controlled the sexual situation and gauged the switches to their level of confidence. If a man felt unsure about having an erection he could just end the experience. But with the more insistent women his sense of adequacy is more vulnerable—the "too much wine" or "not enough sleep" explanations become suspect; better to be cautious and "not that interested." Even young and otherwise competent adult men report that sexually assertive women give them the feeling of performance anxiety—that too much may be demanded (Gillies, 1984). This factor applies even more to older people. The increased sexual liberation and activity of the elderly, including singles, the widowed and divorced, make sexual encounters (particularly in new relationships) more prone to bringing the male fear of failure to the surface and disrupting relationships. Consequently, older women as well as men will have to cope with the male preoccupation with the firm erection as a prerequisite for sexual and social relationships; both would benefit from a focus on pleasuring.

## SEXUALITY IN THE FUTURE

What will the social and sexual life of the elderly look like in the year 2000 and beyond? Many of the social problems of the elderly will very likely remain the same. For example, women will probably continue to outnumber men. Currently, there are four single women for every single man over age 65 (Corby & Zarit, 1983). Life expectancies for newborns in 1982 still show a seven-year gap between men and women (*Statistical Abstracts of the United States*, 1984). The greater longevity of women and the tendency of women to marry men older than themselves contribute to the fact that three-quarters of all married women will be widows at some point in their lives. Glick (1979) recommends that women marry men eight years younger than themselves to deal with the problem. Surely older women (as well as older men) welcome the idea of younger lovers—85 percent of women endorsed the idea in the Starr–Weiner survey. But there is no indication, apart from the widely publicized cases of famous people, that there is any flood-tide in this direction. On the contrary, whereas women marry men 2.5 years older than themselves (median gap), on remarriage they marry men 3.4 years older than themselves (Glick, 1979). Further swelling the ranks of the single elderly (largely female) in the future is the present trend toward the single lifestyle and the current high divorce rate among young and middle-aged adults (*Statistical Abstracts of the United States*, 1984). Also, divorce is increasing at about 10 percent each year, and this affects one out of three families (Santrock, 1985). The disproportionate ratio of older men and women will continue to give men more social and sexual options than women.

But surely there will be changes. As we have pointed out, today's elderly have come a long way from their Victorian upbringings to adopt attitudes and, in some respects, behaviors influenced by the social changes and revolutions they have lived through. Yet although their vistas have been liberalized and broadened, many still live in the grips of irrational guilt over practices such as masturbation, and still others are quick to relinquish their sexuality rather than explore alternatives or seek professional help (Starr & Weiner, 1981). But future generations of elderly are likely to bring into the later years a different set of expectations rooted in their earlier life styles, mores, and attitudes toward personal fulfillment. Older women, for example, are more likely to forge new solutions—some more maverick than others—rather than resign themselves to sublimation, denial, or frustration experienced by older women alone today (Starr & Weiner, 1981). Kemmack and Roff (1980) also point out that older people are much more open to heterosexual alternatives to marriage. But younger people, as their study indicates, are even more open to a variety of alternatives which they suggest will be carried into the later years.

What form will these new solutions take? Obviously, anything that one can say on this matter is speculative and possibly limited by our own assumptions and inhibitions of vision. However, there is evidence pointing to a number of directions.

## Masturbation

Clearly the taboo surrounding this practice has evaporated. In fact, sex therapy programs incorporate self and mutual masturbation as basic to exploring and developing sexual awareness (Gochros & Fisher, 1980; Kaplan, 1974; Kass & Strauss, 1975; Kassorla, 1980; LoPiccolo & Lobitz, 1978; Sviland, 1978). Feminist writers have encouraged women to masturbate to explore their orgasmic potential as well as to provide an important sexual outlet for those without partners (Dodson, 1972; Hite, 1976). Respected professionals have even recommended masturbation (manual and with the use of mechanical devices such as vibrators) either alone or in conjunction with intercourse (Butler & Lewis, 1976; Comfort, 1976; Kaplan, 1984). The pendulum has swung so far that this practice once thought to cause blindness if not madness is now almost a mandated activity, or as Tavris and Sadd (1977) humorously quipped, "The activity once thought to cause warts is now recommended to all but cure them" (p. 94). But despite these enthusiastic endorsements of masturbation and the fact that this will be a common practice for the future elderly without partners (and not burdened by guilt), for many elderly without partners masturbation exacerbates feelings of loneliness and frustration over the absence of physical and emotional intimacy. Masturbation may provide an easily accessible outlet for sexual release, but it does not solve the broader intimacy needs.

## Sharing and Affairs

While affairs for older married people do not currently appear to be rampant, they do exist. Brecher (1984) gives some vivid descriptions from reports of his subjects. Certainly sexual activity among older singles, divorced, and widowed is commonplace, and these trends are likely to continue. For example, in the Duke University sample of the

1950s, only 7 percent of unmarried subjects were sexually active (Newman & Nichols, 1960). In the Starr–Weiner sample of the 1980s, 79 percent of men and women over age 60 were sexually active while only 47 percent were married. Therefore, a large percentage of singles, divorced, and widowed were sexually active. An even larger number indicated the desire for sexual relationships if a suitable partner were available. Similarly, in the Consumer Union Survey (Brecher, 1984) over 50 percent of the unmarried women and over 75 percent of the unmarried men in their 60s and 70s were sexually active.

Also, when we read about the extent of sexual activity reported for younger adults both married and single, it is not unreasonable to assume that these behaviors will be carried into the later years (Hite, 1976, 1978; Pietropinto & Simenauer, 1979; Tavris & Sadd, 1977; Wolfe, 1980). Communal forms of living and other forms of sharing may be more palatable to future generations of elderly accustomed to sharing apartments, having numerous premarital sexual experiences, and/or monogamous or serial monogamous relationships outside of marriage. Comfort (1976) even suggests that future generations of elderly carrying their liberated sexuality into the later years may be more amenable to "eroticizing" friendship relationships to satisfy sexual and physical needs.

## Homosexuality

It is well known that in sexually deprived environments such as prisons, homosexuality is rampant among those who were previously exclusively heterosexual. Will the unavailability of men for many older women encourage them to pursue homosexual relationships? Men are not likely to turn in this direction after age 60 because their heterosexual options are even greater than when they were younger.

While there is no substantial evidence that today older women without partners are routinely turning to lesbianism, there is some persuasive evidence that this choice may be more commonplace in the future. First, there is greater openness about homosexuality. Surprisingly, both Starr & Weiner (1981) and Brecher (1984) found older people quite accepting of homosexuality in principle or as a person's private business. Among younger populations homosexuality has not only become more open and visible, but it is rapidly becoming a widely accepted if almost unremarkable aspect of everyday life. In *The Bisexual Option*, Klein (1978) suggests that bisexuality is much more widespread than generally believed. According to MacDonald (1981), bisexuality has increased in the general population but especially among women. In the *Hite Report* (1976) many women wrote that they would like to try a sexual relationship with another woman. Apparently many young people are experimenting with bisexuality in the spirit of freedom and androgyny. This should not be surprising since Kinsey found that by age 40, 19 percent of the women in his sample had a conscious homosexual experience in which one or both of the participants were actively seeking erotic arousal. The number of bisexuals may be hidden by their tendency to be less open, fearing rejection from both heterosexuals and homosexuals who are more exclusive in their sexual preference and orientation (MacDonald, 1981).

Therefore, it would appear fairly safe to speculate that future generations of older people will be even more accepting of homosexuality and many may have had homosexual experiences. Will homosexuality become a viable choice for older women without partners to satisfy their sexual, physical contact, and intimacy needs? Starr and Weiner presented the case of a 72-year-old woman who turned to homosexual experiences in the later years not out of preference—she clearly preferred heterosexual relationships—but out of need. Will others make a similar choice as one answer to the dilemma of older women alone?

### Sexual and Social Counseling

New options mean new problems. As new generations of elderly bring with them their more varied lifestyles and personal demands for fulfillment, there will be greater recognition of sexual and social problems along with the expectation that they be addressed. The "what? at *your* age!" raised eyebrow reaction to the elderly who take their needs and right to grow seriously will evaporate, we hope. Older people and the professionals who serve them will come to view the elderly as fullfledged adults with all the potential for personal fulfillment as well as the concomitant problems. Consequently, relationships in the later years will be seen in the context of adult relationships in general. For example, loss of sexual desire among married couples and the cessation of sex is not unique to older couples. Edwards (1981) reports that in his survey of 365 husbands and wives (75 percent were between the ages of 20 and 39), one-third had stopped having sexual relations for a definable period of time. Marital discord was the most frequent explanation. We have erroneously concluded that older couples who "lose interest" or cease sexual relations do so because of aging rather than for relationship problems or other psychodynamic reasons (Epstein, 1981).

As the pleasuring principle becomes more widely accepted, women will not be as willing to relinquish their sexuality either to male impotence or the male fear of failure. Changes are already apparent. LoPiccolo (1985) recently reported that women of all ages are increasingly pressuring their husbands into seeking sex therapy for low sexual desire. One can anticipate a host of problems in sexual relationships as couples cope with the physiologic changes and psychological crises in aging and their desire for continued sexual activity.

Other problems can also be anticipated. If homosexuality becomes a pull or choice for many women, the emotional complexities of these nontraditional relationships will have to be dealt with. Then there are the dating and new relationship problems which will be a more open concern of the elderly. Renshaw (1982) received thousands of letters and questions from older people after a talk show discussion of sexuality and sex problems. The mere mention of these topics at senior centers and other settings of actively involved older people causes the questions to flow: "How do you say no to a man who just keeps coming on?" "All these men want is to check right into a motel. How do you handle that?" "My wife doesn't like sex any more. She thinks I'm crazy because I want sex three times a week. What do you advise?" "Do you think it's O.K. to bring a man into my house on the first date?" There is nothing remarkable about the questions except the ages of the people asking them: 71, 68, 73, and 67. But where can these people turn for help? In most senior centers that Starr and Weiner visited across the United States they found that sex had never been discussed openly.

If the speculations about the future become realities, then there will be a greater need for mental health specialists in gerontology who can address sexual and social problems. But more importantly, we will need much more data and research about the emerging social and sexual lives of older people in order to develop useful techniques and strategies to help forge appropriate solutions.

## REFERENCES

Abramson, P.R, & Mechanic, M.B. Sex and the media: Three decades of best selling books and major motion pictures. *Archives of Sexual Behavior*, 1983, *12*, 185–206.

Beck, A. Sexuality and depression. *Medical Aspects of Human Sexuality*, 1968, *2*, 44–51.

Bennett, A.H., & Rivard, D.J. Male impotence. *New York State Journal of Medicine*, 1982, *82*, 1676–1683.

Bishop, J.M., & Krause, D.R. Depictions of aging and old age on Saturday morning television. *Gerontologist*, 1984, *24*, 91–94.

Botwinick, J. *Aging and behavior*. New York: Springer, 1984.

Brecher, E. *Love, sex and aging*. Boston: Little, Brown, 1984.

Butler, R.N., & Lewis, M.I. *Love and sex after sixty*. New York: Harper & Row, 1976.

Christenson, C.V., & Gagnon, J.H. Sexual behavior in a group of older women. *Journal of Gerontology*, 1965, *20*, 351–356.

Comfort, A. *A good age*. New York: Crown, 1976.

Corby, N., & Zarit, J.M. Old and alone: The unmarried woman in later life. In R.B. Weg (Ed.), *Sexuality in the later years: Roles and behavior*. New York: Academic Press, 1983

Demos, V., & Jache, A. When you care enough: An analysis of attitudes toward aging in humorous birthday cards. *Gerontologist*, 1981, *21*, 209–215.

Denney, N.W., Field, J.K., & Quadagno, D. Sex differences in sexual needs and desires. *Archives of Sexual Behavior*, 1984, *13*, 233–245.

Dodson, B. *Liberating masturbation*. Published and distributed by Betty Dodson, 1972.

Edwards, J.N. How prevalent is lack of sexual desire in marriage? *Medical Aspects of Human Sexuality*, 1981, *15*, 73–74.

Epstein, N. How partners collaborate to avoid sex. *Medical Aspects of Human Sexuality*, 1981, *15*, 68.

Farkas, G.M., Sine, L.F., & Evans, I.M. Personality, sexuality, and demographic differences between volunteers and nonvolunteers for a laboratory study of male sexual behavior. *Archives of Sexual Behavior*, 1978, *7*, 513–520.

Felstein, I. Dysfunction: Origins and therapeutic approaches. In R. Weg (Ed.), *Sexuality in the later years: Roles and behavior*. New York: Academic Press, 1983.

Finkle, A. Research: Status, gaps, and design. In R. Weg (Ed.), *Sexuality in the later years: Roles and behavior*. New York: Academic Press, 1983.

Finkle, A.L., Moyers, T.G., & Tobenkin, M. Sexual potency in aging males. *Journal of the American Medical Association*, 1969, *207*, 113–115.

Freeman, J.T. Sexual capacities in the aging male. *Geriatrics*, 1961, *16*, 37–43.

George, L.K., & Weiler, S.J. Sexuality in middle and late life. *Archives of General Psychiatry*, 1981, *38*, 919–923.

Gillies, J. *Men on women*. New York: Dodd Mead, 1984

Glick, P.C. The future marital status and living arrangements of the elderly. *The Gerontologist*, 1979, *19*, 301–309.

Gochros, H.L., & Fischer, J. *Treat yourself to a better sex life*. New York: Prentice-Hall, 1980.

Green, R. Endocrine therapy for erectile failure. In G. Wagner & R. Green (Eds.), *Impotence*. New York: Plenum, 1981a.

Green, R. Psychological theories and erectile failure. In G. Wagner & R. Green (Eds.), *Impotence*. New York: Plenum, 1981b.

Green, R. Psychotherapy of erectile failure. In G. Wagner & R. Green (Eds.), *Impotence.* New York: Plenum, 1981c.

Hite, S. *The Hite report.* New York: Dell, 1976.

Hite, S. *The Hite report on male sexuality.* New York: Alfred A. Knopf, 1978.

Kaplan, H.S. *The new sex therapy.* New York: Brunner/Mazel, 1974.

Kaplan, H.S. *Disorders of sexual desire.* New York: Brunner/Mazel, 1979.

Kaplan, H.S. Sexuality: The vibrator—a misunderstood machine. *Redbook,* May 1984.

Kass, D.J., & Strauss, F.F. *Sex therapy at home.* New York: Simon & Schuster, 1975.

Kassorla, I. *Nice girls do, and you can too!* Los Angeles: Stratford Press, 1980.

Kemmack, L., & Roff, L. Heterosexual alternatives to marriage. *Alternative Lifestyles,* 1980, *3,* 137–148.

Kinsey, A.C., Pomeroy, W.B., & Martin, C.R. *Sexual behavior in the human male.* Philadelphia: W.B. Saunders, 1948.

Kinsey, A.C., Pomeroy, W.B., & Martin, C.R. *Sexual behavior in the human female.* Philadelphia: W.B. Saunders, 1953.

Klein, F. *The bisexual option.* New York: Arbor House, 1978.

Laury, G.V. Ejaculatory changes in aging men. *Medical Aspects of Human Sexuality,* 1981, *15,* 136–137.

Leviton, D. The significance of sexual activity as a deterrent to suicide among the aged. *Omega,* 1973, *4,* 163–174.

LoPiccolo, J. Direct treatment of sexual dysfunction. In J. LoPiccolo & L. LoPiccolo (Eds.), *Handbook of sex therapy.* New York: Plenum, 1978

LoPiccolo, J. Paper presented at the meeting of the Society for the Scientific Study of Sex, Palm Springs, California, January, 1985.

LoPiccolo, J., & Lobitz, C. The role of masturbation in the treatment of orgasmic dysfunction. In J. LoPiccolo & L. LoPiccolo (Eds.), *Handbook of sex therapy.* New York: Plenum, 1978.

Ludeman, K. The sexuality of the older person: Review of the literature. *Gerontologist,* 1981, *21,* 203–208.

MacDonald, A.P. Bisexuality: Some comments on research and theory. *Journal of Homosexuality,* 1981, *6,* 21–35.

Martin, C.E. Factors affecting sexual functioning in 60–79-year-old married males. *Archives of Sexual Behavior,* 1981, *10,* 399–420.

Masters, W.H., & Johnson, V.E. *Human sexual response.* Boston: Little, Brown, 1966.

Masters, W.H., & Johnson, V.E. *Human sexual inadequacy.* Boston: Little, Brown, 1970.

McCarthy, B.W. *What you don't know about male sexuality.* New York: Thomas Y. Crowell, 1977.

McCarthy, B.W. Strategies and techniques for the treatment of inhibited sexual desire. *Journal of Sex and Marital Therapy,* 1984, *10,* 97–104.

Morgan, W. Housing for the elderly in the United States. In A.M. Warnes (Ed.), *Geographical perspectives on the elderly.* London: Wiley, 1982.

Newman, G., & Nichols, C.R. Sexual activities and attitudes of older persons. *Journal of the American Medical Association*, 1960, *173*, 117–119.

Norton, G.R., & Jehu, D. The role of anxiety in sexual dysfunction: A review. *Archives of Sexual Behavior*, 1984, *13*, 165–183.

Pfeiffer, E. Sexual behavior in old age. In E.W. Busse & E. Pfeiffer (Eds.), *Behavior and adaptation in late life*. Boston: Little, Brown, 1969.

Pfeiffer, E., & Davis, G.C. Determinants of sexual behavior in middle and old age. *Journal of the American Geriatrics Society*, 1972, *20*, 151–158.

Pfeiffer, E., Verwoerdt, A., and Wang, H.S. Sexual behavior in aged men and women. *Archives of General Psychiatry*, 1968, *19*, 753–758.

Pfeiffer, E., Verwoerdt, A., & Wang, H.S. The natural history of sexual behavior in a biologically advantaged group of aged individuals. *Journal of Gerontology*, 1969, *24*, 193–198.

Pietropinto, A., & Simenauer, J. *Husbands and wives*. New York: Times Books, 1979.

Pocs, D., Godow, A., Tolone, W.L., & Walsh, R.H. Is there sex after 40? *Psychology Today*, June 1977, 54.

Renshaw, D.C. Sex and older women. *Medical Aspects of Human Sexuality*, 1982, *16*, 132, 134, 139.

Rubin, I. *Sexual life after sixty*. New York: Basic Books, 1965.

Santrock, J.W. *Adult development and aging*. Dubuque, IO: Wm. C. Brown, 1985.

Sherfy, M.J. The nature and evolution of female sexuality. New York: Random House, 1973.

Smith, M.D. The portrayal of elders in magazine cartoons. *Gerontologist*, 1979, *19*, 408–412.

Starr, B.D., & Weiner, M.B. *The Starr-Weiner report on sex and sexuality in the mature years*. New York: McGraw-Hill, 1981.

Sviland, M.A.P. Helping elderly couples become sexually liberated: Psychosocial issues. In J. LoPiccolo & L. LoPiccolo (Eds.), *Handbook of sex therapy*. New York: Plenum, 1978.

Tavris, C., & Sadd, S. *The Redbook report on female sexuality*. New York: Delacorte, 1977.

U.S. Department of Commerce. *Statistical Abstracts of the United States*, 1984.

Verwoerdt, A., Pfeiffer, E., & Wang, H.S. Sexual behavior in senescence: Changes in sexual activity and interest of aging men and women. *Journal of Geriatric Psychiatry*, 1969, *2*, 163–180.

Verwoerdt, A., Pfeiffer, E., & Wang, H.S. Sexual behavior in senescence II. Patterns of sexual activity and interest. *Geriatrics*, 1969, *24*, 137–154.

Wagner, G. Methods of differential diagnosis of psychogenic and organic erectile failure. In G. Wagner & R. Green (Eds.), *Impotence*. New York: Plenum, 1981a.

Wagner, G. Surgical treatment of erectile failure. In G. Wagner & R. Green (Eds.), *Impotence*. New York: Plenum, 1981b.

Wagner, G. Erection. In G. Wagner & R. Green (Eds.), *Impotence*. New York: Plenum, 1981c.

Wagner, G., & Green, R. General medical disorders and erectile failure. In G. Wagner & R. Green (Eds.), *Impotence*. New York: Plenum, 1981.

Wagner, G., Hilsted, J., & Jensen, S.B. Diabetes mellitus and erectile failure. In G. Wagner & R. Green (Eds.), *Impotence*. New York: Plenum, 1981.

Wolfe, L. The sexual profile of the Cosmopolitan girl. *Cosmopolitan*, Sept., 1980, 254.

## CHAPTER 4

# Activities and Leisure

M. POWELL LAWTON, PH.D.
PHILADELPHIA GERIATRIC CENTER
PHILADELPHIA, PENNSYLVANIA

Leisure is one of the oldest topics addressed by students of human behavior. These philosophical issues are dealt with by many authors (deGrazia, 1962; Gordon & Gaitz, 1976; Kaplan, 1975) and will not be discussed in this chapter other than to call the reader's attention to the fact that one may discern varying mixtures of elitist and democratic conceptions of leisure as characterizing the attitudes and behaviors of writers in different periods of history. Most Western cultures appear to have insisted on a sharp dichotomy between leisure and work, a distinction that has fostered the view that "leisure" is either higher on the value scale than work, or a reward earned only by those who have successfully competed in the contest to obtain the financial means to support nonwork pleasures. This chapter will argue that the term *leisure* has become packed with such diverse meanings that we shall do better to consider all types of activity as candidates for the pleasure and self-realization ascribed to leisure. It will further suggest that "meaning" requires multidimensional definition. Finally it will argue, in agreement with Kaplan (1975), that the contemporary world is in a position to support the most democratic merging of "leisure" and "work" that has yet been possible, and that cohorts of the aged in the near future will be major beneficiaries of the situation.

An overall perspective, which will be discussed repeatedly in the sections that follow, is that of leisure and activities as life-course phenomena whose understanding requires both a contemporary and a life-span view. It will be seen that while the evidence is slim regarding true age-related changes in activity, their possibility cannot be ruled out. Both biological changes and social structures specific to different

127

ages are known to affect the ways people spend their time. To this extent, activity patterns may be viewed as age-related, but these are different processes from those that might be considered developmental in a psychological sense. The values, attitudes, and expectations that older people hold toward appropriate uses of time are highly dependent on both history and current norms. Thus we begin with the recognition that time use and the attitudes and feelings associated with it are multiply determined by individual need as it changes or persists over time, social and cultural learning specific to one's age cohort, and the contemporary context, including both broad social institutions and the personal, social, and physical environment in which the person lives.

Some of the terms already used, as well as others that will recur, require definition. This chapter will discuss activities, obligatory and discretionary behaviors, and leisure. These terms are related to one another in complex ways and no promise is extended that each will be defined and satisfactorily distinguished from the others. *Activity* is the most general of the terms. All externally observable behavior may be assigned to some descriptive category of activity. The time budget is one type of framework into which all behavior may be classified and measured by the time allocated to each. One such categorization consists of work and nonwork, where the fact of remuneration defines work, leaving nonwork as the residual category. All activities have also been dichotomized as *obligatory* versus *discretionary*. This dichotomy has caused much definitional distress, to this writer's mind for no good reason. It is suggested here that the subjective meaning of an activity be abandoned for this definition, and that for objectivity's sake we define obligatory activities as paid work and maintenance of self and home and leave a residual category, "free time," to define discretionary behavior. For this dichotomy subjective meaning, the source of definitional distress, is abandoned in favor of a multidimensional conception of meaning that can be applied to all behavior; meaning will be considered at some length.

This leaves us with *leisure*, and here it is suggested that the subjective definition is all-important. Kaplan (1979) writes that leisure is "free time that is seen as leisure by participants, that is psychologically pleasant in anticipation and recollection, that potentially covers the whole range of commitment and intensity, that contains characteristic norms and constraints, and that provides opportunities for recreation, personal growth, and service to others" (p. 26). This definition conveys both the subjective nature of leisure and also its multidimensional character. That is, whether an activity is properly designated as leisure depends first on its perception by the behaver, though one could no doubt find considerable consensus among external observers as to whether some activities would be likely to be experienced as leisure (for example, card playing, watching television, or needlepoint). Second, dimensions by which activities can be classified include, in Kaplan's view, hedonic tone (pleasantness), time referent (past recollection, contemporary experiencing, and future expectation), investment of energy (commitment), intensity of affect, amount of external control (norms and constraint), and content or personal meaning (for example, recreation, growth, service).

The point of view taken here is that the literature has amply demonstrated the personal quality and multidimensionality not only of leisure, but of all activity. As in every sector of the human system, whether it be person and environment (Lawton, 1982a) or quality of life (Campbell, Converse, & Rodgers, 1976), it is essential to define parameters in as objective a way as possible while allowing subjective dimensionality (congruent in varying degrees with objective dimensions) to flow out of the empirical study of the structure of many individuals' experiences. One empirical approach to the meaning of leisure was that of Gordon and Gaitz (1976), who gave primacy to a single subjective dimension of leisure in their definition, "leisure is personally expressive discretionary activity, varying in intensity of involvement from relaxation and diversion at the low end of the continuum, through personal development and creativity at higher levels, up to sensual transcendence at the highest levels of cognitive, emotional, and physical involvement" (p. 316). Despite the creative ideas and new knowledge generated by their approach, the single dimension of expressive involvement is too procrustean and also is not in accord with the multidimensionality found by other research. To this author's mind, the "discovery" of dimensions by which any activity may be classified is necessary in order to deal adequately with some of the persistent conceptual problems characterizing the field of leisure research. For example, discretionary behavior may have obligatory aspects, work may share conceptual or affective space with leisure, and so on.

Despite this plea for subjecting all activity to the same type of analysis, most research on work, time budgets, and leisure has been performed in three corresponding separate streams. It is largely the research in leisure that has begun to give shape to the subjective dimensionality of activity. Nonetheless, one must bear in mind that work and leisure have rarely been subjected to simultaneous and parallel analysis (important exceptions are Havighurst, 1961; Kabanoff, 1980; Pierce, 1980a, 1980b, 1980c), and the subjective aspects of maintenance activities have often been totally disregarded.

There have been three high points in the literature on aging and leisure. Havighurst and his colleagues (Donald & Havighurst, 1959; Havighurst, 1961; Havighurst & Feigenbaum, 1959) led the way in applying social-science methods to the study of aging and leisure and in giving conceptual shape to this area of inquiry. Close upon Havighurst's initial efforts came the multi-authored volume edited by Kleemeier (1961), in which the last word of the era was written by the leaders in the general study of leisure and time use. It took another 15 years for the substantial theoretical contribution and accompanying empirical data of Gordon and Gaitz (1976) to appear. While leisure and aging has not been neglected totally since then, additions to the literature have been spasmodic and much of it either so practice-related or atheoretical that systematic knowledge-building did not occur. An additional problem is the bifurcation of leisure research in general and the major theoretical developments in psychology or sociology. A favorable more recent turn includes the attempt of leisure researchers to incorporate life-span considerations into their approach (Gordon & Gaitz, 1976; Kleiber & Kelly, 1980) and the call for integration of leisure research into mainstream social-science theory (Iso-Ahola, 1980; Wilson, 1980).

Despite the major contributions made by the investigators named above, none can be said to have constituted a review of relevant literature. Thus to some extent, the present chapter begins at zero. However, because Gordon and Gaitz (1976) did to some extent anchor their original contribution in the knowledge base on leisure and aging, this chapter will concentrate on reviewing the literature since 1975 and attempt to give it greater meaning within a theoretical framework. The discussion will include the more general area of activities and time use, rather than leisure alone. This effort will be preceded, however, by a more general consideration of the place of leisure research within the social and behavioral sciences.

## PERSONAL AND SOCIAL BASES
## FOR UNDERSTANDING LEISURE

Until recently leisure has been more likely to have been investigated as a social phenomenon rather than as an internal experience. For example, Gordon, Gaitz, and Scott (1973) suggested that leisure behavior is "very largely determined by our social roles, family contexts, financial resources, level of education, and immediate situational forces" (p. 21). Attempts have been made recently to integrate individual psychological processes with social psychological and macrosocial processes (see Iso-Ahola, 1980; Neulinger, 1974). In fact, a great deal of theoretical and empirical work in personality and social psychology is relevant to leisure and time use and to life-span and gerontological issues, but has been infrequently applied to either leisure or gerontology. The most thought-provoking discussion of general motivation theory and aging has been provided by Wigdor (1980). While she considered leisure behavior only in passing, her entire chapter deals with material basic to the concerns of the present chapter.

Before considering activity in its broadest ecological framework, motivational factors in activity will be discussed in both intrapersonal and social psychological terms. An attempt will be made to understand why people sometimes are motivated to behave in ways for which there is no obvious external reward.

## Motivation in Intrapersonal Terms

Drives and needs have been ever-present as subjects of psychological research despite their occasional eclipse by some varieties of stimulus-response and cognitively oriented theories. Neglected for many years in favor of tension-reduction as the primary motive for behavior were curiosity and exploration as human needs; empirical evidence overwhelmingly supports the idea that both animals and people will create activity where none exists, as if the void of doing nothing or the same thing for too long was as aversive as having too many demands (Berlyne, 1977; Fisk & Maddi, 1961). Thus curiosity and exploratory behavior have taken their rightful places among hunger, thirst, sex, pain-avoidance, and other more obviously physiologic motives as determinants of behavior.

Berlyne (1977) suggested that exploratory behavior could be understood by considering three issues: The characteristics of the external events preceding the behavior, the consequences of the behavior, and intrapersonal factors in the behaver. Much of Berlyne's and others' research was devoted to the specification of stimulus properties associated with behavior, especially what he called their "collative properties," that is, relations among the components of the environmental stimulus, or its differing aspects over time, that resulted in novelty, complexity, ambiguity, and variability. These properties create conflict in the behaver that is measurable as physiologic arousal and frequently as psychological interest or pleasure. He was thus able to measure the "arousal potential" of a stimulus (Berlyne, 1978).

The consequences of such arousal may be purely affective or they may be behavioral. Pleasure and interest (shown to be different by Berlyne, 1978, but for convenience considered together here) at the moment of performing the activity seem to be what Gordon and Gaitz (1976) identify as the "expressive" aspects of leisure behavior. It is suggested, however, that some pleasures derived from the performance of the activity may be instrumental, to the extent that they relate to long-range goals.

Other investigators have described intrapersonal factors that cause the behaver to respond differentially to stimuli of different physical or collative properties. Thus, the extravert seeks greater variety and intensity of stimuli (Eysenck, 1973). Some people show greater preference for complexity (Walker, 1964), stimulus-screening behavior (Mehrabian, 1977), or a propensity for sensation-seeking (Zuckerman & Link, 1968).

Central to understanding exploratory behavior is understanding the effects of the stimulus and the ensuing behavior in changing the person's arousal level, which in turn affects the experience of pleasure. Helson's (1964) concept of adaptation level helps explain some of the dynamics of the change. Adaptation level (AL) is seen as the average or resting state of sensory or hedonic activity under ordinary conditions of stimulation; at AL the psychological experience is indifference, for example, neither bright nor dark, loud nor soft, pleasant nor unpleasant. A change in stimulus intensity or quality of sufficient magnitude will remove the experience of indifference and introduce awareness of the quality in terms of much or little, pleasant or unpleasant. Within limits, continued stimulation at the new level will result in the establishment of a new adaptation level and a drift toward a judgment of indifference in characterizing an unchanging stimulus at this new level. Helson demonstrated that the stimulus level at which adaptation occurs was determined, not only by the intensity and duration of the focal stimulus, but also by the context in which the stimulus was presented and the past experiences of the person with similar or different stimuli ("residual factors"). As applied to a life-span view of activity, residual factors clearly include both personal and cohort-related experiences. While some (e.g., Walker, 1973) have argued that an optimal level of "psychological complexity" exists as an intraindividual preference whereby pleasure can be maximized, others (Berlyne, 1978) suggest that change, rather than absolute level, is the critical determinant of pleasure and therefore that individual preference plus the prevailing stimulus intensity and state of adaptation to it will all influence preference. Research has also shown negative effects associated with changes in stimulus intensity, as in excessively high levels of stimulation (unpleasantness, perceived strain, e.g., Glass & Singer, 1972) or excessively low levels (sensory deprivation, e.g., Bexton, Heron, & Scott, 1954).

Recent research has been converging to suggest that enduring personality characteristics such as those investigated by Eysenck (1973), Mehrabian (1977), Walker (1973), and others need to be accounted for in predicting a person's responses to specific situations. This stream of research underlines three important facts: First, that both stimulus and intrapersonal factors may affect exploratory behavior. Second, that pleasure comes both from the direct experience of stimulus change and as a consequence of exploratory behavior. Third, that exploratory behavior may increase or reduce the amount of stimulation. This intrapersonal approach to motivation usually deals with a short time period (typically the length of a laboratory testing session) and a small environmental scale (a carefully selected visual, auditory, or other stimulus). The relevance of this stimulus-bound approach to longer and more complex behaviors such as a day's activity or leisure participation in the post-retirement period is more hypothetical than empirical. However, the interaction of intrapersonal and microenvironmental factors is what produces exploration, the search for novelty, preference for complexity. These behaviors clearly characterize people's performances in some leisure activities as well as nonleisure activities. It thus seems worthwhile to search further to identify those properties of activities and those properties of people that lead to exploratory behavior and pleasure.

## The Social Psychology of Motivation

The social psychology of motivation has generated the most published material of any topic in present-day psychology. This level of motivation differs from the intrapersonal level, first, in ostensibly dealing with motives that are more explicitly social than individual. Second, the time referent ranges from the immediate to the very long range. Finally, rather than investigating "the stimulus," one is likely to be concerned about context or environment on a larger scale, such as the environment created by community resources, significant others, social norms, or cultural values.

While there are many subtopics and "mini-theories" that fall into this social motivational category, those that are particularly salient to activity choice and experience deal with the stream of action (Atkinson & Birch, 1970), intrinsic versus extrinsic motivation (Deci, 1975), and personal causation (deCharms, 1968).

### Long-range Goals

In an effort to understand the human achievement motive, Atkinson has among other issues dealt with time as an essential element in the person's pursuit of goals. Rather than being concerned with motivations as they determine a single contemporary behavioral act, Atkinson and Birch (1970) see behavior as a stream extending over time, where individual acts are construed by the person as elements of varying relevance to the achievement of long-term goals. In this conception change in level of motivation and in the way behaviors relate to the long-term goals is perpetual, as are changes in the goals themselves. Nuttin (1973) links this long-term goal-directed behavior to the reinforcing pleasurable experience through the construct "means pleasure," referring to a consequence of behavior that might be experienced out of context as indifferent or even aversive, but which gains a positive hedonic tone because it is related to the expectation of future goal attainment. The experience and consequences of a particular, time-limited behavior sequence may differ substantially from those associated with the long-term goal. Thus multiple functions may be served by a single behavioral act. This observation argues against conceiving of time use or leisure along any single dominant dimension like expression/instrumentality. Evidence to be reviewed later shows that some activities usually thought of as leisure activity may be enjoyed for instrumental reasons.

### Intrinsic and Extrinsic
### Motivation

The duality of intrinsic versus extrinsic satisfaction as a basis for motivation has been with us for a long time. Interest in this concept has grown recently with demonstrations that many behaviors cannot be explained by the usual reward–punishment–drive–reduction paradigms. This line of research has been particularly concerned with the relationship between intrinsic and extrinsic motivations directed simultaneously to the same goal. Research (reviewed in Deci, 1975) has shown that when an extrinsic reinforcement contingency is superimposed on an existing intrinsically motivated behavior, that behavior may diminish. Is this finding relevant to the frequent situation where an activity programmer attempts to create incentives for an older person to increase her level of participation in an activity that is already in the person's behavior repertory?

It is of interest to note that apparently the simple provision of information relevant to the behavior and usable by the person (as contrasted with providing a reinforcement contingency) does not seem to have this effect (Deci, 1975). By contrast, the dampening effect on existing behavior is especially strong if the external reinforcer is perceived as existing specifically to control the person's behavior. This finding leads to a topic of critical importance to the present chapter, the area of perceived control and personal causation.

**Perceived Control**

The personality characteristic locus of control, an expectation that behavioral reinforcement originates from internal versus external sources, has been with us for a while (Rotter, 1966), and a literature showing favorable outcomes associated with control among older people has been accumulating (Reid & Zeigler, 1981). Probably even more productive may be predictions based upon a less static construct than locus of control, that is, the person's perception of the degree of personal control possible in a given situation—the extent to which the self is seen as the active agent. Nuttin's (1973) revision of the adaptation-level position is that "event production," rather than change in stimulation level per se, may be responsible for the favorable effects observed in some micropsychological experiments (Nuttin, 1973). He refers to this phenomenon as "causality pleasure." Another familiar related construct is "learned helplessness" (Seligman, 1975), a state of passivity and unwillingness to attempt problem solutions following repeated unsuccessful attempts to control environmental contingencies. Among the most frequently cited studies in social gerontology are those demonstrating favorable outcomes associated with experimentally induced instrumentality among nursing home residents (Langer & Rodin, 1976; Schulz, 1976).

Intrinsically motivated behavior is likely to be perceived as personally caused. Of all the characteristics of leisure described by contemporary researchers (Iso-Ahola, 1980; Kelly, 1972; Neulinger, 1974) and reviewed by Gordon & Gaitz (1976), this aspect of perceived freedom to create the activity or to choose to participate is agreed upon by all as an essential characteristic that distinguishes leisure from non-leisure.

To summarize this introduction to our topic, the following generalizations may be repeated:

1. Curiosity and exploratory behavior characterize all people.
2. Stimulus characteristics, whether in small or large environmental contexts, are capable of motivating exploratory behavior.
3. Intrapersonal characteristics, whether viewed as traits, learned
   expectations, or perceptions of the external situation, also
   motivate or condition exploratory behavior.
4. The immediate consequences of exploratory behavior, if pleasurable, reinforce that behavior.
5. A change in stimulus characteristics may be caused by external
   factors or by personal effort.
6. The perception of personal causation may both motivate behavior and condition the perceived hedonic outcome.
7. A time dimension is necessary to account for sustained motivational states and variations in the hedonic tone of the consequences of behavior. A tentative hypothesis is suggested that
   pleasurable affect is strongest during the performance of desired activities, while means pleasure (Nuttin, 1973), a more
   cognitively based experience, is a time-enduring result of activity that is related to the stream of life-goal attainment. Both
   may be subsumed under what people refer to as the enjoyment of leisure and other activities.

The next section will attempt to link these generalizations regarding the motivations for behavior more closely and apply them more
explicitly to the activities of older people.

## A MODEL OF ACTIVITY
## AND ITS OUTCOME

Because most of the research underlying the preceding review was done
on presumably healthy younger people, one essential aspect of the intrapersonal system, personal competence, has been dealt with in less depth
than is desirable. In old age one cannot assume a behaving individual
with totally intact biological, sensory, psychomotor, or cognitive ability.
Thus the attribute of "personal competence" (Lawton, 1972) must be
added to the set of factors necessary to understand activity and its

consequences. Even among the healthy, where the demands of an activity are extreme, correspondingly extraordinary competence may be required for adequate task performance. If an activity is to be intrinsically rewarding, the person's skills must be closely matched to the demands of the activity (Csikszentmihalyi, 1975). It is suggested here that means pleasure is gained from the performance of some activities because their performance affirms perceived competence.

With this essential ingredient, competence, added, some of the motivational elements discussed above may be placed into the ecological model of Lawton and Nahemow (1973), which is very similar to the totally independently developed model developed by Csikszentmihalyi (1975) to illustrate the "flow" state (to be described later). The surface of Figure 4.1 locates the projections from an unpictured third dimension of all hedonic outcomes (pleasant to unpleasant) associated with the

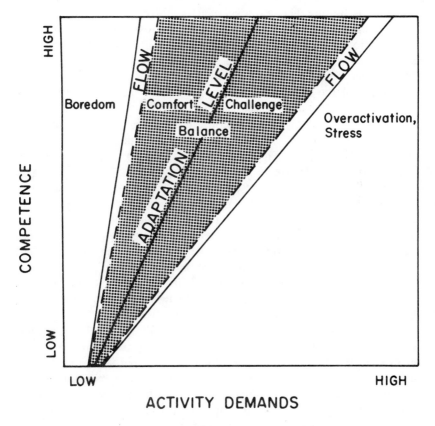

**Figure 4.1**    A model of personal competence and activity demands.

behavior of people of varying degrees of competence as they perform activities of varying levels of difficulty, or task demand. "Activity demand" is a general term to cover properties of activity including, but not limited to, their physical energy-expenditure requirements, physical stimulus qualities, and collative characteristics (complexity, novelty, others; Berlyne, 1978). The third unpictured dimension represents the evaluative dimension, pleasure, satisfaction, interest, or positive-to-negative affect distributed as shown in cross section (Figure 4.2) as it varies with stimulation level around the neutral state associated with adaptation level (Wohlwill, 1966). As Lawton and Nahemow (1973) suggested when discussing their ecological model, the "point" representing the psychological outcome associated with a person's performing a task is rarely stable. Although AL is the resting point, either the demands of tasks change or the exploratory need of the person evokes behavior designed to vary that steady state (that is, to increase or decrease stimulation). The new level of activation once achieved may itself then become perceived as steady; a reversion to a higher or lower level of activation may again be sought. A dialectic process is thus suggested as the means by which maximum enjoyment is attained, rather than a concept like "optimal state of activation."

Areas of the Figure 4.1 surface have been labeled. Clearly, task demands too stringent for the person's competence evoke a state of overactivation (anxiety, tension), while underdemand leads to boredom. The maximum points on the curve of Figure 4.2 are seen as subsuming the areas of Figure 4.1 labeled "comfort" and "challenge." That is, a mild increase in demand is experienced as challenging, a mild decrease as comfortable or relaxing, and both as pleasant. The narrow sectors labeled "flow" represent extremes of expressive behavior as defined by Csikszentmihalyi (1975), which for a few people in high states of challenge or relaxation represents a peak affective experience. The characteristics of flow are (1) a merging of action and awareness, (2) extreme focus of attention on the task, (3) a subjective "loss of ego," (4) a feeling of total control of one's actions and the environment, (5) automatic response to task demands, and (6) the limitation of experienced rewards to the intrinsic type.

It will be noted that Figures 4.1 and 4.2 do not include the other critical element of activity, its internality versus externality. This element is represented by the related dimensions of personal versus external causation and intrinsic versus extrinsic rewards, the former the perceived determinant of activity and the latter the perceived consequence. Personal causation and intrinsic reward act so as to increase pleasure and motivate the repetition of the behavior.

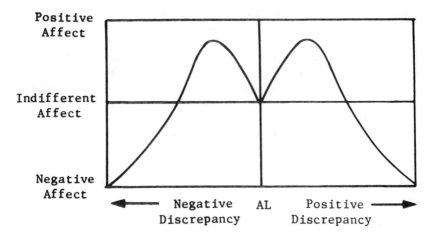

**Figure 4.2**   Affective response and discrepancy from adaptation level. (Reprinted from Wohlwill, 1966, p. 35. © 1966 Society for the Psychological Study of Social Issues. Reproduced with permission.)

It should also be noted that this conception applies to all activity, not simply to leisure. Even flow can be experienced in relation to work, as Csikszentmihalyi (1975) showed in his study of surgeons. While there are many reasons for studying the relationship between work and leisure (Kabanoff, 1980), to designate some activities as inherently more expressive than others, as did Gordon & Gaitz (1976), seems to ignore the demonstrated ability of some "instrumental" behaviors to be perceived as self-chosen, intrinsically rewarding, and enjoyed totally for their own sake. It must be emphasized that the present conception of leisure insists that it should be capable of application to any behavior as long as the behavior meets the subjective criteria for leisure mentioned at the beginning of this chapter.

## Age-related Aspects of the Model

Among the topics that Wigdor (1980) reviewed in her treatment of motivation, a major unresolved question regarding whether the activation level or reactivity of normal older people differs from that of younger people remains, with some evidence favoring underreactivity (Shmavo-nian & Busse, 1963) and other evidence favoring overreactivity (Eis-dorfer, Nowlin, & Wilkie, 1970). It seems clear that where pathologic changes have occurred in any of the sectors of competence, there is a higher risk of anxiety (overactivation in Figure 4.1) and a narrower band where pleasurable challenge may occur. Thus the match of activity to competence becomes a critical matter. Wigdor (1980) notes, however, that the optimum-arousal-level principle may be of use in the resolution of this conflict. An intriguing related suggestion was advanced by Jarvik and Russell (1979) regarding the maintenance of arousal at a tolerable level. They ask whether, in addition to the traditional alternative re-sponses to stress, flight versus fight, there may be a "third emergency reaction" that they call "freeze." To become passive and reduce one's level of reactivity through energy conservation is seen as adaptive, given the internal limitations on competence and the external constraints on the behavior of older people. Some people's reductions in activity during the aging process may thus involve an overgeneralized "freeze" reaction that inappropriately limits pleasurable as well as aversive situations. Wigdor (personal communication) has pointed out, however, that a "freeze" reaction in real life is very short-lived and likely to quickly assume the characteristics of an avoidance, or flight, response.

Is maintenance of the balanced state of adaptation level a more desired goal for older people than for others? Data are not at hand to answer the question of whether activities that are viewed as familiar are judged by older people to be any more pleasant than they would be by those of other ages. However, there is evidence from general psychol-ogy that mere familiarity with a stimulus, in the absence of any reward value, may evoke liking (Zajonc, 1968). It is at least thinkable that familiarity with an activity could increasingly become a strong determi-nant of willingness to participate as age increases. If this is true, there might be some basis for deliberately designing activity programs for the elderly so as to maximize the number of familiar elements.

The social position of the aged in our society selectively reduces the level of activity demands made of them and increases the risk of boredom (underdemand with respect to competence). The loss of in-come, the removal of social ties to sources of knowledge about activity opportunities, and restrictive social attitudes regarding what activities are appropriate for older people effectively reduce activity demands (see Ward, 1979a, pp. 235–270). In a similar manner, opportunities for personal causality may be reduced; it takes money, good health, and social connectedness to create access to many leisure activities.

Whether intrinsic motivation for the activities that are chosen is greater among the aged is questionable. To the extent that the intra-personal manifestations of disengagement (Cumming & Henry, 1961) characterize a person, there should be some liberation from social normative constraints, allowing the older person to choose activities for the sake of pure enjoyment. However, there has been so little study of the subjective meaning of activities to the older person, to say nothing of their study in longitudinal research, that one can only raise the question as one worthy of study.

Is there any change with aging in the extent to which activities in the "comfort" range are sought or enjoyed? Sitting-and-watching be-havior (Lawton, 1974), the rocking-chair lifestyle (Reichard, Livson, & Petersen, 1962), reminiscence (Giambra, 1974), and environmental fantasy (Rowles, 1978) have been documented as being actively en-joyed by some older people, but their relative age-prevalence has never been tested. In sum, it would be very hazardous to conclude that "passive activity" is any more appropriate to healthy older people than to any other broad population group.

## THE SUBJECTIVE
## EXPERIENCE OF ACTIVITY

Considerable recent research has been devoted to determining the important subjective features of activity. While very little of recent research in this area has dealt with aging (Havighurst's earlier work was very much concerned with these issues), future theory develop-ment in activity and aging must take this work into account (a more extended discussion of some of these constructs will be found in Lawton, 1982b).

One problem is the loose and varying nomenclature that has been attached to the subjective aspects of activity. Lawton (1982b) sug-gested that subjective attributes of activity be grouped under the terms *needs, meaning, activity satisfaction,* and *activity preferences. Needs* are primary in the classical sense (hunger, thirst, sex, curiosity). They are the basis for the generalized arousal that establishes and energizes the secondary needs (e.g., aggression, affiliation, power, etc.). However, some leisure researchers have attempted to match particular secondary needs with particular leisure activities (Neulinger, 1974; Tinsley, Bar-rett, & Kass, 1977). Such leisure-specific "needs" seem more properly to belong in the "meaning" category below.

**Activity Meaning**

The meaning of activity is a topic that is still very diffusely articulated. A great variety of terms have been applied to presumed dimensions of meaning. Crandall (1980), for example, identified four dimensions of leisure on which much research has been performed: (1) why people engage in specific activities, (2) which personal needs are fulfilled by leisure, (3) the motivations for leisure, and (4) the satisfactions gained from leisure. These categories are extremely difficult to differentiate conceptually. Therefore, a general term is suggested for the entire category, with subcategories. First, it is suggested that *activity meaning* be the general term for a person's judgment (cognitive or affective) of an activity. Sometimes the judgment is made by the person performing the activity and sometimes by the researcher (for example, the researcher who, like McKechnie, 1974, factored frequency of participation data among activities but then himself applied names to the factors—a judgment that, like all factor naming, imposes the researcher's meaning on the pattern of covariation of objective data).

Meaning is jointly determined by the characteristics of the person making the judgment and the characteristics of the activity itself. This predominance of inner versus outer factors is the basis for the two subcategories of meaning. The term *perceived activity function* will be applied to the aspects of meaning that are more closely related to the person. Those related more closely to the activity itself will be called *perceived activity characteristics.*

*Perceived activity functions* have been called "leisure satisfactions" (Beard & Ragheb, 1980; Pierce, 1980a), "meaning" (Donald & Havighurst, 1959), and "need-satisfying characteristics" (Tinsley et al., 1977; Tinsley & Kass, 1978). All of the data that produced these dimensions were provided by subject-judges. Researcher-generated activity functions have been identified by Bishop and Witt (1970), Dumazedier (1974), Meyersohn (1972), and Neulinger ("activity press," 1974). Perhaps the easiest criterion for the perceived activity function is whether it answers the question, "What does the activity do for me (or for people)?" This class of meanings thus subsumes two constructs, secondary needs and sources of reinforcement; these two classes perhaps should be, but have not to date been, empirically differentiated.

*Perceived activity characteristics,* while purporting to describe the activity in a stimulus-focused manner, are still judgments made by people. Although a relatively high degree of consensus may be obtained for some such characteristics, the range for interindividual variation is great enough to view this category as properly being an aspect of meaning. Pierce (1980c), for example, asked subjects to characterize their favorite activities (such as requires physical strength, do alone, risky, requires knowledge of rules). Factor analysis of these ratings yielded factors that he named physical challenge, stimulation, autonomy, and others. Statistical clustering approaches were used to organize researcher-designated activity characteristics by Gudykunst, Morra, Kantor, and Parker (1981) and McKechnie (1974). Ritchie (1975) had subjects supply characterizations of clusters of activities that had been obtained by multidimensional scaling. Berlyne's (1978) collative properties belong in this class of researcher-generated activity characteristics. Perceived activity characteristics may be used, when consensus is high, to represent activity demand in the model of Figure 4.1.

Unaccounted for among the meanings reviewed above are the dimensions suggested earlier as being of central importance for the understanding of activity (challenge/comfort, perceived control, and intrinsic/extrinsic motivation). Another major dimension is the expressive versus instrumental dimension, the one on which Gordon and Gaitz (1976) based their model of leisure activity. While little empirical research has been done to determine how these attributes relate to concrete behaviors, these concepts appear to be higher-order abstractions than those reviewed above; conceivably they might appear as second-order factors were the relationships among some of the first-order factors analyzed.

As far as research on older people's ascriptions of meaning to their activities goes, very little has happened since Donald and Havighurst's (1959) study. One of the few attempts to determine subjective meaning located in more recent literature offered subjects the Donald and Havighurst categories to characterize their "reasons for enjoying" voluntary associations (Ward, 1979b). Other researchers asked older people to state their reasons for enjoying a local closed-circuit television service (Felton, Moss, & Sepulveda, 1980), educational television programs (Daniel, Templin, & Shearon, 1977), or learning opportunities (Hiemstra, 1972, 1976). In each of these studies roughly equal proportions of seemingly expressive and instrumental choices of reasons were made.

However, no adequate estimate has been made of the distribution of expressive and instrumental meanings accorded most of the usual activities engaged in by older people. A similar lack of inquiry exists regarding the other higher-order meaning dimensions.

**Activity Satisfaction**

Activity satisfaction is not a class of construct that imposes meaning on activities. Rather, it represents a person's amount of pleasure obtained from performing or having performed an activity: how much one enjoys, is satisfied with, or likes an activity. This construct is a combination of the affective and cognitive components of attitude toward an activity (Crandall & Slivken, 1980). This hedonic dimension that applies equally well to content other than leisure should not be confused with "sources of leisure satisfaction." Such an attempt to identify why a particular activity is satisfying is an example of a perceived activity function. By contrast, activity satisfaction represents the affective-cognitive outcome of the person–activity demand transaction schematized in Figures 4.1 and 4.2. Satisfaction derived from an activity is reprocessed so as to influence the motivation to perform a particular activity. Thus, especially as accumulated over time, activity satisfactions will directly determine "preference."

*Activity preference* is the potential behavioral component of attitude toward an activity, the readiness or intention to perform an activity if facilitating factors allow. Preferences are typically measured by asking people how much they would like to have a series of activities available, or to rank activities in order of enjoyment.

This topic of activity meaning has been dealt with poorly in the research literature of social gerontology. The recent research in aging to be reviewed below is remarkable for ignoring meaning, perhaps under the tacit mistaken assumptions that (1) the presence of an opportunity to engage in an activity ensures its performance and (2) the performance of a "desirable" activity ensures an increment of psychological well-being.

It will be helpful to think of activity as an element in a dynamic model where the types of activities are determined by a wide variety of factors including elements from person and environment, from past and future, from ascribed and achieved statuses, and other sources. Wherever such causal priority is plausible, it is instructive to seek multivariate determinants of activity. Activity of all kinds, whether health behavior, activities of daily living, cognitive functioning, effectance, or social behavior (Lawton, 1972), in turn has consequences in terms of other behavior and psychological state. Thus another stream of relevant research is the examination of how participation in various activities affects such outcomes as health, popularity, or life satisfaction.

Activity meaning in turn adds a further complication to the behavioral system. The historical and contemporary meaning of an activity to a person may determine whether the person lives in an environment that affords the choice of that activity, or whether the person perceives an available activity as salient. Meaning is in addition a critical intervening factor between the performance of an activity and the outcomes as discussed above.

The research review to follow is organized so as to consider under the determinants of activity the topics of age changes in activities, socialization to leisure, and environmental and personal determinants of activity. Then outcomes of activity participation will be considered: activity satisfaction, leisure meaning, perceived competence, and psychological well-being. Finally, research on a number of specific types of leisure activity will be briefly reviewed.

## DETERMINANTS OF ACTIVITY

### Age Changes in Activity

Only recently has a substantial body of research developed that reports longitudinally on individual activity patterns. The Bonn Longitudinal Study (Schmitz-Scherzer, 1976) revealed a modest number of changes in frequency of activities over a six-year period. There was a slight decrease in some social activities (being visited and entertainment with others) and an increase in time spent reading the newspaper, watching television, and gardening; no systematic longitudinal change was noted in eight other activities.

The two major Duke Longitudinal Studies to some extent aggregated activity types, so that Palmore (1981) reported a general overall drop in level of social activities in both studies. However, this statistically significant decline must be viewed in a way that also acknowledges the finding (from the second six-year study) that 17 percent of their subjects showed no change and 32 percent increased the number of hours spent in social activity. The type of activity was important: Organizational activity changed very little, and church attendance showed a substantial decline only after age 80 (Cutler, 1977).

These data thus show only mild decline in some formal and informal leisure activities and no change or increase in others. Cross-sectional studies tend to highlight decline. For example, in their large sample of Houston residents, Gordon and Gaitz (1976) found steep apparent declines in the majority of activity types from ages 20–29 to age 75 and over, but little change in a few other, more sedentary activities. A cross-sectional study of different types of organizational membership showed that some not surprisingly peaked in middle age (unions, occupational, and school-related groups), others increased with age (fraternal and church-related), and only one decreased with age (sport-related).

The only time-budget study that obtained data by age on a national probability sample, including 157 people 65 and over, yielded definitive cross-sectional activity data (Hill, 1981). Compared to earlier adulthood (ages 25–44), people 45–64 and 65 + increased slightly their time spent in household activity and "active leisure" and increased considerably the time spent in personal care and passive leisure. Slight increases or no changes were seen in time spent in shopping, education, organizational activity, or social entertainment.

Leisure satisfaction has been reported from several large representative samples to be positively correlated with age (Herzog & Rodgers, 1981), a relationship that remained under most conditions of controlling for other variables. Thus at the very least, the mild overall decline in some forms of activity with age does not appear to undermine older people's satisfaction with what they do in their spare time.

## Socialization to Leisure and Its Effects

While the development of play, interests, and skills over the first two decades of life has received considerable attention, little is known about the long-term persistence of interests or leisure behaviors (Kleiber & Kelly, 1980). Nonetheless, many writers have concluded that continuity in activity is the rule (Atchley, 1977; Kelly, 1977; Palmore, 1981; Troll, 1982). If we accept the decline in some activities that require substantial energy expenditures, the longitudinal data cited above support the idea that people otherwise tend to continue doing what they have done in the past. Snow and Havighurst (1977) added more evidence that retired academics tend to continue to work in their area of expertise; almost half of their sample were classed as "maintainers" of their roles in scholarly work.

There are unquestionably effects of history on activities and the meaning accorded activities. For example, a major change in lifestyle is implied in the fact that employed workers in our time have been shown to have 1,200 hours more free time per year than did workers in 1890 (Kreps, 1977). A hint of the strength of cohort effects was provided by a study of people who experienced the depression of the 1930s (Elder, 1974); those who were economically deprived then accorded less importance to leisure as a contemporary value than did those who had not been economically deprived then. This chapter will only note the probability of a major future change in the extent to which leisure is valued (this topic is discussed at length in Kaplan, 1979). It seems virtually certain that future aged cohorts, having had very different socialization experiences with leisure activities, will have greatly enlarged expectations for the quality and content of leisure. It is possible to overgeneralize in a stereotypic manner—for example, that older people resist new activities or that familiar activities are the only ones that can give pleasure. It is nonetheless important to understand how strong may be the effects of early learning and one's socialization to values regarding leisure (see Gordon & Gaitz, 1976, for an extended discussion of a theory of stagewise life-span socialization to activities).

The main classes of determinants of activity may be grouped into personal, social, and environmental factors.

## Personal Determinants

In studies of older people, *age* often is not associated with activity variations, perhaps because of the restrictions in range of age of subjects in many studies. However, in a time-budget study of the aged (Lawton, Moss, & Fulcomer, in press), which controlled for a number of demographic and health-related factors, higher age was independently associated with more time spent in eating, religious activity (excluding church attendance), rest and relaxation, and time alone, with less time in family interaction and time away from home. Adult education programs report more participants among the younger-old than the old-old (Hooper & March, 1978).

Relationships between *sex* and leisure participation are more notable for their absence than presence, with conflicting findings sometimes appearing. For example, women were found by George (1978) and Hill (1978) to be more active in organizations, but Babchuk, Peters, Hoyt, and Kaiser (1979) found no sex difference and Robertson (1978) found women to belong to fewer groups than did men. Blazer and Palmore (1976) and Hill (1981) reported women to be more active in religious activities. Sex-typed behavior showed much more clearly in obligatory behaviors, where women spent more time in personal care, housework, and cooking, but traveled and were away from their residences less than men (Hill, 1981; Lawton et al., in press). The same studies showed that women spent less time reading and listening to the radio, but the sex difference in time spent shopping was small.

*Race* differences are especially marked in religious behavior (primarily church-related social activities rather than attendance at services), where Blacks were more active (Arling, 1976; Lawton et al., in press). The latter study also showed Blacks to spend less time cooking and eating.

Only a few studies have investigated the effects of *cognitive* factors on activities, but these have found their effects to be substantial. Maintenance of the original level of nonreligious leisure activities was enhanced among those with higher cognitive ability (Palmore, 1981), while general activity level at baseline was higher among the more intelligent in the Bonn study (Schmitz-Scherzer, 1976). People with substantial cognitive impairment spent less time eating, listening to the radio, watching television, or being alone; they spent more time resting, with household family, and inside the dwelling (Lawton et al., in press).

*Health* impairment always is reported to have a depressing effect on active leisure activities (Arling, 1976; Clemente, Rexroad, & Hirsch, 1975; Covey, 1980; George, 1978; Gordon et al., 1973; Lawton et al., in press; Schmitz-Scherzer, 1976). It is thus clear that any research seeking to identify determinants of activity that does not control for health is doomed to ambiguous meaning. Lawton et al. (in press) found those in poor health to spend less time in most obligatory activities except personal care (more) and eating (equal to the healthy). Poor health conditions were independently associated with spending more time alone, but poor health in the form of functional impairment in basic activities of daily living was associated with spending less time alone, no doubt because of the need for assistance or surveillance.

The effects of other *intrapersonal factors* have been explored in less depth than have the foregoing background characteristics. Gordon et al. (1973) found that personal value orientations added some predictability to overall level of leisure participation: Low scores on "ease and contentment" as a life goal were associated with high overall activity participation for both older men and women, as was high religious orientation for women. George (1978) found that scores on the 16 Personality Factor Inventory (Cattell, Eber, & Tatsuoka, 1970) predicted leisure activity level minimally. In both of these studies the effects of background personal and social factors were much greater than were the effects of personality variables. However, considering the substantial predictability for variables other than leisure behavior shown by the higher-order factor intraversion-extraversion among younger people (Eysenck, 1973) or older people (Costa & McCrae,

1980), it is clearly necessary to investigate further the effects of such personality styles on activities. Some personality characteristics or "cognitive styles" also may have close relationships to the motivations underlying leisure behavior: sensation-seeking (Zuckerman & Link, 1968), stimulus screening (Mehrabian & Russell, 1974), complexity (Walker, 1973), and others deserve exploration in this manner.

## Social Characteristics

Socioeconomic status has been shown to have a particularly strong effect on leisure behavior. Without exception, the overall level of the more active or intellectually demanding leisure activities is greatest among those with more income, more education, and higher occupational attainment. The effect is especially strong in determining who participates in adult learning endeavors (Bynum, Cooper, & Acuff, 1978; Covey, 1980; Hooper & March, 1978; Knowlton, 1977), findings that affirm the continuity hypothesis of leisure behavior (Atchley, 1977). By contrast, greater use of television in both informal fashion (Lawton et al., in press) and in a community closed-circuit demonstration (Felton et al., 1980) was observed among those with less education. In other time-budget categories, those with less education spent less time in housework, reading, and recreation and more time cooking and interacting with family and friends (Lawton et al., in press). The only recent study to examine the relationship between the meaning of leisure for older people and SES was Ward's (1979b) study of organizational participation. Those of lower SES belonged more frequently to recreational and informal social organizations, while those of higher SES belonged to those classified as having age-related programs, requiring active participation, and volunteer activities. A descriptive tabulation of reasons given by the subjects for participation showed that low-SES people mentioned passing time and status reasons more frequently while high-SES participants mentioned creative goals and helping others.

Clearly needed is more idiographic research on the meaning of different ways of spending time in a framework that avoids better than does existing research the trap of social-class bias (Lawton, 1978). One needs to know whether freedom, expressive behavior, intrinsic motivation, and challenge are class-related criteria by which activity is evaluated. Are the satisfactions accruing from leisure activities as lopsidedly distributed among the privileged as are the participation rates?

The handful of reports that include *marital status* as an independent variable indicate that married older people tended to be slightly more active in organizations (Robertson, 1978; Trela & Jackson, 1979). The latter authors further differentiated people in terms of their social-role obligations and found that married people with parental roles were more active in community roles than married people without parental roles; this consistency was seen as a "spillover effect," perhaps related to the fact that functioning in one role generated a thirst for activity in other roles. However, where role deprivation had occurred, that is, among widows, those with a parental role were less active in the community, as if a single compensation were enough to satisfy the person or was all that the deprived person could utilize.

Only scattered findings concern the variation in activity associated with other aspects of social structure or social integration. One problem hampering attempts to determine how activity participation fits in with other forms of social behavior is that sometimes (1) organizational activity, (2) active leisure, (3) passive leisure, (4) interaction with friends, and (5) interaction with family are grouped together or in different combinations by different investigators for data analysis. Perhaps the reason for this indiscriminate grouping, in turn, lies in the lack of a conceptual taxonomy of activities, or even an empirical taxonomy that is offered as a model for other researchers until some better scheme comes along. For the time being, the above general categories are suggested as being of heuristic value. These and perhaps subcategories of each should be identified in research, even if they are aggregated for some data analyses.

**Environmental Determinants**

While household composition is related to marital status, it is considered here to be an environmental variable. Moss and Lawton (1980) found that older people who live alone spend about 13 hours of the waking day alone, as compared to 8 hours for those living as marital pairs and 9.5 hours for those living in a younger person's household; those living alone spend more time with friends than do the other two groups. Live-alones spend slightly more time on media and less time in rest and relaxation. Those living with younger family spend less time in obligatory activities generally, interaction with friends, and recreation, and most in family interaction and rest/relaxation. Overall, however, except for time alone, similarities among living-arrangement groups were more striking than differences. The combination of the demands for obligatory activities and the lack of opportunities for more varied behavior among many older people perhaps leads to an overall inelasticity of time use such that people living in very different family situations still manage to deploy their time fairly similarly.

Not surprisingly, much of the research relating activity to environment has been done on older people living in special housing conditions, beginning with the demonstrations by Carp (1966, 1978–1979) and Lawton and Cohen (1974) that a move to age-segregated federally assisted housing resulted in a gain in overall social and leisure activity participation. A similar gain was observed when the move was to nonassisted housing in retirement areas of the country (Bultena & Wood, 1970; Oliver, 1971). A higher age concentration within the housing site (Lawton, Nahemow, & Yeh, 1980) and within the local neighborhood where the housing was located (Lawton & Nahemow, 1979) was associated with greater organized activity participation by tenants, as was housing location in neighborhoods of better quality and single-family-home predominance.

Notable by its absence is any attempt to assess the effects of building type, decor, visual image, environmental legibility, or many other microenvironmental features on specific types of activity participation.

## OUTCOMES OF LEISURE
## AND ACTIVITY PARTICIPATION

While many evaluations of experimental activity programs have appeared in the literature, almost none of them have met minimum quality criteria (i.e., at least a two-occasion study with experimental and control groups and plausible effect indicators). Therefore, this section is limited primarily to cross-sectional, correlational, and naturalistic studies, none of which can legitimately be claimed to have constituted an unequivocal test of whether participation had an effect on the outcome measure.

### Leisure Satisfaction

Relatively little research in aging has systematically dealt with leisure or activity satisfaction either in its own right or as a construct to be included in a more general model of the determinants of well-being. It is of interest to note, however, that in their national survey of perceived quality of life, Campbell et al. (1976) found that satisfaction with spare-time activities was one of the best predictors of overall life satisfaction for the elderly no less than the young.

Csikszentmihalyi and Graef (1980) did not study older people, but their method of "experimental time sampling" is unique and deserves application with the aged. Their subjects were signaled in a random manner through an electronic monitoring device to stop and write down at that moment what they were doing, where they were, why they were doing it, and the extent of their wish to be doing something else (interpreted as "intrinsic motivation" by the researcher, though it appears to this author to more properly represent satisfaction). Freely chosen activities were rated as much more satisfying by this method. Among all activities that were rated as being less freely chosen, leisure behaviors performed at home were the most palatable, while among those that were self-chosen, leisure was more satisfying (whether at home or in public places) than other behaviors (that is, working at home or at work, nonwork behavior at work, or transportation).

Perceived opportunity for recreation was among the most important determinants of community satisfaction among older people in 28 planned and unplanned communities (Toseland & Rasch, 1978).

It is suggested that, following the precedent of Campbell et al. (1976), any research dealing with perceived quality of life consider the domain of leisure satisfaction; in addition, the subaspects of satisfaction with one's own leisure behavior and satisfaction with the existing resources for leisure behavior should be represented.

Some research among the little dealing with meaning is relevant to the instrumental versus expressive meaning construct. Since this construct was accorded such a central position by Gordon and Gaitz (1976), it is of interest to see how activities are viewed in these terms by older people asked to state what they enjoy about or why they perform an activity. Hiemstra (1972, 1976) directly measured older people's preferences for learning behaviors that had been classed as expressive or instrumental; preference was greater for the instrumental category. Of the reasons for studying given by a large group of extension students 60 and over the most frequent choice was "to learn more things of interest," a meaning clearly more expressive than instrumental. However, 7 of the 10 most frequent choices were instrumental (meet interesting people, contribute more to society, improve social life, etc.). A similar weighting toward the instrumental side was seen in senior center participants' choices of reasons for participation (contact with friends, pass time, benefit to society), although a large minority again made more expressive choices (new experience, just for the pleasure; Ward, 1979b).

The main conclusion possible from such traces of knowledge affirms the fact that people do find many kinds of meaning in the same behavior; the results alert us to the need for more in-depth study of meaning.

## Perceived Competence

While Atchley's (1977) suggestion that leisure competence constitutes a major source of affirmation of self-worth in later life is highly plausible, little has been done to test this idea. The approach of Czikszentmihalyi and Graef (1980) is again of potential interest to the gerontologist. Among the other questions, their subjects were also asked to rate their skills in the activity being performed at the moment of enquiry. In general, skills were rated as greater in nonleisure situations than in leisure situations. However, "public leisure" activities, when also rated as self-chosen, were accompanied by much higher skill ratings than were public leisure activities that the person felt she had to do. Thus, the importance of perceived competence and perceived freedom is illustrated within an overall social structure where work does, by its very nature, usually exercise skills more. For the older person, the main nonemployment nonleisure category would be "work at home." After retirement, opportunities to affirm one's competence may be offered primarily by self-maintaining and home-maintaining obligatory behaviors. Again, it behooves us to inquire more deeply into the meaning of these behaviors.

Relevant to this last point is Altergott and Eustis' (1981) study of satisfaction with amounts of time spent in seven activity categories by three groups of older people receiving home care, intermediate institutional care, and skilled nursing care. Those receiving home care were least satisfied in general, wishing to spend more time in all discretionary activity categories. The fact that the most competent (the home-care group) were the least satisfied was cited as evidence of the persistence of the motivation to display competent behavior. By contrast, the institutionalized had accommodated to the loss of competence and therefore expressed greater satisfaction with the way their time was allocated.

## Psychological Well-being

Pursuit of the answer to one of the critical questions concerned with activity theory, "Does activity lead to psychological well-being?" does not abate, nor has the question become conclusively answered despite the steady stream of additions to this literature.

In Larson's (1978) review of the correlates of life satisfaction, the weight of the evidence suggests that leisure activity is related to life satisfaction, though consensus among studies was by no means complete. Ambiguity is particularly great in the case of voluntary associations, despite the fact that multivariate analyses seemed at one point to have shown that with income and health controlled, no relationship remained between organizational activity and life satisfaction (Bull & Aucoin, 1975; Cutler, 1973). Distinguishing among type of organizations led Cutler later (1976) to the conclusion that religious organizational activity, but no other, was related to life satisfaction and happiness. Yet Ward (1979b) found that recreational organizational activity remained a mildly significant predictor of life satisfaction after controlling for other variables, as did Markides and Martin (1979). The only longitudinal test of this hypothesis came from the Duke studies (Palmore, 1981). The first study showed that among women, a leisure index that included organizational activity predicted later positive change in psychological well-being; among men, higher organizational activity at baseline predicted later absolute level of well-being (Palmore, 1981). Several other correlations involving organizational behavior and psychological well-being were not significant. It does appear that the relationship is weak, at best, but worth pursuing with better differentiation of type of organizational participation.

Other demonstrations of direct relationships between nonorganizational leisure behavior and psychological well-being have been presented by Palmore (1981) and Sauer (1977). Even with controls exerted on health and income, Peppers (1977) found that participants in "active social" pursuits were highest in life satisfaction, while those whose activities were "sedentary isolated" were lowest.

As earlier research had indicated with scholars (Rowe, 1973, 1976) a retrospective study of retired academic administrators showed that a substantial number had maintained their academic lifestyles following retirement (Snow & Havighurst, 1977). However, the group that had substituted new interests ("transformers") were slightly less "bored" and "lonely" than the "maintainers."

The importance of considering meaning was demonstrated by Liang, Dvorkin, Kahana, and Mazian (1980), who found no direct relationship between a measure of objective social integration (which included organizational activity as one of its components) and morale, but an indirect relationship through an index of perceived level of social integration. It is necessary for the future researcher in this area to be aware, however, of the ambiguity in results such as these, which depend on relationships between two subjective (and therefore statistically confounded) variables, perceived social integration and perceived psychological well-being (morale). While the need to include subjective meaning variables in activity research is clear, it is also desirable to attempt to represent every subjective variable with an objective cognate, in this case, perhaps observer-judged psychological well-being.

# RESEARCH ON SPECIFIC
# TYPES OF LEISURE ACTIVITIES

Space does not permit a complete review of literature dealing with the many informal and formal ways in which older people use their discretionary time. Such a review needs especially to be done from a practitioner's point of view. However, research in these areas is just beginning to develop in both quantity and quality.

Perhaps the most advanced area in terms of research development is *television*. The most recent data show that older people watch television as a primary activity about 2.6 hours per day (Hill, 1981). This estimate includes those who never watch; nonetheless, it is considerably less than the Nielson survey estimates quoted by Kubey (1980, p. 17) of 25–35 hours per week per person 50 and over. While self-estimates may underestimate, as Kubey indicates, Nielson-type estimates err in the opposite direction, since they include only viewers and include all turned-on time, rather than "primary-activity" time. The interested reader can find an in-depth treatment of the multiple functions of television for the elderly in Davis (1975) and a very comprehensive literature review by Kubey (1980). Felton et al. (1980) studied a specific demonstration designed to enlarge the usefulness of television for a small city's older population. *Reading* is another medium beginning to receive more formal attention by researchers, as seen in the appearance of a monograph on this subject (*Educational Gerontology*, 1979, Whole No. 3).

Another "boom" area is *educational experiences*, where a combination of growing demand by an increasingly educated older population and the desire by educators to utilize educational resources designed for a dwindling young student population has occasioned a great deal of published work in this area. The Harris Survey (National Council on the Aging, 1981) showed that while only 5 percent of older people had been enrolled in an educational program during the past year, 16 percent of older college graduates had—unquestionably a portent of future increased demand as the older cohort becomes better educated. At the present time, the main conclusion from research in this area has been to validate the principle of continuity, namely, that past experiences of learning are the major determinants of participation in old age (Covey, 1980; Hooper & March, 1978; Knowlton, 1977). A recent state-of-the-art review may be found in Peterson (1981).

Volunteer activity is another endeavor of high interest to professionals and to politicians. The appeal of volunteerism to older people is merely in the process of being tested, during a period when more opportunities for participation have been recently created. In the 1975 time-use study (Hill, 1981) an average of 8 minutes per week per person 65+ was devoted to volunteer work, while at about the same time, 22 percent of older people reported doing *some* volunteer work (National Council on the Aging, 1975). Since that time there has been further growth in national programs; the Foster Grandparents, Retired Senior Volunteer Program, and the Senior Companion Program together counted 321,000 participants in 1981 (Lidoff, Dunbar, & Fogelman, 1981). Despite the growth in opportunities, by 1981 only 23 percent reported participating in volunteer activities (National Council on the Aging, 1981), a growth of just 1 percent since 1974.

## CONCLUSION

This review has portrayed the present disjuncture of research in motivational psychology, leisure, and aging. It has also suggested that the returns may be substantial for pursuing research that integrates all of these streams and in addition utilizes the more substantial body of knowledge already generated from social gerontological approaches to leisure research.

The recent empirical research reviewed for this chapter does relatively little to adumbrate the special meanings and consequences, if any, of participation in particular activities by older people as compared to younger. It seems time to move beyond the strategy of relating crude aggregates of activity types to possible determinants and consequences. What are needed are more in-depth studies of how particular activities are experienced by and fit into the lifestyles and personalities of older people.

Age-specific effects or meanings of activity have been suggested primarily in speculative fashion. Further effort is required both in the search for age-specific knowledge and in the application of existing knowledge to policy issues:

**1.** The lack of a work role for many older people means that satisfaction of some basic needs such as the affirmation of competence must be sought in leisure or in nonwork obligatory activities. A major research issue concerns how such needs are satisfied or frustrated. While national policy has fostered the growth of some opportunities for leisure such as senior activity centers, it has neglected any consideration of how new modes for changing capabilities may be developed.

**2.** Pleasure clearly can be derived from both obligatory and instrumental activities. "Leisure" and other highly valued activity may involve both immediate affective pleasure ("flow" and other forms of high-intensity experience) and enjoyment based on their perceived contributions to the attainment of long-range goals (instrumental functions). We particularly need to understand how the immediate and long-range experiences of activity are related to one another and to overall psychological well-being. Our national programs have tended to be unidimensional and unresponsive to subgroup needs or to changing cohorts of aged.

3. Economic deprivation greatly conditions the types of discretionary activities engaged in by older people. If the range of opportunities is thus narrowed, is older people's micropsychological experience of activities changed also? No evidence has been offered that boredom is greater or that activities are liked less by the aged. However, some elderly must adapt to lower levels of stimulation or to unchanging stimulation and thus experience less pleasure. How do they cope with this situation and what effects do these changes have on overall psychological well-being? Coming generations of older people will very likely have enlarged expectations for meaningful activity. National policy needs to be directed toward encouraging continuity in this respect.

4. The expectations of our society are for greater inactivity and passivity in older people than they see in themselves (National Council on the Aging, 1981). To what extent does this expectation reduce opportunities for older people to have varied uses of time and to "keep in practice" on the "challenge" side of the person–environment model (Figure 4.1)? Not only public policy but the efforts of consumer industry need to be attuned to providing opportunities for challenge.

5. A variety of failures of competence become more frequent with age. How do these intraindividual changes affect the ability of the impaired person to reap competence-affirming benefits and pleasures from participation in particular activities? This need to match competence and activity demand is particularly relevant to activity programming in agencies and institutions. A strong effort to mandate programming for meaningful activity in institutions and planned residences for the aged is necessary.

6. All available knowledge underlines the preeminence of the feeling of personal autonomy in determining the quality of perceived outcome. Deserving of more specific investigation with respect to the activities of older people are the related constructs of personal causation, intrinsic motivation, and perceived locus of control.

# REFERENCES

Altergott, K., & Eustis, N.A. Evaluation of everyday life. Paper presented at the annual meeting of the Gerontological Society, Toronto, November, 1981.

Arling, G. Resistance to isolation among elderly widows. *International Journal of Aging and Human Development*, 1976, *7*, 67–86.

Atchley, R.C. *The social forces in later life*, 2nd ed. Belmont, CA: Wadsworth, 1977.

Atkinson, J.W., & Birch, D. *The dynamics of action*. New York: Wiley, 1970.

Babchuk, N., Peters, G., Hoyt, D.R., & Kaiser, M. The voluntary associations of the aged. *Journal of Gerontology*, 1979, *34*, 579–587.

Beard, J.G., & Ragheb, M.B. Measuring leisure satisfaction. *Journal of Leisure Research*, 1980, *12*, 20–33.

Berlyne, D.E. The vicissitudes of aplopathematic and thelematoscopic pneumatology. In D.E. Berlyne & K.B. Madsen (Eds.), *Pleasure, reward, and preference*. New York: Academic Press, 1977.

Berlyne, D.E. Curiosity and learning. *Motivation and Emotion*, 1978, *2*, 97–175.

Bexton, W.A., Heron, W., & Scott, T.H. Effects of decreased variation in the sensory environment. *Canadian Journal of Psychology*, 1954, *8*, 70–76.

Bishop, D.W., & Witt, P.A. Sources of behavioral variance during leisure time. *Journal of Personality and Social Behavior*, 1970, *16*, 352–360.

Blazer, D., & Palmore, E. Religion and aging in a longitudinal panel. *Gerontologist*, 1976, *16*, 82–85.

Bull, C.N., & Aucoin, J.B. Voluntary association participation and life satisfaction: a replication note. *Journal of Gerontology*, 1975, *30*, 73–76.

Bultena, G., & Wood, V. Leisure orientation and recreational activities of retirement community residents. *Journal of Leisure Research*, 1970, *2*, 3–15.

Bynum, J.E., Cooper, B.L., & Acuff, F.G. Retirement reorientation: Senior adult education. *Journal of Gerontology*, 1978, *33*, 253–261.

Campbell, A., Converse, P.E., & Rodgers, W.L. *The quality of American life: Perceptions, evaluations, and satisfactions*. New York: Russell Sage Foundation, 1976.

Carp, F.M. *A future for the aged*. Austin: University of Texas Press, 1966.

Carp, F.M. Effects of the living environment on activity and the use of time. *International Journal of Aging and Human Development*, 1978–1979, *9*, 75–91.

Cattell, R.B., Eber, H.W., & Tatsuoka, M.M. *Handbook for the Sixteen Personality Factor Questionnaire*. Champaign, IL: Institute for Personality and Ability Testing, 1970.

Clemente, F., Rexroad, P., & Hirsch, C. The participation of the Black aged in voluntary associations. *Journal of Gerontology*, 1975, *30*, 469–472.

Costa, P.T., & McCrae, R.R. Influence of extraversion and neuroticism on subjective well-being: Happy and unhappy people. *Journal of Personality and Social Psychology,* 1980, *38,* 668–678.

Covey, H.C. An exploratory study of the acquisition of a college student role by old people. *Gerontologist,* 1980, *20,* 173–181.

Crandall, R. Motivations for leisure. *Journal of Leisure Research,* 1980, *12,* 45–54.

Crandall, R., & Slivken, K. Leisure attitudes and their measurement. In A.E. Iso-Ahala (Ed.), *Social psychological perspectives on leisure and recreation.* Springfield, IL: Charles C. Thomas, 1980.

Csikszentmihalyi, M. *Beyond boredom and anxiety.* San Francisco: Jossey-Bass, 1975.

Csikszentmihalyi, M., & Graef, R. The experience of freedom in daily life. *American Journal of Community Psychology,* 1980, *8,* 401–414.

Cumming, E., & Henry, W.E. *Growing old: The process of disengagement.* New York: Basic Books, 1961.

Cutler, S.J. Voluntary association participation and life satisfaction: A cautionary research note. *Journal of Gerontology,* 1973, *28,* 96–100.

Cutler, S.J. Membership in different types of voluntary associations and psychological well-being. *Gerontologist,* 1976, *16,* 335–339.

Cutler, S.J. Aging and voluntary association participation. *Journal of Gerontology,* 1977, *32,* 470–479.

Daniel, D.E., Templin, R.G., & Shearon, R.W. The value orientation of older adults toward education. *Educational Gerontology,* 1977, *2,* 33–42.

Davis, R.H. Television communication and the elderly. In D. Woodruff & J.E. Birren (Eds.), *Aging: Scientific perspectives and social issues.* New York: Van Nostrand, 1975.

deCharms, R. *Personal causation.* New York: Academic Press, 1968.

Deci, E.L. *Intrinsic motivation.* New York: Plenum, 1975.

deGrazia, S. *Of time, work, and leisure.* New York: Twentieth Century Fund, 1962.

Donald, M.N., & Havighurst, R.J. The meanings of leisure. *Social Forces,* 1959, *37,* 355–360.

Dumazedier, J. *Sociology of leisure.* New York: Elsevier, 1974.

Eisdorfer, C., Nowlin, J., & Wilkie F. Improvement of learning in the aged by modification of autonomic nervous system activity. *Science,* 1970, *170,* 1327–1329.

Elder, G. *Children of the great depression.* Chicago: University of Chicago Press, 1974.

Eysenck, H.J. Personality and the law of effect. In D.E. Berlyne & K.B. Madsen (Eds.), *Pleasure, reward, and punishment.* New York: Academic Press, 1973.

Felton, B.J., Moss, M.L., & Sepulveda, R.J. Two-way television: An experiment in interactive programming for the elderly. *Experimental Aging Research,* 1980, *6,* 29–45.

Fiske, D.W., & Maddi, S.R. (Eds.). *Functions of varied experience.* Homewood, IL: Dorsey, 1961.

George, L.K. The impact of personality and social status factors upon levels of activity and psychological well-being. *Journal of Gerontology,* 1978, *33,* 840–847.

Giambra, L.M. Daydreaming across the life span: Late adolescent to senior citizen. *Aging and Human Development,* 1974, *5,* 115–140.

Glass, D.C., & Singer, J.E. *Urban stress: Experiments in noise.* New York: Academic Press, 1972.

Gordon, C., & Gaitz, C.M. Leisure and lives: Personal expressivity across the life span. In R.H. Binstock & E. Shanas (Eds.), *Handbook of aging and the social sciences.* New York: Van Nostrand Reinhold, 1976.

Gordon, C., Gaitz, C.M., & Scott, J. Value priorities and leisure activities among middle-aged and older Anglos. *Diseases of the Nervous System,* 1973, *34,* 13–26.

Gudykunst, W.B., Morra, J.A., Kantor, W.I., & Parker, H.A. Dimensions of leisure activities: A factor-analytic study in New England. *Journal of Leisure Research,* 1981, *13,* 28–42.

Havighurst, R.J. The nature and values of meaningful free-time activity. In R.W. Kleemeier (Ed.), *Aging and leisure.* New York: Oxford, 1961.

Havighurst, R.J., & Feigenbaum, K. Leisure and lifestyle. *American Journal of Sociology,* 1959, *63,* 152–162.

Helson, H. *Adaptation level theory.* New York: Harper & Row, 1964.

Herzog, A.R., & Rodgers, W.L. Age and satisfaction: Data from several large surveys. *Research on Aging,* 1981, *3,* 142–165.

Hiemstra, R. Continuing education for the aged: A survey of the needs and interests of older people. *Adult Education,* 1972, *22,* 100–109.

Hiemstra, R. Older adult learning: Instrumental and expressive categories. *Educational Gerontology,* 1976, *1,* 227–236.

Hill, M.S. Patterns of time use. In F.T. Juster & F.P. Stafford (Eds.), *Essays in the use of time in American households.* Draft reports of work in progress, Institute for Social Research. University of Michigan, 1981.

Hooper, J.O., & March, G.B. A study of older students attending university classes. *Educational Gerontology,* 1978, *3,* 321–330.

Iso-Ahola, S.E. (Ed.). *Social psychological perspectives on leisure and recreation.* Springfield, IL: Charles C. Thomas, 1980.

Jarvik, L.F., & Russell, D. Anxiety, aging, and the third emergency reaction. *Journal of Gerontology,* 1979, *34,* 197–200.

Kabanoff, B. Work and nonwork: A review of models, methods, and findings. *Psychological Bulletin,* 1980, *88,* 60–77.

Kaplan, M. *Leisure: Theory and policy.* New York: John Wiley, 1975.

Kaplan, M. *Leisure: Lifestyle and lifespan.* Philadelphia: W.B. Saunders, 1979.

Kelly, J.R. Work and leisure: A simplified paradigm. *Journal of Leisure Research,* 1972, *4,* 50–62.

Kelly, J.R. Leisure socialization: Replication and extension. *Journal of Leisure Research,* 1977, *9,* 121–132.

Kleemeier, R.W. (Ed.). *Aging and leisure.* New York: Oxford, 1961.

Kleiber, D.A., & Kelly, J.R. Leisure, socialization, and the life cycle. In S.E. Iso-Ahola (Ed.), *Social psychological perspectives on leisure and recreation.* Springfield, IL: Charles C. Thomas, 1980.

Knowlton, M.P. Liberal arts: The Elder Hostel plan for survival. *Educational Gerontology,* 1977, *2,* 87–93.

Kreps, J.M. Economics of retirement. In E.W. Busse & E. Pfeiffer (Eds.), *Behavior and adaptation in later life.* Boston: Little, Brown, 1977.

Kubey, R.W. Television and aging: Past, present, and future. *Gerontologist,* 1980, *20,* 16–35.

Langer, E., & Rodin, J. The effects of choice and enhanced personal responsibility for the aged. *Journal of Personality and Social Psychology,* 1976, *34,* 191–198.

Larson, R. Thirty years of research on the subjective wellbeing of older Americans. *Journal of Gerontology,* 1978, *33,* 109–125.

Lawton, M.P. Assessing the competence of older people. In D. Kent, R. Kastenbaum, & S. Sherwood (Eds.), *Research, planning and action for the elderly.* New York: Behavioral Publications, 1972.

Lawton, M.P. The human being and the institutional building. In J. Lang, C. Burnette, W. Moleski, & D. Vachon (Eds.), *Designing for human behavior.* Stroudsburg, PA: Dowden, Hutchinson, & Ross, 1974.

Lawton, M.P. Leisure activities for the aged. *The Annals,* 1978, *438,* 71–80.

Lawton, M.P. Competence, environmental press, and the adaptation of older people. In M.P. Lawton, P.G. Windley, & T.O. Byerts (Eds.), *Aging and the environment: Theoretical approaches.* New York: Springer, 1982a.

Lawton, M.P. Time, space, and activity. In G. Rowles & R.J. Ohta (Eds.), *Aging and milieu.* New York: Academic Press, 1982b.

Lawton, M.P., & Cohen, J. The generality of housing impact on the well-being of older people. *Journal of Gerontology,* 1974, *29,* 194–204.

Lawton, M.P., Moss, M., & Fulcomer, M.E. Objective and subjective uses of time by older people. *International Journal of Aging and Human Development,* in press.

Lawton, M.P., & Nahemow, L. Ecology and the aging process. In C. Eisdorfer & M.P. Lawton (Eds.), *Psychology of adult development and aging.* Washington, D.C.: American Psychological Association, 1973.

Lawton, M.P., & Nahemow, L. Social areas and the well-being of tenants in planned housing for the elderly. *Multivariate Behavioral Research,* 1979, *14,* 463–484.

Lawton, M.P., Nahemow, L., & Yeh, T.-M. Neighborhood environment and the wellbeing of older tenants in planned housing. *International Journal of Aging and Human Development,* 1980, *11,* 211–227.

Liang, J., Dvorkin, L., Kahana, E., & Mazian, F. Social integration and morale: A reexamination. *Journal of Gerontology,* 1980, *35,* 746–757.

Lidoff, L.S., Dunbar, M.E., & Fogelman, C.J. Long term care and voluntarism. Washington, DC: Action, 1981.

Markides, K.S., & Martin, H.W. A causal model of life satisfaction among the elderly. *Journal of Gerontology*, 1979, *34*, 86–93.

McKechnie, G.E. The psychological structure of leisure: Past behavior. *Journal of Leisure Research*, 1974, *6*, 27–45.

Mehrabian, A. Individual differences in stimulus screening and arousability. *Journal of Personality*, 1977, *45*, 237–250.

Mehrabian, A., & Russell, J.A. *An approach to environmental psychology.* Cambridge, MA: MIT Press, 1974.

Meyersohn, R. Leisure. In A. Campbell & P.E. Converse (Eds.), *The human meaning of social change.* New York: Russell Sage Foundation, 1972.

Moss, M., & Lawton, M.P. Use of time in different types of households. Paper presented at the annual meeting of the Gerontological Society, San Diego, CA, November, 1980.

National Council on the Aging. *The myth and reality of aging in America.* Washington, DC: National Council on the Aging, 1975.

National Council on the Aging. *Aging in the eighties: America in transition.* Washington, DC: National Council on the Aging, 1981.

Neulinger, J. *The psychology of leisure.* Springfield, IL: Charles C. Thomas, 1974.

Nuttin, J.R. Pleasure and reward in human motivation and learning. In D.E. Berlyne & K.B. Madsen (Eds.), *Pleasure, reward and preference.* New York: Academic Press, 1973.

Oliver, D.B. Career and leisure patterns of middle aged metropolitan out-migrants. *Gerontologist*, 1971, *11*, 13–20.

Palmore, E. *Social patterns in normal aging: Findings from the Duke Longitudinal Study.* Durham, NC: Duke University Press, 1981.

Peppers, L.G. Patterns of leisure and adjustment to retirement. *Gerontologist*, 1977, *16*, 441–446.

Peterson, D.A. Participation in education by older people. *Educational Gerontology*, 1981, *7*, 245–256.

Pierce, R.C. Dimensions of leisure. I: Satisfactions. *Journal of Leisure Research*, 1980a, *12*, 5–19.

Pierce, R.C. Dimensions of leisure. II: Descriptions. *Journal of Leisure Research*, 1980b, *12*, 150–163.

Pierce, R.C. Dimensions of leisure. III: Characteristics. *Journal of Leisure Research*, 1980c, *12*, 273–284.

Reichard, S., Livson, F., & Petersen, P.G. *Aging and personality.* New York: Wiley, 1962.

Reid, D.W., & Ziegler, M. Longitudinal studies of desired control and adjustment among the elderly. Paper presented at the annual meeting of the Gerontological Society, Toronto, November, 1981.

Ritchie, J.R. On the derivation of leisure activity types—a perceptual mapping approach. *Journal of Leisure Research*, 1975, *7*, 128–140.

Robertson, J.F. Activity preferences of community-residing aging as a guide for practical emphases. *Journal of Gerontological Social Work*, 1978, *1*, 95–109.

Rotter, J.B. Generalized expectancies for internal versus external control of reinforcement. *Psychological Monographs*, 1966, *80* (1, Whole No. 609).

Rowe, A.R. Scientists in retirement. *Journal of Gerontology*, 1973, *28*, 345–350.

Rowe, A.R. Retired academics and research activity. *Journal of Gerontology*, 1976, *31*, 456–461.

Rowles, G.D. *Prisoners of space? Exploring the geographical experience of older people*. Boulder, CO: Westview Press, 1978.

Sauer, W. Morale of the urban aged: A regression analysis by race. *Journal of Gerontology*, 1977, *32*, 600–608.

Schmitz-Scherzer, R. Longitudinal change in leisure behavior of the elderly. *Contributions to Human Development*, 1976, *3*, 127–136.

Schulz, R. Effects of control and predictability on the physical and psychological well-being of the institutionalized aged. *Journal of Personality and Social Psychology*, 1976, *33*, 563–573.

Seligman, M.E.P. *Helplessness: On depression, development, and death*. San Francisco: Freeman, 1975.

Shmavonian, B.M., & Busse, E.W. The utilization of psychophysiological techniques in the study of the aged. In R.H. Williams, C. Tibbitts, & W. Donahue (Eds.), *Processes of aging: Social and psychological perspectives*. New York: Atherton, 1963.

Snow, R.B., & Havighurst, R.J. Life style types and patterns of retirement of educators. *Gerontologist*, 1977, *17*, 545–552.

Tinsley, H.E., Barrett, T.C., & Kass, R.A. Leisure activities and need satisfaction. *Journal of Leisure Research*, 1977, *8*, 110–120.

Tinsley, H.E.A., & Kass, R.A. Leisure activities and need satisfaction: A replication and extension. *Journal of Leisure Research*, 1978, *10*, 191–202.

Toseland, R., & Rasch, J. Factors contributing to older persons' satisfaction with their communities. *Gerontologist*, 1978, *18*, 395–402.

Trela, J.E., & Jackson, D.J. Family life and community participation in old age. *Research on Aging*, 1979, *1*, 233–251.

Troll, L.E. *Continuations: Adult development and aging*. Monterey, CA: Brooks/Cole, 1982.

Walker, E.L. Psychological complexity as a basis for a theory of motivation and choice. *Nebraska Symposium on Motivation*, 1964, *13*, 47–95.

Walker, E.L. Psychological complexity and preference: A hedgehog theory of behavior. In D.E. Berlyne & K.B. Madsen (Eds.), *Pleasure, reward, and preference*. New York: Academic Press, 1973.

Ward, R.A. *The aging experience*. New York: J.B. Lippincott, 1979a.

Ward, R.A. The meaning of voluntary association participation to older people. *Journal of Gerontology*, 1979b, *34*, 438–445.

Wigdor, B.T. Drives and motivations with aging. In J.E. Birren & R.B.

Sloane (Eds.), *Handbook of mental health and aging.* New York: Prentice-Hall, 1980.

Wilson, J. Sociology of leisure. *Annual Review of Sociology,* 1980, *6,* 21–40.

Wohlwill, J.F. The physical environment: A problem for a psychology of stimulation. *Journal of Social Issues,* 1966, *22,* 29–38.

Zajonc, R.B. Attitudinal effects of mere exposure. *Journal of Personality and Social Psychology.* Monograph supplement, 1968, *9* (Whole No. 2).

Zuckerman, M., & Link, K. Construct validity for the sensation-seeking scale. *Journal of Consulting and Clinical Psychology,* 1968, *32,* 420–426.

## CHAPTER 5

# The Elderly Who Live Alone and Their Social Supports

ROBERT L. RUBINSTEIN, PH. D.
PHILADELPHIA GERIATRIC CENTER
PHILADELPHIA, PENNSYLVANIA

In 1980, more than seven million elderly Americans, some 30 percent of the population of older Americans, lived alone (U.S. Senate, 1982). This percentage is part of a decades-long series of population trends which have seen increases in the absolute number of elderly, in overall longevity, and in the percentage of elderly who live alone (Belcher, 1967; Chevan & Korson, 1972; Glick, 1979; Siegel, 1980). As is well known, six out of every ten older Americans are women and the ratio of women to men increases with age over 65. Not surprisingly, then, the trend toward living alone especially concerns women. In 1960, only about 25 percent of older women lived alone, while by 1980 this figure was about 40 percent. (In 1960, 12 percent of older men lived alone; in 1980, 15 percent.) These patterns are also age stratified. For example, in 1980, about 35 percent of women aged 65–74 and more than 50 percent of women aged 75 and older lived alone.

Living alone is a desired lifestyle for many older persons, offering highly valued independence and a sense of control over one's own affairs. But by its very nature, living alone can make certain demands of individuals or bring about conditions not part of other lifestyles. Among these are the greater possibility of isolation and loneliness; some degree of physical distance in relationships; and the need to develop and implement rules, structures, and routines which one must enforce by oneself.

When a person is vigorous and healthy, the independence gained through living alone may be viewed by an individual as generally beneficial and desirable. At the onset of a variety of deleterious conditions sometimes associated with or occurring in old age, the independence of living alone can be problematic; and, further, such independence may be impossible if conditions worsen. At all points along this continuum of independence, the presence of social supports is necessary for most individuals so that they may live their lives as they wish. By social supports we mean here the giving and receiving (Lopata, 1975) of any of the possible range of human contacts, interactions, or services, whether instrumental, expressive, or multidimensional in nature. This process enables older individuals to maintain themselves, despite change, so that needs of various kinds are met and, further, so that their sense of self and meaning in the world can endure.

In examining living alone in old age as a specific phenomenon, we can distinguish three areas in which the gerontological and other literature may be grouped. The first focal area concerns those factors antecedent to living alone in old age such as fertility, gender, marital status, and the ethnic and cultural values which give further meaning for living alone. A predominant form of antecedent state is the elderly marital dyad, the death of one member of which leads to living alone for the survivor. This chapter argues that one rationale for living alone is the desire on the part of older people for the benefits of continued independence, as variously defined.

The second focal area encompasses social correlates to living alone in old age, those events and experiences that are part of living alone. Such correlates have been generally examined from the perspective of social support in old age. They may also be examined from either a general perspective without regard to specific events or from an event-specific perspective (for example, after events such as spousal loss or illness). While the differential effects of various post-loss living arrangements have not been of central importance to the study of event-related phenomena such as bereavement, living arrangements have had an implicit role in the study of ongoing social support. While such support is recognized to be a positive contribution to living alone in late life, we know very little about the daily experiences of living alone in old age.

The third focal area concerns the life satisfaction outcomes of living alone in old age. Two possible paths to these outcomes may be ascertained. The first concerns the direct effects of various antecedent factors on the psychological well-being of older persons who live alone. The interpretation of such direct effects is hampered by the confounding, indirect, and interactive effects of bereavement, marital status, gender, and other factors previously mentioned. The second path leads from such antecedent factors to the well-being of those living alone, as mediated by social relations and social support.

In addition, each of these three focal areas, antecedents, correlates, and outcomes, relates to a particular theme which will be in evidence throughout this review. The first theme, concerning antecedent factors, is that the desire for independence is an important subjective contributing element to living alone. The second theme, concerning the correlates to living alone, is that the quality of social support is crucial for the successful maintenance of living alone. The third theme concerning outcomes associated with living alone is that it appears to represent a mixed blessing for older persons. While this style of living is associated with such positive elements as independence and with fewer functional disabilities, this living arrangement is also associated with such negative outcomes as lower income, a greater structural potential for isolation, and diminished housing quality. As each dimension and theme is discussed, difficulty will be experienced in separating out specific factors which contribute to the well-being of those elderly who do live alone.

This chapter then will be organized around these three dimensions—antecedents, correlates, and outcomes—and their associated themes, each of which will be treated separately below. However, we will begin by providing some basic information about older people who live alone, in the areas of demography, income, housing, and health.

## BACKGROUND

### Demography

About 95 percent of the 22.5 million older persons counted in 1980 have married once, and only a small percentage of these individuals have been divorced (U.S. Senate, 1982). Remarriage in late life after the death of a spouse is relatively infrequent for both the divorced and the widowed (only 5 percent of the women widowed after the age of 55 and 25 percent of the men widowed after the age of 65 ever remarry (Cleveland & Gianturco, 1976). While the majority of older persons living alone are widows, there is a small but significant number of older widowers living alone. Besides the widowed and the separated/divorced, the remainder of the population of elderly living alone may be found among the approximately 5 percent of the elderly population which has never married (U.S. Senate, 1982). Marital sta-

tus influences living arrangements, but there is no one-to-one correspondence between the two. About 65 percent of widowed elderly—
or about 5.5 million persons—live alone. About 15 percent of widowed elderly head a family while an additional 15 percent are non-
heads, in a family. About 5 percent live with non-relatives (Lawton,
1981, p. 60).

The separated and divorced make up about 5 percent of the total
population of elderly. Of these about 60 percent of separated and 66
percent of divorced elderly live alone. About 14 percent of the divorced elderly are heads of families, some 16 percent are non-heads,
living in a family, and about 5 percent live with an unrelated person
(Lawton, 1981, p. 60).

Fifty-six percent of elderly men and 51 percent of elderly women
who have never married live alone. These are the smallest percentages
living alone of any of the not-married statuses. Of the never married
elderly, about 11 percent live with a nonrelative, 21 percent of men
and 24 percent of women live as non-heads in a family, and 11 percent
of men and 15 percent of women are heads of a family (Lawton, 1981,
p. 60).

## Income

The median family income in 1980 for older, nonmarried women
was about $4,630, less than that of nonmarried men ($5,570) and
considerably less than that of married couples ($12,020; Grad,
1983). Widowed women had the lowest median income for older
marital status groups ($4,620), as compared with separated/divorced
women ($4,680), never-married men ($4,830), never-married women
($5,340), separated/divorced men ($5,590), and widowers ($5,800),
who have the highest median income (about 125 percent of the
median income of elderly widows; Grad, 1983, p. 21). Of interest
here is the very vulnerable financial position of older widows living
alone. We can also imagine that the elderly who live alone are
much less likely to receive the many bonuses, in the form of entertainment, transportation, and the like, which might be available to
them if they resided in a household, such as that of a child, in
which the aggregate income might be considerably higher. On the
subjective side, Fengler, Danigelis, and Little (1983) found that widows living alone were more likely than married women or those
living with others to feel that the money they did have did not take
care of their needs well.

## Housing

Lawton (1981) has described some of the housing consequences of living arrangements for the elderly. He found that housing occupied by older persons who live alone tends to be of poorer quality. He also found that housing occupied by not-presently-married elderly men is of worse quality than that occupied by not-presently-married older women, a "paradoxical" finding given men's generally greater income and their socially accepted role as housing maintainers. Fundamental gender patterning and cohort experiences probably influence housing maintenance behaviors. Such findings demand further inquiry to understand their dynamics.

## Health

The relationship between health status and the ability to live alone is important. Table 5.1 presents data (from 1974) on health status and living arrangements of persons age 65 and older.

These data highlight the need for social supports for those elderly living alone. The majority (about 65 percent) have slight or no limits to activity, but the remainder have limitations in a major activity due to

**Table 5.1**
Percent Distribution of Persons by Activity Limitation due to Chronic Conditions, According to Living Arrangements, Age 65 and Older, United States, 1974[a].

|  | With No Limitations in Activity | Limited, but not in Major Activity | Limited in Amount or Kind of Major Activity | Unable to Carry on Major Activity |
|---|---|---|---|---|
| All living arrangements | 54.1 | 6.6 | 22.1 | 17.1 |
| Living alone | 54.9 | 9.3 | 26.2 | 9.6 |
| Living with spouse | 56.4 | 5.5 | 19.3 | 18.8 |
| Living with relatives/ other | 47.1 | 5.8 | 24.5 | 22.7 |

[a]*Note:* Although Feller (1981, 1983) updates these figures, they are not disaggregated by living arrangements.
*Source:* From Wilder (1977), Table 24.

chronic conditions. The proportions of elderly living alone who have relatively few or no limitations in activity are slightly higher than elderly in other living arrangements; conversely, the proportion of elderly living alone who are unable to carry on a major activity is significantly less than that of the elderly in other living arrangements. That is to say, while living alone is roughly correlated with better health, there are many elderly with severe limitations who have no other residential option than to live alone or who choose to retain their autonomy and "tough it out." Since the institutional residence rate is highest for socially nonaffiliated elderly, this suggests that a housemate functions to delay the institutionalization of marginally healthy persons. Tissue and McCoy (1981) have described living alone as a "luxury" for those elderly who can "meet the physical demands of independence" (cf. Tissue, 1979).

## ANTECEDENTS OF LIVING ALONE

Our focus in this section is the various factors antecedent to living alone, such as fertility, gender, marital status, ethnic and cultural values, and other pressures toward or away from forming independent households. Older persons' decisions to live alone are shaped by the structural possibilities engendered by a particular sociocultural system, by economic constraints, by culturally located values, by the long-term implications of fertility, and by individual predilection. Many older people live alone because they can—it is economically and socially feasible—and they want to; others because they can and they have no one to live with. Indeed, the trend toward living alone is not just confined to the elderly, but is occurring with increased frequency among many adult age groups (Kobrin, 1976; Michael, Fuchs, & Scott, 1980; Pampel, 1983).

### Fertility

Thomas and Wister (1984) in a study of Canadian elderly, found that fertility, along with ethnicity, is the major determinant of whether or not older women live alone, living alone being less frequent as the number of children increases. Previously, Kobrin (1976) had suggested that an increase in the number of one-woman households was in part due to a decline in the number of adult daughters. Given the degree of reliance by older persons on children, particularly on daughters, any drop in the number of daughters per older individual will decrease the number of potential available coresidential households.

## Gender

Since women tend to live longer than men, gender per se is an important antecedent to living alone in old age. Many older women prefer to live alone in their own households, given the great value placed on independence, given the relative lack of unattached men, and given the cultural perception that the household is structurally arranged around the marital unit and its transformations. Berardo (1968, 1970), in writing about gender differences specifically among the widowed, suggested that problems of widowers were more severe than those of widows and that there were fundamental differences in their social supports. While the empirical nature of these differences and their effects are being debated in the gerontological literature (see below), they arise from a culturally based system of gender-meaning which organizes the various functions of men and women, possibly engendering differential coping skills.

## Marital Status

Because most elderly couples live without others in the household, spousal loss is most often followed by living alone. Bowling and Cartwright (1982) found that 78 percent of a sample of 361 elderly surviving spouses were living alone when they were interviewed about six months after the death of a spouse. About a third of these found living alone "very difficult" to accept and an additional third found it "fairly difficult" to accept.

Upon the death of a spouse, solitude may be mitigated for a time as friends and relatives come to visit (Heinemann, 1983), but eventually, as the most intense grief lessens, the surviving spouse continues on alone. Unfortunately, research on the social supports of older persons from the time immediately following and up to one year after the death of a spouse has rarely made reference to living arrangements. Bowlby (1980, pp. 187–189) reviewed the limited literature on the effects of spousal bereavement by living arrangement and asserted that those who live alone fare worse. In her study of Chicago-area widows of all ages, Lopata (1979) noted that it is "surprising in view of the women's backgrounds . . . that so many are able to live alone, once they become widows" (p. 37). Yet she offers no analysis of the role of living alone at any age for these women.

Concerning the never-married, Spreitzer and Riley (1974) analyzed factors associated with singlehood and found differences between never-married men and women. Women show higher educational and occupational levels, while poor relationships with parents and siblings "predispose" males to lifelong singlehood (p. 541). Poor family relationships for these men do not bode well for the maintenance of family-based social networks, nor does the childlessness of never-married older persons in general, since children quite often act in important support positions.

There is almost no literature on the living arrangements of the divorced elderly (Hennon, 1983). Uhlenberg and Myers (1981) have examined some of the population trend data concerning divorce among the elderly and noted that only 1 percent of the divorces in 1975 were to persons age 65 and older, but they expect this to rise substantially in the future. They note that divorce in old age "will frequently disrupt family and kinship ties which form critical links in the support system" (p. 280), but they present no data on divorce and living alone.

**Ethnic and Cultural Values**

Many elderly prefer to maintain their own households rather than live with family members (Troll, 1971). The prospect of sharing a household may involve fears of intergenerational conflict, the loss of independence (Lopata, 1971), or an increase in the experience of what are considered excessive demands or decreased privacy (Hughes & Gove, 1981). Of equal significance are the positive values attached to maintaining one's own household, such as independence (Kerckhoff, 1966), mastery, control, familiarity (Rowles, 1978), and the expression of self-identity.

Living alone, for many elderly, is the last or next-to-last household stage in the life cycle and can represent an expression of the pervasive sense of self-reliance and individualism which are major themes in American culture. Like all individually undertaken projects, living alone may be a gamble for older individuals in that whatever is gained must be measured against the structurally induced possibility of isolation. Hughes and Gove (1981, p. 69) speculate about whether people who live alone compensate for their relative isolation by developing

especially rewarding behaviors. Clark's (1972) analysis of the concept
of dependency in old age in the United States provides an informative
framework within which to examine living alone. In American culture,
dependence is negatively valued. She notes that independence or lack
of dependency is a frequent criterion of self-esteem among the elderly,
and she cites the fear of dependency as a central concern of old age.
Independence may be the most important advantage to living alone,
one which compensates for any number of disadvantages.

Closely related to the desire for independence and autonomy is
the desire to "not be a burden." In my own work with older men living
alone (Rubinstein, in press), I have found this to be the most consistently voiced statement which expressed the "bottom line" of living
alone: maintaining one's own household means that one is not a
burden to children or to others. The idea that one should not be a
burden can involve complex and emotional arrangements with family
over what will and will not be provided. For some, there is an unstated
fear that the family will only go through the motions of caring (Francis,
1984); staying independent puts off the day of discovering whether
such fears are true. The processes by which family members anticipate
that they will provide care or services to an infirm elder who lives
alone are worthy of detailed investigation. How arrangements are set
up or put off, the value of potential support, the anxiety over its costs
or possible denial all constitute aspects of independence.

The meaning of living alone may vary on the basis of marital
status, gender, ethnicity, or other categories. For example, as Braito
and Anderson (1983) comment, "freedom is an important word to the
ever-single [i.e., never-married] elderly woman" (p. 202). Some
studies have examined aspects of living arrangements by ethnicity.
Thomas and Wister (1984), in an analysis of the residential patterns of
some 7,000 older widowed and divorced women, found that while
fertility was the major determinant of whether or not older women
lived alone, ethnicity was the second major factor. In contrasting British, French, Jewish, and Italian subsamples, they found significantly
more coresidence by members of older generations among the French
and Italians, in comparison to the British and Jewish, an effect they
attribute to differences in "cultural or normative structures, as measured by ethnicity" (p. 302). Manuel and Reid (1982) reported on the
family status of elderly by ethnicity (Black/White/Hispanic), noting
that for elderly who live alone or with nonrelatives, the proportion of
Black men aged 65 to 74 so residing was higher than that of White
men, while the percentage of Black and Hispanic women aged 75 and
older in such a living arrangement was significantly lower than that of

comparable White women. These differences no doubt variously reflect gross health differences, economic and social distinctions, as well as cultural values. Johnson (1983), in an account of cross-generational ties in Italian-American families, noted that sharing a household with a child was not a highly valued option among her sample of elderly; some 78 percent of those who were not living with offspring said they would not want to consider this possibility. Rather, maintaining one's own household in relative proximity to that of a child was considered an "ideal situation." Johnson considers this solution a compromise between traditional cultural values and the value placed on independence in America. Cohler (1982), too, has emphasized the mix of transgenerational closeness and the possible strain-in-closeness within multigenerational Euro-American ethnic families.

We have concentrated our discussion of antecedents on cultural and ethnic values which influence living alone in late life. Such emphasis is appropriate because the maintenance of independent households is the behavioral outcome of a strongly felt antecedent ethos modified within particular ethnic groups. The value placed on independence is one reason why older persons might want to maintain independent households in the first place; such a high value on independence has its basis in a particular cultural system and is clearly not universal (cf. Goldstein, Schuler, & Ross, 1983). The other antecedents to living alone, such as fertility, gender, and prior marital status, modify the workings out of this ethos in ways that are not yet clear.

## THE SOCIAL CORRELATES
## TO LIVING ALONE

By correlates to living alone, we mean those events and processes which occur at the same time as one is living alone. One important correlate is social support. The quality of social support is crucial for the maintenance of an effective and satisfying lifestyle while living alone. More generally, the system of support, which generally includes family, friends, and neighbors, is a major factor contributing to the well-being of older persons (Cantor, 1980; Lowenthal & Robinson, 1976; Wentowski, 1981). Support is implicit in living arrangements. Generally, those who coreside have built-in support. While we do, in fact, know a good deal about social support in old age, sadly, we know little about the daily experiences of older persons who live alone, and their meanings.

Generally, studies of correlates to living alone in old age have proceeded from two perspectives. The first perspective is the event-oriented study, which includes support surrounding and following such dramatic events as bereavement and illness. Within this type of study, researchers have looked at support at a single point during the larger event, at several points, or more or less continuously during a relatively longer period (one to two years) of adjustment to the event. The second perspective is the study of social support without reference to any event, the more typical study of social support in old age. Unfortunately, there appear to be no studies over a long period of time that attempt to track responses to ongoing events the subjects are experiencing (e.g., a study of how a support system expands, contracts, and changes over time and how these changes are related to life events).

**Social Correlates to Living Alone:**
**Theoretical Background**

In our discussion of correlates to living alone, we will examine the social networks and supports of elderly living alone. The discussion will begin by considering some differences in perspectives used to study older persons who live alone.

One may discern two views in the study of social support and social relations in old age. The first, rather more standard in gerontological research, enquires generally about which specific family members, friends, and neighbors a subject views as important or who contribute to social support. This perspective looks primarily for positive aspects of social relations. The other approach, more characteristic of a social network perspective to social relations, seeks out domains of social interaction beyond the family, friends, and neighbors triad. The network approach does not necessarily assume that relations are entirely supportive, but rather that these qualities and functions remain to be specified. This latter approach may be more useful in understanding the elderly in nonstandard situations. From the friends, family, and neighbors point of view, support relations are rather exclusive. Almost everyone comes with relatives; neighbors are a function of our living circumstances; friends or close friends may be a rather restricted collection of all the people we know, and their definition in an interview situation may be dependent on "middle-class" notions of friendship.

Generally, asking about friends, family, and neighbors and their respective support functions enables us to learn a good deal about the social support of the elderly. But consider the following case: an older man living alone in a small center city apartment. He has few close relatives (20 percent of persons age 65 and older have no living children; Johnson & Catalano, 1981); he does not know his neighbors very well; and his definition of close friendship does not categorize his current acquaintances. Yet this man might have a large number of other social contacts, many supportive in a variety of senses; these would not be picked up by restricting questions to friends, family, and neighbors. Clearly, a social network approach, for example, mapping the domains of people with whom this man habitually interacts or those he usually sees at least once a week, would more accurately portray his social world. Thus there is a restricted view of social relations which concentrates on specific domains of friends, family, and neighbors. There is also a less restricted view, often accessed through network techniques, which includes these domains as well as others and which may best help us understand social relations in a variety of nonstandard communities in which the elderly live. Wellman (1981) has noted that viewing social support through the medium of social network analysis "opens up the consideration of supportive ties anywhere in an individual's social network and does not assume that social support is available only from corporate groups . . . or specified social categories (e.g., kin)" (p. 173). A social network may be thought of as "persons who are important to me in some way" or "persons with whom I habitually interact."

This network perspective has three other advantages compared to the more limited perspective of the supportive aspects of family, friends, and neighbors. First, we are able to see clearly ties of both a supportive and nonsupportive nature. As Wellman (1981, p. 172) has also noted, there is a problem in assuming that a certain set of ties constitutes a "support system" in advance of our knowledge of the precise nature of such ties; if one looks only for supportive ties, one will find just those. Human relations are, in fact, complex and multidimensional. Second, such an approach may enable us to learn more about what might be supportive in everyday experiences. The greater the need for support on the part of the older person, the more events and interactions may be defined specifically in terms of their supportive nature. For example, a common interaction such as going to the neighborhood market and chatting with the sales clerk, once viewed matter-of-factly when a person was in good health, may in ill-health be competence-affirming and therefore a supportive kind of interaction. Third, within the social network approach, a successful individual is viewed as a virtuoso who can "operate," "manage," or "mobilize" her network (Ross, 1983; Rubinstein, 1984). Connections of all sorts are purposeful and may aid an individual in achieving personal goals and plans.

These issues have four important implications for the study of older persons who live alone. First, they help to map accurately domains and features of social interaction. For example, Sokolovsky and Cohen (1981; Sokolovsky, 1980), in a study of older single-room-occupancy (SRO) residents, found it useful to divide social network linkages into six "fields" of interaction (tenant–tenant, tenant–nontenant, tenant–kin, tenant–manager, tenant–public agency, tenant–social institution) which accurately portrayed patterns of habitual interactions. Moreover, use of such techniques were prominent in their reassessing the social isolation said to be experienced by SRO elderly who live alone. They found, in opposition to the popular image of these persons as fully isolated and always alone, a surprising amount of social interaction.

Second, this approach allows for an interest in the actual or potential negative aspects of relationships, which may in fact be a certain reality for some older persons living alone. Having avoided coresidence with family and others, they may find something of greater value in the diffuse set of contacts characteristic of daily living. Third, such techniques may more accurately assess social relations and support from the full range of social settings in which the elder participates. Finally, this view of the individual as virtuoso may in fact better enable us to focus on the day-to-day activities of the older person, about which we really know very little.

**Social Correlates to Living Alone:**
**Social Relations without**
**Reference to Any Event**

Most measures of social relations and support of the elderly have been made without sensitivity to the specific events which have occurred prior to the measurement and which might have affected the array of supportive persons mentioned in an interview. Unfortunately, we do not have as much information as we might need specifically on family, friends, and neighbors in relation to older persons who live alone. We shall thus rely here on general discussions of these domains to extrapolate about older persons who live alone.

*Children and Other Family.*   By far the greatest amount of research has been on family interaction and support. Shanas (1979) suggested that elderly in need of care or help turn first to family, then to friends, then to neighbors. Family aid will be modified by residential proximity (Leigh, 1982). "The family," often conceptualized as a unitary concept, has been shown to be otherwise in terms of the support it renders: it is made up of a central supporting cast of primary kin, including a spouse, if living, and children, with other relatives more peripheral (Babchuk, 1978; Gottlieb, 1979). Lopata (1978) notes the high frequency with which children are mentioned and the very low frequency with which extended family relatives (siblings, cousins, nieces, nephews, and grandchildren) are listed in widows' support networks. On the other hand, Anderson (1984) found that siblings and other extended kin continue to be important to the widow. Other recent studies (Cicirelli, 1983; Lang & Brody, 1983; Quinn, 1983; Stoller, 1983; Walker & Thompson, 1983) have shown the fundamental importance of adult children and children-in-law in the support systems of elders. A recent study of older persons living alone conducted at the Philadelphia Geriatric Center examined the social supports and relations of elderly widows, widowers, and never-married men and women living alone. Thirty of 33 widowers and 30 of 35 widows living alone who had children listed all their children as among those they felt the closest to. In contrast, never-married older men and women tended to list siblings, nieces, and nephews as among their closest relatives (unpublished data).

*Friends.*    Recent studies have also considered friends as a source of important social support for the elderly. Arling (1976), for example, assessed the differential impact that friendship and neighbor and family involvement had on elderly widows and their morale. He found that family contact, especially contact with children, did little to improve the morale of his sample of widows, while friendship was associated with well-being. Wood and Robertson's (1978) data demonstrated the significance of friends, in contrast to grandchildren, for the morale of the elderly. The specialness and nuances of the friend relationship have also been explored by Matthews (1983), who suggested that whether an individual views friends as irreplaceable individuals or replaceable relationships will influence the form of friend relations in old age. Cohen and Rajkowski (1982) were concerned with definitions of friendship in an SRO sample; among SRO residents, most of whom live alone, the concept of friendship was viewed as centering around both material and nonmaterial aspects of social relationships. In New York, Cantor (1979) found that about 40 percent of her elderly inner-city sample was able to name a significant nonkin friend and that the vast majority were proximate (same-city). These individuals were clearly an important source of social support. In the Philadelphia study noted above, 68 percent of the never-married older men and 50 percent of the never-married older women living alone placed at least one friend in a closest-persons category (among several categories of "importance"); while only 31 percent of widowers and 33 percent of widows named friends as among the closest persons to them.

*Neighbors.*   In Cantor's study (1979), neighbors form another potential support group; almost two-thirds of her inner-city sample know a neighbor "well" and those respondents living alone (almost 40 percent of the total sample) were more likely to know a neighbor than were elderly living with a spouse or others. She notes, "the level of mutual help occurring with neighbors is substantial" (p. 446) and lists several kinds of instrumental and affective help carried out by neighbors.

These findings would suggest a hierarchy of relationships on the part of older persons, so that neighbors are turned to when family is less proximate or when the use of social capital in seeking help from the family may be too "expensive."

Arling (1976) reported a high degree of satisfaction with neighbor relations among his sample of elderly widows. Rosel (1983) described a closely knit network of mutual assistance and support ("old people helping old people") which developed among the oldest residents of a neighborhood. Huckfeldt (1983) examined the influence of neighborhood social contexts on social networks, suggesting that "associational opportunities and constraints" influence neighborhood friendships. Clearly, neighborhood ties (Greenbaum, 1982) are significant elements in maintaining an independent household for an older person living alone.

**Social Support
as Event-related:
Bereavement and Illness**

Research which has examined spousal bereavement in late life has stressed phases or stages of bereavement, although there has been some criticism of stage models (Barrett & Schneweis, 1980; Bettis & Scott, 1981; Bowlby, 1980; Bugen, 1977; Glick, Weiss, & Parkes, 1974; Hardt, 1978; Parkes, 1972; Parkes & Weiss, 1983). There is little information on the interrelation and effects of living arrangements, types of social support networks, and the stage of bereavement on the bereavement experience (although see Bankoff, 1983). We do know of the very central role of children in giving comfort and practical help to a grieving elderly parent (Bowling & Cartwright, 1982). In addition, Clayton, Halikas, and Maurice (1971) found that interaction with children helped prevent depression in elderly bereaved. Shanas (1979) noted that children, especially, provide help at the time of loss and thereafter. We assume that many bereaved elderly are living alone, but we know little about the overall social networks of elderly bereaved persons. Parkes and Weiss (1983) and Vachon, Lyale, Rogers, Freedman-Letofsky, and Freeman (1980) have reported that the presence of supportive others can sometimes have only minimal effect on how one recovers from bereavement. Such findings seem to suggest that living arrangements may have no necessary influence on the social support which aids in recovery or, at least, on the specifically internal aspects of recovery from bereavement (cf. Bowlby, 1980). This view is opposed by a recent study which suggests that living alone is associated with a higher degree of mortality (certainly a "poor recovery") for widowers. Helsing, Szklo, and Comstock (1981) studied some 4,000 adults who were widowed between 1963 and 1974 and an equal number of married persons, matched for age, sex, race, and geographic residence. In comparing the widowed and married groups, they found that mortality rates were about the same for widowed and married women, but were significantly higher for widowed men than for married men. They found that living alone was associated with a higher mortality for both widowed men and women. They hypothesized that the continued availability of a coresident for support "may be even more effective than a large number of friends or relatives who visit less frequently" (p. 808). They found further that the mortality rate for men who remarried after being widowed was much lower than that for those who did not remarry (although as Goldman and Lord, 1983, have shown, a typical widower who remarries in his 50s faces a four to one chance that he will be outlived by his spouse). Helsing and his colleagues found no difference in mortality for widowed women who did or did not remarry.

While there is very little information on the effects of living arrangements and social support on bereavement per se, we must note that any positive effects of social support on the bereaved are most accessible to those who live with others.

Social support during the time of health crises is of crucial importance to those elderly who live alone, since these persons are most vulnerable at such a time. The presence of another person in the home almost automatically ensures help when needed. The mere existence of a social network outside the home does not always ensure the prompt availability of help. There is a gap between in-home and out-of-home support. While numerous studies have demonstrated the ability of adequate social supports to moderate potential negative effects of health and other crises, "there is no certainty about how exactly supportive ties keep people healthy" (Alcalay, 1983), and living arrangements are not always specified in such studies.

Again, the support-in-home/support-out-of-home distinction is most crucial for older persons living alone. Generally, the potential negative effects of living alone are mitigated by regular phone or face-to-face contact with family or neighbors or even by a system of signals to neighbors ("I'm O.K. if the shade is up by nine o'clock"). The fear of dying alone and not being discovered for days was articulated by some older men living alone whom I interviewed. Whatever success there has been for various in-home medical alert systems is due in part to the increasing numbers of persons living alone and the gap between in-home and out-of-home support.

While many studies have documented the importance of social support for older persons, our continued study of this phenomenon should pay greater attention to living arrangements and the implications of such living arrangements.

## LIVING ALONE AND ITS CONSEQUENCES FOR WELL-BEING

Studies of the effects on well-being of living alone in old age have shown no consistent set of positive findings. Rather, living alone appears to be a mixed blessing. Some research has illustrated mental health and well-being outcomes directly attributable to such variables as health, effects of early life fertility, gender, and marital status while other research has viewed well-being as an outcome mediated by social relations and social supports, but not always as a direct consequence of living arrangements. Here we will review some of these findings.

### Direct Effects of Antecedent Factors on the Well-being of Those Living Alone

*Effects of Health on the Well-being of Those Living Alone.*   As we have seen above in Table 5.1, about 25 percent of older people living alone are limited in the amount or kind of activity they can perform, while almost 10 percent are unable to carry out a major activity and may be largely dependent on others for help. Studies of the overall well-being of the elderly have generally shown health to be a major determinant of well-being. As Tissue and McCoy (1981) have noted, functional capacity and health are the most important determinants of a change in living arrangements for the elderly, poorer health necessitating a residential change. Newman (1976) found that such moves are usually to the home of a child or to an institution, rather than to any other type of household.

*Effects of Differential Fertility on the Well-being of Those Living Alone.* Because of the importance of children for support, childlessness may especially affect the well-being of those elderly who live alone, and as was noted above, about one-fifth of the elderly population has no living children. Johnson and Catalano (1981), who studied childless unmarried persons, reported that the childless widowed and never-married elderly they interviewed nonetheless had a high degree of contact with kin, especially siblings. They suggest that childless unmarried elderly "rehearse" for a time when they will need more involved care by building up potential support networks over time. Singh and Williams (1981) documented the lower satisfaction of childless elderly over the age of 70 with their family life, in comparison to those of the same age with children. This finding says something of the quality of the support available to childless elderly. Bachrach (1980) found a strong relationship between childlessness and social isolation in old age; childless elderly are more likely to live alone and, if living alone, were less likely to have had social contact in the previous day or two.

*Direct Effects of Gender on the Well-being of Those Living Alone.* In general, research on gender and well-being has dealt with a limited set of people living alone, namely, those who have lost a spouse. Since widows and widowers live in a variety of arrangements, this stream of research does not speak directly about those living alone. Berardo (1968, 1970) reported large differences in the life satisfaction of widowers and widows. He reported that widowers were less likely than widows to be living with children or to have a high degree of kin or friend interaction. He suggested that widows encounter less stress in the transitions accompanying the death of a spouse. By contrast, a higher degree of strain experienced by widowers is manifest in their higher degree of suicide, mental illness, social isolation (including living alone), and mortality. He suggested that women traditionally take the role of kinkeeper and social organizer, in part managing their husbands' contacts, networks, and affective ties, functions many widowers will not take on with ease or comfort. Such differences may arise from the culturally based system of gender-meaning which socially organizes the complementary and unique functions of men and women.

Conclusions supporting profound gender-based differences in responses to bereavement have been challenged in several recent papers. Gallagher, Breckenridge, Thompson, and Peterson (1983) compared bereaved elderly two months after the death of a spouse to a nonbereaved control group. They found differences in distress between the bereaved and nonbereaved, but no sex-based differences within the bereaved group "that could be attributed directly to the loss of a spouse" (p. 569). Arens (1982), in an examination of national survey data on the elderly, noted a lower level of well-being among the widowed but suggested this is not due to the effects of widowhood per se, but rather to the effects of age, poor health, and "less active" social ties in comparison to the married. Lower levels of social participation for widowers as compared to widows were not found. Ferraro and Barresi (1982, p. 242; see below) also found no evidence to indicate that widowhood led to a comparative decrease in social relations for widowers as compared to widows. They examined changes in family, friend, and neighbor relations of elderly persons prior to and after widowhood based on panel data from a national survey. Widows were classified by the amount of time that had passed since the spouses' deaths and were compared to a continuously married group. They found a good deal of stability in the family relations of recently widowed persons, but for those widowed four or more years, "lower levels of social interaction were observed on measures of family contact" (p. 227). This finding also affirms the suggestion made earlier that assistance may drop off following the support offered earlier during the period of adjustment to loss. In this study, time, not gender, greatly affected levels of social interaction.

*Direct Effects of Marital Status on the Well-being of Older Persons Living Alone.*   While logically marital status is antecedent to living arrangements, each does not necessarily equate with the other and therefore each can act as a confound when attempting to understand the consequences of the other. Not only does marital status confound living arrangements, but some marital statuses and living arrangements may also be the residuals of other events such as bereavement, ethnic traditions, and socioeconomic status.

It has been known for some time that the experiences of depression and psychological distress vary by marital status (Kessler & Essex, 1982; Pearlin & Johnson, 1977). The best-replicated finding is that the married experience fewer such symptoms than marital groups who are likely to live alone. Hughes and Gove (1981) examined relationships among living alone, mental health, and social integration and suggested that living alone does not appear to be especially problematic for many people and, in fact, may be a better, less stressful arrangement for some. They emphasize that previous studies of social integration have noted the benefits but ignored the costs of coresidence as a form of social integration: Family roles may have a negative effect on mental health if such roles are stressful or overly demanding. Kivett and Learner (1982) in a study of rural elderly found no significant differences in morale between elders living with one or more child and those in other living arrangements including living alone. They suggest that explanations of the difference between their findings and those of other researchers rests on the rural nature of their sample and the fact that in many cases the child joined the household of the elder rather than the opposite. From a social support perspective, despite a belief that support in the form of ties with relatives and friends helps personal adjustment and reduces stress, Cohler and Lieberman (1980), in a study of elderly from three ethnic groups, found little relationship between the availability of significant others and mental health and some indication that increased interpersonal involvement was associated with an increased level of stress. Hyman (1983), in studying the "enduring effects" of widowhood over time, found that the isolation of living alone "does not significantly affect the feelings of widows, except in the area of satisfaction with finances where those who live alone are less satisfied" (p. 44).

Clayton (1975) sought to assess the relative influence of living arrangements and marital bereavement on depression, and concluded that bereavement, rather than either living alone or social isolation, influenced the occurrence of depressive symptoms. However, they found that one year after the death of a spouse, 27 percent of survivors living alone showed signs of depression in comparison with only 5 percent who lived with others. Further, in their study of the life satisfaction of the elderly by living arrangement, Fengler et al. (1983) noted that "the widow who lives alone may also have a network of supportive kin living nearby but she might still lack the immediacy and constancy of that support" (p. 364).

While the morale of elderly widows living alone seems to be relatively poor, little is known about the direct effects of divorce on the well-being of those who live alone rather than with others. Hyman (1983) documented the comparatively low general morale shown by divorced or separated older persons (60–79) in his samples. Among divorced and separated women he found, among other things, lower satisfaction with family life and greater disagreement with the idea that "most people can be trusted" than in comparison with married or widowed women (Hyman, 1982, p. 32). Among divorced or separated older men he found less satisfaction with family life, less use of TV, greater use of taverns, and significantly more agreement with the state-ment that one was "not at all satisfied with the present situation" in comparison to married or widowed men (Hyman, 1983, p. 91). While his sample of divorced and separated men is too small for an analysis by residential patterns, there is no reason to expect that the well-being of divorced elderly living alone should be better than that of those in other living arrangements.

Other recent studies have described further negative and mixed effects of living alone on the well-being of the elderly in different marital statuses. Fengler et al. (1983) examined the relationship between life satisfaction and household structure of some 1,400 elderly. The marital status and living arrangement categories included widows living alone, couples with no one else in the household, and elders living with "others." The life satisfaction measured for widows living alone was found to be significantly lower than that of the married couples or elders living with others. A significantly fewer number of elders living alone reported having "someone to care for" them. Fengler and Danigelis (1982) also noted that "the more urban the residence of the widow living alone, the lower life satisfaction" (p. 129). This finding suggests that interaction between living arrangements, morale, and the urban–rural continuum may be worth exploring further.

Mixed advantages and disadvantages to living alone were also found in the Lawton, Moss, and Kleban (1984) analysis of three large data sets. Examined were older persons living alone, married couples "alone," married couples with child, spouseless elderly individuals with a child, and "others." They found that the "live-alones are seen . . . to have an interesting mix of advantages and disadvantages" (p. 336). For those living alone, they found fewer disabilities in func-tion, higher cognitive competence, and greater interaction with friends than for those in other living arrangements. Presumably those favor-able features were what enabled them to live alone. However, they were also relatively more isolated from family, showed less satisfaction with family relations than the other residential categories, and had lower objective housing quality and subjective well-being.

**Well-being of Those Living
Alone as Mediated
by Social Relations**

Living alone clearly means that less time is spent with other people. Certain activities are no doubt substituted for in-home social relations, but for some a paucity of in-home social contacts leads to loneliness.

However, the amount or number of contacts seems to be very poorly correlated, if at all, with the experience of loneliness.

Loneliness and social isolation are often viewed as important aspects of living alone, but as has been apparent since the seminal work of Townsend (1968), we know that these two states do not have a perfect correspondence. It has generally been found that variations in living arrangements do not usually translate into differences in loneliness; and we have some evidence that living alone is no more associated with loneliness than are other living arrangements (Revenson & Johnson, 1984), yet such findings seem counterintuitive. Perhaps it is that living alone provides less immediate opportunity for the amelioration of loneliness by face-to-face interaction, if such is desired. An increased interest in the phenomenon of loneliness is testified to by the number of recent publications on this topic (Hartog, Audy, & Cohen, 1980; Peplau & Perlman, 1982; Weiss, 1980; Wood, 1978). Peplau, Bikson, Rook, and Goodchilds (1982) have examined the line of popular reasoning which equates being old with living alone and living alone with being lonely. They note that while being old is frequently associated with living alone, living alone does not necessarily entail loneliness for the elderly. The reason is that old people living alone are not separated from their families and, indeed, isolation from families is generally rare (Fischer & Phillips, 1982). Further, they note that "marital status and household composition . . . are not good indicators of the quality of social interaction" (p. 330). They further review several studies which document the conclusion that older persons are not especially vulnerable to loneliness and conclude that "for many, the experience of being old and living alone is less lonely and more rewarding than we imagine" (p. 343). A similar conclusion has been made by Revenson and Johnson (1984), who found that loneliness decreased across the adult life span, with individuals over the age of 65 experiencing the least. However, as Lopata, Heinemann, and Baum (1982, p. 316) and others have reported, a large proportion of widowed persons do experience loneliness upon the death of a spouse and such loneliness can be enduring.

Living alone may itself not induce loneliness and low life satisfaction, but it may eventuate in a degree of social estrangement which in turn has been found to be associated with reduced life satisfaction (Liang, Dvorkin, Kahana, & Mazian, 1980). One study (Brown & Chiang, 1983) found substance abuse among the elderly to be associated with living alone. Rundall and Evashwick (1982) constructed a typology of network relations across dimensions of perceived and desired levels of social involvement. They discerned four types of social relations: engaged, disengaged, abandoned, and trapped. They found that more than 40 percent of their sample of elderly persons felt abandoned by or disengaged from family and attributed this to the fact that many of these individuals "are widowed or . . . never married and . . . live alone" (p. 223).

In concluding this section we must emphasize again the mixed blessing theme in understanding the consequences of living alone for well-being. Good health is generally a prerequisite for living alone, although living alone can accommodate a number of health statuses. One study found those living alone to have a higher cognitive competence. Childlessness reduces residential options and therefore may increase the likelihood of living alone. It seems clear that the married experience fewer depressive and distress-related symptoms; the life satisfaction of widows living alone has been found to be lower than that of those in other marital status/living arrangement categories. While relatively more isolated from family members, elderly living alone may have greater interaction with friends.


## CONCLUSION

This chapter has sought to isolate some antecedents to, correlates of, and outcomes associated with living alone in old age. Associated with these topics have been three themes: that a desire for independence often motivates persons' subjective acceptance of living alone; that social supports and relations are important for the maintenance of this independent lifestyle; and that objectively, living alone mixes positive and negative features.

We need further research on these topics for several reasons. We need to disentangle the separate components of our analytic variables so as to further explore the various effects of living arrangements, marital status, gender, ethnicity, fertility, and personality. We should continue to be both more inclusive and more precise in our analyses of what constitutes social support and the fabric of social relationships. There is a need for the continuing investigation of what we have called here the correlates to living alone, such as the daily routines of older persons who live alone, the meaning of social interactions to them, and changes in social relationships over time. The trend toward living alone will undoubtedly continue and as researchers and practitioners we must come to know more of this phenomenon.

## REFERENCES

Alcalay, R. Health and social support networks: A case for improving interpersonal communications. *Social Networks*, 1983, *5*, 71–88.

Arens, D. A. Widowhood and well-being: An examination of sex differences within a causal mode. *International Journal of Aging and Human Development*, 1982, *15*, 27–40.

Arling, G. The elderly widow and her family, neighbors, and friends. *Journal of Marriage and the Family*, 1976, *38*, 757–768.

Anderson, T. B. Widowhood as a life transition: Its impact on kinship ties. *Journal of Marriage and the Family*, 1984, *46*, 105–114.

Babchuk, N. Aging and primary relations. *International Journal of Aging and Human Development*, 1978, *9*, 137–151.

Bachrach, C. A. Childlessness and social isolation among the elderly. *Journal of Marriage and the Family*, 1980, *42*, 627–636.

Bankoff, E. A. Social support and adaptation to widowhood. *Journal of Marriage and the Family*, 1983, *45*, 827–839.

Barrett, C. J., & Schneweis, K. M. An empirical search for stages of widowhood. *Omega*, 1980, *11*, 97–104.

Belcher, J. C. The one-person household: A consequence of the isolated nuclear family? *Journal of Marriage and the Family*, 1967, *29*, 534–540.

Berardo, F. M. Widowhood status in the United States: Perspectives on a neglected aspect of the family life cycle. *Family Coordinator*, 1968, *17*, 191–203.

Berardo, F. M. Survivorship and social isolation: The case of the aged widower. *Family Coordinator*, 1970, *19*, 11–25.

Bettis, S. K., & Scott, F. G. Bereavement and grief. *Annual Review of Gerontology and Geriatrics*, 1981, *2*, 144–159.

Bowlby, J. *Loss: Sadness and depression.* (Vol. III of *Attachment and loss.*) New York: Basic Books, 1980.

Bowling, A., & Cartwright, A. *Life after death: A study of the elderly widowed.* London: Tavistock, 1982.

Braito, R., & Anderson, D. The ever-single elderly woman. In E. W. Markson (Ed.), *Older women: Issues and prospects.* Lexington, MA: Lexington Books, 1983.

Brown, B. B., & Chiang, C. Drug and alcohol abuse among the elderly: Is being alone the key? *International Journal of Aging and Human Development*, 1983, *18*, 1–12.

Bugen, L. A. Human grief: A model for prediction and intervention. *American Journal of Orthopsychiatry*, 1977, *47*, 196–206.

Cantor, M. H. Neighbors and friends: An overlooked resource in the informal support system. *Research on Aging*, 1979, *1*, 434–463.

Cantor, M. H. The informal support system: Its relevance in the lives of the elderly. In E. F. Borgatta & N. G. McCluskey (Eds.), *Aging and society: Current research and policy perspectives.* Beverly Hills, CA: Sage, 1980.

Chevan, A., & Korson, J. H. The widowed who live alone: An examination of social and demographic factors. *Social Forces*, 1972, *51*, 45–53.

Cicirelli, V. G. Adult children's attachment and helping behavior to elderly parents: A path model. *Journal of Marriage and the Family*, 1983, *45*, 815–825.

Clark, M. Cultural values and dependency in later life. In D. O. Cowgill & L. D. Holmes (Eds.), *Aging and modernization*. New York: Appleton-Century-Crofts, 1972.

Clayton, P. J. The effects of living alone on bereavement symptoms. *American Journal of Psychiatry*, 1975, *132*, 133–137.

Clayton, P. J., Halikas, J., & Maurice, W. The bereavement of the widowed. *Diseases of the Nervous System*, 1971, *32*, 597–604.

Cleveland, W. P., & Gianturco, D. T. Remarriage probability after widowhood: A retrospective method. *Journal of Gerontology*, 1976, *31*, 99–103.

Cohen, C. I., & Rajkowski, H. What's in a friend? Substantive and theoretical issues. *Gerontologist*, 1982, *22*, 261–266.

Cohler, B. J. Stress or support: Relations between older women from three European ethnic groups and their relatives. In R. C. Manuel (Ed.), *Minority aging*. Westport, CT: Greenwood Press, 1982.

Cohler, B. J., & Lieberman, M. A. Social relations and mental health. *Research on Aging*, 1980, *2*, 445–469.

Feller, B. A. Health characteristics of persons with chronic activity limitations: United States, 1979. *Vital and Health Statistics*, Series 10, Data from the National Health Survey, Number 137. DHHS Publication Number 82-1565. Washington, DC: U. S. Government Printing Office, December, 1981.

Feller, B. A. Americans needing help to function at home. National Center for Health Statistics, *Advance Data*, Number 92, September 14, 1983. DHHS Publication Number 83-1250. Hyattsville, MD: Public Health Service.

Fengler, A. P., & Danigelis, N. Residence, the elderly widow and life satisfaction. *Research on Aging*, 1982, *4*, 113–135.

Fengler, A. P., Danigelis, N., & Little, V. C. Late life satisfaction and household structure: Living with others and living alone. *Ageing and Society*, 1983, *3*, 357–377.

Ferraro, K. F., & Barresi, C. M. The impact of widowhood on the social relations of older people. *Research on Aging*, 1982, *4*, 227–247.

Fischer, C. S., & Phillips, S. L. Who is alone? Social characteristics of people with small networks. In L. A. Peplau & D. Perlman (Eds.), *Loneliness: A sourcebook of current theory, research, and therapy*. New York: Wiley, 1982.

Francis, D. *Will you still need me, will you still feed me, when I'm 84?* Bloomington: Indiana University Press, 1984.

Gallagher, D. E., Breckenridge, J. N., Thompson, L. W., & Peterson, J. A. Effects of bereavement on indicators of mental health in elderly widows and widowers. *Journal of Gerontology*, 1983, *38*, 565–571.

Glick, I. O., Weiss, R. D., & Parkes, C. M. *The first year of bereavement.* New York: Wiley, 1974.

Glick, P. The future marital status and living arrangements of the elderly. *Gerontologist,* 1979, *19,* 301–309.

Goldman, N., & Lord, G. Sex differences in life cycle measures of widowhood. *Demography,* 1983, *20,* 177–195.

Goldstein, M. C., Schuler, S., & Ross, J. L. Social and economic forces affecting intergenerational relations in extended families in a Third World country: A cautionary tale from south Asia. *Journal of Gerontology,* 1983, *38,* 716–724.

Gottlieb, B. H. The primary group as supportive milieu: Applications to community psychology. *American Journal of Community Psychology,* 1979, *7,* 469–480.

Grad, S. Income of the population 55 and over, 1980. U. S. Department of Health and Human Services, Social Security Administration, SSA Publication Number 13-11871. Washington, DC: U. S. Government Printing Office, 1983.

Greenbaum, S. D. Bridging ties at the neighborhood level. *Social Networks,* 1982, *4,* 367–384.

Hardt, D. V. An investigation of the stages of bereavement. *Omega,* 1978, *9,* 279–285.

Hartog, J., Audy, J. R., & Cohen, Y. (Eds.). *The anatomy of loneliness.* New York: International Universities Press, 1980.

Heinemann, G. D. Family involvement and support for widowed persons. In T. H. Brubaker (Ed.), *Family relationships in later life.* Beverly Hills, CA: Sage, 1983.

Helsing, K. J., Szklo, M., & Comstock, G. W. Factors associated with mortality after widowhood. *American Journal of Public Health,* 1981, *71,* 802–809.

Hennon, C. B. Divorce and the elderly: A neglected area of research. In T. H. Brubaker (Ed.), *Family relationships in later life.* Beverly Hills, CA: Sage, 1983.

Huckfeldt, R. R. Social contexts, social networks, and urban neighborhoods: Environmental constraints on friendship choice. *American Journal of Sociology,* 1983, *89,* 651–669.

Hughes, M., & Gove, W. Living alone, social integration, and mental health. *American Journal of Sociology,* 1981, *87,* 48–74.

Hyman, H. H. *Of time and widowhood: Nationwide studies of enduring effects.* Duke Press Policy Studies. Durham, NC: Duke University Press, 1983.

Johnson, C. L. Interdependence and aging in Italian families. In J. Sokolovsky (Ed.), *Growing old in different societies.* Belmont, CA: Wadsworth, 1983.

Johnson, C. L., & Catalano, D. J. Childless elderly and their family supports. *Gerontologist,* 1981, *21,* 610–618.

Kerckhoff, A. C. Family patterns and morale in retirement. In I. H. Simpson

& J. C. McKinney (Eds.), *Social aspects of aging.* Durham, NC: Duke University Press, 1966.

Kessler, R. C., & Essex, M. Marital status and depression: The importance of coping resources. *Social Forces,* 1982, *61,* 484–507.

Kivett, V. R., & Learner, R. M. Situational influence on the morale of older rural adults in child-shared housing: A comparative analysis. *Gerontologist,* 1982, *22,* 100–106.

Kobrin, F. The fall in household size and the rise of the primary individual in the United States. *Demography,* 1976, *13,* 127–138.

Lang, A. M., & Brody, E. M. Characteristics of middle-aged daughters and help to their elderly mothers. *Journal of Marriage and the Family,* 1983, *45,* 193–202.

Lawton, M. P. An ecological view of living arrangements. *Gerontologist,* 1981, *21,* 59–66.

Lawton, M. P., Moss, M., & Kleban, M. H. Marital status, living arrangements, and the wellbeing of older people. *Research on Aging,* 1984, *6,* 323–345.

Leigh, G. K. Kinship interactions over the family lifespan. *Journal of Marriage and the Family,* 1982, *44,* 197–208.

Liang, J., Dvorkin, L., Kahana, E., & Mazian, F. Social integration and morale: A re-examination. *Journal of Gerontology,* 1980, *35,* 746–757.

Lopata, H. Z. Widows as a minority group. *Gerontologist,* 1971, *11* (Number 1, Part 2), 67–77.

Lopata, H. Z. Support systems of the elderly: Chicago of the 1970's. *Gerontologist,* 1975, *15,* 35–41.

Lopata, H. Z. Contributions of extended families to the support systems of metropolitan area widows: Limitations of the modified kin network. *Journal of Marriage and the Family,* 1978, *40,* 355–364.

Lopata, H. Z. *Women as widows.* New York: Elsevier, 1979.

Lopata, H. Z., Heinemann, G. D., & Baum, J. Loneliness: Antecedents and coping strategies in the lives of widows. In L. A. Peplau & D. Perlman (Eds.), *Loneliness: A sourcebook of current theory, research, and therapy.* New York: Wiley, 1982.

Lowenthal, M. F., & Robinson, B. Social networks and isolation. In R. H. Binstock & E. Shanas (Eds.), *Handbook of aging and the social sciences.* New York: Van Nostrand Reinhold, 1976.

Manuel, R. C., & Reid, J. A comparative demographic profile of the minority and nonminority aged. In R. C. Manuel (Ed.), *Minority aging: Social and social psychological issues.* Westport, CT: Greenwood Press, 1982.

Matthews, S. H. Definitions of friendship and their consequences in old age. *Ageing and Society,* 1983, *3,* 141–156.

Michael, R. T., Fuchs, V. R., & Scott, S. R. Changes in the propensity to live alone: 1950–1976. *Demography,* 1980, *17,* 39–53.

Newman, S. J. Housing adjustments of the disabled elderly. *Gerontologist,* 1976, *16,* 312–317.

Pampel, F. C. Changes in the propensity to live alone: Evidence from consecutive cross-sectional surveys, 1960–1976. *Demography*, 1983, *20*, 433–447.

Parkes, C. M. *Bereavement: Studies of grief in adult life*. New York: International Universities Press, 1972.

Parkes, C. M., & Weiss, R. S. *Recovery from bereavement*. New York: Basic Books, 1983.

Pearlin, L. I., & Johnson, J. S. Marital status, life strains and depression. *American Sociological Review*, 1977, *42*, 704–715.

Peplau, L. A., Bikson, T. K., Rook, K. S., & Goodchilds, J. D. Being old and living alone. In L. A. Peplau & D. Perlman (Eds.), *Loneliness: A sourcebook of current theory, research and therapy*. New York: Wiley, 1982.

Peplau, L. A., & Perlman, D. (Eds.). *Loneliness: A sourcebook of current theory, research and therapy*. New York: Wiley, 1982.

Quinn, W. H. Personal and family adjustment in later life. *Journal of Marriage and the Family*, 1983, *45*, 57–73.

Revenson, T. A., & Johnson, J. L. Social and demographic correlates of loneliness in late life. *American Journal of Community Psychology*, 1984, *12*, 71–85.

Rosel, N. The hub of a wheel: A neighborhood support network. *International Journal of Aging and Human Development*, 1983, *16*, 193–200.

Ross, H. K. The neighborhood family: Community mental health for the elderly. *Gerontologist*, 1983, *23*, 243–247.

Rowles, G. D. *Prisoners of space? Exploring the geographical experience of older people*. Boulder, CO: Westview Press, 1978.

Rubinstein, R. L. Old men living alone: Social networks and informal supports. In W. H. Quinn & G. A. Hughston (Eds.), *Independent aging: Family and social system perspectives*. Rockville, MD: Aspen, 1984.

Rubinstein, R. L. The construction of a day by elderly widowers. *International Journal of Aging and Human Development*, in press.

Rundall, T. G., & Evashwick, C. Social networks and help-seeking among the elderly. *Research on Aging*, 1982, *4*, 205–226.

Shanas, E. The family as a social support system in old age. *Gerontologist*, 1979, *19*, 169–174.

Siegel, J. S. On the demography of aging. *Demography*, 1980, *17*, 345–364.

Singh, B. K., & Williams, J. S. Childlessness and family satisfaction. *Research on Aging*, 1981, *3*, 218–227.

Sokolovsky, J. Interaction dimensions of the aged: Social network mapping. In C. Fry & J. Keith (Eds.), *New methods for old age research*. Chicago: Loyola University Center for Urban Policy, 1980.

Sokolovsky, J., & Cohen, C. I. Measuring social interaction of the urban elderly: A methodological synthesis. *International Journal of Aging and Human Development*, 1981, *13*, 233–244.

Spreitzer, E., & Riley, L. E. Factors associated with singlehood. *Journal of Marriage and the Family*, 1974, *36*, 533–542.

Stoller, E. P. Parental caregiving by adult children. *Journal of Marriage and the Family*, 1983, *45*, 851–858.

Thomas, K., & Wister, A. Living arrangements of older women: The ethnic dimension. *Journal of Marriage and the Family*, 1984, *46*, 301–311.

Tissue, T. Low-income widows and other aged singles. *Social Security Bulletin*, 1979, *42*, 3–10.

Tissue, T., & McCoy, J. L. Income and living arrangements among poor aged singles. *Social Security Bulletin*, 1981, *44*, 3–13.

Townsend, P. Isolation, desolation and loneliness. In E. Shanas, P. Townsend, D. Wedder, H. Friis, P. Milhøj, & J. Stehouwer (Eds.), *Old people in three industrial societies*. New York: Atherton Press, 1968.

Troll, L. E. The family of later life: A decade review. *Journal of Marriage and the Family*, 1971, *33*, 263–290.

Uhlenberg, P., & Myers, M. P. Divorce and the elderly. *Gerontologist*, 1981, *21*, 276–282.

United States Senate, Special Committee on Aging. *Developments in Aging: 1981*, Vol. 1. Senate Report 97-314. Washington, DC: U. S. Government Printing Office, 1982.

Vachon, M. L. S., Lyale, W. A. L, Rogers, J., Freedman-Letofsky, K., & Freeman, S. J. J. A controlled study of self-help intervention for widows. *American Journal of Psychiatry*, 1980, *137*, 1380–1384.

Walker, A. J., & Thompson, L. Intimacy and intergenerational aid and contact among mothers and daughters. *Journal of Marriage and the Family*, 1983, *45*, 841–849.

Weiss, R. S. *Loneliness: The experience of emotional and social isolation*. Cambridge, MA: MIT Press, 1980 [1973].

Wellman, B. Applying network analysis to the study of support. In B. H. Gottlieb (Ed.), *Social networks and social support*. Beverly Hills, CA: Sage, 1981.

Wentowski, G. J. Reciprocity and the coping strategies of older people: Cultural dimensions of network building. *Gerontologist*, 1981, *21*, 600–609.

Wilder, C. S. Limitation of activity due to chronic conditions, United States, 1974. *Vital and Health Statistics*, Series 10, Data from the National Health Survey, Number 111. DHEW Publication Number 77-1537. Washington, DC: U. S. Government Printing Office, June, 1977.

Wood, L. A. Guest editorial: Perspective on loneliness. *Essence*, 1978, *2*, 199–201.

Wood, V., & Robertson, J. F. Friendship and kinship interaction: Differential effect on the morale of the family. *Journal of Marriage and the Family*, 1978, *40*, 367–375.

## CHAPTER 6

# Family Caregiving to the Frail Elderly

Amy Horowitz, D.S.W.
The Lighthouse: New York Association for the Blind
New York, New York

Over the past several years we have witnessed an explosion of professional and scholarly interest in the family relationships of older people and in the implications of these relationships for both the care of the frail elderly and the well-being of their caregiving families. As a result, what had previously been a scant and scattered body of literature is now growing at a rapid rate. Relevant references have appeared in a wide range of scholarly journals and reflect the variety of disciplines concerned with the nature of family relationships and family caregiving in old age.

In Volume I of this series, Tobin and Kulys (1980) noted that caregiving by families had ". . . invariably been investigated by gathering data from small and select samples of family caregivers who provide home care to the impaired" (p. 371). While small, descriptive studies remain predominant, there has been a noticeable increase in studies that utilize relatively larger data sets and that focus on understanding and explaining the complexities of the caregiving phenomenon (e.g., Brody, Johnsen, Fulcomer, & Lang, 1983; Cantor, 1983; Cicirelli, 1981a; Horowitz, 1982c; Lang & Brody, 1983; Montgomery, Gonyea, & Hooyman, in press; Noelker & Poulshock, 1982; Robinson, 1983; Stoller, 1983). National and/or probability samples of family caregivers remain rare, however, and we must rely on representative studies of older people (e.g., Shanas, 1979a, 1979b; Shanas et al., 1968) for national data.

The purpose of this chapter is to review the current state-of-the-art as it concerns the critical issues and empirical research regarding family caregiving to the frail elderly. A basic assumption underlying this review is that the caregiving relationship is differentiated from typical family exchanges and is defined by the existence of some degree of physical, mental, emotional, or economic impairment on the part of the older person which limits independence and necessitates ongoing assistance. Hence, a caregiving situation begins with the older person's need for assistance and cannot be defined by any specified set of behaviors on the part of the caregiver. The variability in these behaviors constitutes a primary area of investigation. Implicit in this underlying assumption is a rather broad definition of the term "frail" elderly. This is a phrase which is commonly used by gerontologists but with great variation in meaning. For example, Shanas (1979a) has used the term to refer to the 10 percent of community elderly who are either bed- or housebound and comparable in impairment to the institutionalized population. Others have equated frailty with the existence of some disability which limits the person's ability to engage in a major activity. Using this definition, approximately one-third of all older people are estimated to be frail in that they require some supportive services (Brody, 1974; Callahan, Diamond, Giele, & Morris, 1980; National Center for Health Statistics, 1979). For the purposes of examining a family member's response to an older relative, it is this second broader definition which is most relevant, defining the conditions under which reciprocal family exchanges begin to shift and the move is made into a caregiving relationship.

The first section of the chapter will provide a historical overview of the development of knowledge in the field. The second section begins the chapter's specific focus on caregiving to the frail elderly and reviews the descriptive data concerning the characteristics of caregivers, caregiving behavior, and caregiving impacts. The third section is concerned with the context and variability in family caregiving. Attention is given to the structural and dynamic forces which have been identified as influencing the course and consequences of the caregiving relationship. Conceptual and methodological issues are also discussed within this section. A discussion of special issues, such as effects on the older person and the process of caregiving over time, follows in the next section. The chapter concludes with a discussion of the critical policy, service, and research issues which face us today.

Throughout the chapter, the focus is on *family* care in the community. However, as noted within the body of this review, friends and neighbors may also be active in the care of the frail aged and familial caregiving does continue in institutional facilities.

## HISTORICAL OVERVIEW:
## THE DEVELOPMENT
## OF KNOWLEDGE

The development of knowledge within this area of inquiry has progressed through four successive but overlapping phases, which may be entitled The Abandoned Elderly; The Elderly as Family Members; The Family as Caregiver; and The Relationship Between Formal and Informal Care of the Aged. The title of each stage reflects the dominant theme in the conceptual and empirical literature. Each will be briefly reviewed below.

### The Abandoned Elderly

The theme of family abandonment and the isolation of older people dominated the literature from the 1930's to the late 1950's. The processes of urbanization, industrialization, social and geographic mobility, and the rise of bureaucracies induced rapid social changes and brought the viability of families to the forefront of sociological thought.

In response to concerns regarding family breakdown, family sociologists, most notably Talcott Parsons, proposed that the family was not dissolving but contracting, becoming more specialized and specific in function. The isolated nuclear family—consisting of husband, wife, and minor children—was identified as the most distinctive feature of the American kinship system (Parsons, 1944). At the same time that Parsonian theory dominated sociology, Freudian theory, which also emphasized the nuclear family structure and the socialization of the child as its primary function, predominated in psychology. Neither of these two approaches had a meaningful place for the middle-aged or aged family members. In fact, Parsons specifically identified the structural isolation of the aged and their loss of function as one of the costs of this family system. While a detailed analysis on *why* this position was so pervasive is beyond the scope of this review, it is important to note that the myth of the abandoned elderly took firm root in both academic and public minds.

### The Elderly as Family Members

However, the research begun in the 1960s and continuing to date challenged this myth and firmly established both the elderly as family members and the modified extended family as the modal family structure in American society (Litwak, 1965; Sussman, 1965; Sussman & Burchinal, 1962). This phase was characterized by large-scale social surveys of the general aged population documenting the type, frequency, and nature of kin interactions and exchange (e.g., Shanas, 1979a, 1979b; Shanas et al., 1968).

These studies firmly established that the elderly are part of family networks: over half are married; 70 percent share a household with another family member; 80 percent have at least one living child; 80 percent have siblings; and only 3 percent of the noninstitutionalized elderly can be considered truly kinless (Shanas, 1979a, 1979b; Shanas et al., 1968; Troll, 1971).

The centrality of family relationships in the lives of older people was indicated not only by the availability of kin but by their proximity, patterns of contact, and mutual aid, as well as by affective relationships (Troll, 1971).

Most older people were found to live close to at least one adult child, with 84 percent nationwide living within one hour's travel time (Shanas, 1979a). At the same time, the clear preference of both generations to live near, but not with each other, was documented in many studies of the aged (Brody & Lang, 1982: Fendetti & Gelfand, 1976; Seelbach, 1977; Seelbach & Sauer, 1977; Sussman, 1977; Wake & Sporakowski, 1972), and gave support to the expression "intimacy at a distance" as characteristic of intergenerational relationships in Western societies (Rosenmayr & Köckeis, 1963).

As indicated by residential proximity, contact between the elderly and their family members is frequent. More than three-fourths of older people see a child at least once a week and approximately half do so almost daily. Contact with siblings is also frequent, especially among the childless elderly (Cantor, 1975; Shanas, 1979b). Furthermore, the Harris survey (1975) found no difference in family contact between people over and under 65, contradicting the assumption that decreased levels of familial interaction characterize typical old age.

Extensive mutual aid and social support systems were also documented. What became clear was that older people give as well as receive services from their families and a *balanced* exchange characterizes the majority of intergenerational relations at any one point in time (Bankoff, 1983; Bromberg, 1983; Cantor, 1975; Cheal, 1983; Harris & Associates, 1975; Lee & Ellithorpe, 1982; Sussman, 1965; Sussman & Burchinal, 1962).

The pattern of reciprocity undergoes a shift only with the deterioration of the financial and/or health status of the older relative. At this

point, the family, and not the social service network, was found to be
the major provider of services and emerged as the primary caregivers
to the frail aged (Shanas, 1979b).

Furthermore, studies found that these relations were characterized
by close affective ties and that satisfying relationships with children
and other relatives are the norm rather than the exception (Adams,
1968; Baruch & Barnett, 1983; Brody, 1974; Brown, 1974; Cantor,
1975; Cicirelli, 1981a; Horowitz & Shindelman, 1983a; Jackson, 1971,
1972; Johnson & Bursk, 1977; Nydegger & Mitteness, 1982; Teresi,
Toner, Bennett, & Wilder, 1980; Troll, Miller, & Atchley, 1979). Lack
of close affective feelings, however, were not found to preclude continued interaction nor the exchange of mutual aid (Adams, 1968; Bromberg, 1983; Brown, 1974; Peterson, 1970; Thompson & Walker, 1982;
Walker & Thompson, 1983; Weishaus, 1980).

## The Family as Caregiver

The recognition that families were providing critical supportive services to the frail elderly in the community raised a new set of questions
regarding patterns of caregiving and the consequences of providing
care for the family unit. Thus, in the mid-1970s, attention was turned
to the families of the elderly and to an examination of the family's role
as caregiver.

Findings continued to accumulate regarding the extent of family
care. A comprehensive study on cost comparisons of home care found
that family and friends were absorbing the largest portion of the cost
compared to expenditure of public dollars (General Accounting Office, 1971). Families provide 80 percent of all home health care for
older people (National Center for Health Statistics, 1975); conversely,
80 percent of all older people with home health care needs depend
primarily on their family (Gurland, Dean, Gurland, & Cook, 1978).
Shanas (1979b) has estimated that for every one older resident in a
nursing home, there are two in the community with similar disabilities
being cared for by families.

Thus, it is not surprising that the support available from families is
one of the most critical factors in preventing or delaying nursing home
utilization and in differentiating nursing home from community populations. Widowhood, living alone, and childlessness have consistently
emerged as significant predictors of nursing home placement (Barney,
1977; Branch & Jette, 1982; Johnson & Catalano, 1981; Palmore,
1976; Prohaska & McAuley, 1983; Shanas & Sussman, 1981; Smyer,

1980; Townsend, 1965; Vicente, Wiley, & Carrington, 1979; Wan & Weissert, 1981). Furthermore, older people with family supports tend to enter nursing homes at much higher levels of impairment than do those who enter without family networks (Barney, 1977; Dunlop, 1980; Townsend, 1965).

At the same time that the academic and professional community began to recognize the strength of families in providing care to the elderly, they also began to realize the family's limitations. Evidence indicated that many families reach a crisis when they can no longer provide the care needed by the older relative (Brody, 1977; Silverstone, 1983). For older people with family, exhaustion of family resources, excessive burden on family members, and change in family circumstances were found to be *more* often the primary precipitant of nursing home placement than was a change in the older person's health status (Arling & McAuley, 1983; Brody, 1966; Dobrof, 1976; Hatch & Franken, 1984; Isaacs, 1971; Kraus et al., 1976; Teresi, Bennett, & Wilder, 1978). In addition, social and demographic trends, such as the increasing growth of the "old" elderly, decreasing family size, increasing labor force participation by women, and increasing divorce rates, had all been identified as limiting the future ability, if not willingness, of families to bear the burden of support alone.

### The Relationship Between
### Informal and Formal Care

Based on the findings cited above, a concurrent theme soon emerged in the literature regarding the role of the formal service sector in supporting families who care for the frail elderly and the proper "mix" of formal and informal services on behalf of the aged (e.g., Brody, Poulshock, & Masciocchi, 1978; Callahan et al., 1980; Carrilio & Eisenberg, 1983; Dunlop, 1980; Lebowitz, 1978; Maddox, 1975; Monk, 1979; Moroney, 1976, 1983; Prager, 1978; Schorr, 1980; Shanas & Sussman, 1977; Treas, 1977; Ward, 1978). The "theory of shared functions," developed by Litwak and his associates (Dobrof & Litwak, 1977; Dono et al., 1979; Litwak, 1965; Litwak & Figueira, 1968; Litwak & Meyer, 1974) provides the conceptual foundation for much of the policy literature on the formal–informal service relationship. Briefly, the theory of shared functions develops the proposition that both primary groups and formal organizations have roles to play in most spheres of social functioning and that, in each sphere, there are tasks that are differentially performed better by either the primary group or the formal organization. By the nature of their structures, the primary group is better adapted to perform the non-uniform aspects of the task and the bureaucracy better able to handle the uniform areas. The latter are those which require concentrated knowledge and/or large-scale resources and which can be easily routinized. Non-uniform tasks, on the other hand, are those which are simple, idiosyncratic, unpredictable, and/or involve many contingencies. Litwak and his associates emphasize that successful achievement of any goal, including the care of the elderly, requires not only the *involvement* of both sectors but the *coordination* of their efforts. Hence, to the extent that an older person can rely only on the formal organization or only on family resources, or to the extent that the two structures work at cross purposes, to that extent will some of the older person's needs remain unmet. As Lebowitz (1978) has noted, this conceptualization ". . . forms the basis for the newest design in social services, the balanced service system" (p. 115–116).

Unfortunately, this realization of a joint responsibility arose at the same time that policy makers and those concerned with rising social and health care costs discovered the family as an "untapped" resource. The current scene (as will be discussed in the last section) is one where those who advocate additional service supports for older people and their families are pitted against those who would like to increase family care in order to reduce public expenditures.

Having provided a general overview of the development of knowledge and issues over the past several decades, it is now appropriate to turn to an examination of the "family as caregiver" in detail.

## THE FAMILY AS CAREGIVER:
## WHO, HOW, AND WITH
## WHAT CONSEQUENCES?

### The Primary Caregiver

While the literature may refer somewhat idealistically to a family caregiving *system,* the research has consistently confirmed that *one* family member occupies the role of primary caregiver and is the primary provider of direct care assistance. Other family members or friends, if involved at all, play secondary roles, and shared responsibility between two or more members of the informal support system is very much the exception to the rule (Cantor, 1980, 1983; Frankfather, Smith, & Caro, 1981; Horowitz, 1982c; Johnson, 1983; Johnson & Catalano,

1981; Kinnear & Graycar, 1984; Noelker & Poulshock, 1982; Sanford, 1975; Stoller & Earl, 1983; Whitfield, 1981).

There is also almost universal consensus about the identity of the primary caregiver, with selection following a hierarchical pattern. Simply, the primary caregiver will be a spouse, if there is one available and capable, and a child if there is not. In the absence of both spouse and children, other relatives (primarily siblings but also grandchildren, nieces, nephews, and cousins) will take on the responsibility of primary caregiver. Only for the minority of older people lacking any functional kin are friends and neighbors identified as the primary caregiver (Arling & McAuley, 1983; Cantor, 1983; Horowitz, 1982c; Johnson, 1983; Johnson & Catalano, 1981; Keith, 1983; Kivett & Learner, 1980; Shanas, 1979a, 1979b; Stoller, 1982; Stoller & Earl, 1983; Teresi et al., 1978; Tobin & Kulys, 1981).

The relationship between the caregiver and frail older person has also been identified as a primary predictor of the pattern of care provided and the stress associated with caregiving. Spouses are usually found to provide the most extensive and comprehensive care and are typically caring for the most disabled older people—findings which suggest that spouses maintain the caregiving role longer and tolerate greater levels of disability than other caregivers (Cantor, 1983; Crossman, London, & Barry, 1981; Horowitz, 1982c; Johnson, 1980, 1983; Johnson & Catalano, 1981, 1983; Soldo & Myllyluoma, 1983). At the same time, several of these same studies have also found that spouses report the highest level of stress compared to other caregivers. Only the findings reported by Johnson are in the opposite direction; that is, spouses tended to report less conflict and stress in their caregiving role than did others.

While adult children also tend to be extensively involved in and affected by caregiving, most research indicates that the involvement is less for children than for spouses. However, the greatest contrast is between spouse and children on one end of the continuum and other relatives, friends, and neighbors on the other. The latter are not only less likely to occupy the role, but when they do, they provide less overall care and less intensive or intimate types of assistance, and experience far less stress in the process. They are also usually found to be caring for the least disabled older people, suggesting that they do not, or cannot, maintain the caregiving role when the demands of the caregiving role increase (Cantor, 1979a, 1983; Horowitz, 1982c; Johnson & Catalano, 1981). In general, other relatives, and especially friends and neighbors, are most willing and able to meet the older person's needs when these needs are relatively less extensive.

It is also clear that caregiving remains a sex-linked activity, with females predominating over males in each kin category as the primary caregiver (Brody, 1981; Cantor, 1983; Horowitz, 1982c; Johnson, 1983; Kinnear & Graycar, 1984; Lee, 1980; Reece, Walz, & Hagebozeck, 1983; Stoller, 1982; Treas, 1979; Troll, 1971; Troll et al., 1979). Thus, given the demography of family structure and gender differences in life expectancy, the usual caregiver for an older man is his elderly wife (typically in her 70s and in fair to poor health herself), and for an older woman, her adult middle-aged or young-old daughter who confronts competing responsibilities from family and/or employment.

One question which has not been extensively addressed is what, in addition to gender, determines the selection of one particular child as caregiver when there are several in the sibling network. Brody and Spark (1966) have hypothesized that a family "burden bearer" emerges to take on the role. Treas, Gronvold, and Bengtson (1980) hypothesized, but failed to confirm, that birth order had strong effects on the parent–child relationship in old age. Horowitz (1982c) found neither birth order effects nor any pattern according to "best or least loved" child. However, in an analysis of sibling availability, she found that less than half of the respondents had a sibling of either sex within close proximity and concluded that it is less often by choice than by necessity that one child takes on primary responsibility for the care of a dependent parent. Ikels (1983) confirms that proximity is a critical variable but goes beyond the immediate time frame to explore why one particular child was more likely than others to remain proximate as well as be the primary provider of care. Her framework specifies, in order of importance: demographic imperatives (i.e., only child or only female child); antecedent events (i.e., special obligations of reciprocity); and situational factors (i.e., child with the least valued competing commitments). Further work on this question is called for and would contribute to a better understanding of how the caregiving role is experienced given different motivating forces.

## Caregiving Behavior

Caregiving, as noted earlier, is defined by the older person's need for assistance rather than any predefined behavior on the part of the caregiver. Therefore, it is not unexpected that most studies find that caregiving activities vary widely among families and can range from occasional errands to round-the-clock care for the bedridden (Archold, 1980; Cantor, 1980; Danis, 1978; Gross-Andrews & Zimmer, 1978;

Horowitz, 1982b; Lang & Brody, 1983; Noelker & Poulshock, 1982). Similarly, caregiver reports of the time they devote to caregiving activities have ranged from an average of three hours weekly to well over 40, with much of this variation a function of the older person's impairment level and/or whether the dyad live together or in separate households (Horowitz, 1982c; Lang & Brody, 1983; Newman, 1976; Noelker & Poulshock, 1982).

The task of identifying typical patterns of care across studies is further complicated by the variation in the types of help examined, the classification systems used to describe tasks, and the fact that some samples include primary relatives of both healthy and disabled older people. While there is great overlap, there is little consensus to date in what the various investigators define as the critical components of caregiving behavior. In an earlier work, this author conceptualized caregiving behavior as falling into four broad categories: emotional support; direct service provision; mediation with formal organizations and providers; and financial assistance (Horowitz, 1982b). Sharing a household was considered to be a special form of caregiving. It may encompass and facilitate the provision of all services within the four general categories but is also a special response in itself. This framework will be used to review the relevant research.

*Emotional Support.*    Emotional support, which includes maintaining social interaction and "cheering up" when depressed, is often taken for granted as part of normal family interactions, and many investigators who study caregiving behavior do not include items to tap this dimension of the caregiving role. However, when included in the inventory of services, emotional support emerges as the most universal caregiving task, engaged in by almost every caregiver (Horowitz, 1982b, 1982c; Lang & Brody, 1983; Sherman, Horowitz, & Durmaskin, 1982). Furthermore, both Horowitz (1982c) and Cicirelli (1983a) found that providing emotional support, regardless of the extensive support and time committed to direct services, was defined by the caregiver as the most important and critical type of assistance offered to their frail relative.

*Direct Service Provision.*    Direct service provision is the core of caregiving support and encompasses a broad range of activities including shopping, doing errands, providing transportation, housekeeping, meal preparation, personal care (bathing, feeding, toileting, transfer, and dressing), financial management, health care (e.g., changing bandages, giving injections), repairs, laundry, administering medications, and continuous supervision. Despite variation across studies in the number of activities asked about and how they are grouped, certain types of tasks do appear to define the majority of caregiving situations.

Danis (1978), for example, found-that for the majority of care-givers, providing care involved frequent errands, transportation for doctor's visits, and daily telephone calls. Frankfather et al. (1981) found that the assistance most frequently provided by family members to their frail elderly relatives were preparing meals, light housekeeping, administering medications, and personal care tasks. Cantor (1980), studying a less severely disabled population, found that shopping, going to the doctor, managing finances, fixing things around the house, and preparing meals were most common. Reece et al. (1983) report that shopping and transportation were also the most commonly provided services but that almost half of the caregivers studied also provided personal care and more than one-third were involved in home health care.

Horowitz (1982c) identified a hierarchy of instrumental assistance. At the very least, the direct service component of caregiving involved the caregiver's being available for shopping/errands, transportation, and financial management. These tasks, requiring intermittent help, represented the basic level of support offered by the majority of caregiving relatives across kin categories. The second level of direct services consists of in-home assistance, that is, meal preparation and household help. These are labor-intensive services requiring regular time commitments. They are not universally provided but are still engaged in by the majority of caregivers. Finally, personal and health care services represent the most intensive and intimate caregiving assistance. They are most likely offered *to* the most impaired and *by* those caregivers closest in relationship and proximity to the older relative.

Overall, the most striking characteristic of the direct service component is, as Cantor (1980) noted, the range of services offered. Families do not specialize or concentrate help in any one or two areas but increase services to meet needs as they arise.

*Mediation with Organizations.*   In addition to providing services directly, the rise in the number and complexity of organizational systems which provide services to the aged has brought attention to a new role for the family that may be variably called linkage, mediation, or management.

Shanas and Sussman (1977) have elaborated on the specifics of the role in that the family can ". . . be a buffer for elderly persons . . . examine the service options provided by organizations; effect entry of the elderly person . . . and facilitate the continuity of the relationship of the aged member with the bureaucracy" (p. 216). Yet in a later article they note that while it is often assumed that the family is more knowledgeable than the older person about the operations of formal organizations, in fact both may be ignorant of the structure of bureaucracies and have difficulty in negotiation (Shanas & Sussman, 1981). As Brody (1979) notes, the aging phase may represent the first time any member of the family has reason to need or use formal service.

Archold (1983) has used this role to dichotomize her caregiving sample as either primarily "care providers" or "care managers." She found that care providers tended to be spouses, while care managers were most likely adult daughters who had greater financial resources with which to purchase direct care services. Horowitz (1982c), on the other hand, found that 70 percent of all caregivers, with little variation by kin relationship, engaged in the linkage role to some degree and concluded that it ". . . is not a role taken on 'instead of' direct assistance [but] added to the repertoire of services in order to maximize the support available for the relative" (p. 184).

Overall, information on the family's role as mediator with formal organizations is limited. As was the case with emotional support, this activity appears to be assumed rather than studied.

*Financial Assistance.*   The greater importance placed by both generations on the socio-emotional rather than financial aspects of their relationship has been documented in every survey of the elderly and their families (Callahan et al., 1980). The elderly do not expect their children to take major responsibility for their income maintenance, and their children concur, consistently placing the responsibility for financial support upon government agencies (Bengtson, Burton, & Mangen, 1981; Cantor, 1980; Harris & Associates, 1975; Schorr, 1980; Simos, 1973).

If one considers only the numbers providing full financial support to aging parents, then the data indicate that behavior is consistent with attitudes toward financial support. Only an estimated 2–3 percent of the aged are reported as full dependents by their children (Schorr, 1980). However, recent evidence suggests that the prevalence of at least some financial assistance to older frail relatives, in cash or in kind, may be more common than previously thought. Morgan (1983) analyzed data from the 1971 and 1975 Longitudinal Retirement Study and found that approximately 10 percent of the men studied, who were between the ages of 60–65 in 1971 and 64–69 in 1975 and who had at least one living parent or parent-in-law, were contributing to the support of this aged relative. Sample studies of caregivers report even larger proportions. Both Reece et al. (1983) and Baumhover and Meherg (1982) report that over one-fourth of their respondents supplemented the older parent's income. Cantor (1980) found that 45 percent of the children provided some regular financial support and Horowitz (1982b, 1982c) reports that 50 percent of the children and 25 percent of the other relatives were helping financially either by cash contributions or by the purchase of household and personal items.

Thus, financial assistance, when provided, tends not to be for basic food, shelter, or health care. These primary needs are covered by the various governmental entitlement programs. Rather, this type of help provides the older relative with what may be called "necessary extras," an extra item of clothing or additional groceries. These contributions often raise the quality of daily life for the older person above a basic subsistence level and their importance should not be underestimated.

*Sharing a Household.* Forming a joint household can be considered a specialized type of caregiving response. However, exactly how common this response is remains uncertain. While national data show that 18 percent of all older people live with a child (Shanas, 1979a), some of these situations represent dependent children living in the household of a parent. At the same time, the data also show that the possibility of living with a child increases among the unmarried and the oldest elderly. Thus, cross-sectional surveys, which capture only one point of time, cannot indicate how prevalent shared households are over the lifetime of either the elderly or the caregiving relative. Beck and Beck (1982), using longitudinal data, suggest that the incidence of extended households over a 10-year period is double that documented at any single point in time. Such data support Noelker and Poulshock (1982), who have referred to the "18 percent fallacy" and have suggested that the proportion of older people *ever* residing within an intergenerational household for caregiving purposes has been consistently underestimated and underdocumented.

Given the preference of both generations to live separately, shared households are usually not a life pattern but a response to extreme circumstances. The primary reasons for forming a joint household are insufficient economic resources and increasing health disabilities which preclude self-care (Troll, 1971). As a result, shared living arrangements are most common when caring for extremely impaired older people and among lower income families. They also tend to be female-linked and two- rather than three-generational households (Horowitz, 1982c; Kivett & Learner, 1982; Lang & Brody, 1983; Moon, 1983; Schorr, 1980; Soldo & Myllyluoma, 1983; Troll, 1971; Troll et al., 1979). While findings from two local studies suggest no difference between whites and non-whites in proportions sharing a household (Horowitz, 1982c; Kivett & Learner, 1982), Soldo and Myllyluoma (1983), using national data from the 1976 Survey of Income and Education, report that multigenerational living among the impaired elderly is more common among non-whites. However, without controls for income or disability, it remains unclear whether this trend is an outgrowth of culture or of necessity. In general, shared households are, as Schorr (1980) has called them, a "lifeboat response," made when help cannot be offered in any other way and reflecting the extent to which families will go to maintain their older frail relatives in the community.

*Caregiving Beyond the Community.*    Caregiving behaviors on the part of family members do not cease when conditions necessitate institutional placement. On the contrary, the evidence indicates that all types of support (with the exception of shared households) can and do continue within institutions (Brody & Spark, 1966; Clark & Pelham, 1983; Dobrof, 1976; Dobrof & Litwak, 1977; Hatch & Franken, 1984; Montgomery, 1982, 1983; Smith & Bengtson, 1979; Tobin & Kulys, 1981; York & Calsyn, 1977). The interested reader is referred to the literature cited for greater detail.

**The Impact of Providing Care**

The provision of the care described above inevitably has some impact on the family unit. There are *both* costs and benefits, although most of the literature has focused on the former. Within this section, we first review the types and relative severity of caregiving problems as identified by the caregivers and then turn to what is known about the positive aspects of the caregiving process.

It is important to keep in mind that not all caregivers experience every problem described below, nor is every problem experienced with the same severity by different caregivers. Just as caregivers have been found to vary in the extent and type of caregiving behavior, so has every study documented extensive variation in the caregiver's evaluation of the experience. Feelings of stress and strain may be absent or may dominate the caregiver's daily existence. While most investigators report that substantial proportions of their respondents are undergoing moderate to extreme stress, they concurrently note that, given the severity of the older person's problems and the demands of the caregiving role, the overall level of burden, disruption, or stress is less than would be expected (Cicirelli, 1981a; Noelker & Poulshock, 1982; Zarit, Reever, & Bach-Peterson, 1980). Overall, most families have been found to have impressive adaptive capabilities.

*The Negative Consequences of Caregiving.*    A fairly consistent finding across the various studies is that the emotional stresses associated with caregiving are the most pervasive and the most difficult for the caregiver to deal with when compared to either the physical or financial aspects of care (Cantor, 1983; Cicirelli, 1980; Horowitz, 1982a). Negative effects on mental and emotional health have been reported by significant proportions of caregivers (Horowitz, 1982a; Noelker & Poulshock, 1982) and increased levels of depression and anxiety as well as lower morale have been documented (Gurland et al., 1978; Rabins, Mace, & Lucas, 1982; Robinson & Thurnher, 1979; Sanford, 1975).

For most caregivers, these emotional strains stem from a constant concern for the older person's health and safety and the need to redefine and come to terms with the changing nature of their relationship with the aging relative. This can be especially stressful in cases of mental deterioration. For spouses, this involves a redefinition of lifelong patterns of roles and responsibilities. For adult children, the emotional stress often involves coping with what Blenkner (1965) has called the "filial crisis," that is, realizing and accepting that the aging parent is no longer the "pillar of strength" from the past. The struggle for "filial maturity" does *not* imply a role reversal but an acceptance of responsibility and an acceptance of what can be done and what cannot be done. It is the struggle to define "what is enough," which often expresses itself as guilt and increases the emotional stress.

Second only to the emotional strains, and often contributing to them, are the restrictions on time and freedom necessitated by caregiving responsibilities. Caregiving activities often require extensive readjustments in previous daily schedules. Disruption of domestic routines, decreased personal time, less time for social and leisure activities, inability to take vacations, rearrangement of work schedules, and restricted mobility are all common indicators of this pervasive problem (Adams, Caston, & Danis, 1979; Archold, 1980, 1983; Arling & McAuley, 1983; Baumhover & Meherg, 1982; Cantor, 1983; Danis, 1978; Frankfather et al., 1981; Horowitz, 1982a; Kinnear & Graycar, 1984; Noelker & Poulshock, 1982; Rabins et al., 1982; Sanford, 1975). Furthermore, restrictions often go beyond daily life and affect changes in long-range plans for retirement and/or relocation (Archold, 1983; Horowitz, 1982a).

Another point on which there is relatively little controversy is the relatively lower stress associated with financial concerns. Although caregiving may involve financial contributions and may objectively strain the economic resources of the family, there is widespread evidence that, when compared to the social and emotional stresses, financial demands are easiest to deal with and least frequently reported as stressful (Adams et al., 1979; Arling & McAuley, 1983; Cancer Care, Inc., 1973; Cantor, 1983; Frankfather et al., 1981; Horowitz, 1982a; Noelker & Poulshock, 1982; Simos, 1973). Not unexpectedly, spouses, who must draw from a joint and often meager financial pool, are most likely to report financial hardship as compared to all other caregiving relatives. Yet even for spouses, it is experienced as less stressful than the other aspects of caregiving (Cantor, 1983; Horowitz, 1982c).

The economic impact of caregiving may, however, be more indirect for other caregivers if it affects their ability to engage in and perform effectively at work. While a major concern in the field (to be discussed later) is the effect of employment on the ability to provide care, there is increasing evidence that the impact of caregiving on ability to work is substantial for significant numbers. Soldo and Myllyluoma's (1983) research suggests that caregiving does deter labor force participation, particularly among older women. Horowitz (1982c) reports that 21 percent of the nonworking caregivers studied had left the labor force to provide care to an older parent; Brocklehurst et al. (1981) reported that 14 percent of their sample had done so; while Cantor (1980) reports that many caregivers either gave up jobs, had to forego job opportunities, or reduced their work schedules. In addition, caregivers have also reported that their performance at work had suffered or that they have had to miss substantial amounts of time at their jobs (Archold, 1983; Horowitz, 1982a, 1982c; Kinnear & Graycar, 1984). Costs of lost wages may be ultimately shared by the public purse in terms of the losses of tax contributions and increased costs of public assistance to a nonemployed population.

The government may also find itself bearing the costs stemming from the increased morbidity of caregivers. The emotional as well as physical drain involved in providing long-term care to a dependent relative has been found to negatively effect the caregiver's health, especially when the caregiver is experiencing his/her own aging and when caregiving involves physical tasks such as bathing and transferring nonambulatory patients (Adams et al., 1979; Archold, 1980; Brocklehurst et al., 1981; Cancer Care, Inc., 1973; Danis, 1978; Frankfather et al., 1981; Horowitz, 1982a; Noelker & Poulshock, 1982; Sainsbury & Grad de Alarcon, 1970; Ward, 1978). This also appears as a particular problem for elderly spouses (Cantor, 1983; Crossman et al., 1981; Fengler & Goodrich, 1979; Horowitz, 1982c). In fact, Satariano, Minkler, and Langhauser (1984) report that the ill-health of one spouse was the strongest predictor of the other spouse's own poor health status.

Many writers have stressed the impact caregiving can have on the marital and family relations of the adult child. Spending time away from their own family and neglecting other family responsibilities emerges as a common concern for substantial proportions of caregivers (Archold, 1983; Arling & McAuley, 1983; Danis, 1978; Horowitz,

1982a; Rathbone-McCuan, 1976). Other studies have found that it is not only a matter of time restrictions for family activities or responsibilities, but that caregivers often reported increased family conflicts and disrupted family relations stemming from the caregiving role (Adams et al., 1979; Kinnear & Graycar, 1984; Noelker & Poulshock, 1982; Rabins et al., 1982). The extent and severity of this problem is, however, a matter of some disagreement. Horowitz (1982a), for example, found that while one-fourth of the adult child caregivers reported reduced time for spouse and children, few reported deteriorated relationships, and these relationships were among the areas least likely to be affected as a consequence of caregiving. This finding is confirmed by Cantor (1980, 1983), who reports minimal family impacts and relations with spouse and children tending to be "jealously guarded."

One possible explanation for this lack of consensus is the failure in some studies to distinguish between nuclear and extended family relationships. The family conflicts reported may not involve spouse and children as much as they involve siblings of the adult child caregiver. The clinical literature does suggest that sibling conflict is a common theme among children of aged parents (Berezin, 1970; Hausman, 1979; Miller, 1981) and when caregivers are asked directly about relations with siblings, significant numbers do report deteriorated relations (Archold, 1980; Frankfather et al., 1981; Horowitz, 1982a; Kinnear & Graycar, 1984).

Several studies indicate that one of the negative consequences of caregiving is strained affective relations between the caregiving relative and the dependent older person (Archold, 1983; Cantor, 1983; Frankfather et al., 1981; Johnson & Catalano, 1983; Kulys & Tobin, 1978; Robinson & Thurnher, 1979). In fact, Noelker and Poulshock (1982), studying caregiving within shared households, report that the caregiver–older person relationship was the second most affected area after personal time restrictions.

Horowitz (1984) has argued that it is important to make the distinction between the effects of caregiving on global affective relationships versus those on the quality of daily interactions. Conflicting needs and the stresses inherent in a caregiving situation may very well affect the ability to get along on a daily basis. However, the effect on more persistent and generalized feelings may be quite different. Data from the Horowitz study indicate that while a substantial minority reported that the ability to get along on a daily basis had deteriorated, very few reported change in their overall affective relationships. Similar findings were also reported by Adams et al. (1979) in a longitudinal study of caregiving dyads, where there was an equal likelihood of both improved and deteriorated relations. Thus, caregiving clearly carries with it the potential of both negative and positive effects on the emotional relationship between caregiver and care receiver. Certain characteristics of the caregiving situation, such as whether the disability is primarily physical or mental, will inevitably influence the direction of the effect. Other factors are clearly operating as well, and further specification in this area is needed.

### The Benefits of Caregiving

As noted earlier, the emphasis has been on the negative aspects of providing care. The research conducted to date has given much less attention to documenting any positive consequences perceived to come from the caregiving role. Yet stressful situations need not have only negative consequences, nor should negative and positive effects be considered mutually exclusive.

The evidence suggests that when asked directly, most caregivers can identify at least one positive aspect associated with providing care and that this aspect primarily involves a feeling of self-satisfaction and increased self-respect stemming from the knowledge that one is successfully fulfilling a responsibility and coping with a personal challenge (Horowitz, 1982a; Reece et al., 1983).

Additionally, as discussed earlier, caregiving may result in an improved relationship with, and understanding of, the aging relative, especially when this relative is a parent. Other positive effects that have been reported include putting other stresses into proper perspective (Danis, 1978); relief from worry that the older relative is being properly cared for (Newman, 1976); and serving as a role model for one's own children (Cancer Care, Inc., 1973).

## VARIATION IN THE CAREGIVING EXPERIENCE: ATTEMPTS AT EXPLANATION

### Conceptual and Methodological Issues

Investigations seeking to explain the variation among families must first define and measure the two primary components of the caregiving phenomenon: caregiving behavior and caregiving effects.

Caregiving behavior is a fairly straightforward concept, almost always referring to the objective level of time and/or task commitment. Studies do, however, differ in the types of tasks they include in their composite measures and in whether caregiving involvement is operationalized as the number of tasks performed, the frequency of specific task performance (i.e., daily, weekly), and/or the actual number of hours consumed in providing assistance. Although these differences are not unimportant and may account for some of the varying findings in the reported research, the concept is uniformly behaviorally based and serves to differentiate caregivers within any one sample in terms of the amount and extent of help provided.

The conceptual and methodological issues involved in the definition and measurement of caregiving effects are more complex and engender greater controversy. The terminology used reflects the lack of consensus. The effects of caregiving and their measures have been variably referred to as caregiving burden (Montgomery et al., 1985; Poulshock & Deimling, 1984; Thompson & Doll, 1982; Zarit et al., 1980; Zarit & Zarit, 1982); caregiver strain (Cantor, 1983; Robinson, 1983); the costs of care (Kosberg, 1983); family inconvenience (Teresi et al., 1978); caregiving consequences (Horowitz, 1982a); personal strains and negative feelings (Cicirelli, 1980, 1981a); stress effects (Noelker & Poulshock, 1982); and caregiving impact (Cantor, 1983; Poulshock & Deimling, 1984).

However named, the effects of caregiving are usually conceptualized as including several distinct elements: the emotional response to the role which may be experienced as depression, demoralization, or negative feelings; adverse effects in various spheres of personal or family life; and difficulties encountered in performing specific caregiving tasks. The primary difference among the existing measures is whether the concept of caregiving effects is operationalized as a unidimensional or multidimensional concept.

Researchers who have used unidimensional measures have either measured only one dimension or made the implicit assumption that all components are interrelated and that the subjective response to the experience will affect the evaluation of objective problems and the degree to which lifestyles are, or are perceived to be, altered (Horowitz, 1982a, 1982c; Kosberg, 1983; Robinson, 1983; Teresi et al., 1978; Zarit et al., 1980).

Others have made the distinction between objective and subjective burden (Cicirelli 1980, 1981a; Montgomery et al., 1985; Thompson & Doll, 1982), with the former reflecting the extent of disruptions or changes in the caregiver's life and the latter reflecting the emotional cost, that is, the caregiver's attitudes toward and emotional reactions to the caregiving experience.

Poulshock and Deimling (1984), however, have criticized the subjective/objective dichotomy as an unsatisfactory solution to the problem and one that adds little to specificity. They argue for the use of the term *caregiving impact* to reflect and measure what has been called *objective burden* and that "burden" be conceptualized and measured as specific to the type of impairment (e.g., activities of daily living versus mental impairment) and reflect the difficulty in coping with the associated needs. The model proposed is one where impairment, burden, and impact are associated but independent, with impairment contributing to burden, which in turn contributes to caregiving impact.

This controversy cannot be resolved within this review, although it is clear that greater specificity of the multiple dimensions of caregiving effects is desirable over gross measures. However, that the controversy exists is itself informative for what it reflects about the state of the field.

First, the controversy is indicative of the relative infancy of this area of enquiry. It is only within the past 15 years that in-depth examinations of family caregiving to the frail elderly have been conducted, and the current debate suggests the growing sophistication with which this stage of the family life cycle is being approached.

Second, some of the disagreement may stem from the largely empirical rather than theoretical nature of the field. While writers often talk about caregiving stress, few explicitly place it within the general context of stress theory and distinguish its components within this framework. A general stress model, such as the one proposed by Dohrenwend and Dohrenwend (1974), would be relevant to the family's response to an older relative. The disability of an older relative can be defined as a potential stressor. The extent to which stress is ultimately experienced and how it is manifested would be a function of the characteristics of the event and the actors, the meaning attached to the event by the family members, and the external and internal resources available to cope with the event. Such a framework may prove extremely fruitful for further study.

Finally, it is interesting to note that even with the variations in definition and measurement, the findings from the various studies have been largely consistent. In many ways a very cohesive body of knowledge regarding family caregiving has developed in a relatively short period of time.

**Major Influences on the**
**Caregiving Experience:**
**A Beginning Explanatory Model**

There are many ways one can categorize the many independent variables that have been mentioned in the literature as being related to both the patterns and consequences of caregiving arrangements. One broad scheme includes two general categories: *structural factors,* focusing on the sociodemographic and health characteristics of the caregiver and the older person which determine the social and economic resources available to meet the needs of the elderly; and *dynamic factors,* focusing on past experiences, attitudes, and feelings which influence the caregiving relationship. As the following review will indicate, both sets of variables appear to play a part in influencing the course and consequences of family caregiving.

The research findings defining our current body of knowledge will be discussed below within six substantive categories: characteristics of the older person and the caregiving context; sociodemographic characteristics of the caregiver; family support; affective relations; prior planning for care; and utilization of formal services. While each is discussed separately, they are interrelated and of differential importance in their influence on caregiving behavior and stress. Emphasis will be given to those variables that tend to be the most salient predictors in multivariate analyses and will be so identified as predictors in the following discussion.

**Demographic and**
**Health Characteristics**
**of the Older Person**

Studies have consistently shown that as the older person's level of functional or mental impairment increases so does *both* the amount of assistance provided by the caregiver (Branch & Jette, 1983; Bromberg, 1983; Cantor, 1975; Cicirelli, 1981a, 1983a; Horowitz, 1982b; Kivett, 1983; McAuley, Jacobs, & Carr, 1984; Noelker & Poulshock, 1982; Seelbach, 1978; Stoller, 1983) *and* the degree of stress experienced (Cicirelli, 1981a, 1983a; Horowitz, 1982a; Johnson & Catalano, 1983; Kosberg, 1983; Mindel & Wright, 1982a; Noelker & Poulshock, 1982; Robinson, 1983; Wilder, Teresi, & Bennett, 1983). Such evidence further indicates that caregivers are responsive to the growing vulnerability of their frail relatives. They will provide more services as needed but will suffer the consequences of doing so.

Recent evidence further suggests, however, that the *type* of help provided may be a more salient predictor of stress than either the total number of tasks or the total number of hours involved in caregiving (Gonyea, Montgomery, & Hooyman, 1982; Montgomery et al., 1985; Noelker & Poulshock, 1982; Reece et al., 1983). Personal care tasks such as bathing, lifting and transferring, dressing, and especially toileting or dealing with incontinence, appear to be both physically and emotionally draining for caregivers and engender the greatest stress. These tasks call for physical resources that older spouse caregivers may not have. For adult children, they require an intimacy that may be considered inappropriate to their lifelong roles.

Similarly, the *type* of impairment has also been identified as a more critical factor than the level of impairment. One basic question is whether mental impairment is more difficult for the caregiving relative to deal with than is physical impairment. The clinical literature has suggested that mental impairment is less expected and more frightening in its implications and manifestations. Much of the research literature supports this view, indicating that it is the appearance or worsening of mental, rather than physical, symptomatology that is most stressful to families (Isaacs, 1971; Noelker & Poulshock, 1982; Robinson, 1983; Robinson & Thurnher, 1979; Smyer, 1980).

Furthermore, the degree of mental impairment appears less critical than the specific disruptive behaviors that stem from it (Noelker & Poulshock, 1982; Wilder et al., 1983). Sleep disturbances have been identified as especially distressing for families (Brocklehurst et al., 1981; Crossman et al., 1981; Gurland et al., 1978; Rabins et al., 1982; Sanford, 1975). Thus, it may not be the fact of dementia that is so stressful for families but rather the manifestations of the disease with which they must cope.

While age and income of the older relative, as indicators of dependency, have been found to be important variables predicting family response in studies of the general aged population (e.g., Branch & Jette, 1983; Bromberg, 1983; Cantor, 1975; Cicirelli, 1981a; Seelbach, 1978), few studies of caregiving to the frail elderly identify either age or socioeconomic status of the older relative as independent predictors of caregiving behavior. Similarly, sex and marital status of the older relative, two highly correlated variables, are most influential in determining *who* will be the caregiver. They act on caregiving behavior and experiences through this relationship, rather than acting directly on the type or amount of support.

The preceding discussion indicates that we are gaining greater specificity in our analyses of the caregiving phenomenon. The latest research has gone beyond gross indicators of impairment and has identified the specific components of the caregiving experience which engender the greatest stress. As a result, the studies suggest the specific areas where formal services may most effectively intervene to reduce the most burdensome aspects of care for the family caregiver.

## Caregivers' Sociodemographic Characteristics

*Gender.*    Gender is one of the most significant factors determining the selection of the caregiving relative, with women predominating over their male counterparts in every kin category. However, men can be found in the role of primary caregiver and the question is: Once in the role do they differ from women in their behavior and experiences?

Most of the evidence suggests that they do, with women offering significantly higher levels of overall assistance (Horowitz, 1981; Kivett, 1983; McAuley et al., 1984; Reece et al., 1983; Stoller, 1983). The differences are most pronounced in all tasks requiring "hands-on" assistance such as domestic and personal care tasks, and less apparent in areas such as decision making, financial management, and linkage functions (Bahr, 1976; Horowitz, 1981; Levav & Minami, 1974; Stoller, 1982, 1983; Treas, 1979).

When it comes to the experiences associated with caregiving, women report higher levels of stress and continue to do so when the amount of care provided and/or level of impairment is controlled (Cantor, 1983; Cicirelli, 1981a; Horowitz, 1981, 1982a; Johnson, 1983; Lieberman, 1978; Noelker & Poulshock, 1982; Robinson & Thurnher, 1979; Zarit, Gatz, & Zarit, 1981).

The question of why this is so is open to interpretation. In regard to the difference between husbands and wives, it has been reported that elderly husband caregivers are more likely to receive greater support from both informal and formal caregivers and that this support may account for lower levels of perceived burden (Johnson, 1983; Zarit et al., 1981). Caregiving may also provide a meaningful role and activity for older retired men. Men, in later life, tend to primarily depend on their wives for social interaction and may more easily accommodate themselves to the more intensive focus involved in caregiving. Wives tend to have wider social contacts outside the marriage and, as a result, feel more of a loss when caregiving limits outside activities (Noelker & Poulshock, 1982).

The subjective experiences of adult daughters as compared to sons have been attributed to the stronger emotional tie daughters usually have with their mothers (Robinson & Thurnher, 1979). The greater stress may also come from being "the woman in the middle" (Brody, 1981). Caregiving daughters are the middle generation, usually middle-aged and subject to competing demands on their time. The daughter is usually expected to hold primary responsibility for homemaking, child rearing, and the emotional support of other family members, often in addition to working full time. The same multiple demands are seldom placed on men. It may be little wonder then that women express greater stress when the care of a parent or spouse is added to these other responsibilities.

*Employment Status.*    The preceding discussion suggests the critical role the employment status of the female caregiver plays in influencing both caregiving behavior and the resultant stress. Many writers (e.g., Schorr, 1980; Treas, 1977), have emphasized that the increasing labor force participation of women will severely undermine the ability of families to provide the types of day-to-day care needed by the very frail elderly.

The elderly and their family members tend to share this fear in that demands from a job tend to be one of the more frequently reported impediments to anticipated caregiving (Baumhover & Meherg, 1982; Johnson, 1980; Pelham & Clark, 1983). Furthermore, a study of attitudes among three generations of women found that all generations believe a woman should not have to quit her job to care for an elderly parent (Brody et al., 1983).

However, the research which has explored this question with current rather than anticipatory caregivers does not provide strong support for these fears. Several studies have reported that the employment status of the caregiver is unrelated to the overall amount of help provided (Brody, 1981; Cantor, 1980; Horowitz, 1981, 1983b; Noelker & Poulshock, 1982; Reece et al., 1983; Sherman et al., 1982). While Lang and Brody (1983) do report that working women provided fewer hours of care, they emphasize that their findings do not indicate any widespread or significant reduction in parent care by working women. Interestingly, Stoller (1983) found that while employment status was the most significant predictor of lower levels of assistance for sons, it was not significant for daughters. Furthermore, Sherman et al. (1982) suggest that parents of working daughters may in fact be *more* advantaged in that they receive similar levels of instrumental help but are more likely than parents of nonworking daughters to receive financial assistance.

Unexpectedly, these same women do not consistently evidence

more stress. While some studies do report significant relationships (Montgomery et al., 1985; Robinson, 1983), many others do not find a relationship between employment status and caregiving burden (Cantor, 1983; Horowitz, 1982a; Horowitz et al., 1983b; Noelker & Poulshock, 1982). It may well be that the lifestyles of these women have always required a balancing of multiple commitments and that they are both skilled at arranging time and accustomed to the necessity of doing so. It is also very possible that employment acts as a "safety valve" for working women. It provides them time out of the house and may represent a welcomed respite from the constant care of the older person (Horowitz, 1982a).

However, the effect of employment may be more complex than would first appear. One problem with all our data is that they are drawn from cross-sectional studies which capture the caregiving situation at only one point in time. Yet caregiving is a dynamic process, involving a series of decisions at different stages of one's caregiving career. There may well have been a "critical point" when decisions were made regarding the ability to continue in the labor force. As we have already seen, significant numbers of caregivers do report leaving the work force to provide care. On the other hand, the critical point may involve the decision of whether one can continue to provide care in light of the need to continue employment. This may well be the case according to the reports of both Soldo and Sharma (1980) and Nardone (1980). Both use aggregate data on a community level and have identified the woman's labor force attachment as a significant factor influencing the rates of institutional care.

In addition, the knowledge that employed women do continue as viable caregivers, at least for some period of time, raises questions regarding both the conditions of their employment which either facilitate or impede caregiving, and the consequences of this competing responsibility for the quality of care afforded the older person. For example, Archold (1983) suggests that women in higher status positions are able, by virtue of their more flexible work schedules, to incorporate caregiving activities with minimal disruptions. Horowitz et al. (1983b) have raised the issue of the quality of care, given that the assistance provided by working women may have to be routinized, that is, given when time permits rather than when the needs or wishes of either party arise. Thus, research on the effects of employment on caregiving is in a relatively early stage of development and these, as well as related questions, represent the issues for future investigations.

*Age.*    The aging of the caregiver has been hypothesized as a critical structural constraint on caregiving behavior. However, while the oldest spouses have been found to do less (Noelker & Poulshock, 1982), the advanced age of the adult child tends to be more strongly associated with an expressed unwillingness to provide care at some future time (Baumhover & Meherg, 1982; Hanson, Sauer, & Seelbach, 1983; Sussman, 1977) than it is with actual caregiving behavior once in the role. When age is found to be related to caregiving behavior, it is usually the *oldest* children who do more and is usually explained by the fact that they are caring for the oldest, probably most disabled parents (Horowitz, 1982b; Kivett, 1983; Lang & Brody, 1983; Noelker & Poulshock, 1982).

The evidence on whether older caregivers experience more stress is mixed, with no relationship being reported by Horowitz (1982c) and Noelker and Poulshock (1982); a positive relationship by Cicirelli (1981a) and Montgomery et al. (1985); and a negative relationship by Robinson (1983).

Overall, the age of the caregiver seems to be less important as an independent factor and more important as an indicator of the physical resources available and the extent to which competing commitments are present. It is the variation in these areas that needs to be controlled across studies to explain the divergent findings.

*Health Status.*    References to the health status of the caregiver in the empirical literature are scarce, except by implication on the basis of the caregiver's age. The available evidence suggests few independent effects (Horowitz, 1982c; Noelker & Poulshock, 1982; Robinson, 1983). Such findings underscore that family members help according to the older person's needs and regardless of their own limitations, and that the primary source of stress is the caregiving situation itself.

*Social Class.*    The social class of the caregiver tends not to affect the *amount* of help given as much as it affects the *type* of assistance. This is primarily due to the greater resources available to the middle class. In the lower classes, caregivers tend to provide more direct services and are more likely to share a household in response to the older person's growing needs (Cantor, 1979b; Sussman, 1965; Sussman & Burchinal, 1962). Caregivers of higher socioeconomic status can afford to purchase direct care services for their aged relative (Archold, 1983; Kinnear & Graycar, 1984; Noelker & Poulshock, 1982). Those with greater financial resources have also been found to be more likely to provide financial assistance to their aged relative (Moon, 1983; Morgan, 1983; Reece et al., 1983).

The evidence on the influence of social class on the reaction to the caregiving role is mixed. Some researchers have found no relationship (Cicirelli, 1980; Noelker & Poulshock, 1982; Poulshock &

Deimling, 1984), while others have reported that higher socioeconomic status is a significant predictor of greater caregiving stress (Horowitz, 1982c; Montgomery et al., 1985). In explaining the latter finding, Horowitz (1982c) has hypothesized that high status offspring may have had higher expectations for their later years in terms of leisure time and retirement opportunities. When the needs of an older relative intrude on these expectations, the strains of providing care are intensified. However, it is probable that social class differences, if they are confirmed by future research, are not as critical as gender or the characteristics of the caregiving situation (Lee, 1980; Troll et al., 1979).

*Race.*   The assumption that the minority elderly have stronger and more extensive family support systems is consistently disproven by the research evidence. Most studies report little difference in the caregiving behavior and/or reactions of black and white families (Bengtson et al., 1981; Cantor, 1979b; Horowitz, 1982c; Jackson, 1971; Kivett & Learner, 1982; Mindel & Wright, 1982b; Mitchell & Register, 1984; Noelker & Poulshock, 1982; Seelbach, 1978). When differences are found, they tend to be between blacks and whites on one hand, and Hispanic families on the other (Bengtson et al., 1981; Cantor, 1979b; Horowitz, 1982c). Hispanics are more likely to live in multigenerational families, have higher filial expectations and interactions, and receive more direct services. However, as Cantor (1979b) points out, ". . . although being Hispanic is likely to increase the chances of receiving help . . . functional ability, current income and social class position are, if anything, even more important determinants of amount and patterns of help" (p. 170).

*Marital Status.*   The marital role represents a very strong competing commitment to the caregiving role and there is evidence that married nonspouse caregivers do have lower levels of caregiving involvement when compared to the unmarried (Horowitz, 1982b; Lang & Brody, 1983; Stoller, 1983). Marital status also appears to be an important factor determining the selection of the primary caregiver. Where there is a choice, families implicitly recognize the pull of the competing marital role and place the responsibility for care disproportionately on never-married or unmarried offspring (Ikels, 1983; Stoller, 1983). Married children, especially those who have had to balance the demands of spouse and minor children, have also been among those reported to be the most negatively affected by the caregiving role (Horowitz, 1978; Noelker & Poulshock, 1982).

The increase in divorce rates has raised some critical questions and concerns about the future patterns of family care for the aged. At the current time, it is estimated that 40 percent of all recent marriages will end in divorce (Furstenberg, 1981; Hagestad, 1982). The implications of this trend for caregiving have only begun to be investigated. Cicirelli (1983b), for example, has reported that offspring with disrupted marriages do provide somewhat, although not drastically, lower assistance to their parents. However, many questions have yet to be addressed. If divorce occurs in the early years and disrupts ongoing relationships with parents, will an offspring feel the same obligation to help the parent as he or she grows older? Will the prevalence of remarriage after divorce create such extended kinship systems that any one child may be faced not only with aging parents and grandparents but with aging step-relations as well? Divorce in the younger generation may cause the middle generation to "reroute" resources such as time, attention, and money that would have been available for an aging parent (Hagestad, 1982). As a result, will the older generation and the younger divorced generation emerge as competitors in the race to fill the "empty nest" of the middle-aged? On the other hand, will the extensive support parents have been found to give to recently divorced and widowed daughters (Bankoff, 1983) create obligations that the former will feel motivated to repay in later years? Such questions are critical, and to date, remain unexplored.

*Living Arrangements.*   In a study of caregiving to an elderly relative, sharing a household can be considered as both an independent and a dependent variable. As one possible response of a child to the needs of the parent, it has been shown that the move into a joint household is influenced by social class, the disability of the parent, and the gender of the parent and child. Most evidence also confirms that the amount of help provided is more extensive when caregiver and care receiver share a household (Horowitz, 1982b; Lang & Brody, 1983; Reece et al., 1983).

As a factor influencing the experience of caregiving, the available evidence indicates that the stresses of caring for an elderly relative are more severe when help is given within a shared household. This is primarily a function of the higher levels of impairment and the more extensive demands on the caregiver's time associated with joint households (Horowitz, 1982b; Reece et al., 1983; Sainsbury & Grad de Alarcon, 1970), but may also be due, as clinicians have noted, to the greater opportunity for open interpersonal conflict (Savitsky & Sharkey, 1972).

**Family Support**

Relatives other than the primary caregivers are rarely found to provide care of any significant extent. The help that is reported primarily centers on social interaction and the less intensive direct services, and not in areas such as personal or home health care (Cicirelli, 1981a; Horowitz, 1982c; Johnson & Catalano, 1981; Kinnear & Graycar, 1984; Noelker & Poulshock, 1982).

Yet the question remains whether assistance from other kin, when it does exist, supplements or substitutes for the care available from the primary caregiver. The available evidence indicates that it is the former, with the amount of care provided by other relatives being unrelated to the amount of care provided by the primary caregiver (Horowitz, 1982b, 1982c; Noelker & Poulshock, 1982). Therefore, it appears to be incorrect to conceptualize the caregiving situation as one where having many active caregivers translates into less work per caregiver. Rather, the primary caregivers do what they feel can and/or must be done. The extent to which other relatives are assisting may enhance the overall amount or quality of care afforded the aged recipient but does little to influence the behavior of the primary caregiver.

Perhaps because the support is minimal and not located in those tasks most stressful for the caregiver, the *amount* of other family assistance fails to act as a buffer on the degree of stress experienced by the primary caregiver (Horowitz, 1982a; Noelker & Poulshock, 1982; Wilder et al., 1983). However, the *perception* of support or of supportive attitudes emerges as a critical variable predicting lower levels of burden (Archold, 1983; Horowitz, 1982a; Noelker & Poulshock, 1982; Rathbone-McCuan, 1976; Sussman, 1979; Zarit et al., 1980, 1981; Zarit & Zarit, 1982). Thus, a primary caregiver operating within what is perceived as a supportive environment and feeling secure in the knowledge that support is available if needed can carry out the caregiving role with relatively less stress, regardless of whether that help is ever activated.

**Affective Relationships**

It has already been noted that family interactions and exchanges over most of the life cycle can and do take place regardless of the quality of affective relationships. It also appears that the assumption of the caregiving role is not dependent upon affective closeness (Horowitz, 1978; Horowitz & Shindelman, 1983a; Kulys & Tobin, 1978). Feelings of obligation and familial responsibility seem to be sufficient motivators and will often override any impediments due to a poor past relationship.

However, once in the role of caregiver, there is some evidence to suggest that affection influences the extent to which one will engage in supportive activities. Horowitz (1982b) found that the quality of affective relations was a significant predictor of the amount of care provided, second only to and controlling for the parent's level of impairment. Affection thus acted as a motivator for higher levels of care.

Affection also appears to mediate the perceived stress of caregiving. When multivariate analyses have been performed, more positive feelings have emerged as significant predictors of less stressful caregiving experiences (Cantor, 1983; Cicirelli, 1983a; Horowitz, 1982a; Robinson, 1983; Zarit, 1983).

### Anticipatory Planning

It has been hypothesized that the more successful cases of family care would be those where family members were able to address the problem before it occurred and to articulate and reach agreement on the alternatives available to them (Schlesinger, Tobin, & Kulys, 1980). This, however, remains primarily an area of speculation. Only one study was found that included this variable, and findings were contradictory to expectations; that is, prior planning was not associated with lower levels of stress but was a significant predictor of higher levels of caregiving assistance (Horowitz, 1982b).

What the literature does show more clearly is that anticipating and planning for the caregiving experience is more the exception than the rule with both generations rarely reporting either family discussions or personal deliberations (Horowitz, 1982c; Kulys, 1983; Kulys & Tobin, 1980; Stoller, 1982). In general, there seems to be an emotional barrier, on both sides, impeding the consideration of the need for care and this denial may further explain why caregiving is so emotionally stressful when it must eventually be confronted.

### Formal Service Utilization

The relationship between formal and informal service providers and how they interact with each other is a very complex issue. However, from the available evidence we can begin to identify some very general patterns in service use that are indicative of the formal–informal service sector relationships.

First, we do know that having family available not only reduces the probability of institutionalization but also reduces the probability of utilizing formal services in the community (O'Brien & Wagner 1980; Starret, Mindel, & Wright, 1983; Wagner & Keast, 1981; Ward, Sherman, & LaGlory, 1984). Second, when formal services are used, the family continues to provide the major portion of care (Greene, 1983; McAuley & Arling, 1984; Pelham & Clark, 1983; Sager, 1983). Third, higher levels of formal service utilization tend to be associated with higher levels of family care, suggesting that it is the very impaired elderly who are receiving extensive assistance from both sectors (Horowitz, 1982c; Noelker & Poulshock, 1982). Fourth, when family caregivers do approach formal service providers, they tend to be very selective and modest in their service requests, often requesting far less than professionals would have recommended (Horowitz, 1982c; Sager, 1983; Zimmer & Sainer, 1978). Fifth, the types of services families report as most needed and desirable typically represent some form of respite from the ongoing responsibility of care (Archold, 1983; Danis, 1978; Horowitz, 1982; Reece et al., 1983; Whitfield, 1981; Zimmer & Sainer, 1979).

The effect that the provision of formal care has on the behavior of family caregivers is one of the major questions at the current time. From a policy point of view this has been labeled the "substitution issue," that is, the extent to which the expansion of publicly provided services will substitute for the care that families would have provided in their absence. From a service provider's perspective, this question might be alternatively posed as whether the service was successful in meeting the goal of respite.

Regardless of the position from which one approaches the question, the available evidence indicates that the provision of formal services does not significantly reduce the previous level of care provided by family caregivers. Evaluations of demonstrations in publicly funded community-based long-term care, utilizing longitudinal and comparison group designs, have found no support for the substitution concern (Horowitz et al., 1983a; Sklar & Weiss, 1983). Gonyea et al. (1982) report that the provision of chore services was unrelated to both the type of tasks families engage in and the number of hours spent in care. Frankfather et al. (1981) found that while there was some reduction in family efforts when homemaker services were introduced, these same families ". . . would adopt new supportive activities that were less intensive but complemented the homemaker's activities" (p. 71). Similarly, Lewis, Beinstock, Cantor, & Schneewind (1980) found that the initiation of service resulted more in a shifting or redirecting of family care rather than a withdrawal of such care. Finally, Gibson (1984), in a cross-cultural review, reports that research in other countries found that formal services complement rather than undercut or substitute for family support.

The issue of whether the introduction of formal services reduces the burden of caregiving upon family caregivers is also somewhat complex. When families are asked directly to evaluate the effects of formal services on their caregiving situations, the qualitative data attest to the many benefits of formal service input in terms of reducing the emotional and physical burdens of care (Frankfather et al., 1981; Horowitz, 1982c; Whitfield, 1981). Yet when quantitative analysis attempts to relate the level of formal service utilization to the level of caregiving stress, no significant associations are found (Gonyea et al., 1982; Horowitz, 1982a; Noelker & Poulshock, 1982). This lack of a relationship has been variously hypothesized to be due to the fact that the amount of formal services remained minimal when compared to the efforts of family members (Noelker & Poulshock, 1982); that the services provided were not directed at the tasks that families found most stressful and therefore did little to affect family stress (Gonyea et al., 1982); and that the quantity of service received is not as critical as the family's perception that this service is adequate to meet their needs (Horowitz, 1982c). Obviously this remains a critical area for future research given that the goal and rationale for formal service intervention is specifically to reduce family stress in order to prolong community care.

**Summary**

The research findings highlight that both structural and dynamic forces are important in understanding the variation in family caregiving to the frail elderly. The strongest influence on the behavior and experiences of families is, as many writers have noted, the caregiving context itself (Cantor, 1983; Cicirelli, 1981a; Noelker & Poulshock, 1982). The older person's type and level of impairment predicts the type and amount of help families provide which, in turn, predicts the stress they experience in the process. Caregiving behavior is further facilitated when the caregiver is female and unencumbered by the structural constraints entailed in occupying the role of spouse. Other structural constraints such as age, health, and employment status appear less important. At the same time, the quality of the affective relationship and the attitudes of other family members emerge as the most salient dynamic variables influencing the caregiving experience. Thus, the context of family caregiving to the frail elderly is neither dominated by objective forces nor determined only by subjective feelings, but like most human situations, represents a complex interaction of the two.

## EFFECTS OF FAMILY CARE
## ON THE FRAIL OLDER PERSON

It is somewhat ironic that when we discovered the family as caregiver we seemed to forget about the older person as the recipient of care. There is a very limited literature on what effects receiving assistance has on the frail older person (other than in the global sense of permitting continued community residence) or on which conditions define more satisfactory caregiving arrangements from the older person's point of view. Streib (1983) has, in fact, labeled the frail elderly the "excluded 20 percent" in terms of being the focus for research.

Dependency is clearly not valued in our society, and it is not surprising that older people report difficulty and dissatisfaction with the dependent role (Fengler & Goodrich, 1979; Noelker & Poulshock, 1982; Teresi et al., 1980). Older people living with others in the latter's households tend to report lower satisfaction than those living independently, but this appears to be more a function of the conditions that brought them into this living arrangement (poor health and low income) than a direct outcome of the living situation itself (Fengler, Danigelis, & Little, 1983; Kivett & Learner, 1982).

Older people who are care receivers do tend to report a general satisfaction with their care arrangements (Johnson, 1980; Noelker & Poulshock, 1982). However, it is of interest that a complaint made by 55 percent of the older people in one study was that the caregiver attempted to do *too much* for them; this finding suggests that families may inadvertently increase the dependency of the older person (Noelker & Poulshock, 1982).

The type of arrangement and the source of care that are most acceptable to the older person are under some dispute. Johnson (1980) reports that receiving services from one's spouse (one's age peer and partner) was found to be more acceptable to the older person and less conflictual than receiving assistance from offspring. Noelker and Poulshock (1982), however, report contradictory findings. Older people living with and receiving care from their offspring were found to be much more satisfied and had higher levels of well-being than did those living with and receiving care from their spouse. Thus, we are left with little consensus on the question.

Finally, while most older people report satisfaction with the care received, we have no objective data on the quality of care families provide to their disabled relatives. This gap in our knowledge was identified in an earlier review (Tobin & Kulys, 1980) and remains true today. Family caregivers often find themselves in the position of providing skilled home health care and/or involved in technical types of assistance for which they have received no training and in which they have little prior experience. Often they have little choice but to learn by trial and error. Whether they are adequately meeting the needs of their older relative remains largely unknown.

## THE CHANGING NATURE
## OF CAREGIVING

Most of the research conducted in family caregiving is cross sectional and provides us only with an isolated picture of a family situation. Yet no one would dispute that caregiving is a dynamic process that goes through stages and changes. The needs of the older person change, as do the internal and external resources available to family members. Involvement and stresses may be different during one phase than during another, and the most salient predictors of these outcomes may also vary at different stages. There is also a decision-making process that families go through regarding caregiving alternatives, which has been relatively unexplored.

Cross-sectional studies seem to indicate that the length of time in the caregiving role is unrelated to the perceived burden of caregiving (Noelker & Poulshock, 1982; Zarit et al., 1980). However, such data are still limited to a sample of caregivers at one point of time and do not indicate whether any one family caregiver will experience change in levels and/or types of stress experienced. Cross-sectional studies also miss caregiving "drop outs," who need to be studied for a more complete understanding of the dynamic nature of the caregiving experience.

References to longitudinal studies in the literature remain scarce, but the few that have been reported give us some evidence of how caregiving experiences and contexts may vary over time. For example, Brocklehurst et al. (1981) report that the role of primary caregiver is not always a continous one. Changes in the primary caregiver were sometimes due to the improvement in the older person's status (as in cases where an elderly spouse was able to take over responsibility of care from a daughter) as well as to the "burn-out" of the previous caregiver. We get little indication or understanding of this phenomenon from cross-sectional studies.

Johnson and Catalano (1983) have reported that the level of support from the primary caregiver also changes over time. Among those older people who continued to exhibit high dependency needs, only about two-thirds of the caregivers maintained or increased support, whereas more than one third decreased their assistance. The latter was more common among children, who were also more likely to turn to formal services, than among spouse caregivers. This finding suggests that there is an attrition of family support over time which may be differentially exhibited as a function of both the type of caregiver and the alternatives available to them.

## DIRECTIONS FOR THE FUTURE: POLICY AND RESEARCH IMPLICATIONS

Our growing body of knowledge in family caregiving to the frail aged continues to confirm two basic facts: one, that most families wish to maintain their involvement with older family members and will respond voluntarily to meet their needs; and two, that families will make extensive personal and financial sacrifices in the process of helping that may eventually lead to the exhaustion of family support.

The critical need for the public sector to respond and work in a cooperative relationship with families cannot be emphasized too strongly. Caregiving to a frail older relative is now a common occurrence in the family life cycle and all evidence indicates that it will become increasingly so in the future. At the current time, 10 percent of the noninstitutionalized elderly are housebound while another 6–7 percent can get out only with difficulty (Shanas, 1979a). Estimates of the proportion who need supportive services, a slightly broader definition, are around the one-third mark, or 8 million people (Brody, 1974; Callahan et al., 1980). With the older population projected to increase to 18 percent of the total population by 2030, and this increase most rapid and pronounced in the 75 and older age group, it is clear that more family members will eventually find themselves with one or more older relatives for whom to care. The woman who is only freed from parent-caring responsibilities in her 70s, just in time to assume this role for her disabled spouse, will no longer be a rarity. From a research perspective, we need to better understand the caregiving phenomenon;

from a public policy perspective, it is becoming increasingly critical that it be addressed.

It is important to note that there has been very little research to date which has directly addressed the long-term effects of either service expansion or service restriction on family caregiving. The discussion that follows, therefore, represents this writer's interpretation of the available evidence that is relevant to evaluating both current trends and proposed policy initiatives.

**Policy Implications**

Ironically, our growing knowledge of the importance of family support to the elderly has been differentially used by two major groups influencing public policy today. On the one hand, there are the advocates of the aged and their families who are urging the development of programs and policies that will be supportive of family care. On the other hand, there are those within the political arena who approach families of the aged from both a conservative ideological perspective and a perspective motivated by concern over the rapid rise in institutional and health care costs.

The first argument made by this latter group is that it is not the place of government to intervene in family life. To do so would risk the disruption of the family unit and take over a function that families obviously desire to retain. However, the government has always intervened in family life and is currently doing so via the policies and programs already in place (Newman, 1980). This intervention is often unintentional and usually to the family's detriment. For example, the Supplemental Security Income program reduces benefit levels by one third when older people live in the household of a family member—a clear disincentive for the formation of an intergenerational household, which some families might desire. Furthermore, Medicaid regulations incorporate a strong disincentive for spouses to continue community care in that eligibility for home care under Medicaid is determined by joint income and assets while eligibility for institutional care is determined only by those resources considered to be independent and available to the disabled spouse. These regulations cannot help but affect the decision-making process regarding the locale of care.

The second argument made is that families will withdraw from the care of their elderly relatives if services are made more available and that this will ultimately result in increased health care costs. This argument wrongly assumes that families would not be involved in caregiving if they were not forced to be. As discussed earlier, there is no evidence to support this concern. Rather, the available evidence indicates that public service supports may in fact enhance the family's ability to maintain the primary caregiving role over time.

The third manifestation of the conservative position is the most disturbing. Given the current concern with rising health care costs for the aged, the family, having been "discovered," is now being viewed as a "cost-containment" resource.

Specifically, this trend is evidenced by the action taken in February 1983 through which, by a reinterpretation of Medicaid policy, the federal regulatory agency attempted to reestablish filial financial responsibility laws. State Medicaid directors were informed they might, if they chose, require adult children and other relatives to provide financial support to aged relatives under statutes of general applicability. The express purpose of this policy is to save public dollars by both raising revenues from relatives of the institutionalized aged and by acting as a deterrent to nursing home placement. Several states have already begun legislative work to enact this provision.

However, in addition to its very questionable legality, this policy rests on a foundation of false assumptions. First, this policy assumes that families are capable of absorbing an even greater proportion of the care than they do now. However, families are currently providing the vast majority of care. Given the projected increases in the elderly population and the decreases in family size, it is extremely questionable whether they can do any more without assistance.

Second, the assumption behind the "deterrent effect" is that alternatives are available to families which have not been pursued prior to the decision to institutionalize. This, however, is far from the typical situation. All research confirms that families approach institutional care as the last resort for the care of their older relatives. They do so only after a long history of community care, after personal and financial resources have been exhausted, and when the older relative's disability requires care beyond that possible in the home (Brody, 1977). With all other options already exhausted, it is highly unlikely that requiring filial financial contributions will effectively act as an additional deterrent to an already undesirable alternative.

Third, the expectation that this policy will generate significant revenues rests on the assumption that there are significant numbers of Medicaid-eligible nursing home residents with adult children capable of, but avoiding, financial support of their aged parents. Even a cursory look at the demographic characteristics of the national nursing home population can refute this assumption. The kinless elderly are clearly overrepresented among nursing home residents: 20 percent are totally kinless, only 12 percent are married, and almost half (46 percent) have no living children (Troll et al., 1979). Furthermore, the fact that the median age of nursing home residents is over 80 suggests that the typical adult child is not the middle-aged individual at the height of his or her earning potential, but the 60+ "young-old" who is, or will soon be, dependent upon a retirement income.

Fourth, even if additional funds could be thus generated, the amount would have to be weighed against the costs of program administration and enforcement. These costs promise to be high given the range of ambiguous administrative issues that need to be addressed. For example, who constitutes a relative? Is it children only or are siblings, cousins, nieces, and nephews to be held responsible? Will it be limited to blood relatives or are step-children and children-in-law also included? How does one divide responsibility among the network of family members? How does one determine income and assets and weigh the competing demands on these resources, such as responsibilities to dependent children? How does one enforce the policy when relatives live in one state and the older person in another? All these complexities make it probable that the administrative costs would equal or exceed any savings generated. The experience of the states that enacted filial responsibility clauses under Old Age Assistance in the 1950s confirm this prediction. Such laws were found difficult and expensive to administer and did *not* lead to financial savings for the states (Schorr, 1980).

Finally, regardless of other objections, the devastating effects of this policy on the quality of relations between adult children and their aging parents would have to be considered. Older people go to great lengths to avoid placing financial burdens on their children and will not request needed help if they perceive that it will reduce the resources available for the middle and younger generations. This proposed policy can potentially pit one generation against the other and may drive a wedge into what is often an already highly charged emotional situation.

The fact is that government can no longer ignore the growing needs of the elderly. Added to the demographic imperatives will be the growing political sophistication of future cohorts and their greater acceptance and expectation of governmental assistance. A systematic national response to the long-term care needs of the elderly and their family caregivers will become increasingly unavoidable. This writer would agree with those who regard as inevitable the extension of Medicare (or the development of a comparable program) to address community-based long-term care.

There is, however, that second group mentioned earlier composed of other federal, state, and local officials and professionals who are advocating the development of programs within our current structure that will support and facilitate family care of the aged. A range of program initiatives has been proposed and/or implemented. They tend to fall into one of two general types: financial or service supports. Most are currently operated as demonstration projects, offered to restricted populations and subject to time-limited funding. They do, however, represent the possible foundations upon which a more systematic national policy for family caregivers can be built.

Examples of financial supports include the State of Maryland's demonstration project offering cash grants to a small number of families who care for an older relative in their own home (Whitfield, 1981); New York State's experience with cash grants through its home attendant program; Florida's Home Care for the Elderly program, which provides subsidies to a caregiving household member for both basic support and for otherwise unreimbursed health care costs; and California's statewide system, which provides relatively high levels of reimbursement for family-based attendant care. In addition to direct cash grants to family members, recommendations for tax relief via "credits" for care have also been proposed as a method of providing economic support to family caregivers (Callahan et al., 1980). Current program initiatives emphasizing service supports most often tend to be local efforts. The majority provide direct homecare services to support and relieve family members. Demonstrations providing institutional respite care, such as those authorized by New York State in 1981, are also being developed to determine the effectiveness of this specific service in deterring institutionalization and supporting families.

Given the lack of controlled evaluation, the relative advantages of these different types of service and financial approaches remain more a subject of debate than of analysis at the current time. However, based on what we do know about family caregiving, the relative effectiveness of financial supports compared to expanded service programs is being seriously questioned (Arling & McAuley, 1983; Cantor, 1983; Horowitz & Shindelman, 1983b; Noelker & Poulshock, 1982; Prager, 1978).

Financial programs assume that families are faced with economic constraints that limit their ability to maintain their older relative at home and that cash incentives will remove these barriers. Yet we have seen that financial stresses are among those least frequently reported by caregivers and least difficult for them to deal with. Unless the amount of the grant was substantial, and there existed a market of services available for purchase, financial supports would not address the most pressing needs of most families. Furthermore, when family caregivers are asked to make a choice, they tend overwhelmingly to select service over economic programs (Horowitz & Shindelman, 1983b; Sussman, 1977, 1979; Whitfield, 1981).

If we are to go the route of service development, several issues must be considered. First, it must be remembered that there are *two* target populations: the elderly and their families. The elderly, due to their vulnerability to chronic disability, have one set of needs. Their families, engaged in the process of helping the older relative, have needs specific to the supportive role they have undertaken. This is not to say that policies providing for services and financial support of the aged do not ultimately relieve the burden of care for the family member, for they certainly do. However, the primary target of these services is the older person, and, more importantly, the criteria for eligibility must depend only on the characteristics of the elderly person and not on the resources of the family network.

In times when resources are perceived to be scarce, there is a tendency to target services, by outcome if not design, to the isolated and kinless elderly. However, to institutionalize such a policy would create a two-tier entitlement system which would, in practice, penalize families for their concern and involvement. Such a system would result in an inequity which is difficult to justify and a program impossible to operationalize (Frankfather et al., 1981; Gonyea et al., 1982; Schorr, 1980).

However comprehensive the network of services for the elderly, the family as the second target population will continue to have unique needs. Programs that provide individual and group counseling, skills training, and in-home and institutional respite will remain important.

Finally, in recognizing that there are two target populations we must also recognize that the needs of each may not always coincide and that ethical considerations may arise when there is conflict. For example, there may eventually come a point when the family cannot realistically provide the round-the-clock care needed by the older person and institutional care is the appropriate placement. The family and the older person may reach this decision jointly or they may not. The older person may be reluctant to make the move or the family may be unwilling to relinquish responsibility even when holding on to it would be clearly destructive to themselves and against the best interests of the older person. It is a dilemma that is not easily resolved, nor one that is uncommon.

**Research Directions**

Throughout this review, an attempt has been made to differentiate those aspects of the caregiving phenomenon on which we have extensive and consistent findings from those that engender controversy and/ or have remained relatively unexplored. What follows, therefore, is a brief summary of our most pressing research concerns.

1. Longitudinal studies should be given priority in the future in order to explore both the dynamic nature of caregiving and the long-term relationship between family care and formal services.
2. Research should continue to explore in depth the effects of divorce on the family's ability and willingness to provide care.
3. The effects of employment on the ability and quality of care as well as the effects of caregiving on ability to engage in employment requires more in-depth analysis.
4. Future research in family caregiving should be more theoretically based in order to better understand the processes by which the need to provide care for a frail older relative may or may not manifest itself as family stress.
5. Investigations should be conducted into the quality of care families provide, with the objective of identifying and differentiating those tasks families are best able to perform from those for which they may need instruction and/or support.
6. There is a critical need for evaluations of interventions in support of families and the older persons for whom they care. Respite care, financial incentives, tax proposals, skill training, and support groups have all been proposed as potential supports for families. Controlled field studies are needed to determine their effects in improving the quality of care and/or reducing the burden of care on families. They also need to specify the types of supports that are most appropriate for different types of families and under varying caregiving conditions.
7. Further psychometric work is needed to establish the reliability and validity of the instruments developed to measure the concept of caregiving stress/burden/impact. Unless we reach some consensus on this issue, we will be forever trying to explain divergent findings that represent not the reality of different situations but the artifact of measurement.

8. Further work is needed to understand the structural and dynamic forces that lead to the selection of one particular child as the caregiver.

9. We need to expand our focus of study and examine the behavior and experience of secondary kin from their own perspective. Our current knowledge about secondary kin is based almost exclusively on reports from primary caregivers. The perspective of a nonprimary caregiver, especially the siblings of an adult child, may prove quite different and offer further insight into the system of family care.

10. The qualitative relationship between the primary caregiver and the older person, and how it affects and is affected by caregiving, requires further specification.

11. Research should further explore the role of families as mediators with formal organizations.

12. Further work is needed to understand how and why families do or do not plan for caregiving and what effect this has on the ultimate course of caregiving when the need does arise.

# REFERENCES

Adams, B.N. *Kinship in an urban setting*. Chicago: Markham, 1968.

Adams, M., Caston, M.A., & Danis, B.G. A neglected dimension in home care of elderly disabled persons: Effect on responsible family members. Paper presented at the 32nd Annual Scientific Meeting of the Gerontological Society, Washington, DC, November, 1979.

Archold, P.G. The impact of caring for an ill elderly parent on the middle-aged offspring. *Journal of Gerontological Nursing*, 1980, *6*, 78–85.

Archold, P.G. The impact of parent-caring on women. *Family Relations*, 1983, *32*, 39–45.

Arling, G., & McAuley, W.J. The feasibility of public payments for family caregivers. *The Gerontologist*, 1983, *23*, 300–306.

Bahr, H.M. The kinship role. In F.I. Nye (Ed.), *Role structure and analysis of the family*. London, Beverly Hills: Sage, 1976.

Bankoff, E.A. Aged parents and their widowed daughters: A support relationship. *Journal of Gerontology*, 1983, *38*, 226–230.

Barney, J.L. The prerogative of choice in long-term care. *The Gerontologist*, 1977, *17*, 309–314.

Baruch, G., & Barnett, R.C. Adult daughters' relationships with their mothers. *Journal of Marriage and the Family*, 1983, *45*, 601–606.

Baumhover, L.A., & Meherg, J.D. Intergenerational helping patterns: Who cares? Paper presented at the Annual Meeting of the Gerontological Society of America, Boston, 1982.

Beck, S.H., & Beck, R.W. The formation of extended households during middle-age: Evidence from a panel study. Paper presented at the Annual Meeting of the Gerontological Society of America, Boston, 1982.

Bengtson, V.L., Burton, L., & Mangen, D. Family support systems and attribution of responsibility: Contrasts among elderly blacks, Mexican-Americans and whites. Paper presented at the Annual Meeting of the Gerontological Society of America, Toronto, Canada, 1981.

Berezin, M.A. The psychiatrist and the geriatric patient: Partial grief in family members and others who care for the elderly patient. *Journal of Geriatric Psychiatry*, 1970, *4*, 53–64.

Blenkner, M. Social work and family relationships in later life. In E. Shanas & G.F. Streib (Eds.), *Social structure and the family: generational relations*. Englewood Cliffs, NJ: Prentice-Hall, 1965.

Branch, L.G., & Jette, A.M. A prospective study of long term care institutionalization among the aged. *American Journal of Public Health*, 1982, *72*, 1373–1379.

Branch, L.G., & Jette, A.M. Elders' use of informal long-term care assistance. *The Gerontologist*, 1983, *23*, 51–56.

Brocklehurst, J.C., Morris, P., Andrews, K., Richards, B., & Laycock, P. Social effects of stroke. *Social Science and Medicine*, 1981, *15A*, 35–39.

Brody, E.M. The aging family. *The Gerontologist*, 1966, *6*, 201–206.

Brody, E.M. Aging and family personality: A developmental view. *Family Process*, 1974, *13*, 23–37.

Brody, E.M. *Long-term care of older people: A practical guide*. New York: Human Sciences Press, 1977.

Brody, E.M. Aged parents and aging children. In P.K. Ragan (Ed.), *Aging parents*. Los Angeles: The University of Southern California Press, 1979.

Brody, E.M. Women in the middle and family help to older people. *The Gerontologist*, 1981, *21*, 471–480.

Brody, E.M., Johnsen, P.T., Fulcomer, M.C., & Lang, A.M. Women's changing roles and help to elderly parents: Attitudes of three generations of women. *Journal of Gerontology*, 1983, *38*, 597–607.

Brody, E.M., & Lang, A. They can't do it all: Aging daughters with aged mothers. *Generations*, 1982, *7*, 18-20.

Brody, E.M., & Spark, G. Institutionalization of the aged: A family crisis. *Family Process*, 1966, *5*, 76-90.

Brody, S., Poulshock, S.W., & Masciocchi, C. The family caring unit: A major consideration in the long term support system. *The Gerontologist*, 1978, *18*, 556–561.

Bromberg, E.M. Mother-daughter relationships in later life: The effect of quality of relationships upon mutual aid. *Journal of Gerontological Social Work*, 1983, *6*, 75–92.

Brown, A.S. Satisfying relationships for the elderly and their patterns of disengagement. *The Gerontologist*, 1974, *14*, 258-262.

Callahan, J., Diamond, L., Giele, J., & Morris, R. Responsibility of the family for their severely disabled elders. *Health Care Financing Review*, 1980, *1*, 24-48.

Cancer Care, Inc. *The impact, costs, and consequences of catastrophic illness on patients and families.* National Cancer Foundation, March, 1973.

Cantor, M. Life space and the social support system of the inner city elderly of New York. *The Gerontologist*, 1975, *15*, 23-34.

Cantor, M. Neighbors and friends: An overlooked resource in the informal support system. *Research on Aging*, 1979a, *1*, 434-463.

Cantor, M. The informal support system of New York's inner city elderly: Is ethnicity a factor? In D.E. Gelfand & A.J. Kutzik (Eds.), *Ethnicity and aging.* New York: Springer, 1979b.

Cantor, M. Caring for the frail elderly: Impact on family, friends, and neighbors. Paper presented at the Scientific Meeting of the Gerontological Society of America, San Diego, November, 1980.

Cantor, M.H. Strain among caregivers: A study of experience in the United States. *The Gerontologist*, 1983, *23*, 597-604.

Carrilio, T.E., & Eisenberg, D.M. Informal resources for the elderly: Panacea or empty promises? *Journal of Gerontological Social Work*, 1983, *6*, 39-47.

Cheal, D.J. Intergenerational family transfers. *Journal of Marriage and the Family*, 1983, *45*, 805-813.

Cicirelli, V.G. Personal strains and negative feelings in adult children's relationships with elderly parents. Paper presented at the 33rd Annual Scientific Meeting of the Gerontological Society of America, San Diego, November, 1980.

Cicirelli, V.G. *Helping elderly parents: The role of adult children.* Boston: Auburn House, 1981.

Cicirelli, V.G. Adult children's attachment and helping behavior to elderly parents: A path model. *Journal of Marriage and the Family*, 1983a, *45*, 815-825.

Cicirelli, V.G. A comparison of helping behavior to elderly parents of adult children with intact and disrupted marriages. *The Gerontologist*, 1983b, *23*, 619-625.

Clark, W.F., & Pelham, A.O. Informal support and nursing home patients. Paper presented at the Annual Scientific Meeting of the Gerontological Society of America, San Francisco, November, 1983.

Crossman, L., London, C., & Barry, C. Older women caring for disabled spouses: A model for supportive services. *The Gerontologist*, 1981, *21*, 464-470.

Danis, B.G. Stress in individuals caring for ill elderly relatives. Paper presented at the Annual Scientific Meeting of the Gerontological Society, Dallas, 1978.

Dobrof, R. *The care of the aged: A shared function.* Unpublished dissertation, Columbia University School of Social Work, 1976.

Dobrof, R., & Litwak, E. *Maintenance of family ties of long-term care patients.* Rockville, MD: National Institute of Mental Health, 1977.

Dohrenwend, B.S., & Dohrenwend, B.P. *Stressful life events.* New York: Wiley, 1974.

Dono, J.E., Falbe, C.M., Kail, B.L., Litwak, E., Sherman, R.H., & Siegel, D. Primary groups in old age: Structure and function. *Research in Aging,* 1979, *1,* 403–433.

Dunlop, B.D. Expanded home-based care for the impaired elderly: Solution or pipe dreams. *American Journal of Public Health,* 1980, *70,* 514–519.

Fendetti, D.V., & Gelfand, D.E. Care of the aged: Attitudes of white ethnic families. *The Gerontologist,* 1976, *16,* 545–549.

Fengler, A.P., Danigelis, N., & Little, V.C. Later life satisfaction and household structure: Living with others and living alone. *Aging and Society,* 1983, *3,* 357–377.

Fengler, A.P., & Goodrich, N. Wives of elderly disabled men: The hidden patients. *The Gerontologist,* 1979, *19,* 175–183.

Frankfather, D., Smith, M.J., & Caro, F.G. *Family care of the elderly: Public initiatives and private obligations.* Lexington, MA: Lexington Books, 1981.

Furstenberg, K.F. Remarriage and intergenerational relations. In R. Fogel, E. Hatfield, S. Kiesler, & E. Shanas (Eds.), *Aging: Stability and change in the family.* New York: Academic Press, 1981.

General Accounting Office. *The well-being of older people in Cleveland, Ohio.* Washington, DC: GAO, 1977.

Gibson, M.J. Caring for the carers: The experience of other developed nations. Paper presented at the Annual Conference of the National Council on the Aging, Washington, DC, 1984.

Gonyea, J., Montgomery, R., & Hooyman, N. The impact of chore services termination on family caregivers. Paper presented at the Annual Scientific Meeting of the Gerontological Society of America, Boston, 1982.

Greene, V.L. Substitution between formally and informally provided care for the impaired elderly in the community. *Medical Care,* 1983, *21,* 609–619.

Gross-Andrews, S., & Zimmer, A.H. Incentives to families caring for disabled elderly: Research and demonstration project to strengthen the natural supports system. *Journal of Gerontological Social Work,* 1978, *1,* 119–133.

Gurland, B., Dean, L., Gurland, R., & Cook, D. The dependent elderly in New York City. *Dependency in the elderly of New York City.* New York: Community Council of Greater New York, 1978.

Hagestad, G.O. Divorce: The family ripple effect. *Generations,* 1982, *7,* 24–25.

Hanson, S.L., Sauer, W.J., & Seelbach, W.C. Racial and cohort variations in filial responsibility norms. *The Gerontologist,* 1983, *23,* 626–631.

Harris & Associates, Inc. *The myth and reality of aging in America.* Washington, DC: National Council on the Aging, 1975.

Hatch, R.C., & Franken, M.L. Concerns of children with parents in nursing homes. *Journal of Gerontological Social Work,* 1984, *7,* 19–30.

Hausman, C.P. Short-term counseling groups for people with elderly parents. *The Gerontologist,* 1979, *19,* 102–107.

Horowitz, A. Families who care: A study of natural support systems of the elderly. Paper presented at the Annual Scientific Meeting of the Gerontological Society of America, Dallas, 1978.

Horowitz, A. Sons and daughters as caregivers to older parents: Differences in role performance and consequences. Paper presented at the Annual Scientific Meeting of the Gerontological Society of America, Toronto, Canada, 1981.

Horowitz, A. The impact of caregiving on children of the frail elderly. Paper presented at the Annual Meeting of the American Orthopsychiatric Association, San Francisco, 1982a.

Horowitz, A. Predictors of caregiving involvement among adult children of the frail elderly. Paper presented at the Annual Scientific Meeting of the Gerontological Society of America, Boston, 1982b.

Horowitz, A. *The role of families in providing long-term care to the frail and chronically ill elderly living in the community.* Final report submitted to the Health Care Financing Administration. New York: The Brookdale Center on Aging at Hunter College, 1982c.

Horowitz, A. Analysis of the caregiver/carereceiver qualitative relationship. Presentation at the Conference entitled: "The Future of Natural Caregiving Networks in Later Life." Sponsored by the University of Buffalo Center for the Study of Aging, Buffalo, 1984.

Horowitz, A., Dono, J., & Brill, R. Continuity or change in informal support: The impact of an expanded home care program. Paper presented at the Annual Scientific Meeting of the Gerontological Society of America, San Francisco, 1983a.

Horowitz, A., Sherman, R., & Durmaskin, S. Employment and daughter caregivers: A working partnership for older people? Paper presented at the Annual Scientific Meeting of the Gerontological Society of America, San Francisco, 1983b.

Horowitz, A., & Shindelman, L. Reciprocity and affection: Past influences on current caregiving. *Journal of Gerontological Social Work,* 1983a, *5,* 5–20.

Horowitz, A., & Shindelman, L. Social and economic incentives for family caregivers. *Health Care Financing Review,* 1983b, *5,* 25–33.

Ikels, C. The process of caretaker selection. *Research on Aging,* 1983, *5,* 491–509.

Isaacs, B. Geriatric patients: Do their families care? *British Medical Journal,* 1971, *4,* 282–286.

Jackson, J.J. Sex and social class variations in black aged parent-child relationships. *Aging and Human Development,* 1971, *2,* 96–107.

Jackson, J.J. Comparative life styles and family and friend relationships among older black women. *Family Coordinator*, 1972, *21*, 477–485.

Johnson, C.L. Obligation and reciprocity in caregiving during illness: A comparison of spouses and offspring as family supports. Paper presented at the Annual Scientific Meeting of the Gerontological Society of America, San Diego, 1980.

Johnson, C.L. Dyadic family relations and social support. *The Gerontologist*, 1983, *23*, 377–383.

Johnson, C.L., & Catalano, D.J. Childless elderly and their family supports. *The Gerontologist*, 1981, *21*, 610–618.

Johnson, C.L., & Catalano, D.J. A longitudinal study of family supports to impaired elderly. *The Gerontologist*, 1983, *23*, 612–618.

Johnson, E.S., & Bursk, B.J. Relationships between the elderly and their adult children. *The Gerontologist*, 1977, *17*, 90–96.

Keith, P.M. Patterns of assistance among parents and the childless in very old age: Implications for practice. *Journal of Gerontological Social Work*, 1983, *6*, 49–59.

Kinnear, D., & Graycar, A. Aging and family dependency. *Australian Journal of Social Issues*, 1984, *19*, 13–25.

Kivett, V.R. Consanguinity and kin level: Their relative importance to the helping network of older adults. Paper presented at the Annual Scientific Meeting of the Gerontological Society of America, San Francisco, 1983.

Kivett, V.R., & Learner, R.M. Perspectives on the childless rural elderly: A comparative analysis. *The Gerontologist*, 1980, *20*, 708–716.

Kivett, V.R., & Learner, R.M. Situational influences on the morale of older rural adults in child shared households: A comparative analysis. *The Gerontologist*, 1982, *22*, 100–106.

Kosberg, J.I. The cost of care index: A case management tool for predicting family abuse of the aged. Paper presented at the Annual Scientific Meeting of the Gerontological Society of America, San Francisco, 1983.

Kraus, A.S., et al. Elderly applicants to long-term care institutions. *Journal of the American Geriatrics Society*, 1976, *24*, 117–125.

Kulys, R. Future crisis and the very old: Implications for discharge planning. *Health and Social Work*, 1983, *8*, 182–195.

Kulys, R., & Tobin, S. The older person's responsible other—child vs. nonchild. Paper presented at the Annual Scientific Meeting of the Gerontological Society of America, Dallas, November, 1978.

Kulys, R., & Tobin, S. Older people and their "responsible others." *Social Work*, 1980, *25*, 138–145.

Lang, A.M., & Brody, E.M. Characteristics of middle-aged daughters and help to their elderly mothers. *Journal of Marriage and the Family*, 1983, *45*, 193–202.

Lebowitz, Barry D. Old age and family functioning. *Journal of Gerontological Social Work*, 1978, *1*, 111–118.

Lee, G.R. Kinship in the 70's: A decade review of research and theory. *Journal of Marriage and the Family*, 1980, *42*, 923–936.

Lee, G.R., & Ellithorpe, E. Intergenerational exchange and subjective well-being among the elderly. *Journal of Marriage and the Family*, 1982, *44*, 217–224.

Levav, I., & Minami, H. Mothers and daughters and the psychogeriatric patient. *The Gerontologist*, 1974, *14*, 197–200.

Lewis, M.A., Bienstock, R., Cantor, M., & Schneewind, E. The extent to which informal and formal supports interact to maintain the older person in the community. Paper presented at the Annual Scientific Meeting of the Gerontological Society of America, San Diego, November, 1980.

Lieberman, G.L. Children of the elderly as natural helpers: Some demographic differences. *American Journal of Community Psychology*, 1978, *6*, 489–498.

Litwak, E. Extended kin relations in an industrial democratic society. In E. Shanas & G.F. Streib (Eds.), *Social structure and the family: Generational relations*. Englewood Cliffs, NJ: Prentice-Hall, 1965.

Litwak, E., & Figueira, J. Technological innovation and theoretical functions of primary groups and bureaucratic structures. *American Journal of Sociology*, 1963, *73*, 468–481.

Litwak, E., & Meyer, H. *School, community, and neighborhood: The theory and practice of school-community relations*. New York: Columbia University Press, 1974.

McAuley, W.J., & Arling, G. Use of in-home care by very old people. *Journal of Health and Social Behavior*, 1984, *25*, 54–64.

McAuley, W.J., Jacobs, M.D., & Carr, C.S. Older couples: Patterns of assistance and support. *Journal of Gerontological Social Work*, 1984, *6*, 35–48.

Maddox, J.L. Families as context and resource in chronic illness. In S. Sherwood (Ed.), *Issues in long-term care*. New York: Halsted Press, 1975.

Miller, D.A. The "sandwich" generation: Adult children of the aging. *Social Work*, 1981, *26*, 419–423.

Mindel, C.H., & Wright, R. Satisfaction in multigenerational households. *Journal of Gerontology*, 1982a, *37*, 483–489.

Mindel, C.H., & Wright, R. Assessing the role of support systems among black and white elderly. Paper presented at the Annual Scientific Meeting of the Gerontological Society of America, Boston, 1982b.

Mitchell, J., & Register, J.C. An exploration of family interaction with the elderly by race, socioeconomic status and residence. *The Gerontologist*, 1984, *24*, 48–54.

Monk, A. Family support in old age. *Social Work*, 1979, *24*, 533–538.

Montgomery, R.J.V. Impact of institutional care policies on family integration. *The Gerontologist*, 1982, *22*, 54–58.

Montgomery, R.J.V. Staff-family relations and institutional care policies. *Journal of Gerontological Social Work*, 1983, *6*, 23–37.

Montgomery, R.J.V., Gonyea, J.G., & Hooyman, N.R. Caregiving and the experience of subjective and objective burden. *Family Relations,* in press.

Moon, M. The role of the family in the economic well-being of the elderly. *The Gerontologist,* 1983, *23,* 45–50.

Morgan, L.A. Intergenerational family support: Retirement age males, 1971–75. *The Gerontologist,* 1983, *23,* 160–166.

Moroney, R. *The family and the state: Considerations for social policy.* London: Longmans, 1976.

Moroney, R. Families, care of the handicapped, and public policy. *Home Health Care Services Quarterly,* 1983, *3,* 188–213.

Nardone, M. Characteristics predicting community care for mentally impaired older persons. *The Gerontologist,* 1980, *20,* 661–668.

National Center for Health Statistics. *Vital statistics of the United States, 1973 life tables.* Rockville, MD: U.S. Government Printing Office, 1975.

National Center for Health Statistics. *Current estimates from the Health Interview Survey, 1978.* Vital and Health Statistics. Series 13. No. 130. Washington, DC: U.S. Government Printing Office, 1979.

Newman, S. Housing adjustments of older people: A report of findings from the second phase. Ann Arbor: Institute for Social Research, University of Michigan, 1976.

Newman, S.J. Government policy and the living arrangements of the elderly. *Home Health Care Services Quarterly,* 1980, *1,* 59–71.

Noelker, L.S., & Poulshock, S.W. *The effects on families of caring for impaired elderly in residence.* Final report submitted to the Administration on Aging. The Margaret Blenkner Research Center for Family Studies, The Benjamin Rose Institute, Cleveland, OH, 1982.

Nydegger, C.H., & Mitteness, L.S. Older fathers and aging children: Marriage as a source of strain. *Generations,* 1982, *7,* 16–17.

O'Brien, J., & Wagner, D. Help seeking by the frail elderly: Problems in network analysis. *The Gerontologist,* 1980, *20,* 78–83.

Palmore, E. Total chance of institutionalization among the aged. *The Gerontologist,* 1976, *16,* 504–507.

Parsons, T. The social structure of the family. In R.N. Anshen (Ed.), *The family: Its function and destiny.* New York: Harper, 1944.

Pelham, A.O., & Clark, W.F. Who is taking care of the poor old widow now? Paper presented at the Annual Scientific Meeting of the Gerontological Society of America, San Francisco, 1983.

Peterson, James A. A developmental view of the aging family. In J.E. Birren (Ed.), *Contemporary gerontology: Concepts and issues.* Los Angeles: University of Southern California Gerontology Center, 1970.

Poulshock, S.W., & Deimling, G.T. Families caring for elders in residence: Issues in the measurement of burden. *Journal of Gerontology,* 1984, *39,* 230–239.

Prager, E. Subsidized family care of the aged: U.S. Senate Bill 1161. *Policy Analysis,* 1978, *4,* 477–490.

Prohaska, T., & McAuley, W.J. The effects of family care and living arrangements in acute care discharge recommendations. *Journal of Gerontological Social Work*, 1983, *5*, 67–80.

Rabins, P.V., Mace, N.L., & Lucas, M.J. The impact of dementia on the family. *Journal of the American Medical Association*, 1982, *248*, 333–335.

Rathbone-McCuan, E. Geriatric day care: A family perspective. *The Gerontologist*, 1976, *16*, 517–521.

Reece, D., Walz, T., & Hageboeck, H. Intergenerational care providers of non-institutionalized frail elderly: Characteristics and consequences. *Journal of Gerontological Social Work*, 1983, *5*, 21–34.

Robinson, B., Validation of a caregiver strain index. *Journal of Gerontology*, 1983, *38*, 344–348.

Robinson, B., & Thurnher, M. Taking care of parents: A family-cycle transition. *The Gerontologist*, 1979, *19*, 586–593.

Rosenmayr, L., & Köckeis, E. Propositions for a sociological theory of aging and the family. *International Social Science Journal*, 1963, *15*, 410–426.

Sager, A. A proposal for promoting more adequate long-term care for the elderly. *The Gerontologist*, 1983, *23*, 13–17.

Sainsbury, P., & Grad de Alarcon, J. The effects of community care on the family and the geriatric patient. *Journal of Geriatric Psychiatry*, 1970, *4*, 23–41.

Sanford, J. Tolerance of debility in elder dependents by supports at home: Its significance for hospital practice. *British Medical Journal*, 1975, *3*, 471–473.

Satariano, W.A., Minkler, M.A., & Langhauser, C. The significance of an ill spouse for assessing health differences in an elderly population. *Journal of the American Geriatrics Society*, 1984, *32*, 187–190.

Savitsky, E., & Sharkey, H. Study of family interaction in the aged. *Journal of Geriatric Psychiatry*, 1972, *5*, 3–19.

Schlesinger, M.R., Tobin, S.S., & Kulys, R.A. The responsible child and parental well-being. *Journal of Gerontological Social Work*, 1980, *3*, 3–16.

Schorr, A. ". . . thy father and thy mother. . ." A second look at filial responsibility and family policy. U.S. Department of Health and Human Services. Social Security Administration Office of Policy, SSA Publication No. 13-11953, July, 1980.

Seelbach, W.C. Gender differences in expectations for filial responsibility. *The Gerontologist*, 1977, *17*, 421–425.

Seelbach, W.C. Correlates of aged parents' filial responsibility expectations and realizations. *Family Coordinator*, 1978, *27*, 341–350.

Seelbach, W.C., & Sauer, W.J. Filial responsibility expectation and morale among aged parents. *The Gerontologist*, 1977, *17*, 492–499.

Shanas, E. Social myth as hypothesis: The case of the family relations of old people. *The Gerontologist*, 1979a, *19*, 3–9.

Shanas, E. The family as a social support system in old age. *The Gerontologist*, 1979b, *19*, 169–174.

Shanas, E., & Sussman, M.B. (Eds.). *Family bureaucracy and the elderly*. Durham, NC: Duke University Press, 1977.

Shanas, E., & Sussman, M.B. The family in later life: Social structure and social policy. In R. Fogel, E. Hatfield, S. Kiesler, & E. Shanas (Eds.), *Aging: Stability and change in the family.* New York: Academic Press, 1981.

Shanas, E., Townsend, P., Wedderburn, D., Friis, H., Milhøj, P., & Stehouwer, J. *Old people in three industrial societies.* New York: Atherton Press, 1968.

Sherman, R., Horowitz, A., & Durmaskin, S. Role overload or role management: The relationship between work and caregiving among daughters of aged parents. Paper presented at the Annual Scientific Meeting of the Gerontological Society of America, Boston, 1982.

Silverstone, B. Informal social support systems for the frail elderly. Paper prepared for the National Research Council/Institute of Medicine, Committee for an Aging Society, The National Academy of Sciences, Washington, DC, 1983.

Simos, B.G. Adult children and their aging parents. *Social Work,* 1973, *18,* 78–85.

Sklar, B.W., & Weiss, L.J. *Project OPEN.* Final report submitted to the Health Care Financing Administration. Mount Sinai Hospital, San Francisco, 1983.

Smith, K.F., & Bengtson, V.L. Positive consequences of institutionalization: Solidarity between elderly parents and their middle-aged children. *The Gerontologist,* 1979, *19,* 438–447.

Smyer, M. The differential usage of services by impaired elderly. *Journal of Gerontology,* 1980, *35,* 249–255.

Soldo, B.J., & Myllyluoma, J. Caregivers who live with dependent elderly. *The Gerontologist,* 1983, *23,* 605–611.

Soldo, B., & Sharma, M. Families who purchase vs. families who provide care services to elderly relatives. Paper presented at the Annual Scientific Meeting of the Gerontological Society of America, San Diego, November, 1980.

Starrett, R.A., Mindel, C.H., & Wright, R. Influence of support systems on the use of social services by the Hispanic elderly. *Social Work Research and Abstracts,* 1983, *19,* 35–40.

Stoller, E.P. Sources of support for the elderly during illness. *Health and Social Work,* 1982, *7,* 111–122.

Stoller, E.P. Parent caregiving by adult children. *Journal of Marriage and the Family,* 1983, *45,* 851–858.

Stoller, E.P., & Earl, L.L. Help with activities of everyday life: Sources of support for the non-institutionalized elderly. *The Gerontologist,* 1983, *23,* 64–70.

Streib, G. The frail elderly: Research dilemmas and research opportunities. *The Gerontologist,* 1983, *23,* 40–44.

Sussman, M.B. Relationships of adult children with their parent in the United States. In E. Shanas & G.F. Streib (Eds.), *Social structure and the family: Generational relations.* Englewood Cliffs, NJ: Prentice-Hall, 1965.

Sussman, M.B. *Incentives and the family environment for the elderly.* Final report to Administration on Aging. AoA Grant #90-A-316, February, 1977.

Sussman, M.B. *Social and economic supports and family environments for the elderly.* Final report to Administration on Aging. AoA Grant #90-A-316 (03), January, 1979.

Sussman, M.B., & Burchinal, L. Kin family network: Unheralded structure in current conceptualization of family functioning. *Marriage and Family Living,* 1962, *24,* 231–240.

Teresi, J.A., Bennett, R.G., & Wilder, D.E. Personal time dependency and family attitudes. In *Dependency in the elderly in New York City.* New York: Community Council of Greater New York, 1978.

Teresi, J.A., Toner, J.A., Bennett, R.G., & Wilder, D.E. Discrepancies between attitudes toward older relatives and attitudes toward elderly in general. Paper presented at the Annual Scientific Meeting of the Gerontological Society of America, San Diego, 1980.

Thompson, E.H., & Doll, W. The burden of families coping with the mentally ill: An invisible crisis. *Family Relations,* 1982, *31,* 379–388.

Thompson, L., & Walker, A.J. Mothers and daughters: Aid patterns and attachment. Paper presented at the Annual Scientific Meeting of the Gerontological Society of America, Boston, 1982.

Tobin, S.S., & Kulys, R. The family and services. In C. Eisdorfer (Ed.), *Annual Review of Gerontology and Geriatrics,* Vol. 1. New York: Springer, 1980.

Tobin, S.S., & Kulys, R. The family in the institutionalization of the elderly. *Journal of Social Issues,* 1981, *37,* 145–157.

Townsend, P. The effects of family structure on the likelihood of admission to an institution in old age: The application of general theory. In E. Shanas & G.F. Streib (Eds.), *Social structure and the family: Generational relations.* Englewood Cliffs, NJ: Prentice-Hall, 1965.

Treas, J. Family support systems for the aged: Some social and demographic considerations. *The Gerontologist,* 1977, *17,* 486–491.

Treas, J. Intergenerational families and social change. In P. Ragan (Ed.), *Aging parents.* Los Angeles: The University of Southern California Press, 1979.

Treas, J., Gronvold, R., & Bengtson, V.L. Filial destiny? The effect of birth order on relations with aging parents. Paper presented at the Annual Scientific Meeting of the Gerontological Society of America, San Diego, November, 1980.

Troll, L.E. The family of later life: A decade review. *Journal of Marriage and the Family,* 1971, *33,* 263–290.

Troll, L.E., Miller, S.J., & Atchley, R.C. *Families in later life.* Belmont, CA: Wadsworth, 1979.

Vicente, L., Wiley, J.A., & Carrington, R.A. The risk of institutionalization before death. *The Gerontologist,* 1979, *19,* 361–367.

Wagner, D., & Keast, F. Informal groups and the elderly: A preliminary examination of the mediation function. *Research on Aging*, 1981, *3*, 325–332.

Wake, S.B., & Sporakowski, M.J. An intergenerational comparison of attitudes towards supporting aged parents. *Journal of Marriage and the Family*, 1972, *34*, 42–48.

Walker, A.J., & Thompson, C. Intimacy and intergenerational aid and contact among mothers and daughters. *Journal of Marriage and the Family*, 1983, *45*, 841–849.

Wan, T.H., & Weissert, W.G. Social support networks, patient status, and institutionalization. *Research on Aging*, 1981, *3*, 240–256.

Ward, R.A. Limitations of the family as a supportive institution in the lives of the aged. *Family Coordinator*, 1978, *27*, 363–374.

Ward, R.A., Sherman, S.R., & LaGory, M. Informal networks and knowledge of services for older persons. *Journal of Gerontology*, 1984, *39*, 216–223.

Weishaus, S. Determinants of affect of middle-aged women toward their mothers. Paper presented at the Annual Scientific Meeting of the Gerontological Society of America, San Diego, November, 1980.

Whitfield, S. Report to the General Assembly on the family demonstration program. State of Maryland, Office on Aging, Mimeograph, August, 1981.

Wilder, D.E., Teresi, J.A., & Bennett, R.G. Family burden and dementia. In R. Mayeux & W.G. Rosen (Eds.), *The dementias*. New York: Raven Press, 1983.

York, J.L., & Calsyn, R.J. Family involvements in nursing homes. *The Gerontologist*, 1977, *17*, 500–505.

Zarit, J.M., Gatz, M., & Zarit, S.H. Family relationships and burden in long-term care. Paper presented at the Annual Scientific Meeting of the Gerontological Society of America, Toronto, Canada, 1981.

Zarit, J.M., & Zarit, S.H. Measuring burden and support in families with Alzheimer's disease elders. Paper presented at the Annual Scientific Meeting of the Gerontological Society of America, Boston, 1982.

Zarit, S.H. Interventions with families of impaired elderly. Paper presented at the Annual Scientific Meeting of the Gerontological Society of America, San Francisco, 1983.

Zarit, S.H., Reever, K.E., & Bach-Peterson, J. Relatives of the impaired elderly: Correlates of feelings of burden. *The Gerontologist*, 1980, *20*, 649–655.

Zimmer, A.H., & Sainer, J.S. Strengthening the family as an informal support for their aged: Implications for social policy and planning. Paper presented at the Annual Scientific Meeting of the Gerontological Society of America, Dallas, November, 1978.

# Social Interventions in Behalf of the Impaired Elderly and Their Families

CHAPTER 7

# Intervention Strategies to Assist Caregivers of Frail Elders: Current Research Status and Future Research Directions

DOLORES E. GALLAGHER, PH.D.
GERIATRIC RESEARCH, EDUCATION AND CLINICAL CENTER (GRECC)
VA MEDICAL CENTER
PALO ALTO, CALIFORNIA
STANFORD UNIVERSITY SCHOOL OF MEDICINE
STANFORD, CALIFORNIA

The purpose of this chapter is to highlight relevant clinical and research issues that emerge when studying the caregiver stress and intervention literature. First, we will review major theoretical perspectives in the study of caregiving that are particularly relevant to the development of intervention programs; second, we will review the most frequently used intervention strategies currently in the literature; third, we will critique this literature in terms of its research methodology, pointing out strengths and limitations of current knowledge; fourth, we will present several research programs that are "in progress" at present that the clinical researcher may wish to follow over time; and finally, we will discuss the kinds of research methodologies needed in the future to address the many unanswered questions in this field. Since an extensive body of research findings does not currently exist, the chapter will serve more as a conceptual and methodological critique than as a research overview. It is hoped that this effort will stimulate future clinical researchers to delve into this area in a thoughtful and rigorous manner.

This work was supported in part by Grant No. AGO4572-01 from the National Institute on Aging, and Grant No. MH37196-04 from the National Institute of Mental Health.

## THEORETICAL PERSPECTIVES

### General Overview

As numerous authors have stated, caregivers are highly responsible agents who provide substantial physical, emotional, social, and economic support to their chronically ill elder relatives (Brody, 1981; Brody, Poulshock, & Masciocchi, 1978; Shanas, 1979; Shanas & Maddox, 1976). However, this situation takes its toll on caregivers who themselves often develop problems in response to the stresses inherent in the caregiving role. For example, it has been found that anxiety, depression, marital and family conflict, embarrassment, and fatigue are frequent consequences of caring for a patient who is suffering from a dementing illness (Blazer, 1978; Koopman-Boyden & Wells, 1979; Sanford, 1975). In addition, the caregiver is likely to suffer from a constriction of social life and reduction in available leisure time (Ross & Kedward, 1977). Caregivers of physically and/or emotionally frail elders have also been reported to feel guilt and resentment (York & Calsyn, 1977), low morale (Fengler & Goodrich, 1979), physical and emotional exhaustion (Farkas, 1980), excessive depression and anxiety (Grad & Sainsbury, 1968), and "strain" (Cantor, 1983), which refers to a sense of deprivation in the spheres of personal desires, individuality, and socialization. An extended review of the caregiving process appears in Horowitz's chapter in this volume. Similar findings have been reported by those studying caregivers of mentally ill persons (see Thompson & Doll, 1982, for an extensive review of that literature) and the chronically ill (Manjoney & McKegney, 1978). Thus, most clinical researchers in the field have concluded that caregiving can be an arduous and debilitating experience (as well as one having distinct positive features for some caregivers). Most intervention programs have been designed to reduce one or several of the above-mentioned negative correlates of chronic caregiving.

### Models of the
### Caregiving Process

Despite our increased understanding of the stresses and strains of caregivers who are caring for a frail elder relative (typically, a spouse or a parent), little conceptual work has been done to develop testable models of caregiver coping that can then form the basis for intervention research. However, studies of caregiving to children with chronic diseases are more prevalent; it is instructive to examine several concepts derived from them, as they provide useful guidelines for the design of interventions likely to be appropriate for our population of interest.

The first of these is the "stage" or "phase" model. For example, Fortier and Wanlass (1984) proposed a five-stage model for adaptation to the crisis of learning that one's child has a chronic disorder. These were: impact, denial, grief, focusing outward, and resource mobilization. While there may very well not be "stages" of adaptation (in the strict sense of the term "stage"), there probably are clear phases or steps to adjusting to one's spouse or parent as a frail elder with increasing needs and dependencies. In the case of Alzheimer's disease, a recent paper by Cohen, Kennedy, and Eisdorfer (1984) defined several likely phases of change as the disease progressed, with corresponding caregiver adaptive mechanisms. They postulated that before diagnosis, recognition and concern were typical of both patient and caregiver. Then denial occurred once the diagnosis was confirmed, followed by anger, guilt, and sadness and varied attempts to cope with the situation. In the terminal phase of the disease, a degree of "maturation" occurred, followed by separation from self (meaning that caregivers accepted the patient as a greatly changed person who would never again be the particular person they loved as parent or spouse). This "phase model" has stimulated development of several intervention programs designed to improve caregiver well-being at specific points in the frail elder's degenerative process; these will be described in the Intervention section that follows. The model may be most appropriate for caregivers of Alzheimer's patients where disease progression is more or less predictable; the model may be a less useful way to view caregiver adaptation when the frail elder's situation is composed of a multitude of physical and/or emotional problems that have a much more indefinite course.

A second useful conceptual framework has emerged from the pediatric literature and has received some attention in the geriatric literature as well. This framework calls attention to the value of mourning in caregivers prior to the actual death of the care-receiver. According to this model, parents coping with childhood leukemia and other malignant diseases fare better if "anticipatory grief" can be acknowledged and experienced (Binger et al., 1969; Chodoff, Friedman, & Hamburg, 1964; Gogan, O'Malley, & Foster, 1977; Knapp & Hansen, 1973). These authors indicate that the process of anticipatory mourning begins when a diagnosis of cancer (or another life-threatening illness) is made; denial, anger, depression, and acceptance of the reality of the death have all been reported as part of this process. The process has been recognized as normal, though sometimes in need of facilitation by professionals. This theoretical framework was first applied to caregivers of geriatric patients by Martin Berezin (1970) who described the process of "partial" or early grief as inherent in the caregiving role, irrespective of diagnosis. He postulated that with aging patients, there was not just a *final* loss (with its expected grief) but also a sense of partial loss which was more or less continuously present in caregivers whom he treated. To him it was absurd to maintain that the concept of loss operated purely on an all-or-none basis; rather, loss might be partial, threatened, or anticipated and lead to clinical reactions such as anxiety and depression in caregivers unless recognized and labeled as such. Berezin (1970) viewed this as a paradoxical situation, since the grief reaction could not really be resolved or worked through to completion while the frail elder relative was still living, yet the partial grief state was clearly present. He recommended that health care professionals be prepared to acknowledge its presence as normal and facilitate as much movement through this state as possible, given the particular circumstances involved. More recently, a popular book by Powell and Courtice (1983) on family issues in Alzheimer's disease has made a similar point.

There is clearly not enough firm knowledge upon which to base a definitive "anticipatory grief" model of caregiving. However, for heuristic purposes, it seems appropriate to suggest that caregiving may be viewed (on a psychological level) as an anticipatory mourning process that warrants recognition and may need facilitation. Adoption of this theoretical framework leads to formulation of quite different caregiver intervention programs than adoption of the "phase" model discussed above; these interventions will be described in subsequent sections of this chapter.

A third important thread from the pediatric distress literature involves study of the naturalistic coping strategies used by parent-caregivers of chronically ill children. Prior research along these lines has emphasized the identification of positive versus negative mechanisms, so that the positive can be strengthened and the more negative or unadaptive coping mechanisms can be evaluated and eventually abandoned, or referrals made to intervention programs designed to help in their amelioration.

McCubbin et al. (1983) developed a coping inventory based on a sample of 100 parents of children with cystic fibrosis. They found that certain specific mechanisms were associated with positive caregiver adjustment; these included caregivers' ability to maintain family integration (despite the debilitating nature of the disease); caregivers' accurate understanding of the medical situation (through appropriate communications with health care staff and other parents); and their ability to secure and maintain an adequate social support network. The last two factors (disease education and maintenance of social support) have been widely emphasized in intervention programs designed for caregivers of frail elders as well. It may be that the inventory developed by this clinical research team would be useful to identify those caregivers with poor initial coping strategies in these spheres so that they could be channeled into these kinds of intervention programs.

Similar studies of the predictive value of specific parental coping patterns were conducted by Kupst et al. (1982) regarding childhood leukemia, and by Morrow, Hoagland, and Carnike (1981) on pediatric cancer. Both studies found that perceived adequacy of the social support network was highly correlated with positive adaptation, while the preexistence of other familial stress and/or mental health problems was associated with negative caregiver adjustment. Thus, as in the work of McCubbin et al. (1983), careful study of caregivers' ability to obtain adequate social support has been underscored; by initially assessing caregiver strength in this domain, one can decide whether or not participation in intervention programs aimed at increasing one's sense of social support would be an appropriate recommendation. Similarly, knowing the caregiver's mental health history would be a valuable aspect of the initial assessment process, so that caregivers thought to be "at risk" could be referred to a suitable resource.

### Prevalence of Mental Health
### Problems in Family Caregivers

Although it was noted earlier that caregivers may report a host of psychological symptoms (e.g., anxiety, depression, social withdrawal and isolation, guilt, low morale, and "strain"), we do not really know the prevalence of diagnosable psychiatric disorders in this group. Rather, we have fragments of information from many studies, none of which was epidemiologic in nature, nor designed to interview caregivers in a comprehensive manner to obtain sufficient information for reliable assessment of the person's overall psychiatric/psychological status. Thus, we do not have a solid data base at present from which to draw conclusions about *typical* psychiatric disturbances likely either to result from, or to be associated with, long-term caregiving. This also means that development of *specific* caregiver intervention programs that target specific mental health problems (e.g., depressive reactions, either singly or in combination with anxiety disorders) has to proceed slowly and await the results of epidemiologic research.

Preliminary data reported by Becker (1984) from an interview study of a relatively small sample of caregivers ($N = 68$) indicated that approximately 40 percent (28 persons) met criteria for some type of depressive disorder, using standard diagnostic criteria. Also noteworthy was the fact that caregivers' total depression scores on a commonly used self-report questionnaire were often lower than expected (given the interview findings), which suggests that they may underreport psychological distress when queried only with self-report forms. Additional analyses of these data are under way at the University of Washington and, when completed, will provide helpful insights into the estimated prevalence of depression as a clinical disorder in caregivers.

Our own work in progress (Yesavage & Gallagher, 1984) uses the Diagnostic Interview Schedule (DIS) developed by Robins et al. (1981), designed to provide a brief yet reliable and valid index of numerous psychiatric disorders. We shall interview approximately 100 caregivers of Alzheimer patients and follow them over at least a two-year period so that changes in psychiatric status may be observed over time. We hope to increase this sample size by also interviewing caregivers of persons with different disorders, so that we may examine the relationship (if any) between caregiver mental health problems and frail elder diagnosis. While this research will not study intervention programs per se, its results should permit more informed development of interventions that are aimed to treat the most common disorders of caregiving.

## Service Versus Research Issues

A major factor that has slowed conceptual and informational progress in this field seems to be the "press for service" that most agencies dealing with older people have experienced in the past five years. A rather sudden surge of requests for services from relatives caring for frail elders began in about 1978 with the development of increasing public awareness about Alzheimer's disease and the concomitant growth of self-help organizations dedicated to working with families of persons with degenerative brain disorders. Most professionals were relatively unprepared for this demand, yet the needs had to be met, particularly in service agencies. It is also true that major research centers and funding sources have only recently focused attention on Alzheimer's disease and some other chronic disorders of aging.

Even more recent is the emphasis on caregiver intervention research; few published studies exist on the efficacy of intervention programs at the present time, and those that are in the literature tend to be pilot studies or anecdotal reports, rather than controlled experiments. Thus, at present, we are in a situation in which social service agencies have been unable to give research high priority and instead have developed intervention programs that were designed exclusively to serve public demands. Now that the historical trends are clear, and most planners and policymakers are fully aware of the "graying of America," we must be responsive to the equally important "press for research" so that informed decisions can be made for the future. Without such collaboration between clinicians and researchers, we will be unable to generate the knowledge needed to design appropriate and cost-effective intervention programs for the ever-increasing caregiver population.

## COMMONLY USED CAREGIVER INTERVENTION STRATEGIES

Programs whose purpose is to treat caregivers' needs may be grouped conceptually in at least two ways: first, according to which model of the caregiving process they are operating from (as noted earlier, phase, anticipatory grief, and coping models have guided some research on assessment and intervention), or second, according to the locus of the intervention (that is, is the focus on caregiver education, on increasing caregivers' social support, on providing services for the frail elder, on providing counseling or psychotherapy for those caregivers who require it, or on some combination of these components?). In this section, we will use the locus of intervention framework for organizing the data currently available on the impact of caregiver intervention. This approach provides a logical way to direct the reader's attention to what has been done, and what remains to be done, in the field. Throughout this discussion, cross-reference will be made to the three models of the caregiving process whenever appropriate (even though, for the most part, intervention research has proceeded without clear delineation of its conceptual underpinnings).

Intervention programs that aim to increase caregivers' knowledge and/or perceived social support typically consist of lecture series, discussion groups, support groups, or some combination of these experiences. Those that offer services (such as respite care, day care, home health care, etc.) for the frail elder do so on the assumption that relieving some of the caregiver's daily responsibilities will result in less caregiver burden and hence in increased caregiver capacity to function effectively in the situation and to maintain themselves in the caregiving role. Psychotherapeutically oriented programs may offer individual counseling or psychotherapy, family meetings, group therapy, or other similar interventions to caregivers who self-identify as clients and who request mental health services. They usually aim to increase the caregiver's ability to cope with specific problems in the family milieu, and often teach cognitive/behavioral skills within a time-limited therapeutic framework. Some caregivers require long-term therapy and/or psychotropic medications in order to maintain themselves, but in general, more has been written about the use of brief, skill-oriented therapies with this group.

Besides these formal interventions, a number of self-help programs have been developed at the grass-roots level by and for caregivers. These programs (e.g., the Alzheimer's Disease and Related Disorders Association, referred to as ADRDA; "stroke clubs," mastectomy volunteers, and the like) generally focus on the provision of information and support, although they may assist members in obtaining referrals to other needed services as well.

In the remainder of this section, each of these kinds of intervention programs will be described in greater detail, along with supporting data (when available) on their efficacy. This section will end with brief descriptions of intervention research in progress.

### Education/Support Programs
### for Caregivers

Generally, such programs are offered on a time-limited basis by professionals in service and/or university settings or by self-help organizations using some professional input. There have been a fair number of papers on the value of such programs for parents coping with chronic illnesses in their children (see Heffron, Bommelaere, & Masters, 1973; Johnson, Rudolph, & Hartmann, 1979; Schilling, Gilchrist, & Schinke, 1984, for a sampling of this literature). Systematic use of such programs with caregivers of frail elders has only recently been reported in the literature, however. A search conducted in 1984 indicated that there were only 18 published reports that both described education and/or support programs designed for caregivers of frail elders and at the same time presented enough detail about subjects, orientation of the group, and comments about its impact to permit the reader both to understand the intervention and to get some sense of whether or not it made a difference to participants. Most of these reports did not provide data (other than anecdotal) on the impact of their interventions. In general, they reported on a specific program (usually designed at the particular center or agency involved, with little cross-reference to other programs) that offered both educational and social support components in a preventive mental health framework.

Theoretically, such programs were operating from the coping model described earlier, in which adaptive strategies for gaining accurate information and for increasing the perceived adequacy of one's support network were identified as important components of positive adaptation. In addition, these methods have theoretical links with the work of Dean and Lin (1977) on the stress-buffering effects of social support, and with the research of Moos and Mitchell (1982) on social networks and adaptation and Billings and Moos (1981) on the complexities of coping responses in adults. The development of educational and supportive programs can also be seen as a response to the growing body of data indicating that family caregivers may be "at risk" for morbid reactions if at least some of their emotional needs are not being met. A common rationale for this kind of program was that if caregivers could be helped to function more effectively and efficiently in their roles, they would be likely to remain caregivers longer. As a result, reliance on formal (and expensive) systems of health care delivery would be reduced. The theoretical bases for these interventions could be formulated into testable hypotheses that could become the basis for controlled program evaluation and/or research efforts.

Groups or classes are typically set up on variable schedules, ranging from once per week for 6–10 weeks, to once or twice per month. Size varies from a low figure of 6 per group to a high of 20 or so, with one program (CARERS in Buffalo) reporting workshops averaging 50 attendees. Participants typically are relatives who respond to advertisements or other solicitations; generally, efforts are not made to limit participation to relatives dealing with specific types of problems (e.g., all strokes, or all Alzheimer's disease), so that considerable heterogeneity is found in the samples used. When content descriptions were given in the reports, one could see that they varied considerably from program to program: some focused more on practical concerns (for example, funeral arrangements or legal questions) and others on feelings (encouragement to talk about depression, grief, or anger). Many programs blend these two components into a semistructured program which begins with a didactic session on a particular topic presumed to be of general interest, followed by a discussion period or group interaction session where feelings and reactions are shared. Nontreated or other control groups were not used in any of these studies.

Outcomes generally are reported in terms of impressions (from leader and/or participants) that such experiences were helpful, rather than as quantitative findings. Sessions are described as "therapeutic" or as enhancing feelings of support (Barnes, Raskind, Scott, & Murphy, 1981; Cohen, 1983; Crossman, London, & Barry, 1981; Hausman, 1979; Safford, 1980); caregivers indicated in some instances that they were "less upset" by the frail elder's behavior or had more confidence in their ability to cope (Barnes et al., 1982; Helphand & Porter, 1981; Roozman-Weigensberg & Fox, 1980; Selan & Schuenke, 1982); members "appeared to function better" to group leaders (Hartford & Parsons, 1982); more knowledge was reported about specific topics pertinent to aging and/or caregiving (Brahce, 1983; Johnson & Spence, 1982; Peck, 1983; Silverman & Brahce, 1979); and two papers indicated that "visiting skills" were improved for families of institutionalized relatives (Brudno, 1964; Fox & Lithwick, 1978).

One study in this group focused exclusively on relatives caring for Alzheimer's patients and used a battery of outcome measures to assess impact rather than relying solely on anecdotal data. Lazarus et al. (1981) reported on a pilot study conducted with seven family members of whom four participated in the 10-week support group and three did not. Even with this very small $N$, significant positive differences were found between participants and nonparticipants. Participants indicated that they experienced a greater sense of control over their lives, and less dissatisfaction with changes in the family unit. There were no differences on self-reported anxiety or depression, however, or on measures of trust or self-esteem. Three of the four participants indicated that the group had helped "somewhat" in their being able to relate to, and cope with, their impaired relative. Co-leaders' clinical observations suggested that the discussion group served a valuable education and supportive function for the participants. Research of this nature is continuing at the Illinois State Psychiatric Institute as part of a larger study on the effects of cholinergic treatment with Alzheimer patients.

Similar research on the effectiveness of information/support interventions is in progress on the CARERS program at SUNY Buffalo (Nowak & Brice, 1984; Peck, 1983); on support groups at the Philadelphia Geriatric Center (Reever, Kepfer, Klein, & Nagele, 1983) and at Montefiore/Albert Einstein College of Medicine (Aronson, 1984; Cohen et al., 1984); on the comparative effectiveness of information versus support at the Palo Alto VA Medical Center (Priddy, 1984);

and at numerous service centers (such as the Benjamin Rose Institute and the Community Service Society of New York) on natural supports utilized by caregivers (see Poulshock, 1982, and Zimmer & Hudis, 1980).

Recently, Gray (1983) reported the results of a pilot study that used a randomized design to evaluate the impact of training in how to give care to the elderly, plus participation in a support group and modest financial reimbursement (to family members for doing chores to assist the frail elder at home) versus reimbursement alone (for charting services rendered at home) compared to a control group that was required to chart services but did not receive reimbursement, training, or opportunity to be in a support group. Fifty-six caregivers were recruited for the study, but only 28 actually completed it, with significant attrition due to death, nursing home admission, and/or dropping out. Results on several measures (e.g., caregiver life satisfaction, knowledge of personal care methods, use of additional services, and frail elder functional status) indicated that there were no significant differences caused by experimental conditions of reimbursement or of training and support. However, Gray (1984), with the support of the Ebenezer Society in Minneapolis, has published a very valuable educational manual containing considerable practical information on how to relate to and care for the frail elderly. This book and others like it (e.g., the extensive manual published by the Family Survival Project for Brain-Damaged Adults) should prove useful to family members and to professionals desiring to develop supportive educational programs for caregivers.

Finally, a controlled randomized experiment has recently begun at the Palo Alto VA to assess the comparative efficacy of classes designed to teach problem-solving skills versus classes to teach methods for enhancing the life satisfaction of caregivers (more broadly conceptualized as ways of coping with stress), compared to a delayed-treatment waiting-list condition. The 10-session interventions are being led by clinicians experienced in each particular modality; projected sample size is over 300 "completers." Statistical analysis will evaluate both short-term and longer term change and identify characteristics of caregivers predictive of good outcome for each kind of intervention (Gallagher, 1984). No data are yet available from that project.

In summary, the literature described above on the effectiveness of caregiver support and/or educational programs can, at best, be regarded as relatively sparse and primarily impressionistic. While pointing out these limitations clearly in their review, Clark and Rakowski (1983) nevertheless concluded that ". . . the consensus among

reports is that at least short-term benefit has accrued to most participants" (p. 640). They point to the value of respite from constant
responsibility, even if only through attendance at a group meeting.
Yet they also have argued strongly for controlled research on the
impact of such programs, with an effort toward specification of persons most likely to benefit from these particular kinds of interventions. Our own impressions were convergent with those reported by
Clark and Rakowski (1983): Given the amount of clinical service of
this type being provided to frail elder caregivers, it is remarkable that
so few publications could be found. Also, it was troublesome to discover the lack of controlled evaluation and/or research currently
available on program impact. Future research efforts will need to
assess these kinds of programs with experimental rigor, and with
reliable outcome instruments, so that their scientific value can be
more precisely determined.

## Programs for the Frail
## Elderly Designed to Reduce
## Caregiver Burden

This category of intervention programs refers to formal service programs such as day care, day health, and inpatient respite, which are
currently used to meet two distinct, but often complementary, goals:
first, they provide specific services to the frail elder, appropriate for his
or her functional status and care plan; and second, they provide caregivers with a "safe" place to leave the care-receiver for varying
amounts of time (depending on the nature of the program), so that
caregivers can be temporarily relieved of their responsibilities. The
category may also include other programs aimed at giving less intensive relief, such as paid homemaker services, part-time Visiting Nursing assistance, or a home health aide. This category could also include
elders who participate in experimental programs aimed at averting
nursing home placement (such as Wisconsin's Community Care Organization project, Applebaum, Seidl, & Austin, 1980; or channeling
programs operating in various states). These programs often coordi-
nate a number of specific services for the identified patient, which
clearly benefit the caregiver in that they provide some degree of respite. However, for purposes of this chapter, we will narrow our focus
to examine only those programs that clearly aim to improve caregiver
functioning through the mechanism of providing services *outside the
home* to the frail elder. Thus, day care, day health, and overnight

respite programs will be discussed, and data presented (when available) as to their impact on caregivers.

These programs reflect at least three converging trends in the field of long-term care: first, aging centers have been developing programs that reflect the notion of a "continuum of care," meaning that a wide range of services are available within that center to care for persons with different levels of functional impairment; as their condition worsens, transfer to the next level of care can be accomplished with a minimum of difficulty (e.g., the Philadelphia Geriatric Center in the private sector, and various Veterans Administration Medical Centers in the public sector, have adopted this model of service provision). Second, some evidence suggests that provision of formal services, at least of some types and under some circumstances, *does* alleviate stress and does aid in raising morale for the informal caregiver (cf. Blenkner, Bloom, & Nielsen, 1971; Dunlop, 1980; Hay, 1979). Third, recent emphasis on the prerogative of *choice* in long-term care has highlighted the fact that many elders (as well as their families) will go to great lengths to avoid or postpone permanent institutional placement; thus alternative programs have been developed to meet this need (Barney, 1977; Kane & Kane, 1980). Currently, there is considerable controversy about whether these alternative programs really do meet this need: Are they merely additional services, or are they really a substitute for institutional care? While this debate seems beyond the scope of this chapter, the interested reader is referred to Dunlop (1980) and Wan, Weissert, and Livieratos (1980) for review of the issues. At present, however, the effectiveness of the programs we have been discussing has yet to be demonstrated. Considerable additional research needs to be done before this question has been answered to the satisfaction of policymakers and financiers.

Day care and day health programs can be distinguished from each other in the type of programming provided: the former utilize a psychosocial model (emphasizing socialization and activities) whereas the latter follow a medical/rehabilitative model in which services such as physical therapy, occupational therapy, and medication monitoring are provided. Both types of programs are often described as "respite" programs because they offer this time away from caregiving to caregivers as well as delivering services to the patient. Evidence regarding the efficacy of these programs for improvement of caregiver functioning can best be described as limited and, once again, primarily anecdotal in nature. The usual methodological limitations found in the early stages of evaluating new programs are evident. The studies to be described used questionnaire data, each center developing its own, with-

out apparent sharing of methods. Standard measures of caregiver function were usually not obtained, although the frail elder patients in
these studies often were carefully evaluated. No control or comparison
groups of caregivers were reported, although several of the adult day
health studies had patient control groups. Evaluation data typically
were not collected by independent observers but rather by program
staff.

    At least three published papers have described the positive im-
pact of *day care programs* on families of frail elders as well as on
the frail elders themselves (Eskew, Sexton, Tars, & Wilcox, 1983;
Rathbone-McCuan, 1976; Sands & Suzuki, 1983). Two others from
the aging research group at the Palo Alto VA Medical Center have
not yet been published, but their data were supportive of these
conclusions (Katz, Gallagher, Zielski, & Bruguera, 1984; Scharlach
& Frenzel, 1982). These studies found that families typically reported satisfaction with services, while staff impressions suggested
that the programs aided families in maintaining their elder relative
in a noninstitutional setting. In addition, Scharlach and Frenzel
(1982) found that low caregiver burden was best predicted by frequent use of both formal and informal social supports, as well as
in-home caregiving assistance.

    To date, there have been three major systematic evaluations of
*adult day health care programs* (Capitman, 1980; Weiler & Rathbone-
McCuan, 1978; Weissert, Wan, & Livieratos, 1980). However, they
have not focused on the presumed impact of this service on caregiver
functioning, but rather have been concerned with patient care issues
and cost-effectiveness. One published report from the Palo Alto Senior
Health Services Project (Hartley, 1981) found that day health did,
indeed, have a significant positive impact on caregivers. Of the 76 frail
elders who attended the day health program, 61 had family members
willing to be interviewed by project staff when the patient was initially
placed. Almost half of them (48 percent) indicated that personal respite was a major reason for selecting this program for their frail elder
relative. After six months, 40 of these caregivers were reinterviewed to
determine the impact of the program. The majority (92% percent)
indicated that the program helped them maintain themselves in their
caregiving role; about one third indicated that the program provided
general support and help in addition to specific skilled and unskilled
services for the frail elder; and about one third said that the program
permitted them to have needed personal time to themselves and respite from their ongoing responsibilities. In addition to the usual day
health services for their impaired relatives, caregivers were encouraged

to attend support group meetings, and a floating "respite bed" was made available to their relatives at a nearby location for occasional planned or emergency stays. Thus, the available data are suggestive, at least, of a positive impact of day health care programs on caregivers of frail elders.

Finally, *inpatient or overnight respite* programs have been developed on a limited scale in this country, but it is likely that they will proliferate rapidly in the next few years. Robertson, Griffiths, and Cosin (1977) described the functioning of one British inpatient respite program that became a model program emulated by others. They indicated that the planned intermittent use of an inpatient bed allowed caregivers to place their frail elder when medical procedures, surgery, or a vacation period were needed. Family members rated these services as "essential" or "very useful," although more detailed evaluation data about the impact of this program on caregiver well-being unfortunately was not reported. No other reports could be found on the impact of inpatient respite. A randomized clinical trial on the efficacy of respite care programs that include all the varieties mentioned above, plus in-home respite care, is currently in progress at the Philadelphia Geriatric Center (Lawton & Brody, 1984). Thus, it is impossible at the present time to comment on the efficacy of respite programs.

For all the different programs mentioned in this section, an obvious direction for future research is to determine for whom the intervention might be most efficacious. It seems likely that *some* caregivers will respond with decreased burden, less morbidity, and more tolerance for their role demands when they are referred to one or more of the aforementioned services; but without carefully controlled evaluation research on the characteristics of who benefits from which type of intervention, we cannot make such referrals with confidence. This issue has been addressed in some detail in the psychotherapy outcome literature (see Barlow, 1981; Doerfler, 1981; Mintz, Steuer, & Jarvik, 1981; Nelson, 1981; Rothblum, Sholomskas, Berry, & Prusoff, 1982; and Yeaton & Sechrest, 1981, for representative papers on diverse aspects of outcome methodology). In the long-term care field, where it has been difficult to "deny" services to clients in need, and where research and/or program evaluation have typically not been high priorities, progress has been less intensive. Also, ethical issues unique to research with this population need to be carefully considered (see Yordi, Chu, Ross, & Wong, 1982, for thoughtful discussion of ethical and methodological issues in long-term care research).

**Psychotherapeutic
Interventions for Caregivers**

In this section we will review a number of intervention strategies that have been used with caregivers, primarily on an individual basis. These types of interventions apply psychotherapeutic principles to improve caregiver well-being and enhance adaptive coping. Although this body of literature is relatively small at present, there seems to be growing interest in such interventions, and several controlled outcome studies are now in progress.

In general these programs have been offered to caregivers who either responded to media announcements informing them of services and soliciting responses, or who have presented themselves to mental health settings for treatment of problems related to their caregiving status. Conceptually, each reflects one or more of the earlier models presented for thinking about the caregiving process. Different emphases are placed on phase notions, anticipatory grief, and strengthening of adaptive coping strategies, according to the orientation and background of the program developer. Specific treatment methods, such as short-term cognitive therapy (Beck, 1974), behavioral therapy (Lewinsohn, 1974) or psychodynamic therapy (Horowitz, 1976), are commonly used in individual work with distressed caregivers. Cognitive and behavioral therapies are examples of coping-based approaches to psychological treatment in that they emphasize the acquisition of practical skills for gaining control over mood, activities, and thinking patterns. The psychodynamic orientation is more introspective and emphasizes increased personal understanding of why one feels a specific way, as well as what actions one could perform to improve one's situation. Psychodynamic therapy has been used with some success for treating the anticipatory grief reactions that some caregivers experience. Any of these orientations could be used within a phase model of caregiving; one could hypothesize that the more coping-focused therapies would be most useful in the early stages of learning that one's elder relative has a debilitating disease, since at that point it is often necessary to mobilize resources and begin to adjust to the fact of the relative's illness. As the disease progresses (and particularly as brain-damaged elders become less able to function cognitively), it may be that a psychodynamic approach is most useful, since it would encourage greater exploration of the grieving process that would be presumed to be occurring at that point. These suggestions are offered in the hope that they will encourage future researchers to generate testable hypotheses when doing intervention/outcome research.

Other ways to treat caregivers in psychological distress include behavioral training of caregivers so that they can serve as therapists to their family members, specific caregiver training in coping skills and problem solving, and use of structured family meetings to increase the informal supports caregivers receive. Some may find these distinctions somewhat artificial, since *all* the psychotherapeutically oriented interventions utilize a blend of information, support, problem-solving, and enhancement of positive coping to accomplish their goals. However, notable differences can be found in the manner in which these therapies are described and conducted that may make these distinctions useful for future investigation.

Our own pilot work at the Center for the Study of Psychotherapy and Aging at the Palo Alto VA has indicated that caregivers who develop a clinically significant depressive reaction may be effectively treated with brief cognitive, behavioral, or psychodynamic psychotherapies. Individual treatment averaged 20 sessions on a once per week basis. We have found that significant improvement in self- and interviewer-rated depression occurred for 11 out of 13 persons so treated; follow-up over a one-year period indicated that only two persons had relapsed into a new episode of clinical depression (Gallagher & Czirr, 1984). The apparent success of these approaches was encouraging and suggested that for caregivers with clinical depression, improvement similar to that reported elsewhere for non-caregiving elder depressives (Gallagher & Thompson, 1982; Thompson & Gallagher, 1984) was possible. Additional pilot work has been done with "late-stage" caregivers experiencing intense anticipatory grief, using brief psychodynamic psychotherapy. Experience has been gained with five such depressed persons. A modification of Horowitz' (1976) approach developed to treat stress response syndromes was used. This dynamic approach was found to have been successful in several clinical trials with patients suffering intense post-bereavement reactions (Horowitz et al., 1984, in press). In this work, caregivers are encouraged to express their grief, to recognize (even though it is painful to admit) that their loved one is a mere shell of what he or she used to be, and to share their fears of the future, along with anticipated relief (and its accompanying guilt). We are again encouraged that this type of intervention may hold promise, at least for some caregivers who are able to acknowledge their painful feelings and to cognitively rehearse for the future. Finally, we have made detailed study of other caregivers' case histories, and found that *both* coping and grief work tended to typify successful treatment, regardless of the predominant modality used (Baum & Gallagher, 1984). This suggests that flexibility may be required in the application of "standardized" treatments for depression, in order to best address the complex and multiple psychological needs of caregivers coming for treatment. While this may be quite appropriate clinically, it complicates one's efforts to do controlled research on the outcomes associated with specific psychotherapies with this population.

Behavioral training for family members (similar to Parent Effectiveness Training programs for management of disruptive child behaviors, as described by Dangel & Polster, 1984) has been advocated by Haley (1983), Rathbone-McCuan and Hashimi (1982), and Linsk and Pinkston (1980, 1981). Each of these authors described the therapist's role as that of an active trainer and consultant to the caregiver, who in turn was taught various behavioral strategies, including procedures for baseline recording, choosing and implementing an appropriate intervention, and monitoring progress. Rathbone-McCuan and Hashimi (1982) did not present data on the efficacy of these interventions. Their reports are devoted to a presentation of the rationale for this position and description of general ways to proceed. Haley (1983) reported several successful case examples, indicating that caregivers treated on a one-to-one basis could successfully learn behavioral management strategies which were based on an operant conditioning model (e.g., positive reinforcement, shaping, and extinction). Linsk and Pinkston (1980, 1981; Pinkston & Linsk, 1984a, 1984b) have presented the most extensive data on this approach, having used it with over 50 caregiver–frail elder dyads enrolled in the Elderly Support Project at the University of Chicago. Their approach has used a combination of contingency contracting, modeling, rehearsal, and feedback procedures, taught to the caregiver and then implemented in the home setting. Generally, 15 to 20 individual sessions per family were required to accomplish the requisite learning. Evaluation of impact has been through single-case methodology, where visual analysis of graphs and charts were the primary ways to assess change. Their 1981 report presented data on the successful treatment of elder depressives; the two more recent reports (Pinkston & Linsk, 1984a, 1984b) summarize data collected over time on the overall sample and present their program in sufficient detail so that it can now be implemented by other clinical researchers in the field.

Based on analysis of 21 frail elders and their caregivers for whom pre and post data were complete (out of a sample of 51 persons referred to the program), they found that most clients improved as a result of the intervention and maintained that improvement for at least six months. Behavior change occurred in the desired direction at clinically significant levels for 60 percent of cases treated. Targeted behaviors included general self-care (e.g., incontinence, eating, hygiene, ambulation), social activities (e.g., time out of the house, number of visitors), other positive behaviors (e.g., reporting positive feelings, reading), and a reduction of negative behaviors (e.g., verbal abuse, fighting). After obtaining a detailed functional analysis of behavioral excesses and deficits, baseline data were recorded by the caregiver, who was trained by project staff in behavioral recording at home. Then interventions were introduced and taught by the caregiver. Most frequently used (and with the most clear positive benefit) were contracting, cueing, and reinforcement. General self-care showed improvement following intervention in 78 percent of the behaviors treated; all social activities improved and 83 percent of negative verbal behaviors improved during the intervention phase. At follow-up, it was found that 78 percent of previously targeted behaviors were maintained at or above post-intervention levels. In addition, most caregivers reported that training in behavioral principles was at least somewhat helpful, and the majority indicated that they understood the principles and felt they could apply them to other aspects of the frail elder's behavior. While the sample size is small, and single-case methodology was used exclusively, the work of Pinkston and Linsk represents a substantial contribution to the field in that they have developed and implemented a systematic approach to teaching caregivers practical coping skills and have obtained reliable data on the impact of this intervention strategy.

Description of a multifaceted cognitive/behavioral intervention program designed to improve caregiver coping skills was found in Levine, Dastoor, and Gendron (1983). They reported the results of a pilot study conducted with 10 caregivers of dementia patients. The aim of this program, called "Supporter Endurance Training" (SET), was to improve specific coping skills in the caregiver by use of motivational enhancement, assertion training, and stress reduction. A fourth component, training in problem-solving, was considered optional, and recommended for use only with caregivers lacking these skills. Motivational enhancement was accomplished by having caregivers watch a videotape of an "ideal" coping model. They were then taught to focus on the content of self-statements they made in stressful situations. Through role-playing and discussion, they were encouraged to use more adaptive self-statements when stress arose in the care of the demented relative. Assertion training also used both cognitive and behavioral elements and situation-specific role-playing. Stress reduction was accomplished by teaching participants meditative relaxation. Although careful preintervention assessment was done (of caregiver coping style, the patient's behavioral problems, and caregiver locus of control), no outcome data were reported. The authors recommend that future research evaluate the comparative effectiveness of SET versus support groups or other currently used interventions.

Preliminary data on the effectiveness of a therapeutic approach combining individual counseling with "family meetings" for caregivers of patients with Alzheimer's disease have recently been reported by Zarit and Zarit (1982, 1983). This program is comprised of three treatment techniques (information, problem solving, and support) that are given in a combination of one-to-one counseling sessions with the primary caregiver and in family meetings. To date, this integrated package (termed IFC, meaning individual and family counseling) has been successfully used with over 50 caregivers. The ongoing research program at the University of Southern California's Ethel Percy Andrus Older Adult Center evolved from Zarit's previous research on the correlates of caregiver burden (Zarit, Reever, & Bach-Peterson, 1980). This approach suggests that primary caregivers are best served by interventions that encourage other members of the natural support system to visit and/or assist the family. The intervention package consists of six sessions of individual counseling; a family meeting is generally held after session five. At the family meeting, information is shared about the nature of the disorder; problem solving is done in the meeting so that all who attend have the opportunity to generate solutions to the problem of how to provide more support to the primary caregiver; finally, a specific plan is developed for caregiver respite, with checkpoints encouraged so that modifications can be made by the family if necessary. Results of IFC have been compared to those obtained from participation in a six-session traditional support group. Zarit (1983) reported that *both* interventions were associated with short-term decline in perceived burden and in emotional distress, but there were no significant differences between conditions on the specific measures used. Those treated with IFC rated several therapeutic aspects of the intervention as having been of more importance to them than did subjects treated in the support group condition, for example, "Feeling supported in what I am doing" and "Knowing I have people to turn to for help." Currently, this research program aims to enroll over 100 caregivers and will continue to compare the effects of these two intervention programs.

In terms of the models of the caregiving process that were described earlier in this chapter, it can be seen that the psychotherapeutic approaches reported in the literature tend to focus predominantly on enhancement of caregiver coping skills, while providing information and support as part of the intervention. Only a few studies have examined the value of anticipatory grieving (though their results are promising), and no controlled work has been done to test the notion that different interventions may be more or less appropriate for a given caregiver, depending on the stage of the frail elder's illness and slope of his or her deterioration. In summary, each of the various psychotherapeutic approaches reviewed above holds promise as an intervention strategy for caregivers of the frail elderly. Although the data presented on behavioral management training were strong relative to the other approaches noted, it should be emphasized that we do not yet know for whom these interventions are most appropriate, nor can we specify the characteristics of successful versus unsuccessful responders for each kind of treatment.

## Self- or Mutual-Help Groups

The final topic of this section focuses on the efficacy of self-help groups (termed by some mutual-help groups, because this mutuality is a major focus and reason to join) for alleviation of caregiver distress. Self-help groups are usually formed on a grass-roots level by persons suffering from particular disabilities or disorders; probably the oldest is Alcoholics Anonymous, which was formed over 30 years ago and which is very strong and active today all over the country. Others, such as "stroke clubs," mastectomy groups, Weight Watchers, Widow-to-Widow programs, and the ADRDA groups and their offshoots, are oriented around the principle that taking increased responsibility for oneself (with its accompanying increased sense of mastery and self-esteem) will enable most persons to receive sufficient support and understanding so that they can cope effectively with their problems. Such programs tend to be set up for people only with the particular disorder or in the particular situation implied by the title. Thus, each group is "special" or unique in its focus, in that the specific problems faced by the individuals in these various groups are, in fact, different. In addition, the specific coping strategies they need to develop in order to deal with their problems may also be distinct. Some general curative factors may be postulated, such as gaining accurate information about one's own or one's family member's condition; being in a supportive atmosphere where feelings can be shared; learning by attending to the experiences of others; and being encouraged to cope actively, rather than passively accepting defeat or giving in to one's problem. However, little research has been done to articulate these factors, either within groups of a particular type, or across groups. In fact, there are no formal evaluations of such groups currently available, although anecdotal reports in the media and in popular books emphasize their helpful effects.

For our purposes, we shall focus on ADRDA (and similar local equivalents). This organization was formed by a woman who was herself a caregiver of a demented spouse and who felt she needed such a group in order to ventilate and obtain support for continuing in her role. Since its inception about seven years ago, ADRDA has become a national organization with chapters in many large and small communities in this country. In the San Francisco Bay area alone, there are over a dozen local chapters; geographic proximity increases the likelihood that caregivers will be able to attend meetings on a regular basis. There are no fees to join; meetings are typically held monthly in a comfortable atmosphere (such as a church hall or a bank community room). Usually an invited speaker will start the meeting, thus providing new information on some aspect of the care of the brain damaged. Then a refreshment break occurs, followed by unstructured time for sharing reactions to the speaker and for more general discussion of how one is feeling at this time. Some offshoots of ADRDA, such as the Family Survival Project in the San Francisco area, have meetings more frequently and offer other services to caregivers, such as professionally led support groups, classes on home health care, and referrals to other services upon request. These groups have been very effective in drawing public attention and resources both to the illness and to caregiver needs.

However, self- or mutual-help groups may have liabilities as well. Some groups that our own staff attended seemed biased against professionals; negative attitudes were expressed that could, if not weighed and sorted, interfere with caregivers' abilities to obtain future needed services from the health care system. We have also found that some caregivers sought out our program because of unpleasant experiences with self-help groups. Typically they complained that they experienced a *lack* of a truly supportive atmosphere (e.g., through subtle or overt cues, some persons learn that they do not exactly "fit in"). Clearly, the advantages and disadvantages of self-help groups need to be more clearly articulated.

Currently, self-help caregiver programs are quite popular. It must nonetheless be recognized that some types of groups (encounter groups, for example) once enthusiastically endorsed by the public and by professionals have not withstood the test of empirical study. For example, Lieberman, Yalom, and Miles (1973) found that some of the most dynamic, charismatic leaders actually had the highest rates of psychological casualties and often were unaware that some group members had worsened during the course of the group. Both the trained and the untrained leaders who emerge from self-help movements are capable of being blind to their own impact. These remarks are not meant to constitute negative commentary specifically on self-help groups. *Any* service program (whether led by professionals or nonprofessionals) has the potential for harm as well as good; future research needs to help delineate profiles of likely "casualties" from each type of intervention program that is studied. Essential new knowledge is provided by the study of failures.

In summary, while it is likely that self-help organizations will be found to provide appropriate and sufficient services for *some* caregivers, we currently have no way to identify those caregivers most likely to benefit from this approach, nor can we weed out those for whom self-help programs are likely to be insufficient or actively negative in effect.

## FUTURE RESEARCH DIRECTIONS

Although numerous references to suggested research have been made throughout this chapter, this final section will attempt to summarize these recommendations and to add several new thoughts. First, epidemiologic studies are very much needed in order to determine the prevalence of psychiatric/psychological disorders in caregiving populations. This is an important point in that such work helps us to define "what is a case" and to know the distribution of cases in the population. Also, it enables us to design different intervention programs to address selectively each of the most common clinical problems noted. Active collaboration between clinicians and researchers is needed to enrich such studies in that selection of measures, sensitivity to issues that may arise in an interview situation, and assessment of caregivers' strengths (as well as weaknesses) are more likely to occur appropriately when both groups design the instruments and develop the research plan. Particular attention should be paid to the distinction between symptoms of distress and clinically diagnosable DSM-III syndromes, since each symptom pattern or clinical disorder may require its own form of intervention strategy.

Second, continued careful work needs to be done on the development and psychometric refinement of the various measurement tools to be used in future research. The work of Zarit and colleagues on measuring burden (Zarit et al., 1980) and Poulshock and Deimling (1984) on the multidimensionality of burden are excellent examples of careful approaches to measurement. They represent efforts to measure specific targets for intervention (rather than being limited to global indices of change). These instruments have the additional advantage of being relevant to caregivers' experience. Too frequently, this issue of relevance has not been seriously considered. Too often, long and tedious generalized outcome batteries have been used that contain many questions of only secondary importance to either the focal problem or the intervention. Some burden measures have been found sensitive to change over time. Other such measures are needed, since nonsignificant evaluation results may be due to the insensitivity of the measures employed rather than to failure of the intervention to effect change (see Nelson, 1981, for fuller discussion of this problem).

Third, controlled experiments need to be designed and conducted to evaluate, in a scientifically rigorous manner, the impact of the various kinds of interventions discussed above, and to assess their theoretical import. We also need to determine *for whom* specific interventions are appropriate. This will not be an easy task, since there are many logistical, practical, and ethical concerns about conducting randomized clinical trials; yet selection of the appropriate methodology, and adherence to protocol, have been essential ingredients of historical scientific progress. An excellent discussion of various research designs that are considered appropriate for studies of long-term care can be found in Sherwood and Morris (1975).

Fourth, it seems obvious that significant advances in knowledge cannot occur without continued active collaboration between clinicians and researchers. As noted earlier, intervention programs have typically developed in response to clinical needs, without including research or evaluation components. It is self-evident that good evaluation will, in turn, improve the quality of clinical practice.

Finally, we would like to indicate several specific considerations that need to be thought out prior to initiation of caregiver intervention research, based on work in our own laboratory with caregiver support groups (Priddy & Gallagher, 1984). First, when doing recruitment and screening with caregivers, it is necessary to assess accurately the potential pool of available subjects; most agency directors significantly underestimated the number of caregivers who might be interested to participate in a research program. Many of those who entered our caregiver support groups were also in numerous other groups that met concurrently. It is difficult to ask such people to refrain from participation in these groups until the research program is completed, yet failure to do so severely compromises the internal validity of the study.

Second, we found that caregivers required a significant amount of time at each meeting to ventilate and share their feelings. Since the purpose of this study was to evaluate different kinds of support groups (an unstructured group, a structured group, and an educational condition), there were frequently times when the leader had to take control over the group in order to remain within the confines of the agreed-upon protocol for that condition. Some participants resented this and dropped out, leading to differential attrition across the conditions. It is suggested that any caregiver intervention program being considered for inclusion in a research design should be carefully pilot-tested, to determine its acceptability to the population of interest. By doing so one can make necessary modifications prior to the research to reduce anticipated dropout from whichever is regarded by caregivers as the least desirable condition.

Third, during the course of the six-session groups, several family crises occurred that required additional individual case management services and/or referral to other health or mental health professionals for immediate action. For example, one care provider in our study had to cope with the death of her daughter in a household accident; in other cases, the frail elder experienced a precipitous decline. Consideration of research versus clinical needs and priorities was frequently required in order to adhere to the protocols as much as possible while still giving good clinical care in emergency situations.

Fourth, we found that most of the caregivers who participated in this research did not want to leave the project when their scheduled group was complete; they asked for regular follow-up sessions. This had not been anticipated, since we had not experienced such demand for additional services in our other intervention research programs. However, it was evident that in order both to obtain scheduled follow-up evaluation data and to respond to the clinical needs of this population, we had to develop a maintenance or after-care program. "Graduates' groups" now meet once per month; they are heavily attended, and as new crises come up, additional services or referrals are provided. We would recommend that the issues outlined above be thoughtfully considered during the planning stage of the research program so appropriate contingency plans can be made to handle the unexpected aspects of working with caregivers in a therapeutic manner.

On a conceptual level, we would like to see intervention research guided more directly by the various theoretical orientations reviewed previously in this chapter. Several of these frameworks seem relevant.

The "phase" model states that caregivers have very different concerns at different points in the progression of their care-receiver's illness, as noted by Cohen et al. (1984) and Gallagher and Czirr (1984). The "anticipatory grief" model views the central problem of debilitating illness to be partial (unexpressed) mourning experienced by the caregiver while the patient is still alive. The various models to enhance coping skills, such as cognitive or behavioral therapy, and the teaching of home-based behavioral management, all focus on increasing one's sense of mastery and ability to cope with day-to-day problems as reflected in the work of Levine et al. (1983) and Pinkston and Linsk (1984a). Finally, the combined information/support/problem solving/ family meeting approach of the Zarits blends a number of important components thought to be responsible for change which, taken together, may have an additive effect. Each of these frameworks posits a different *model* of change and identifies different critical ingredients as potentially responsible for whatever change ensues. Thus, by designing intervention programs that test specific theories, we can obtain greater understanding of the mechanisms of change, not merely describe that change has occurred, although we are not sure why or how. The issue of identification of change mechanisms is critical to outcome research in other fields (e.g., the psychotherapy literature), and warrants careful consideration here as well.

We would like to suggest that Bandura's work on self-efficacy theory may hold particular promise for caregiver intervention research (Bandura, 1982). According to this theory, change occurs when the client's sense of perceived self-efficacy (or overall judgment of competency to perform capably in given situations) is strengthened. Self-efficacy judgments are based on a balanced appraisal of all relevant available information; thus, they have been found to be better predictors of new behavior than any other single piece of information (such as prior behavior or mere exposure to new learning). Modification of self-efficacy perceptions is best accomplished through a combination of modeling, rehearsal, and performance-based feedback; thus *any* interventions that contain these ingredients and do in fact modify self-efficacy perceptions may be viewed as resulting in positive outcome. Therefore, self-efficacy becomes a critical mediating variable that may be responsible for change (regardless of the particular content or form of the intervention). On the other hand, critics have commented that the theory is so general that it would be impossible to disconfirm, and that there are inherent measurement problems to be addressed (e.g., "halo effects" in obtained ratings). Still, on balance, this theoretical orientation may prove to be a heuristic way to account for change in future intervention research.

The last point concerns the need for intervention research that better recognizes the multivariate nature of caregiving, interventions, and their effects. It is clear that caregiving is not a unitary process, and that caregivers are very different from each other in the ways in which they cope (or fail to cope) with the demands of the caregiver role. Multiple factors impinge upon their ability to respond favorably to any intervention offered. At the very least, one needs to assess and model the effects of adequacy of the social support network, the nature of the care-receiver's disability, previous coping history of the caregiver, intercurrent stressful life changes, and caregiver physical and mental health, before concluding that specific positive effects are *due to* a specific intervention. This kind of research usually requires large samples, so that relevant variables can be assessed with enough power to detect impact. It is therefore costly and time-consuming to do and can easily be dismissed as an unnecessary "luxury" that cannot be afforded when services need to be rendered in the here-and-now. Yet it is only by thoughtfully considering the interrelationships among variables that one can develop fine-grained answers to the questions we have been posing in this chapter. Hopefully, the next 10 years will witness considerable growth and refinement of our knowledge of *which* intervention strategies are most likely to benefit particular caregivers in specific, complex life situations.

## REFERENCES

Applebaum, R., Siedl, F. W., & Austin, C. The Wisconsin Community Care Organization: Preliminary findings from the Milwaukee experiment. *The Gerontologist,* 1980, *20,* 350–355.

Aronson, M. And who will care for the caregiver? Paper presented at the conference on Alzheimer's Disease: Assessment and Treatment of Patients and Caregivers, Palo Alto, CA, June, 1984.

Bandura, A. Self-efficacy mechanism in human agency. *American Psychologist,* 1982, *37,* 122–147.

Barlow, D. H. On the relation of clinical research to clinical practice: Current issues, new directions. *Journal of Consulting and Clinical Psychology,* 1981, *49,* 147–155.

Barnes, F., Raskind, M., Scott, M., & Murphy, C. Problems of families caring for Alzheimer patients: Use of a support group. *Journal of the American Geriatrics Society,* 1981, *29,* 80–85.

Barney, J. The prerogative of choice in long-term care. *The Gerontologist,* 1977, *17,* 309–314.

Baum, D., & Gallagher, D. Issues and observations on psychotherapy with depressed caregivers. *Clinical Gerontologist* (in press).

Beck, A. T. The development of depression: A cognitive model. In R. Friedman & M. Katz (Eds.), *The psychology of depression.* Washington, DC: Winston, 1974, pp. 3–20.

Becker, J. Depressive reactions in the spousal caregivers of Alzheimer patients. Paper presented at the conference on Alzheimer's Disease: Assesment and treatment of patients and caregivers, Palo Alto, CA, June, 1984.

Berezin, M. A. The psychiatrist and the geriatric patient: Partial grief in family members and others who care for the elderly. *Journal of Geriatric Psychiatry,* 1970, *4,* 53–64.

Billings, A., & Moos, R. H. The role of coping responses and social resources in attenuating the stress of life events. *Journal of Behavioral Medicine,* 1981, *4,* 139–157.

Binger, C., Ablin, A., Fewerstein, R., Kushner, J., Zoger, S., & Mikkelsen, C. Childhood leukemia: Emotional impact on patient and family. *The New England Journal of Medicine,* 1969, *280,* 414–418.

Blazer, D. Working with the elderly patient's family. *Geriatrics,* 1978, *33,* 123.

Blenkner, M., Bloom, M., & Nielsen, M. A research and demonstration project of protective services. *Social Casework,* 1971, *52,* 483–499.

Brahce, C. Creating partnerships with family caretakers. In M. Smyer & M. Gatz (Eds.), *Mental health and aging.* Beverly Hills, CA: Sage, 1983, pp. 185–196.

Brody, E. M. "Women in the middle" and family help to older people. *The Gerontologist,* 1981, *21,* 471–480.

Brody, S. J., Poulshock, S. W., & Masciocchi, C. F. The family caring unit: A major consideration in the long-term support system. *The Gerontologist,* 1978, *18,* 556–561.

Brudno, J. J. Group programs with adult offspring of newly admitted residents in a geriatrics setting. *Geriatrics,* 1964, *12,* 385–394.

Cantor, M. H. Strain among caregivers: A study of experience in the United States. *The Gerontologist,* 1983, *23,* 597–604.

Capitman, J. *Evaluation of adult day health care programs in California.* Sacramento, CA: Office of Long Term Care and Aging, Department of Health Services, 1980.

Chodoff, P., Friedman, S., & Hamburg, A. Stress, defenses, and coping behavior: Observations in parents of children with malignant disease. *American Journal of Psychiatry,* 1964, *120,* 743–749.

Clark, N. M., & Rakowski, W. Family caregivers of older adults: Improving helping skills. *The Gerontologist,* 1983, *23,* 637–642.

Cohen, D., Kennedy, G., & Eisdorfer, C. Phases of change in the patient with Alzheimer's dementia: A conceptual dimension for defining health care management. *Journal of the American Geriatrics Society,* 1984, *32,* 11–15.

Cohen, P. M. A group approach for working with families of the elderly. *The Gerontologist,* 1983, *23,* 248–250.

Crossman, L., London, C., & Barry, C. Older women caring for disabled spouses: A model for supportive services. *The Gerontologist*, 1981, *21*, 464–470.

Dangel, R. F., & Polster, R. A. (Eds.). *Parent training: Foundations of research and practice*. New York: Guilford Press, 1984.

Dean, A., & Lin, N. The stress-buffering role of social support. *Journal of Nervous and Mental Disease*, 1977, *165*, 403–417.

Doerfler, L. A. Psychological research on depression: A methodological review. *Clinical Psychology Review*, 1981, *1*, 119–137.

Dunlop, B. D. Expanded home-based care for the impaired elderly: Solution or pipe dream? *American Journal of Public Health*, 1980, *70*, 514–519.

Eskew, R., Sexton, R., Tars, S., & Wilcox, F. Day treatment program evaluation. In M. Smyer & M. Gatz (Eds.), *Mental health and aging*, Beverly Hills, CA: Sage, 1983, pp. 63–84.

Family Survival Project for Brain-Damaged Adults. *Learning to survive*. San Francisco: Author (Available from: 1736 Divisadero St., San Francisco, CA, 94115), 1981.

Farkas, S. W. Impact of chronic illness on the patient's spouse. *Health and Social Work*, 1980, *5*, 39–46.

Fengler, A. P., & Goodrich, N. Wives of elderly disabled men: The hidden patients. *The Gerontologist*, 1979, *19*, 175–183.

Fortier, L. M., & Wanlass, R. Family crises following the diagnosis of a handicapped child. *Family Relations*, 1984, *6*, 13–24.

Fox, M., & Lithwick, M. Groupwork with adult children of confused institutionalized patients. *Long-Term Care and Health Services Administration*, 1978, *2*, 121–131.

Gallagher, D. Enhancing caregivers' capacity to care for frail elders. Research grant (#AG 04572-01) funded by the National Institute on Aging. Veterans Administration Medical Center, Palo Alto, CA, 1984.

Gallagher, D., & Czirr, R. Clinical observations on the effectiveness of different psychotherapeutic approaches in the treatment of depressed caregivers. Paper presented at the meeting of the Gerontological Society, San Antonio, TX, November, 1984.

Gallagher, D., & Thompson, L. W. Treatment of major depressive disorder in older adult outpatients with brief psychotherapies. *Psychotherapy: Theory, Research and Practice*, 1982, *19*, 482–490.

Gogan, J. L., O'Malley, J., & Foster, D. J. Treating the pediatric cancer patient: A review. *Journal of Pediatric Psychology*, 1977, *2*(2), 42–48.

Grad, J., & Sainsbury, P. The effect that patients have on their families in a community care and a control psychiatric service: A two year follow-up. *British Journal of Psychiatry*, 1968, *114*, 265–278.

Gray, V. K. Providing support for home care givers. In M. Smyer & M. Gatz (Eds.), *Mental health and aging*. Beverly Hills, CA: Sage, 1983, pp. 197–214.

Gray, V. K. (Ed.). *Caresharing: How to relate to the frail elderly*. Minneapolis: Ebenezer Center for Aging and Human Development, 1984.

Haley, W. D. A family-behavioral approach to the treatment of the cognitively impaired elderly. *The Gerontologist,* 1983, *23,* 18–20.

Hartford, M., & Parsons, R. Groups with relatives of dependent older adults. *The Gerontologist,* 1982, *22,* 394–398.

Hartley, W. *A better way.* Final report of the Senior Health Services Project. Palo Alto, CA: Midpeninsula Health Services, Inc., and the Senior Coordinating Council, Palo Alto, 1982.

Hausman, C. P. Short-term counseling groups for people with elderly parents. *The Gerontologist,* 1979, *19,* 102–107.

Hay, D. Some observations of long-term health care facilities in Great Britain. *Long-Term Care and Health Services Administration,* 1979, *3,* 58–71.

Heffron, W., Bommelaere, K., & Masters, R. Group discussions with the parents of leukemic children. *Pediatrics,* 1973, *52,* 831–840.

Helphand, M., & Porter, C. M. The family group within the nursing home: Maintaining family ties of long-term care residents. *Journal of Gerontological Social Work,* 1981, *4,* 51–62.

Horowitz, M. J. *Stress response syndrome.* New York: Jason Aronson, 1976.

Horowitz, M. J., Marmar, C., Weiss, D., DeWitt, K., & Rosenbaum, R. Brief psychotherapy of bereavement reactions. *Archives of General Psychiatry,* 1984, *41,* 438–448.

Horowitz, M. J., Weiss, D., Kaltreider, N., Krupnick, J., Marmar, C., Wilner, N., & DeWitt, K. Reactions to the death of a parent: Results from patients and field subjects. *Journal of Nervous and Mental Disease.* (In press.)

Johnson, E., & Spence, D. L. Adult children and their aging parents: An intervention program. *Family Relations,* 1982, *31,* 115–122.

Johnson, F. L., Rudolph, L. A., & Hartmann, J. Helping the family cope with childhood cancer. *Psychosomatics,* 1979, *20,* 241–251.

Kane, R. L., & Kane, R. A. Alternatives to institutional care of the elderly: Beyond the dichotomy. *The Gerontologist,* 1980, *20,* 249–259.

Katz, S., Gallagher, D, Zielski, E., & Bruguera, M. A pilot study of medical and psychosocial factors related to participation in a Day Respite program. Manuscript submitted for publication, 1984.

Knapp, V. S., & Hansen, H. Helping the parents of children with leukemia. *Social Work,* 1973, *18,* 70–75.

Koopman-Boyden, P. G., & Wells, L. F. The problems arising from supporting the elderly at home. *New Zealand Medical Journal,* 1979, *89,* 265–269.

Kupst, M. J., Schulman, J., Honig, G., Maurer, H., Morgan, E., & Fochtman, D. Family coping with childhood leukemia: One year after diagnosis. *Journal of Pediatric Psychology,* 1982, *7,* 157–174.

Lawton, M. P., & Brody, E. M. A multi-service respite program for family caregivers of patients with Alzheimer's disease. Research program funded by the Pew Foundation and the Hartford Foundation to the Philadelphia Geriatric Center, Philadelphia, 1984.

Lazarus, L. W., Stafford, B., Cooper, K., Cohler, B., & Dysken, M. A pilot

---

study of an Alzheimer patients' relatives discussion group. *The Gerontologist,* 1981, *21,* 353–358.

Levine, N. B., Dastoor, D. P., & Gendron, C. Coping with dementia: A pilot study. *Journal of the American Geriatrics Society,* 1983, *31,* 12–18.

Lewinsohn, P. M. A behavioral approach to depression. In R. Friedman & S. Katz (Eds.), *The psychology of depression.* Washington, DC: Winston, 1974, pp. 157–176.

Lieberman, M., Yalom, I., & Miles, M. B. *Encounter groups: First facts.* New York: Basic Books, 1973.

Linsk, N. L., & Pinkston, E. Introducing community-based behavioral techniques to families of the impaired elderly. Paper presented at the National Conference on Social Welfare, Cleveland, OH, May, 1980.

Linsk, N. L., & Pinkston, E. Home-based behavioral family treatment of depression in the elderly. Paper presented at the Association for Behavior Analysis, Milwaukee, WI, May, 1981.

Manjoney, D., & McKegney, F. Individual and family coping with polysystic kidney disease: The harvest of denial. *International Journal of Psychiatry in Medicine,* 1978, *9,* 19–31.

McCubbin, H., McCubbin, M., Patterson, J., Cauble, A., Wilson, L., & Warwick, W. CHIP—Coping health inventory for parents: An assessment of parental coping patterns in the care of the chronically ill child. *Journal of Marriage and the Family,* 1983, *45,* 359–370.

Mintz, J., Steuer, J., & Jarvik, L. Psychotherapy with depressed elderly patients: Research considerations. *Journal of Consulting and Clinical Psychology,* 1981, *49,* 542–548.

Moos, R. H., & Mitchell, R. E. Social network resources and adaptation: A conceptual framework. In T. A. Wills (Ed.), *Basic processes in helping relationships.* New York: Academic Press, 1982, pp. 213–231.

Morrow, G., Hoagland, A., & Carnike, C., Jr. Social support and parental adjustment to pediatric cancer. *Journal of Consulting and Clinical Psychology,* 1981, *49,* 763–765.

Nelson, R. O. Realistic dependent measures for clinical use. *Journal of Consulting and Clinical Psychology,* 1981, *49,* 168–182.

Nowak, C., & Brice, G. CARERS (Caregivers Assistance and Resources for the Elderly's Relatives Series). Unpublished manuscript, University of Buffalo Center for the Study of Aging, Buffalo, NY, 1984.

Peck, R. L. Home caregiver: Toward a new partnership with doctors. *Geriatrics,* 1983, *38,* 124–128.

Pinkston, E., & Linsk, N. L. *Care of the elderly: A family approach.* New York: Pergamon Press, 1984a.

Pinkston, E., & Linsk, N. L. Behavioral family intervention with the impaired elderly. *The Gerontologist,* 1984b, *24,* 576–583.

Poulshock, S. W. The effects on families of caring for impaired elderly in residence. Unpublished manuscript, Margaret Blenkner Research Center for Family Studies of the Benjamin Rose Institute, Cleveland, OH, 1982.

Poulshock, S. W., & Deimling, G. T. Families caring for elders in residence: Issues in the measurement of burden. *Journal of Gerontology*, 1984, *39*, 230–239.

Powell, L. S., & Courtice, K. *Alzheimer's disease: A guide for families*. Reading, MA: Addison-Wesley, 1983.

Priddy, J. M. Structured versus process support groups for families of the cognitively impaired elderly. Unpublished doctoral dissertation, Virginia Commonwealth University, Richmond, VA, 1984.

Priddy, J. M., & Gallagher, D. Clinical and research issues in the study of caregiver support groups. Paper presented at the meeting of the Gerontological Society, San Antonio, TX, November, 1984.

Rathbone-McCuan, E. Geriatric day care—A family perspective. *The Gerontologist*, 1976, *16*, 517–521.

Rathbone-McCuan, E., & Hashimi, J. *Isolated elders*. Rockville, MD: Aspen Systems Press, 1982.

Reever, K., Kepfer, C., Klein, J., & Nagele, D. Caregivers of dementia and psychological well-being. Paper presented at the meeting of the Gerontological Society, San Antonio, TX, November, 1983.

Robertson, D., Griffiths, A., & Cosin, L. Z. A community based continuing care program for the elderly disabled. *Journal of Gerontology*, 1977, *32*, 334–339.

Robins, L., Helzer, J., Croughan, J., Williams, J. B., & Spitzer, R. L. *NIMH Diagnostic Interview Schedule* (version III). Available from the first author at Washington University School of Medicine, St. Louis, 1981.

Roozman-Weigensberg, C., & Fox, M. A groupwork approach with adult children of institutionalized elderly: An investment in the future. *Journal of Gerontological Social Work*, 1980, *2*, 355–362..

Ross, H. E., & Kedward, H. B. Psychogeriatric hospital admissions from the community and institutions. *Journal of Gerontology*, 1977, *32*, 420–427.

Rothblum, E. D., Sholomskas, A., Berry, C., & Prusoff, B. Issues in clinical trials with the depressed elderly. *Journal of the American Geriatrics Society*, 1982, *30*, 694–699.

Safford, F. A program for families of the mentally impaired elderly. *The Gerontologist*, 1980, *20*, 656–660.

Sands, D., & Suzuki, T. Adult day care for Alzheimer patients and their families. *The Gerontologist*, 1983, *23*, 21–23.

Sanford, J. R. Tolerance of debility in elderly dependents by supporters at home: Its significance for hospital practice. *British Medical Journal*, 1975, *3*, 471–473.

Scharlach, A. E., & Frenzel, C. Correlates of psychological stress in wives of disabled adults. Paper presented at the meeting of the Western Psychological Association, Sacramento, CA, April, 1982.

Schilling, R., Gilchrist, L., & Schinke, S. P. Coping and social support in families of developmentally disabled children. *Family Relations*, 1984, *6*, 47–54.

Selan, B., & Schuenke, S. The Late Life Care Program: Helping families cope. *Health and Social Work,* 1982, *7,* 192–197.

Shanas, E. The family as a social support system in old age. *The Gerontologist,* 1979, *19,* 169–174.

Shanas, E., & Maddox, G. L. Aging, health, and the organization of health resources. In R. Binstock & E. Shanas (Eds.), *Handbook of aging and the social sciences.* New York: Van Nostrand Reinhold, 1976.

Sherwood, C. C., & Morris, J. Strategies for research and innovation. In S. Sherwood (Ed.), *Long-term care: A handbook for researchers, planners and providers.* New York: Spectrum Publications of John Wiley & Sons, 1975, pp. 639–722.

Silverman, A. G., & Brahce, C. "As parents grow older": An intervention model. *Journal of Gerontological Social Work,* 1979, *2,* 77–85.

Thompson, E., & Doll, W. The burden of families coping with the mentally ill: An invisible crisis. *Family Relations,* 1982, *31,* 379–388.

Thompson, L. W., & Gallagher, D. Efficacy of psychotherapy in the treatment of late-life depression. *Advances in Behavior Research and Therapy,* 1984, *6,* 127–139.

Wan, T. T., Weissert, W. G., & Livieratos, B. Geriatric day care and homemaker services: An experimental study. *Journal of Gerontology,* 1980, *35,* 256–274.

Weiler, P. G., & Rathbone-McCuan, E. *Adult day care: Community work with the elderly.* New York: Springer, 1978.

Weissert, W. G., Wan, T. T., & Livieratos, B. Effects and costs of day care and homemaker services for the chronically ill: A randomized experiment (DHHS Publication No. PHS 79-3258). Washington, DC: U.S. Government Printing Office, 1980.

Yeaton, W.H., & Sechrest, L. Critical dimensions in the choice and maintenance of successful treatments: Strength, integrity, and effectiveness. *Journal of Consulting and Clinical Psychology,* 1981, *49,* 156–167.

Yesavage, J., & Gallagher, D. Clinical research center for the study of senile dementia; subproject on Caregivers' correlates of primary degenerative dementia (Grant No. MH40041). Funded by the National Institute of Mental Health, 1984.

Yordi, C., Chu, A., Ross, K. M., & Wong, S. Research and the frail elderly: Ethical and methodological issues in controlled social experiments. *The Gerontologist,* 1982, *22,* 72–77.

York, J. L., & Calsyn, R. J. Family involvement in nursing homes. *The Gerontologist,* 1977, *17,* 500–505.

Zarit, S. H. Interventions with caregivers: Do they help and why? Paper presented at the meeting of the Gerontological Society, San Francisco, November, 1983.

Zarit, S. H., & Zarit, J. M. Families under stress: Interventions for caregivers of senile dementia patients. *Psychotherapy: Theory, Research and Practice,* 1982, *19,* 461–471.

Zarit, S. H., & Zarit, J. M. Cognitive impairment. In P. M. Lewinsohn & L. Teri (Eds.), *Clinical geropsychology*. New York: Pergamon Press, 1983, pp. 38–80.

Zarit, S. H., Reever, K., & Bach-Peterson, J. Relatives of the impaired elderly: Correlates of feelings of burden. *The Gerontologist*, 1980, *20*, 649–655.

Zimmer, A. H., & Hudis, I. E. Education for caregivers of the aged: A developmental view. Paper presented at the meeting of the Gerontological Society, San Diego, November, 1980.

CHAPTER 8

# Mental Health Interventions in the Nursing Home Community

Michael A. Smyer, Ph.D. and Margaret Frysinger, B.S.
Department of Individual and Family Studies
College of Human Development
The Pennsylvania State University
University Park, Pennsylvania

## INTRODUCTION

Approximately 15 percent of community-dwelling elderly are sufficiently impaired to require psychological services (Romaniuk, McAuley, & Arling, 1983). Perhaps most notable among the psychological impairments is the cognitive deterioration accompanying organic brain diseases which increase in prevalence across the life span (Kay & Bergmann, 1980). Despite significant levels of impairment, however, older adults remain underrepresented in the caseloads of traditional mental health settings (Redick & Taube, 1980; Smyer & Pruchno, 1984). In contrast, older adults with mental health impairments (particularly cognitive impairment) are overrepresented in the patient population of nursing home settings (Levine, 1981). Within these settings, however, there are few organized intervention efforts on a scale comparable to the community mental health system's offerings for community-dwelling elderly.

This chapter has two major themes. First, long-term care settings should be viewed as communities that could benefit from mental health interventions. In viewing such settings as communities, we high-

We appreciate the helpful comments of Margy Gatz, Pat Piper, Rachel Pruchno, and the editors on an earlier version of this chapter. Partial support for this chapter was provided by Grant No. 2 T32 AG00048-06 from the National Institute on Aging and Grant No. 1 T24 MH17422-02 from the National Institute of Mental Health.

light mental health interventions for three subgroups of community members: patients, patients' relatives, and staff members. The chapter's second theme is that there are a variety of mental health approaches that can be effective with each subgroup of the community.

The chapter is organized into five sections. In the first section, we review briefly indicators of the need for mental health intervention found in nursing home settings. In the next three sections we present examples of interventions aimed at patients, patients' relatives, and staff members. In the final section, we discuss potential changes in the health care system that will affect the attention given to the mental health needs of those whose lives are touched by long-term care settings.

Throughout the chapter, we will emphasize possible areas for consultation and education, as well as demonstrate the existing and potential range of interventions that could be useful in this setting. We emphasize consultation approaches because of two elements: (1) the relative scarcity of professionals trained in clinical gerontological intervention skills (Santos & VandenBos, 1982); and (2) the relatively greater efficiency of indirect service approaches when compared to one-to-one therapeutic interventions (Albee, 1959). Since there are few doctoral level professionals specifically trained in clinical gerontology, our assumption is that consultation approaches may allow those who are experienced in this area to have their maximum impact on the well-being of older adults, their family members, and their caregivers. Thus, this chapter is designed for professionals who are in direct service roles, consultation roles, and staff development roles. In addition, researchers, nursing home administrators, and those concerned with the development and implementation of mental health policy should find the chapter useful.

The definition of nursing home settings used here will include both skilled nursing facilities and intermediate care facilities, as defined by federal and state guidelines. (See Shadish & Bootzin, 1981, for a more complete description of the two types of nursing home care.) This definition will therefore include a more heterogeneous group of settings than simply homes that provide complete 24-hour nursing care.

Our definition of mental health intervention is similar to the description provided by Gatz and her colleagues when defining "psychological intervention":

> . . .a planned interpersonal intervention which is intended to have a psychotherapeutic impact of a preventive, curative, or palliative nature. Its goals and strategies are based to varying degrees on psychological theory. Psychotherapy is the prototypal psychological intervention, yet the em-

pirical literature on clinical intervention with the aged tends to emphasize nontraditional and institutional programs. . . . (Gatz, Popkin, Pino, & VandenBos, 1985, p. 755.)

Unlike Gatz et al., we will not focus on individual psychotherapy in our review. Instead, we will highlight programmatic intervention efforts aimed at the diversity of community members within nursing homes.

## Indicators of the Need for Mental Health Intervention in Nursing Homes

In the 1970s, nursing homes replaced state mental hospitals as the major receiving site for mentally ill elderly (see Gatz, Smyer, & Lawton, 1980, for a discussion of these developments). Estimates vary, but somewhere between 50 and 80 percent of the elderly in nursing homes are believed to have some degree of mental health impairment (Gottesman, 1977).

Some facts about nursing home use place these mental health statistics in perspective. At any one point in time, 5 percent of the entire elderly population is found in institutional settings—the majority of them in nursing homes. The most recent statistics available, for example, suggest that 1.3 million elderly were in nursing homes in 1977 (National Center for Health Statistics, 1981). Another way of thinking about the nursing home setting is that the lifetime chance of spending time in an institution is about one in four (Palmore, 1976). Thus, the potential number of elderly whose mental health needs may be influenced by or recognized in nursing home settings is potentially very large. As the number of elderly, especially the very old, continues to increase, the number with mental health impairments in nursing homes will undoubtedly grow.

The elderly are not the only ones who are being transferred from state mental hospitals to nursing homes. Many persons under age 65 are also turning up in nursing home settings, especially in intermediate care facilities (summarized in Shadish & Bootzin, 1981). In fact, it has been argued that rather than a national policy of deinstitutionalization, most mental patients are being treated in an institutional setting (Kiesler, 1980), and that nursing homes are "the centerpiece of that national policy" (Shadish & Bootzin, 1981, p. 490). Nursing home staff, however, are inexperienced and untrained in dealing with mental health problems (Jones, 1975; More, 1977).

It is useful for mental health professionals to consider nursing homes as communities with a variety of opportunities for consultation and treatment. Just as communities vary in their resources, so too do nursing homes range from resource-rich to resource-starved. Thus, a first task in mental health intervention in the nursing home setting is an assessment of the community and the potential indicators of impairment. These indicators are often a barometer for the mental health of the members of the nursing home community as a whole. In addition to staff, long-term care settings are communities composed of various subpopulations (patients, families); the institution is a special environment within which these subpopulations interact and affect each other. Most research in this area has concentrated on only one direction of effect, the influence of staff and the setting on the mental health of the residents.

While staff perceptions and staff philosophy may have a direct impact on patient care and ward atmosphere (Pierce, Trickett, & Moos, 1972; Smyer, Siegler, & Gatz, 1976), the institutional setting of the nursing home also affects the people who work there. Federal legislation and control have forced professionals to spend much of their time in clerical duties, leaving less well-trained personnel to deal with the patients (Wack & Rodin, 1978). These entry-level personnel in nursing home settings often have difficult life situations of their own, which detract from their on-the-job performance (Edinberg, 1982). In addition, they often find that bias and discrimination result in a general underestimation of their capabilities.

Staff turnover is one indicator of the negative effects that nursing homes can have on employees. The problem of staff turnover has been a persistent economic and interpersonal difficulty for the nursing home industry (Knapp & Harissis, 1981; Schwartz, 1974). It not only leads to disruption in the continuity of care for residents but also results in lowered morale for the remaining staff.

To the mutual influence between patients and staff must be added another source of influence. This third subgroup involved in the nursing home community is the families of the patients.

Families are a major source of support for older adults (Callahan, Diamond, Giele, & Morris, 1980). (See Bengtson & Treas, 1980, for a review of the role of family support of the elderly.) As Sussman (1977) has pointed out, family members serve as buffers between the impaired elderly and the several service bureaucracies from which they seek help. In the case of institutionalization, it is clear that family members are often involved in the placement decision (Smyer, 1980) and that they maintain frequent contact after the placement has been made. It has been suggested that the impact of placing a parent in an institution can intensify any ongoing family conflicts (Brody & Spark, 1966). Some families, however, have found some positive consequences of institutionalization (Smith & Bengtson, 1979). Whatever the consequences are for an individual family, it is evident that they, too, are involved in the nursing home community and are affected by the institutionalization of a family member.

Before considering specific interventions, however, several cautionary notes should be emphasized. First, our knowledge base on the epidemiology of mental health problems and impairments among older adults is inadequate. Second, even less is known about the impairment levels of caregivers of older adults—both institutional staff members and family members. Similarly, we have few studies of roles and influence of family members following the institutionalization of their older relative. Thus, the perspective offered here proceeds from sketchy data regarding mental health impairment and caregiving concerns. Better epidemiologic inquiry is needed to document levels of impairment and subsequent changes over time in response to intervention.

In addition to epidemiologic study, however, it is important to achieve some consensus regarding the appropriate terminology and implicit philosophy to be assumed when considering mental health interventions. For example, some colleagues assert that documented impairment is a direct indication of need for mental health services. Others caution, however, that need for services is a judgment, often reflecting the judge's own professional training and self-interest (e.g., Rappaport, 1977). In this chapter, we have tried to focus our discussion on the concept of impairment of functioning—both psychological and interpersonal functioning—without assuming automatically that such impairment signals a need for treatment. In addition, we have emphasized mental health, not solely mental illness. Thus, when considering, for example, the functioning of individual patients, we stress the existential stress involved in adaptation to a nursing home, in addition to the traditional mental illness concerns of standard diagnostic approaches.

With this background information on the potential targets of intervention, specific efforts aimed at different populations within the nursing home setting will now be considered. Each section includes a table summarizing illustrative interventions from the literature. The text is devoted more to a description of problems and interventions that have been or could be used in nursing homes.

**The Elderly Patient**

A variety of interventions have been used in nursing home settings that are geared to the elderly patient. While the main purpose of this section is to discuss examples of patient-focused intervention, it is important to remember that the process of institutionalization begins before the person actually enters the nursing home (Tobin & Lieberman, 1976).

Gurland (1980) suggested three common pathways to mental health problems for older adults: problems with self-care activities, lack of an effective social support network, and the presence of concomitant medical disorders. These three elements also constitute the most likely precipitants of institutional placement. Many residents use nursing homes as the treatment site of last choice, after experiencing the deficits identified by Gurland (Smyer, 1980). The mental health professional in the nursing home setting, therefore, must assess the previous history of adaptation of the impaired older patient, as well as the previous resources already depleted prior to the nursing home placement. The following example, written by a 34-year-old professional, described the dilemmas faced by his family. It illustrates the strains felt by the person entering the nursing home as well as demonstrating its effects on other family members.

> About five years before my mother entered a nursing home, I began to be concerned about her health and about my dad's own health. My mother seemed to be deteriorating, sometimes not knowing the date, sometimes retelling the same story several times during a conversation. She had begun to be confused in her own home, at times leaving the stove on. At other times, she was unable to get around within the house, especially after she fractured her hip. Her combination of arthritis and obesity made her vulnerable to falls and subsequent panic attacks, when she cried for help and no one came to her aid. My dad had begun to curtail his business, moving into semiretirement. In large part, he did this to be at home more, to provide physical care and emotional support for my mother.
>
> I was concerned that both of my parents were beginning to decline. My mother seemed to be getting worse, and my dad's health didn't seem up to the physical and emotional strain of caring for my mom. I suggested that they consider a nursing home now—now when it was not a crisis, now when they had some time to choose, now while there were still some options available. I mentioned it during our annual visit at Thanksgiving. No one did much with the idea.
>
> Things continued in the same way for a couple of years—everyone slowly getting a little worse, no one willing to do anything about it.

Finally, on another visit home I talked with my dad and told him that I was selfishly concerned about what would happen to mom if he died. It seemed to me that he would not be helping anyone if he killed himself, albeit slowly, through his devoted care of my mother. I outlined a likely scenario—he dies, my mother is forced to seek institutional care since neither my sister nor I could provide the quality and quantity of care he'd been providing, and my mother is forced to take whatever bed she can find. He agreed that this wasn't a good path, so he and my mother began to discuss the possibility of nursing home care. With my sister's help, they looked around for a year. They eventually found a home which was good, close to home, Catholic, and potentially available in the near future. My mother was placed on the waiting list. When a bed became available, however, she refused to enter the home. She didn't feel that her own situation warranted that type of treatment. In the meantime, she had begun calling my sister quite often, asking her to visit, to rescue her when she fell or became confused, and making more demands on my sister's time and energy than Sis could handle. The combination of a retarded son and a needy mother was almost too much for her. At the same time, my dad's health began to fail. He was not sleeping well (because my mother awoke frequently at night) and his legs were bothering him, from the strain of lifting my mother in and out of bed, in and out of chairs, etc.

Finally, a family council was called. I made a special visit home to talk about the family's option . . . I talked with both of my parents about the importance of making choices before things became a crisis. My mother agreed, with great hesitation, to enter a nursing home if I thought it was the right thing to do. Within a couple of months, through a variety of intercessions, my mother entered the nursing home she had passed up a year earlier. (Smyer, 1983, pp. 2–3)

With this general understanding of the process of institutionalization, we will now consider examples of interventions focused on the patients of long-term care institutional settings. Table 8.1, while not an exhaustive search of all the options available, offers an overview of several ways mental health interventions have been used for residents in the nursing home setting.

Several elements are important to consider when reviewing the entries in Table 8.1. First, three general types of intervention are described in successive sections of Table 8.1: individual, group, and program interventions. Individual interventions are those that involve just the therapist or staff member, and the patient. Group interventions are those that try to involve several patients. Those listed as program interventions are efforts that attempt to be more widespread in their impact.

The information on each intervention effort has been divided into

**Table 8.1**
A Sample of Intervention Approaches for Nursing Home Residents.

| Author | Intervention Approach | Desired Outcome | Evaluation Approach |
|---|---|---|---|
| I. Type: *Individual Treatment* | | | |
| Berger (1979) | Interpersonal skill training | Ability to use adaptive interpersonal skills to negotiate major role changes | 1. An assessment measure: judges rated responses in role plays<br>2. Control group |
| Brink (1977) | Brief psychotherapy | Improved mental health | None (clinical example) |
| Brink (1980) | Behavioral treatment of paranoia (reality therapy & verbal nonreinforcement) | Behavioral change (decrease in paranoid behavior) | Reports from others about person (but used only one clinical example) |
| Carstensen & Fremouw (1981) | Behavioral clinical approach to treatment of paranoia | Relieve paranoia | None (one clinical example) |
| Feier & Leight (1981) | A communication-cognition program | Compensation for diminished abilities & raised level of communication & cognitive functioning | Performance judged on anecdotal records & observations |
| Godbole & Verinis (1974) | Psychotherapy for reaction to physical illness | Increased patient improvement | Comparison groups (3) |
| Goldstein & Baer (1976) | Behavioral approach to increase letter-writing & receiving | Decrease loneliness | Pre & post comparison (3 subjects) |
| Hanley (1981) | Reality orientation through:<br>1. Active orientation training<br>2. Sign posting | Lower ward disorientation | ABABA single-case design for training alone;<br>ABC single-case design for sign posting |

| Study | Approach | Goal | Design |
|---|---|---|---|
| MacDonald (1978) | Behavioral approach | Increase verbalization | Comparing mean rates of verbalization in 4-minute blocks (single-subject, baseline-contingency-reversal-contingency design) |
| MacDonald & Butler (1974) | Behavioral modification | Produce walking behaviors | Baseline—contingency I, Reversal—contingency II |
| Nigl & Jackson (1981) | Behavioral management program (use of reinforcement by tokens) | Increase social functioning & social behaviors | ABA design (baseline-reinforcement-withdraw-reinforcement) |
| Penner et al. (1983) | Learning-based self-care skills training program | Deinstitutionalization or prevent institutionalization | (Quasi-experimental design) 1. Periodic assessments for each skill module, & behavior change assessments for individuals 2. After discharge: comparison group & one-year follow-up of those discharged |
| Power & McCarron (1975) | Interactive-contact approach to depression (use of body contact & social interaction) | Reduced depression | Pre- & post-tests & 6-week follow-up control group |
| Rinke et al. (1978) | Behavior therapy: prompting & reinforcement | Increased self-bathing | Control group & comparisons with baseline |

**Table 8.1** *(continued)*

| Author | Intervention Approach | Desired Outcome | Evaluation Approach |
|---|---|---|---|
| Sherr & Goffi (1977) | Early psychosocial intervention | Prevention of crippling mental & emotional disability; decrease need for hospitalization | (Clinical) |
| II. Type: *Group Treatment* | | | |
| Berger & Rose (1977) | Interpersonal skill training | Development of competence in social interactions | Control group & comparison group (discussion group); post-treatment assessment |
| Berland & Poggi (1979) | Expressive group psycho-therapy | Increased self-awareness & chance for behavior change | None (clinical description) |
| Corbin & Nelson (1980) | Use of discussion-stimulating board games | Ameliorate social isolation & sensory deprivation | Pre- & post-test questionnaire-directed interview; control group |
| Garrison (1978) | An educational approach to stress management | 1. Cognitive understanding of stress & relaxation 2. Ability to relax 3. Ability to extend relaxation skill to real-life stress situations | Self-report questionnaire; report of stress-related symptoms |
| Lesser et al. (1981) | Reminiscence group therapy with psychotic inpatients | Group cohesiveness | None (observations & impressions) |

| Study | Intervention | Goals | Method |
|---|---|---|---|
| McClannahan & Risley (1975) | Recreational materials for severely disabled | Interaction with environment | Observers recording number of times persons "appropriately" participated with their environment (with & without recreation materials) |
| Rathbone-McCuan & Levenson (1975) | Socialization therapy in day-care setting | Increase social risks | None (clinical examples) |
| Reinke et al. (1981) | A "friendly visitor" program | Improve morale & cognitive functioning | Comparison & control groups; Pre- & post-tests with several measures |
| Rodin & Langer (1977) | Emphasizing personal responsibility | Increase feelings of choice & personal responsibility | Comparison & control groups |
| Saul & Saul (1974) | Group psychotherapy | 1. Motivation to live<br>2. Memory improvement<br>3. Communication skill improvement<br>4. Improvement of self-awareness<br>5. Increased social skills & social identity<br>6. Improved self-control<br>7. Develop a sense of camaraderie<br>8. Development of a role & identity in the setting | None (clinical examples) |
| Thompson et al. (1983) | Psycho-educational model for coping with depression | Reduced psychological distress | Pre- & post-tests with several measures of depression |

Table 8.1 (continued)

| Author | Intervention Approach | Desired Outcome | Evaluation Approach |
|---|---|---|---|
| Wallach et al. (1979) | Intergenerational visiting using high school students | Decreased social isolation | Pre-post test |
| III. Type: *Program Interventions* | | | |
| Brickel (1979) | Therapeutic roles of animal mascots | Increased morale | None |
| Carroll (1978) | Use of alcohol in a daily "social hour" | Increased socialization | Comparison groups (drinkers vs. nondrinkers at same function) |
| Citrin & Dixon (1977) | Reality orientation programming | Improve orientation to environment & behavioral functioning | Pretest–posttest control group |
| Cornbleth & Cornbleth (1979) | Reality orientation classes | Increase verbal orientation & improvement in independent functioning | Pre- & post-tests |
| Jason & Smetak (1983) | Environmental intervention with resident participation | Increase social involvement | Compared observer-rated interaction levels at baseline & after treatment; Also post-treatment questionnaire |
| Jenkins et al. (1977) | An activities program with recreational materials | Increase levels of engagement | Compared observer-rated levels of engagement during activity, with level at baseline |
| Kalson (1976) | A program of social interaction with mentally retarded adults | Increase morale Increase general social interaction patterns Express feelings of role | Control group |

| | | | |
|---|---|---|---|
| | | satisfaction in being useful & helpful | |
| | | Show a more positive attitude toward retarded persons | |
| MacDonald & Settin (1978) | Reality orientation vs. sheltered workshops | Evaluate the effects of the two types of treatment | Comparison of 2 treatment groups; control group |
| Powell et al. (1979) | Recreational activity: An indoor gardening program | Increase residents' level of engagement | Compared engagement levels in comparison groups & also comparison (nongardening) times |
| Reichenfeld et al. (1973) | Group-oriented activity programs | 1. Improve discharge rates & status at discharge 2. Improve level of functioning 3. Improve staff attitudes | Control group; Post-test only |
| Salter & Salter (1975) | A combined program of reality orientation, environmental stimulation, and activities | Improvement in orientation to reality & motivation | None (just notes end-status of participants) |
| Schulz (1976) | Personal visitation program | Improved physical and mental health through predictability and control of the schedule | Comparison & control groups |
| Solon et al. (1977) | Program linking young & old institutionalized persons | Decrease institutional isolation | None |
| Whitley et al. (1976) | Adopted grandparent program | Increase interaction between age-groups | None |

several columns: author(s), intervention approach, desired outcome, and evaluation approach. The approach column briefly describes the type of treatment and, if applicable, the model used. The outcome column describes the outcome(s) the researchers were hoping to achieve. As we will see, the outcome that is emphasized by the various interventions reflects a variety of assumptions about the role which the nursing home will play for the patient. The evaluation column briefly describes the study design and the form in which the data were evaluated. The significance of this column will be discussed later.

The examples shown in Table 8.1 indicate the diversity of ways that interventions have been attempted in long-term care institutions such as nursing homes, as well as indicating that the same approach (e.g., behavioral) can be used for each of the three types of interventions. Just within the individual intervention type there are efforts aimed at decreasing specific problems (e.g., paranoia—Carstensen & Fremouw, 1981; depression—Power & McCarron, 1975) or increasing specific behaviors (e.g., verbalization—MacDonald, 1978; walking—MacDonald & Butler, 1974; self-bathing—Rinke, Williams, Lloyd, Smith-Scott, 1978).

Apart from the variability within each type of intervention, the wide range of target problems considered in the examples of Table 8.1 also indicates that different interventions may lead to different outcomes for nursing home residents. Some approaches (e.g., Berger, 1979) focus on helping the patient adapt to the significant role changes that occur with institutionalization (Laird, 1979). The majority are concerned with increasing the patient's adaptation to the environmental demands of the nursing home. For example, Hanley (1981) tried to help residents regain or maintain their orientation to their surroundings. Nigl and Jackson (1981) helped withdrawn patients to increase their social activities within the nursing home. Wallach, Kelley, and Abrahams (1979) used visits from high school students to decrease feelings of social isolation for residents. Other interventions are designed to decrease specific problems or increase specific behaviors. A few interventions are designed either to prevent institutionalization or to prepare patients for a return to the community (e.g., Penner, Eberly, & Patterson, 1983; Reichenfeld, Csapo, Carriere, & Gardner, 1973).

These different substantive emphases reflect different assumptions about the role the nursing home will play for the patient—a point of entry in the support system; a final home and environment to which they must accommodate; or a replacement that should be followed with subsequent discharge and resumption of residence in the patient's former community. Whether recognized or not, the patient and those involved in the placement will have their own feelings about the role the setting will play. Assessment of those perceptions is an important aspect involved in choice of intervention.

Patient, staff, and family members' perceptions may be linked to the patient's prior history of adaptation. Kahn (1975) pointed out that there are two general categories of older adults with mental impairments: those who have had a lifelong history of adjustment problems, and those who have developed impairments as a concomitant of old age. The treatment approaches, prospects for success, and goals for treatment will vary depending upon the patient's prior history and experience of impairment.

In addition to denoting a variety of substantive concerns, the entries in Table 8.1 also vary in terms of their research designs and sophistication. Some offer no evaluation of their interventions, preferring instead clinical case descriptions of their approach (e.g., Brink, 1977; Saul & Saul, 1974; Sherr & Goffi, 1977). Others offer evaluation approaches that incorporate control or comparison groups (e.g., Penner et al., 1983; Rinke et al., 1978; Rodin & Langer, 1977). Still others have used single-case designs to assess the efficacy of their approaches (e.g., Hanley, 1981).

Evaluative research must be integrated with mental health interventions in long-term care institutional settings. The number of entries in this table and the diversity of the interventions that have been evaluated lead to the conclusion that we now have a wide range of available mental health interventions that can be effective with nursing home residents. With continued use of appropriate methodologies, we should begin to focus more on matching the appropriate intervention with the various concerns of elderly nursing home residents.

## The Families of
## Institutionalized Elderly

As mentioned previously, families are strongly involved as intermediaries with service institutions in behalf of their older members, they are involved in placement decisions, and they maintain contact after the older person enters the institution. The mental health professional working with families of mentally impaired elderly should be aware of several facts.

First, it is important to realize that families turn to institutionalization only after trying everything else. In contrast to the myth that family members abandon their elderly relatives to the warehouse of the nursing home, the evidence suggests that more frequently the decision to seek institutional care is made only after significant emotional and economic resources have been depleted by maintaining the older adult in the community (Maddox, 1977; Smyer, 1980). Second, it is important to be aware that "family" in this case refers to a diversity of family forms, and can include a spouse, children, nieces, nephews, and grandchildren (U.S. Department of Commerce, 1978). Third, as with individually oriented treatment, there are several different family tasks which may be aided by mental health intervention.

Pruchno and Smyer (1984) suggested that family caregivers of mentally impaired elderly face four major challenges; the same is true for relatives of institutionalized elderly. The four tasks they outlined were differential diagnosis; grieving; caregiving; and personal development.

The first challenge is the difficult process of establishing a diagnosis, or answering the seemingly simple question of what is wrong with the older relative. Oftentimes, this differential diagnostic enquiry is broken into several subquestions by the family members: Is this part of normal aging? What is the likely outcome? Is it hereditary (especially if the older adult's difficulties appear to be caused by an organic brain disorder)?

A second major task facing family members is personal grieving for the lost relationship and lost functioning of the older person they once knew. Again, in the case of an organically impaired relative, the grieving may be the result of a pattern of decline, in many cases lasting several years (Butler, 1984). Despite this long opportunity for adjustment, however, oftentimes the crisis of institutionalization begins or heightens a grieving response by family caretakers. As Cohen (1984) noted, in the case of Alzheimer's patients, there are almost always two patients—the demented older adult and a depressed relative.

The third challenge facing family members is that of the caregiving itself. The nature of caregiving may change as the older adult moves through a continuum toward increasing dependence and increasingly complicated services. Direct caregiving is the most prevalent challenge, but obtaining help from outside services frequently becomes necessary. Negotiating the maze of human services and government programs can in and of itself be a frustrating experience for family caregivers.

The fourth task that faces each family caregiver is the challenge of continuing her or his own personal development, despite the loss and grief over the impaired relative. For although lives are interwoven within families (Pruchno, Blow, & Smyer, 1984), each individual must inevitably face many such problems alone in later life. The challenge associated with following this solitary path and the need for continued personal development often become clearer and perhaps more threatening for caregivers once a long-term care setting has been sought for their dependent relative.

Bloom (1983) provided an excellent example of the still-important role family members play as "buffers" between the frail, impaired relative and the service system. He described a 42-year-old professional whose mother had been hiring a home health nurse following a severe fall that had briefly put her into the hospital:

> Halfway through this experience, it was obvious that
> 1. my mother was not improving and
> 2. she was bankrupting herself.
>
> And I began to look for advice. I opened the phone book and called the Department on Aging. What I wanted to know was
> 1. Could my mother receive government assistance to defray the cost of the home aides?
> 2. Precisely when could I apply for welfare on her behalf?
> 3. Could she stay in her present apartment and receive welfare? I spent one entire working day on the phone and by the end of the day I had received every conceivable shade of answer. The major amount of time was spent determining not what I should do but whom I should call. For instance, the fact that I lived in Evanston and my mother lived in Glenview would give rise to conversations such as this:

> VOICE: Would you rather apply for aid in Evanston or in Glenview?
> ARTHUR: Is there any difference?
> VOICE: Well, it's a different provider.
> ARTHUR: Well, can I apply through Evanston for service for someone who lives in Glenview?
> VOICE: I don't know. We can try.
> ARTHUR: Well, that way all the business affairs could be done through my address and we wouldn't have to bother my mother.
> VOICE: O.K. What zone are you in?
> ARTHUR: Is that like my zip code?
> VOICE: No, it's your health zone.
> ARTHUR: I don't know. Can you find out?
> VOICE: I might be able to call downtown. I don't have an Evanston map. I only have a Glenview map.
> ARTHUR: Why don't we try that? What zone is my mother in?

> VOICE:   Where in Glenview does she live?
> ARTHUR:  2600 Golf Road.
> VOICE:   No, the map doesn't show streets. It only shows zones, like east, west, north. Does she live in North Glenview?
> ARTHUR:  I don't know. How far north does Glenview go?
> VOICE:   I don't know. I don't have a street map.

By the end of the day, what I felt I needed was a tour guide through the labyrinth. Fortunately I got one. The Council for Jewish Elderly said that for $100 they would do an assessment of my mother's physical and emotional state, make recommendations for her future, and help me contact the necessary agencies. What they did was

1. conduct a lengthy interview with Rena (my wife) and me,
2. conduct two interviews with my mother, one in her home,
3. have her medical records examined,
4. have her examined by a nurse practitioner,
5. have her examined by a psychiatrist (this part was waived because of the difficulties in transporting my mother),
6. conduct a wrap-up session with Rena and me, and
7. provide a list of referral agencies.

The family in this situation eventually sought a nursing home placement for their mother. The decision, and its implementation, however, only took place after many weeks of weighing options, reviewing family history and assets, and assessing the mental and physical strain continued caregiving would require. What did this service provide?

1. Nothing for my mother. It turned out to be a service for Rena and me.
2. An impartial viewpoint that gave me a lot of personal support. I was able to see my situation in relation to others. I was able to get an opinion not only of my mother's condition but also of my perception of and reaction toward it.
3. A sense of alternatives. (pp. 4–6)

In summary, the process of seeking institutional care affects not only impaired older adults, but also the caregivers whose lives are integrally linked to them (Brody, 1981; Brody & Spark, 1966; Hagestad, 1981). The transition of institutionalization creates a variety of "countertransitions" for family members (Riley & Waring, 1976). Mental health professionals can be of assistance to family members who are seeking, not only to provide care and comfort for their impaired relatives, but also to continue to cope with their own daily life demands as well. Specifically, mental health professionals can help in each of the four family tasks outlined above (differential diagnosis; grieving; caregiving; and personal development).

A sample of intervention approaches for families of residents of long-term care settings is provided in Table 8.2. Several aspects of Table 8.2 are noteworthy. First, there are fewer entries here than in the first table. While neither listing is an exhaustive compilation, the relative size of the work in the two areas is reflected in the number of entries. Clearly, much more work has been done with the older resident than with family members as a focus.

Another important aspect of Table 8.2 is the range of problems reflected by the programs listed. Three of the four family tasks are well-represented. For example, several of the offerings focus on differential diagnosis by providing accurate information about the aging process and the underlying cause of the patient's difficulty (e.g., Manaster, 1967; Safford, 1980; Zarit & Zarit, 1982). Similarly, some of the interventions highlight the importance of working on the caregivers' own reactions, such as grief, to the older adults' impairments (e.g., Hausman, 1979; Manaster, 1967; Zarit & Zarit, 1982). Finally, for the caregiving task, many of the intervention programs listed are aimed at increasing the abilities of the caregivers to provide optimal care for impaired relatives (e.g., Breslin, 1978; Hausman, 1979; La-Wall, 1981). Perhaps not as well represented are interventions aimed at assisting the continued personal growth and development of the individual caregivers, although some of the approaches included these elements (e.g., Reifler, Larson, Cox, & Featherstone, 1981; Zarit & Zarit, 1982).

In terms of staff involvement, the range of approaches represented in Table 8.2 includes both individual therapists as well as aides, nursing staff, and others active in the day-to-day programming of nursing homes. What is noteworthy, however, is that only one example of joint programming for both family members and staff was found in our review of the literature. Breslin's (1978) effort focused on developing rapport between staff and family members, clearly acknowledging the interdependence and mutual support that they could provide to each other. Most approaches, however, focus solely on family members as service recipients, rather than as active collaborators in the caregiving process. This philosophical difference has obvious ramifications in the family members' self-assessment and perceptions of self-efficacy in caregiving within the nursing home setting.

The sample of interventions in Table 8.2 also reflects the need for increased evaluative rigor in the domain of family intervention in long-term care. There are good examples of well-evaluated programs geared to family caregivers (e.g., the study of Frankfather, Smith, & Caro, 1981, of the effects of aging services on family support of im-

**Table 8.2**
A Sample of Intervention Approaches for Families of Nursing Home Residents.

| Authors | Intervention Approach | Desired Outcome | Evaluation Approach |
|---|---|---|---|
| Breslin (1978) | Inservice training with both family members and nursing home staff | Open dialogue between two groups | Questionnaires after each session |
| Hausman (1979) | Short-term counseling groups for children of elderly parents | 1. Participants to find balance between responsibility to self, own family, & parents<br>2. Make specific decisions about extent of obligation to parents & what attendant behavior will be<br>3. Learn to deal with parents in a mature way | General evaluation questionnaire at last meeting |
| LaWall (1981) | Conjoint therapy with elderly couples | Utilizing spouse as co-therapist | None (clinical examples) |
| Lewis (1980) | A continuum of services for families of institutionalized aged, including pre-admission groups, post-admission counseling, and discussions | Helping families cope | None (article discusses possibilities) |
| Manaster (1967) | Group therapy for family members | 1. Awareness by family of reasons for patient's behavior | None |

| | | | |
|---|---|---|---|
| | | 2. Awareness of own feelings & reactions about putting older person in home & how affects their relationship<br>3. Clearer understanding of entire field of aging | A variety of pre- and post-tests |
| Reifler et al. (1981) | A comprehensive evaluation & treatment program that includes support, counseling, & practical advice for referring family members | Physical & mental improvement | |
| Safford (1980) | An educational & support program approach to the issues which arise for families of mentally impaired aged | Increased knowledge about mental impairment and effects on family; help families deal with issues & help assume a responsible role in improved care for mentally impaired aged | None |
| Zarit & Zarit (1982) | Interventions for caregivers of patients with senile dementia, including information & counseling | Reducing caregiver burden and strain through providing accurate information about senile dementia; problem-solving in individual and group sessions; providing support through group meetings | None—program description without evaluation |

paired elderly in the community). However, there is still a relative dearth of well-designed investigations into effective mental health interventions with family members of impaired elderly who are living in long-term care institutions.

## The Staff

In addition to the 1.3 million residents in nursing homes in 1977, there were over 647,000 employees providing direct health-related care (National Center for Health Statistics, 1981). This figure, however, actually underestimates, for a couple of reasons, the number of individuals working in these settings. First, it does not include several categories of workers who provide indirect service (e.g., custodial staff, nutrition and food service staff, or laundry personnel). Second, it is based on full-time equivalents. When the total number of full- and part-time employees is considered, the total number of personnel increases substantially.

Just as family members face a variety of mental health challenges as part of their caregiving, so too do nursing home staff. Thus, mental health interventions aimed at staff may focus on several different areas: the staff members' own well-being and morale; skill-building to improve patient well-being and morale; and increasing the cooperation between patients and staff to enhance the well-being of all members of the nursing home community.

If one focuses on staff members' well-being, the logical target group is nurses aides. They are the largest subgroup within the staff. This group also has more contact with residents and visiting family members than other nursing home employees, and they may have the first opportunity to recognize any changes in patient functioning (Pavur & Smith, 1983). Their role in determining a patient's quality of care is, therefore, very important.

The staff turnover rate, however, is greatest among the nurses' aides (Kasteler, Ford, White, & Carruth, 1979). As noted earlier, they also are more likely to have difficult life situations and job morale problems from employee turnover and lowered work status. Thus, mental health interventions may be useful for improving the aides' well-being as well as that of their patients.

In Table 8.3, a sample of intervention approaches for nursing home staff members is presented. Interventions with the staff have generally taken two approaches: programs to improve staff morale and functioning (e.g., Breslau, 1978/1979; Kramer, 1977; Tallmer, Mayer, & Hill, 1977), and programs that are designed to train staff to improve patient morale and functioning (e.g., Fergus, 1979; Pavur & Smith, 1983; Sperbeck & Whitbourne, 1981).

Kastenbaum's work (1965, 1972) is a good example of an intervention designed to affect *both* patients and staff. He and his colleagues designed several programs intended to help decrease the us–them distinction that often locks the staff and the residents into constricted and predictable relationships. Their programs, designed to increase mutual gratification, attempted to discover whether staff and patients could be encouraged to seek each other out, not just out of necessity, but because they enjoyed each other's company. Kastenbaum and his colleagues found that rather than programs developed by "experts," the changes that were most successful were ones that spontaneously grew out of the program changes his studies created. For example, wine and beer social hours were instituted six afternoons a week in wards with socially isolated and confused patients. Increases in patient–staff interactions and patient–patient interactions were noteworthy. In addition, decreases in patients' use of psychotropic medications were recorded.

The changes thus created had several positive results: they helped decrease the us–them distinction that is so often present in institutional settings between staff and patients; they helped increase job satisfaction for staff; and they led to spontaneous actions between residents and aides, which helped the nurses' aides to feel more involved and more a part of the community.

In contrast to these findings, nursing home staff expectations and attitudes have often been found to focus on the negative behaviors of the older patient. For example, when resident self-care behaviors are observed, the staff has been found to reward independent behaviors infrequently, while dependent behaviors were inadvertently encouraged because it was easier to do things for patients than to foster independent self-care (Baltes, Burgess, & Stewart, 1980). Behaviors such as wandering, which pose difficulties for staff, are seen as problems and are often responded to by restraints. This can then hide other symptoms or increase the anxiety that created the behavior in the first place (Snyder, Rupprecht, Pyrek, Brekhus, & Moss, 1978). Chemical and physical restraints are often used to treat the symptom behavior, ignoring underlying problems (Covert, Rodrigues, & Solomon, 1977). Homes for the aged have also been found to have the highest scores on alienation and conditional freedom when compared to other types of residential organizations (Dudley & Hillery, 1977). Staff are more likely to label behavior as senile if the behavior is annoying and if they are busy (Gubrium, 1978).

The tendency of staff to interpret patient behavior by how it af-

**Table 8.3**
A Sample of Intervention Approaches for Nursing Home Staff Members.

| Author | Intervention Approach | Desired Outcome | Evaluation Approach |
|---|---|---|---|
| Breslau (1978/1979) | Development of weekly staff meetings | Combat staff alienation, interunit competition, & other problems | None |
| Connell & Smyer (1984) | Teleconference training of nursing home staff in skills to manage moods | Skills in mood monitoring, behavioral charting, & improved affect | Formative evaluation of substantive & procedural issues; no control group |
| Fergus (1979) | Teaching milieu therapy to staff & using telephone consultation as follow-up | Increased program implementation by staff who receive telephone consultation | Random assignment to groups for those who took workshop: control group, comparison group, & follow-up consultation Pre- & post-test |
| Jason & Smetak (1983) | Environmental alteration of lounge spaces, painting, and seating arrangements | Increased social interaction among patients, staff, and family members | Pre-post intervention comparisons, using control groups |
| Kastenbaum (1965 & 1972) | Implementation of beer and wine social hours in ward settings | Improved social interactions between patients and staff and among patients; improved patient well-being | Pre-post observations of social interacting patient behaviors, psychotropic medications |

| | | |
|---|---|---|
| Kramer (1977) | Utilization of a core group of administrators to improve staff relations & attitudes | Keep struggles in the open so solutions can be found | None (article chronicles one home's experiences) |
| Pavur & Smith (1983) | Training nurses aides | Improve job performance & improve quality of care for residents | Comparison group; pre- & post-tests on numerous measures |
| Pierce et al. (1972) | Staff discussion of perceived ward environment & appropriate subsequent changes | Enhancing ward atmosphere | Pre- & post-test of ward atmosphere compared to staff view of "ideal ward" |
| Soskis (1981) | Small group discussion focused on federally mandated patients' rights in nursing homes | Increase staff's understanding of patients' rights from federal & state regulations | None |
| Sperbeck & Whitbourne (1981) | Training staff in the principles of behavior analysis, focusing on cognitive & attitudinal restructuring | Increase independence & decrease dependence of residents | Trained observers recorded behaviors at baseline & post-treatment for treatment group, modified control group, and control group |
| Tallmer et al. (1977) | Workshop for nurses aides with emphasis on how attitudes are formed & reinforced by cultural differences | Increase aides' awareness of their attitudes toward older people, & implications for job performance | Self-administered questionnaires on workshop impact |

fects their job should not be surprising. Such a tendency can, however, be important in determining patient outcome, even when the staff has earlier defined different interpretations as being more successful (Smyer et al., 1976). This tendency of the staff to interpret and label behavior is affected by staff attitudes toward nursing home patients, an attitude which has been found to be generally negative. Staff have been found to assume that debilitation always occurs (Gubrium, 1978), and in some cases that senility is inevitable (Smithers, 1977). In addition, a medical model that does not expect the patient to recover and accepts the use of many drugs may be used (Wack & Rodin, 1978). It has been suggested that the segregation of the severely impaired elderly implies a doomed status role where the patient is unable to seek help or participate in achieving a state of wellness (Maxwell, 1979). Kastenbaum's work, however, is a good indication that alternatives are available.

Another set of interventions has focused on enhancing the skills of nurses aides to affect not only their own mental health but also the well-being of their patients. Connell and Smyer (1984), for example, used an educational approach to mild depression. Their program was a modification of earlier work by Thompson and his colleagues (Thompson, Gallagher, Nies, & Epstein, 1983), based on Lewinsohn's cognitive-behavioral approach to depression (Lewinsohn, Munoz, Youngren, & Zeiss, 1978). The program adopted a "train-the-trainers" approach, aimed at providing nursing home staff members with skills and information to use in their personal lives and with their patients (Danish & D'Augelli, 1976; Danish et al., 1978).

Using a teleconference format, staff members in 14 acute- and extended-care facilities throughout Pennsylvania were trained in four one-hour sessions. The focus of the training was a behavioral assessment of the links between moods and positive or negative events in the staff member's life. The program focused on coping with depression for two reasons: first, previous analyses of nursing home staffs' life circumstances suggested that aides typically experience a fair amount of dysphoria in their personal and professional lives; second, depressive symptoms are one of the major mental health problems of older adults (Gurland, 1976). In addition, Thompson and his colleagues found few differences in classes taught by professionals and nonprofessionals (Thompson et al., 1983). Thus, this approach might easily be implemented with nursing home staff, especially aides, in the role of teachers.

Connell and Smyer's (1984) evaluation suggested that the staff members found the training useful for their own moods, but felt that they needed additional training to teach their newly learned skills to patients. When effective, such approaches offer one way to affect the mental health of both staff and patients with a single intervention.

While not directly tested with nursing home personnel, several colleagues have recently begun to investigate the possibility of training lower-level community staff in techniques of mental health intervention with older adults. The programs developed by Griffin and Gottesman (1983) and by Santos and his colleagues (1983) are examples of programs that could be applied easily to the nursing home administration and staff.

Griffin and Gottesman (1983), for example, pointed out that it is essential to engage the administrative level in training. In addition to the political support they can provide, they also need the knowledge that is offered in many of the training programs. Moreover, it is clear that nurses aides can benefit from the paraprofessional training developed for other groups, such as the materials and designs developed by Santos and his co-workers (1983).

In addition to training the staff, others have attempted to affect the atmosphere of the setting in two primary ways—either by focusing on the interpersonal, psychological atmosphere of the setting (e.g., Breslau, 1978–1979) or by focusing on the physical environment of the setting itself (e.g., Jason & Smetak, 1983). Breslau's program concentrated on giving the staff a weekly staff meeting as a way to work out any problems they might be having in their own or other wards. Jason and Smetak's study showed that residents and staff of a nursing home could work together in raising the money to physically improve the lounge areas. The outcome of this improvement was increased interaction among the staff, the residents, and the residents' family. This study illustrates that an intervention aimed primarily at one group, the residents, can affect the other groups within the nursing home community as well.

In such attempts, however, it is essential to clarify the desired outcome and to measure patient and staff performance on this dimension adequately. Jason and Smetak's (1983) work is a good example of a carefully designed and evaluated environmental intervention aimed at improving the socialization of residents and their visitors. They carefully recorded a variety of resident behaviors (e.g., reading, talking in conversation, or socially isolated television watching). Through careful pre–post comparisons, they were able to document the effectiveness of a seemingly small environmental improvement on social functioning in the setting.

The size of Table 8.3 indicates that the number of studies aimed at assisting nursing home staff is not very large. Most of those interventions that do exist were designed to help nursing home staff learn ways to improve the atmosphere in the facility and to improve the quality of care for the residents. Although emphasized in our discussion here, far less has been done to investigate ways to improve the quality of life for the staff within the nursing home setting.

## The Nursing Home as Part of the National Health Care System

It is important to place mental health interventions in nursing homes within a broader context of health care for the elderly (Vladeck & Firman, 1983). As a nation, we are beginning to consider the costs involved in providing medical care for an aging population. For example, in 1967, Medicare reimbursements totaled $4.2 billion; in 1978, it was $24.2 billion. The projected figure for 1984 is $72.9 billion, a 200 percent increase from the 1978 figure (Jones, 1984).

As Lave and Silverman (1983) point out, there are several ways to reduce the costs of the Medicare and Medicaid programs: decrease the size of the eligibility groups; change the types of services covered; decrease the reimbursement to providers; and increase the personal financial liability of those receiving services. Each of these aspects has been at least discussed if not implemented in the recent public debate on health care provision for the elderly (Bayer, 1984). Each of these changes would have an important impact on the mental health interventions discussed thus far.

As an example, consider the recently initiated Medicare prospective payment system of Diagnosis Related Groupings (DRGs) (Office of Technology Assessment, 1983). Under this system, the government specifies in advance what it will pay for various medical conditions and treatments. For example, in one Pennsylvania hospital, Medicare will reimburse $2,733 for treating heart failure, one of the 467 DRGs. (The reimbursement rates vary within and between states.) If the hospital's treatment costs less, the hospital keeps the profit; if it costs more, the hospital must absorb the loss.

The DRG may have an important impact on long-term care settings for two reasons: It may affect the type of patient sent to nursing homes; and it may eventually affect the type of services paid for under Medicare and Medicaid reimbursement procedures. As Jones (1984) points out, the DRG system will encourage hospitals to specialize in the most cost-effective procedures and to avoid the most debilitated clientele. Moreover, the DRG will encourage hospitals to release elderly patients to the care of family members and long-term care settings much sooner than in the past. This means that long-term care settings could be facing a much sicker patient population requiring a high level of care at the same time that the public commitment to funding health care for older adults is seeking to limit the government's fiscal responsibility.

Apart from the potentially changed patient profile for nursing homes, DRGs will focus increased attention on the types of services provided and required by older patients. Many of the interventions discussed in this chapter are not currently eligible for public reimbursement under Medicare or Medicaid sources. Two major obstacles to public funding are the nursing home setting and types of mental health problems typically found among nursing home patients. In terms of setting, the reimbursement patterns, history, and philosophy of the nursing home have been linked exclusively to physical health problems and models of treatment. Thus, psychological or nonmedical psychiatric interventions have not been included for reimbursement. In addition, many of the causes of cognitive impairment that lead to nursing home admissions are often labeled as psychiatric illnesses and, therefore, not appropriate for reimbursement in a nursing home setting. For example, senile dementia of the Alzheimer's type (SDAT) is not an acceptable primary diagnosis for Medicare reimbursement.

The treatment setting and nomenclature issues are of specific concern for those working with older adults. An additional obstacle is the lack of public support for preventive interventions (such as staff or family training), or efforts aimed at the caregivers of impaired elderly (such as family members). With a funding system focused on remedial efforts aimed only at the identified patient, many of the approaches outlined here will remain ineligible (Smyer, 1984).

Lack of funding is a major barrier to implementing additional mental health programming in the long-term care setting. Given the current climate of public debate about the appropriateness of investing funds in impaired elderly (e.g., Avorn, 1984; Bayer, 1984), it is unlikely that additional mental health services will be readily added to the Medicare- or Medicaid-eligible list.

This brief discussion of the financing of health care is designed to point out one important area for further research, in addition to work on the specific interventions reviewed earlier in the chapter: the economic impact of mental health intervention in the nursing home setting. Mental health practitioners must be aware of the fiscal constraints placed upon nursing homes and long-term care settings. They must include some assessment of the total costs of the intervention—psychological *and* economic—and address the economic feasibility issue when assessing the effects of the intervention. Unfortunately, few of the interventions listed in this chapter have taken into account the economic dimension of the long-term care setting.

Researchers should also focus on the *physical* health effects of *mental* health interventions. For example, Rodin's recent work (Rodin, 1980; Rodin & Langer, 1977) suggests that increasing the older adult's sense of control, even in an institutional setting, may improve physical health outcomes (see also Chapter 1, this volume).

Thus, those who are concerned with incentives and barriers to financing mental health interventions in nursing homes must assess three types of outcomes—psychological, economic, and physical—of their interventions. Only with such integrated program assessments will the entire value of approaches like Kastenbaum's "cocktail-hour therapy" (1965, 1972) and others be appreciated and supported.


## CONCLUSION

In summary, we have tried to focus increased attention on the importance of mental health consultation and intervention for the nursing home setting. We have offered examples of current work in these settings, along with suggestions of some of the shortcomings of these efforts. Where appropriate, we have made suggestions for extending approaches tried in other settings to long-term care institutions. Throughout the chapter, we have tried to show that the nursing home should be viewed as a community with a variety of potential beneficiaries of mental health consultation: patients, their relatives, and the diversity of staff members who work in the setting. The functioning of each of these groups affects the functioning of the others, and all should be considered when contemplating mental health in the nursing home community. Although we have discussed intervention approaches for the three groups in separate sections, the distinctions are somewhat artificial. For example, some interventions focused on patient well-being (e.g., Jason & Simetak, 1983) clearly affect the well-being of the other community members. Similar examples of "ripple effects" are apparent with each of the other subgroups (families, staff).

In closing, we would agree with Rosenfeld's (1978) assessment of mental health issues in long-term care settings:

We are in an awkward stage in the development of institutional care for the elderly. Our nursing homes—and the funding arrangements that support them—are geared to providing physical health care to the aged. They have not been structured to care for the mentally ill or to provide an environment conducive to sustaining mental health and well-being in their aged residents. As a result, many mental health problems and needs go undetected and unheeded and sometimes worsen in an inhospitable environment. The widespread incidence of mental impairment among the institutionalized elderly, estimated to run as high as 50 percent, represents, in part, their advanced age and preexisting conditions that initially led to their institutionalization. But it may also represent the effect of living in an environment that provides little stimulation or motivation to keep alert, intact, and growing (pp. 109–110).

## REFERENCES

Albee, G. W. *Mental health manpower needs*. New York: Basic Books, 1959.

Avorn, J. Benefit and cost analysis in geriatric care: Turning age discrimination into health policy. *The New England Journal of Medicine*, 1984, *310*, 1294–1301.

Baltes, M. M., Burgess, R. L., & Stewart, R. B. Independence and dependence in self-care behaviors in nursing home residents: An operant-observational study. *International Journal of Behavioral Development*, 1980, *3*, 489–500.

Bayer, R. Will the first Medicare generation be the last? *The Hastings Center Report*, 1984, *14*, 17.

Bengtson, V. L., & Treas, L. The changing family context of mental health and aging. In J. E. Birren & R. B. Sloane (Eds.), *Handbook of mental health and aging*. Englewood Cliffs, NJ: Prentice-Hall, 1980.

Berger, R. M. Training the institutionalized elderly in interpersonal skills. *Social Work*, 1979, *24*, 420–423.

Berger, R. M., & Rose, S. D. Interpersonal skill training with institutionalized elderly patients. *Journal of Gerontology*, 1977, *32*, 346–353.

Berland, D. I., & Poggi, R. Expressive group psychotherapy with the aging. *International Journal of Group Psychotherapy*, 1979, *29*, 87–108.

Bloom, A. W. My experience with health care delivery systems for the elderly. Unpublished manuscript prepared for the W. K. Kellogg Foundation National Fellows Program, 1983.

Breslau, L. Toward an integrated approach to the institutionalized aged: An encounter with the medical model. *International Journal of Psychiatry in Medicine*, 1978–1979, *9*, 71–81.

Breslin, L. Aging: A family dilemma. *Psychiatric Quarterly*, 1978, *50*, 55–58.

Brickel, C. The therapeutic roles of cat mascots with a hospital-based geriatric population: A staff survey. *The Gerontologist*, 1979, *19*, 368–372.

Brink, T. L. Brief psychotherapy: A case report illustrating its potential effectiveness. *Journal of the American Geriatrics Society,* 1977, *25,* 273–276.

Brink, T. L. Geriatric paranoia: Case report illustrating behavioral management. *Journal of the American Geriatrics Society,* 1980, *28,* 519–522

Brody, E. M. "Women in the middle" and family help to older people. *Gerontologist,* 1981, *21,* 471–480.

Brody, E. M., & Spark, G. M. Institutionalization of the aged: A family crisis. *Family Issues,* 1966, *5,* 76–90.

Burnside, I. M. (Ed.). *Working with the elderly: Group processes and techniques.* North Scituate, MA: Duxbury Press, 1978.

Butler, R. N. Senile dementia: Reversible and irreversible. *Counseling Psychologist,* 1984, *12,* 75–80.

Callahan, J. J., Jr., Diamond, L. D., Giele, J. Z., & Morris, R. Responsibility of families for their severely disabled elders. *Health Care Financing Review,* 1980. Winter, 29–48.

Carroll, P. The social hour for geropsychiatrics patients. *Journal of American Geriatrics Society,* 1978, *26,* 32–35.

Carstensen, L. L., & Fremouw, W. J. The demonstration of a behavioral intervention for late life paranoia. *Gerontologist,* 1981, *21,* 329–333.

Citrin, R. S., & Dixon, D. N. Reality orientation: A milieu therapy used in an institution for the aged. *Gerontologist,* 1977, *17,* 39–43.

Cohen, G. D. A national perspective on mental health and aging. Paper presented at "A New Partnership in Service: Aging and Mental Health." State College, PA, June, 1984.

Connell, C. M., & Smyer, M. A. Training in mental health: Evaluation of the telephone conference network. Paper presented at the annual meeting of the Gerontological Society of America, San Antonio, TX, November, 1984.

Corbin, S., & Nelson, T. M. Using angels and devils: A board game developed for play in nursing homes. *International Journal of Aging and Human Development,* 1980, *11,* 243–250.

Cornbleth, T., & Cornbleth, C. Evaluation of the effectiveness of reality orientation classes in a nursing home unit. *Journal of the American Geriatrics Society,* 1979, *27,* 522–524.

Covert, A. B., Rodrigues, L., & Solomon, K. The use of mechanical and chemical restraints in nursing homes. *Journal of American Geriatrics Society,* 1977, *25,* 85–89.

Danish, S. J., & D'Augelli, A. R. Rationale and implementation of a training program for paraprofessionals. *Professional Psychology,* 1976, *7,* 38–46.

Danish, S. J., D'Augelli, A. R., Brock, G. W., Conter, K. R., & Meyer, R. J. A symposium on skill dissemination for paraprofessionals: Models of training, supervision, and utilization. *Professional Psychology,* 1978, *9,* 16–38.

Dudley, C. J., & Hillery, G. A. Freedom and alienation in homes for the aged. *Gerontologist,* 1977, *17,* 140–145.

Feier, C. D., & Leight, G. A communication-cognition program for elderly nursing home residents. *Gerontologist*, 1981, *21*, 408–416.

Fergus, E. O. Telephone change agentry in the diffusion of a program for the elderly. *Journal of Community Psychology*, 1979, *7*, 270–277.

Frankfather, D. L., Smith, M. J., & Caro, F. G. *Family care of the elderly.* Lexington, MA: Lexington Books, 1981.

Garrison, J. E. Stress management training for the elderly: A psychoeducational approach. *Journal of the American Geriatrics Society*, 1978, *26*, 397–403.

Gatz, M., Popkin, S. J., Pino, C. D., & VandenBos, G. R. Psychological interventions with older adults. In J. E. Birren & K. W. Schaie (Eds.), *Handbook of the psychology of aging.* New York: Van Nostrand Reinhold, 1985, pp. 755–785.

Gatz, M., Smyer, M. A., & Lawton, M. P. The mental health system and the older adult. In L. W. Poon (Ed.), *Aging in the 1980's: Selected contemporary issues in the psychology of aging.* Washington, DC: American Psychological Association, 1980.

Godbole, A., & Verinis, J. Brief psychotherapy in the treatment of emotional disorders in physically ill geriatric patients. *The Gerontologist*, 1974, *14*, 143–148.

Goldstein, R. S., & Baer, D. M. RSVP: A procedure to increase the personal mail and number of correspondents for nursing home residents. *Behavior Therapy*, 1976, *7*, 348–354.

Gottesman, L. E. Clinical psychology and aging: A role model. In D. Gentry (Ed.), *Geropsychology.* Cambridge, MA: Ballinger, 1977.

Griffin, L. W., & Gottesman, L. E. Training professionals in aging and mental health. In M. A. Smyer & M. Gatz (Eds.), *Mental health and aging: Programs and evaluations.* Beverly Hills, CA: Sage, 1983.

Gubrium, J. F. Notes on the social organization of senility. *Urban Life*, 1978, *7* (1), 23–44.

Gurland, B. J. The comparative frequency of depression in various adult age groups. *Journal of Gerontology*, 1976, *31*, 283–292.

Gurland, B. J. The assessment of the mental health status of older adults. In J. E. Birren & R. B. Sloane (Eds.), *Handbook of mental health and aging.* Englewood Cliffs, NJ: Prentice-Hall, 1980.

Hagestad, G. O. Parent and child: Generations in the family. In T. Field (Ed.), *Human development.* New York: Wiley, 1981.

Hanley, I. G. The use of signposts and active training to modify ward disorientation in elderly patients. *Journal of Behavior Therapy and Experimental Psychiatry*, 1981, *12*, 241–247.

Hausman, C. P. Short-term counseling groups for people with elderly parents. *Gerontologist*, 1979, *19*, 102–107.

Jason, L., & Smetak, S. Altering the design of a nursing home. In M. A. Smyer & M. Gatz (Eds.), *Mental health and aging: Programs and evaluations.* Beverly Hills, CA: Sage, 1983.

Jenkins, J., Felce, D., Lunt, B., & Powell, L. Increasing engagement in activity of residents in old people's homes by providing recreational materials. *Behaviour Research and Therapy*, 1977, *15*, 429–434.

Jones, A. A. Perspective payment: Curbing medicare costs at patients' expense. *Generations*, 1984 (Fall), *9*(1), 19–21.

Jones, M. Community care for chronic mental patients: The need for a reassessment. *Hospital and Community Psychiatry*, 1975, *26*, 94–98.

Kahn, R. L. The mental health system and the future aged. *Gerontologist*, 1975, *15*(1), 24–31.

Kalson, L. MASH: A program of social interaction between institutionalized aged and adult mentally retarded persons. *Gerontologist*, 1976, *16*, 340–348.

Kasteler, J. M., Fort, M. H., White, M. A., & Carruth, M. L. Personnel turnover: A major problem for nursing homes. *Nursing Homes*, 1979, *28*, 20–25.

Kastenbaum, R. Wine and fellowship in aging: An exploratory action program. *Journal of Human Relations*, 1965, *13*, 266–276.

Kastenbaum, R. Beer, wine, and mutual gratification in the gerontopolis. In D. P. Kent, R. Kastenbaum, & S. Sherwood (Eds.), *Research, planning, and action for the elderly*. New York: Behavioral Publications, 1972, pp. 365–394.

Kay, D. W. K., & Bergmann, K. Epidemiology of mental disorders among the aged in the community. In J. E. Birren & R. B. Sloane (Eds.), *Handbook of mental health and aging*. Englewood Cliffs, NJ: Prentice-Hall, 1980.

Kiesler, C. A. Mental health policy as a field of inquiry for psychology. *American Psychology*, 1980, *35*, 1066–1080.

Knapp, M., & Harissis, K. Staff vacancies and turnover in British old people's homes. *Gerontologist*, 1981, *21*, 76–84.

Kramer, J. R. Education and consultation on mental health in long-term care facilities: Problems, pitfalls, and solutions: A process approach to staff training and consultation. *Journal of Geriatric Psychiatry*, 1977, *10*, 197–213.

Laird, C. *Limbo*. Novato, CA: Chandler & Sharp, 1979.

Lave, J. R., & Silverman, H. A. Financing the health care of the aged. *The Annals of the American Academy of Political and Social Science*, 1983, *468*, 149–164.

LaWall, J. Conjoint therapy of psychiatric problems in the elderly. *Journal of the American Geriatrics Society*, 1981, *29*, 89–91.

Lesser, J., Lazarus, L. W., Frankel, R., & Havasy, S. Reminiscence group therapy with psychotic geriatric in-patients. *Gerontologist*, 1981, *21*, 291–296.

Levine, M. *The history and politics of community mental health*. New York: Oxford, 1981.

Lewinsohn, P. M., Munoz, R. F., Youngren, M. A., & Zeiss, A. M. *Control your depression*. Englewood Cliffs, NJ: Prentice-Hall, 1978.

Lewis, K. Services for families of the institutionalized aged. *Aging,* 1980, No. 309–310, 14–19.

MacDonald, M. L. Environmental programming for the socially isolated aging. *Gerontologist,* 1978, *18,* 350–354.

MacDonald, M. L., & Butler, A. K. Reversal of helplessness: Producing walking behavior in nursing home wheelchair residents using behavior modification procedures. *Journal of Gerontology,* 1974, *29,* 97–101.

MacDonald, M. L., & Settin, J. M. Reality orientation versus sheltered workshops as treatment for the institutionalized aged. *Journal of Gerontology,* 1978, *33,* 416–421.

Maddox, G. The unrealized potential of an old idea. In A. N. Exton-Smith & J. G. Evans (Eds.), *Care for the elderly: Meeting the challenge of dependency.* New York: Grune & Stratton, 1977.

Manaster, A. The family group therapy program at Park View Home for the Aged. *Journal of the American Geriatrics Society,* 1967, *15,* 302–306.

Maxwell, R. J. Doomed status: Observations on the segregation of impaired old people. *Psychiatric Quarterly,* 1979, *51,* 3–14.

McClannahan, L. E., & Risley, F. R. Activities and materials for severely disabled geriatric patients. *Nursing Homes,* 1975, *24,* 10–13.

More, M. T. Education and consultation on mental health in long-term care facilities: Problems, pitfalls, solutions: An administrator's point of view. *Journal of Geriatric Psychiatry,* 1977, *10,* 151–162.

National Center for Health Statistics. Employees in nursing homes in the United States: 1977 National Nursing Home Survey. *Vital and Health Statistics,* Series 14, No. 25, 1981.

Nigl, A. J., & Jackson, B. A behavior management program to increase social responses in psychogeriatric patients. *Journal of the American Geriatrics Society,* 1981, *29,* 92–95.

Office of Technology Assessment. *Diagnosis related groups (DRGs) and the Medicare Program: Implications for medical technology—a technical memorandum.* Washington, DC: U.S. Congress Office of Technology Assessment, OTA-TM-H-17, July, 1983.

Palmore, E. Total risk of institutionalization among the aged. *Gerontologist,* 1976, *16,* 504–507.

Pavur, E. J., Jr., & Smith, P. C. Absenteeism, turnover, and an inservice program. In M. A. Smyer & M. Gatz (Eds.), *Mental health and aging: Programs and evaluations.* Beverly Hills, CA: Sage, 1983.

Penner, L. A., Eberly, D. A., & Patterson, R. L. Skills training for community living. In M. A. Smyer & M. Gatz (Eds.), *Mental health and aging: Programs and evaluations.* Beverly Hills, CA: Sage, 1983.

Pierce, W. D., Trickett, E. J., & Moos, R. H. Changing ward atmosphere through staff discussion of the perceived ward environment. *Archives of General Psychiatry,* 1972, *26,* 35–41.

Powell, L., Felce, D., Jenkins, J., & Lunt, B. Increasing engagement in a home for the elderly by providing an indoor gardening activity. *Behaviour Research and Therapy*, 1979, *17*, 127–135.

Power, C. A., & McCarron, L. T. Treatment of depression in persons residing in homes for the aged. *The Gerontologist*, 1975, *15*, 132–135.

Pruchno, R. A., Blow, F. C., & Smyer, M. A. Life events and interdependent lives. *Human Development*, 1984, *27*, 31–41.

Pruchno, R. A., & Smyer, M. A. *Therapeutic intervention with adult caregivers.* Paper presented at The Future of Natural Caregiving Networks in Later Life: Policy, Planning, Research, and Intervention Workshop, Buffalo, NY, April, 1984.

Rappaport, J. *Community psychology: Values, research, action.* New York: Holt, 1977.

Rathbone-McCuan, E., & Levenson, J. Impact of socialization therapy in a geriatric day-care setting. *Gerontologist*, 1975, *15*, 338–342.

Redick, R. W., & Taube, C. A. Demography and mental health care of the aged. In J. E. Birren & R. B. Sloane (Eds.), *Handbook of mental health and aging.* Englewood Cliffs, NJ: Prentice-Hall, 1980.

Reichenfeld, H. F., Csapo, K. G., Carriere, L., & Gardner, R. C. Evaluating the effect of activity programs on a geriatric ward. *The Gerontologist*, 1973, *13*, 305–310.

Reifler, B. V., Larson, E., Cox, G., & Featherstone, H. Treatment results at a multi-specialty clinic for the impaired elderly and their families. *Journal of the American Geriatric Society*, 1981, *29*, 579–582.

Reinke, B. J., Holmes, D. S., & Denny, N. W. Influence of a "friendly visitor" program on the cognitive functioning and morale of elderly persons. *American Journal of Community Psychology*, 1981, *9*, 491–504.

Riley, M. W., & Waring, J. Age and aging. In R. K. Merton & R. Nisbet (Eds.), *Contemporary social problems* (4th ed.). New York: Harcourt, Brace, and Jovanovich, 1976.

Rinke, C. L., Williams, J. J., Lloyd, K. E., & Smith-Scott, W. The effects of prompting and reinforcement on self-bathing by elderly residents of a nursing home. *Behavior Therapy*, 1978, *9*, 873–881.

Rodin, J. Managing the stress of aging: The role of control and coping. In S. Levine & H. Ursin (Eds.), *Coping and health.* New York: Plenum, 1980.

Rodin, J., & Langer, E. J. Long-term effects of a control-relevant intervention with the institutionalized aged. *Journal of Personality and Social Psychology*, 1977, *35*, 897–902.

Romaniuk, M., McAuley, W. J., & Arling, G. An examination of the prevalence of mental disorders among the elderly in the community. *Journal of Abnormal Psychology*, 1983, *92*, 458–467.

Rosenfeld, A. H. *New views on older lives: A sampler of NIMH-sponsored research and service programs.* Washington, DC: U.S. Government Printing Office, DHEW Publication No. (ADM) 78-687, 1978.

Safford, F. A program for families of the mentally impaired elderly. *Gerontologist*, 1980, *20*, 656–660.

Salter, C., & Salter, C. Effects of an individualized activity program on elderly patients. *Gerontologist*, 1975, *15*, 404–406.

Santos, J. F., Burdick, D. C., Hubbard, R. W., & Santos, M. A. Training in mental health outreach. In M. A. Smyer & M. Gatz (Eds.), *Mental health and aging: Programs and evaluations*. Beverly Hills, CA: Sage, 1983.

Santos, J. F., & VandenBos, G. R. (Eds.). *Psychology and the older adult: Challenges for training in the 1980's*. Washington, DC: American Psychological Association, 1982.

Saul, S. R., & Saul, S. Group psychotherapy in a proprietary nursing home. *Gerontologist*, 1974, *14*, 446–450.

Schulz, R. The effects of control and predictability on the physical and psychological well-being of the institutionalized aged. *Journal of Personality and Social Psychology*, 1976, *33*, 563–573.

Schwartz, A. N. Staff development and morale building in nursing homes. *Gerontologist*, 1974, *14*, 50–53.

Shadish, W. R., Jr., & Bootzin, R. R. Nursing homes and chronic mental patients. *Schizophrenia Bulletin*, 1981, *7*, 488–498.

Sherr, V., & Goffi, M. On-site geropsychiatric services to guests of residential homes. *Journal of American Geriatrics Society*, 1977, *25*, 269–272.

Smith, K. F., & Bengtson, V. L. Positive consequences of institutionalization: Solidarity between elderly parents and their middle-aged children. *The Gerontologist*, 1979, *19*, 438–447.

Smithers, J. A. Institutional dimension of senility. *Urban Life*, 1977, *6*, 251–276.

Smyer, M. A. The differential usage of services by impaired elderly. *Journal of Gerontology*, 1980, *35*, 249–255.

Smyer, M. A. Choosing a nursing home: A family decision. Unpublished manuscript prepared for the W. K. Kellogg Foundation National Fellows Program, 1983.

Smyer, M. A. Health-care costs: Roots are still there. *Philadelphia Inquirer*, July 1, 1984, p. 7F.

Smyer, M. A., & Pruchno, R. A. Service use and mental impairment among the elderly: Arguments for consultation and education. *Professional Psychology*, 1984, *15*, 528–537.

Smyer, M. A., Siegler, I. C., & Gatz, M. Learning to live in a therapeutic community: A study of elderly inpatients. *International Journal of Aging and Human Development*, 1976, *7*, 189–193.

Snyder, L. H., Rupprecht, P., Pyrek, J., Brekhus, S., & Moss, T. Wandering. *Gerontologist*, 1978, *18*, 272–280.

Solon, J. A., Amthor, R. P., Rabb, M. Y., & Shelley, J. C. Linking young and old institutionalized people. *Public Health Reports*, 1977, *92*, 57–64.

Soskis, C. W. Teaching nursing home staff about patients' rights. *Gerontologist*, 1981, *21*, 424–430.

Sperbeck, D. J., & Whitbourne, S. K. Dependency in the institutional setting:

A behavioral training program for geriatric staff. *Gerontologist,* 1981, *21,* 268–275.

Sussman, M. B. Family, bureaucracy, and the elderly individual: An organizational/linkage perspective. In E. Shanas & M. B. Sussman (Eds.), *Family, bureaucracy, and the elderly.* Durham, NC: Duke University Press, 1977.

Tallmer, M., Mayer, M., & Hill, G. Education and consultation on mental health in long-term care facilities: Problems, pitfalls, and solutions: Cross-cultural issues in nursing home settings. *Journal of Geriatric Psychiatry,* 1977, *10,* 173–189.

Thompson, L. W., Gallagher, D., Nies, G., & Epstein, D. Evaluation of the effectiveness of professionals and nonprofessionals as instructors of "Coping with Depression" classes for elders. *Gerontologist,* 1983, *23,* 390–396.

Tobin, S. S., & Lieberman, M. A. *Last home for the aged.* San Francisco: Jossey-Bass, 1976.

U.S. Department of Commerce, Bureau of the Census. 1976 survey of institutionalized persons: A study of persons receiving long term care. *Current Population Reports,* Series P-23, No. 69, 1978.

Vladeck, B. C., & Firman, J. P. The aging of the population and health services. *The Annals of the American Academy of Political and Social Science,* 1983, *468,* 132–148.

Wack, J., & Rodin, J. Nursing homes for the aged: The human consequences of legislation-shaped environments. *Journal of Social Issues,* 1978, *34,* 6–21.

Wallach, H. F., Kelley, F., & Abrahams, J. P. Psychosocial rehabilitation for chronic geriatric patients: An intergenerational approach. *Gerontologist,* 1979, *19,* 464–470.

Whitley, E., Duncan, R., & McKenzie, P. Adopted grandparents: A link between the past and future. *Educational Gerontology,* 1976, *1,* 243–249.

Zarit, S. H., & Zarit, J. Families under stress: Interventions for caregivers of senile dementia patients. *Theory, Research, and Practice,* 1982, *19,* 461–471.

# Index

# Index